The Management of Equity Investments

The Management of Equity Investments

Capital markets, equity research, investment
decisions and risk management with case studies

Dimitris N. Chorafas

ELSEVIER
BUTTERWORTH
HEINEMANN

AMSTERDAM • BOSTON • HEIDELBERG • LONDON • NEW YORK • OXFORD
PARIS • SAN DIEGO • SAN FRANCISCO • SINGAPORE • SYDNEY • TOKYO

332.6
C551 m

Elsevier Butterworth-Heinemann
Linacre House, Jordan Hill, Oxford OX2 8DP
30 Corporate Drive, Burlington, MA 01803

First published 2005

British Library Cataloguing in Publication Data
A catalogue record for this book is available from the British Library

Library of Congress Cataloguing in Publication Data
A catalogue record for this book is available from the Library of Congress

ISBN 0 7506 6456 8

For information on all Elsevier Butterworth-Heinemann finance
publications visit our website at http://books.elsevier.com/finance

Typeset by Newgen Imaging Systems (P) Ltd, Chennai, India
Printed and bound in Great Britain

Working together to grow
libraries in developing countries

www.elsevier.com | www.bookaid.org | www.sabre.org

ELSEVIER   BOOK AID
International   Sabre Foundation

Contents

Foreword   ix

Preface   xi

Abbreviations   xv

Part One: The art of investing   **1**

1 Golden rules of investing   3
    1.1   Introduction   3
    1.2   Asset classes of investing   6
    1.3   Investors, speculators, risk and return   10
    1.4   Savings down the drain: the Eurotunnel fiasco   12
    1.5   Understand the difference between investing, trading and speculating   15
    1.6   Caveat emptor and human nature   19
    1.7   A golden rule for private investors, but not necessarily for all
          professionals   22
    1.8   Income, growth and control of exposure   25

2 The area where professional asset managers and private investors meet   30
    2.1   Introduction   30
    2.2   Investments through private banking   32
    2.3   Betting on the challenger and learning to diversify   36
    2.4   Increasing the visibility of one's investments   39
    2.5   The 5 percent rule about assets at risk   43
    2.6   Challenges faced by pension funds   47
    2.7   Are mutual funds a good alternative?   51

Part Two: Capital markets and their players   **57**

3 Capital markets and the securities industry   59
    3.1   Introduction   59
    3.2   Securities and their legal protection   61
    3.3   Investment banking and underwriting   64
    3.4   Investment bankers and primary dealers   67
    3.5   Correspondent banks   70
    3.6   The globalized securities market   72
    3.7   Risk of global contagion   76

4   The trading of equities   79
    4.1   Introduction   79
    4.2   Equities, stock exchanges and over-the-counter operations   80
    4.3   Basic facts about equities: common and preferred stock   83
    4.4   Convertible bonds defined   86
    4.5   The funding competition between capital markets and
          commercial banks   89
    4.6   Stock markets and equity prices   93
    4.7   Stock market indices: Dow Jones, S&P and NASDAQ   96
    4.8   European market indices   102
    4.9   Appendix: The Paper Ships Index   105

5   Regulation and operation of the exchanges   107
    5.1   Introduction   107
    5.2   Role of a regulatory authority   108
    5.3   Self-regulation by the exchanges and conflicts of interest   111
    5.4   Role of specialists in a stock exchange   114
    5.5   Bid, ask, large blocks and the third market   117
    5.6   Cash and margin accounts   120
    5.7   Short sales and reverse/forward splits   123

Part Three: Performance criteria and quoted equities   129

6   Technical and fundamental analysis   131
    6.1   Introduction   131
    6.2   Fundamental analysis defined   133
    6.3   Technical analysis defined   137
    6.4   Theory behind the art of charting   139
    6.5   The bolts and nuts of charting   142
    6.6   Financial analysis and future price of a commodity   146
    6.7   Learning how to detect and analyze market trends   149
    6.8   The role of rocket scientists   152
    6.9   Appendix: Microsoft's 2004 Huge Dividend   154

7   Quantitative criteria for equity performance   156
    7.1   Introduction   156
    7.2   An equity's valuation and need for stress tests   158
    7.3   Equity as an option and dividend discount model   162
    7.4   Earnings per share and creative accounting solutions   166
    7.5   Earnings before interest, taxes, depreciation, and amortization   168
    7.6   Price to earnings ratio and its challenges   171
    7.7   Using return on equity as a guide   175
    7.8   Appendix: the Tobin Q-ratio   178

8   Transparency in financial statements and reputational risk   180
    8.1   Introduction   180
    8.2   Goals of transparent financial reporting   181
    8.3   Transparency role of an audit committee   185
    8.4   Transparency and corporate governance   189

	8.5	Forward-looking statements	191
	8.6	Virtual balance sheets and risk management	194
	8.7	Compliance with the Sarbanes-Oxley Act	197
	8.8	Appendix: the European Union's version of the Sarbanes-Oxley Act	200
9	**A private investor's self-protection**		**202**
	9.1	Introduction	202
	9.2	Investing in large caps versus small caps	204
	9.3	A prudent policy for investors: equities versus bonds	209
	9.4	Data analysis is at the core of the investor's homework	211
	9.5	Investors should always consider the contrarian's advice	215
	9.6	Value stocks, growth stocks and intrinsic value	219
	9.7	Importance of the investment horizon	221
	9.8	Factors affecting return on investment	224

Part Four: Execution risk and damage control   **229**

10	**Investors' responsibility in risk management**		**231**
	10.1	Introduction	231
	10.2	Risk management requires a lot of homework	232
	10.3	The importance of rigorous risk management standards	236
	10.4	Investors should never hesitate to cut losses	240
	10.5	Damage control through limits and profit targets	243
	10.6	Flexibility is one of the investor's best friends	247
	10.7	Using mathematical tools and appreciating they are not fail-safe	250

11	**Independent equity research and management risk**		**255**
	11.1	Introduction	255
	11.2	The bottleneck is at the top of the bottle	256
	11.3	Legal risk in equity research and analysis	258
	11.4	Quality of corporate governance affects investors and the companies themselves	262
	11.5	Can independent research be an effective solution?	265
	11.6	Very often, analysts' pickings are mediocre	267
	11.7	Buy-side asymmetries in the experts advice	270

12	**Volatility, liquidity, leverage, and their impact on investments**		**274**
	12.1	Introduction	274
	12.2	Volatility, volume of transactions, and volatility index	276
	12.3	The concept of implied volatility and its use	279
	12.4	Solvency and liquidity feed upon one-another	283
	12.5	Liquidity management and risk control	287
	12.6	Risks associated with multiply-connect leverage	291

13	**Methods for judging quoted equities**		**296**
	13.1	Introduction	296
	13.2	Rethinking the metrics which we use	297

13.3   New measures for judging equity performance   301
13.4   Business risk and brand name   303
13.5   A new method for measuring business risk   307
13.6   Fair value accounting and its impact on equities   311
13.7   Globalization increases the complexity of evaluating equity
        performance   314

Part Five: Case studies in investments   319

14   Case studies on equity values   321
     14.1   Introduction   321
     14.2   Risk management, damage control, and hedging   323
     14.3   Two technology companies: Cisco Systems and IBM   326
     14.4   Investors' appetite for Internet stocks   329
     14.5   Old-established companies, too, can be highly volatile   333
     14.6   Equity values of service firms also plunge   337

15   Parmalat: a case study on leveraging corporate assets   341
     15.1   Introduction   341
     15.2   Parmalat as a speculative hedge fund   342
     15.3   A bird's-eye view of Parmalat's scam   345
     15.4   Taxpayers, investors, and the control of malfeasance   348
     15.5   Mr Fixit and the challenges of a turnaround   351
     15.6   It is not easy to get out of bankruptcy unscathed   354
     15.7   The banks of Parmalat   357
     15.8   Conflicts of interest and reputational risk   361
     15.9   Management accountability   364
     15.10   Parmalat bites back banks and auditors   367
     15.11   Epilog   368

Acknowledgements   371

Index   395

Foreword

First there was an e-mail politely requesting a meeting. It had arrived with one of my colleagues at the IMA – she ducked, adding 'I think that this must be one for you?' Then there was a phone call – 'I am coming to London in a few weeks' time, could we meet to talk about the twenty golden rules for investing?' Intrigued I agreed, then panic set in. Twenty golden rules? – if only it were true. But if it was true that these existed, and if everyone followed them, then of course it wouldn't be true as they could offer no advantage to any single market participant: markets are a zero sum game, aren't they?

When we met, Dimitris handed me a single sheet which was to form the basis of our discussion over the next two hours. And there were his twenty golden rules, exactly as set out at the beginning of this book. But for me worse was to follow as Dimitris added 'Do you think that the rules are different between professional and retail investors?' I noticed the extra columns and the tick boxes, one for the retail investor, one for the professional investor. What followed was an invigorating and challenging conversation as one by one the rules were articulated, my opinions sought and the contradictions in my opinions exposed, gently but exposed all the same.

This book explores the usefulness and limitations of these rules by examining current market structures and recent market failures. If there is one single message that investors might take from this book, it is 'think before you act and don't act without knowledge'. The golden rules are a framework of knowledge you should have and thinking you should do.

Gordon Midgley
London
October 2004

Preface

The past is not behind us but within us, like rings in a tree. This past is part of the knowledge we have of ourselves and of what we are doing, as well as of what we might be doing in the future. Therefore, we have no choice but to probe into this past. This is particularly true of investments if we want to be in a position to cure ourselves of our dangerous lunacies about risk-less rewards.

Based on extensive research in the USA, the UK and continental Europe, this book brings to the reader's attention lessons learned about the art of investments. To help make them comprehensible, these research results have been crystalized into twenty rules, presented and documented in the fifteen chapters of the book.

Behind all of these rules lies the fact that there is not only reward but also risk with investments. Therefore, it is important to evaluate any investment's risk factors before entering into it. Since investments are typically made up of common stocks and debt instruments, the risks I am talking about are those inherent in equities and bonds. Though this volume addresses equities rather than bonds, the principles are similar:

- The value of any position in one's portfolio fluctuates, and
- This value can be higher or lower than the value on the day the securities were bought, or deposited with trustees.

The challenge is to put in place a methodology which allows the investor to be ahead of the game, and equip him or her with the tools to implement this methodology. This is precisely where experience from past practices and their aftermath is invaluable. Without it, the market's twists can have a shocking impact on the complacent investor.

This book is designed for professionals, individual investors and the academic market, particularly senior-level and graduate studies in Finance, Business Administration and Management, in colleges and universities. In regard to the professional market, the book addresses practitioners in business and industry responsible for managing funds and for investing.

Typical readers will be treasurers and financial officers of manufacturing companies and merchandising firms, institutional investors, financial analysts, traders, investment bankers and brokers, commercial bankers, personal bankers, investment advisers, funds managers and trustees – but also high and medium net worth individuals.

The text outlines and documents the benefits sound investment management can provide in gaining confidence in equity investments, as well as lessons on prudence which can be learned from the market bubble of the late 1990s, the 2000–02 market depression, the start of recovery in 2003, and doubts which cast their shadow upon the market in 2004.

The fact that successful investing is to a large extent an art does not mean that it is deprived of rules and guidelines. The text examines investment rules within the perspective of each investor's goals and challenges, as well as ways and means for implementing these rules in an able manner.

Based on research results and on the author's own investment experience, the book's contents demonstrate that risk and return varies widely from one deal to the next, shareholder value is usually being paid lip service, there are serious risks associated with leveraging, and near-sighted management can destroy an investment's prospects. Furthermore, obsolete skills and dubious deals are among the investor's worst enemies.

The text also demonstrates how, why and when there is an upside and a downside with investments. The upside is more likely when sound rules are observed and one is doing lots of homework. An investor's ability to analyze facts and figures helps in avoiding the slippery path which ends with a loss of most of the investor's capital.

To help in explaining what underpins a dependable method, the book outlines the way capital markets work and equity research is done. It also pays attention to forces propelling economic growth or downturn. The focal point is *markets* and, as the reader should appreciate, markets are difficult to read no matter what kind of expert one claims to be.

The book is divided into five parts. Part One addresses the art of investing. Chapter 1 outlines three of the golden rules of investing – *golden* because over the years they have proved their worth not on one but on many occasions. Behind these rules is a certain sense of consensus from bankers who left their mark in the financial industry of the twentieth century. The text also brings the reader's attention to the significant differences between investing, trading and speculating.

Chapter 2 provides evidence that there is a common landscape where professional asset managers and private investors live and work together. Private banking is one of the examples and pension funds is another; mutual funds is a third case with common interests between investment professionals and retail investors. But are the golden rules of investing truly shared among all parties? The case studies in this chapter provide the answer to this question.

The theme of Part Two is capital markets and their players. Chapter 3 introduces the reader to the notions of capital markets and their impact. After examining the sense of the word 'securities', it explains the functions of investment bankers, underwriters, primary dealers, correspondent banks and globalized financial markets. The theme of Chapter 4 is trading in equities, including transactions in stock exchanges and over the counter (OTC), as well as the competition between capital markets and commercial banks. Chapter 4 also explains stock market indices – Dow Jones and many others.

Chapter 5 concentrates on regulation and operation of stock exchanges, looking at them as pivot points of capital markets. The text also examines the role of supervisory authorities and of the exchanges' self-regulation, functions of specialists in a stock exchange, bid-ask system, notion of trading in large blocks, and what lies behind cash and margin accounts.

The four chapters of Part Three concentrate on performance criteria for private equities. Chapter 6 explains the nuts and bolts of fundamental and technical analysis – the latter with particular emphasis on charting. Chapter 7 outlines quantitative criteria needed for evaluating equity performance, including challenges posed by an equity's valuation. Price/earnings, return on equity and treating equity as an option are among the chapter's subjects.

While performance criteria and analytical processes are necessary, they can deliver only *if* the financial statements on which they are applied are reliable. Transparency in financial statements and reputational risk correlate, as Chapter 8 suggests. Chapter 9 adds to this theme by advancing some basic principles and associated mechanisms for investors' protection. It also explains the difference between value stocks and growth stocks, as well as the concept underpinning intrinsic value.

Part Four, also, has four chapters, which concentrate on risk embedded in a portfolio and on damage control. Chapter 10 outlines the investor's own responsibility in risk management – from ways and means for controlling exposure to the establishment of an effective risk control system. Because a sound risk management policy is enhanced through prognostication, Chapter 11 examines whether independent equity research is really of help.

Behind practically every market opportunity, but also every market risk, is volatility. This is the subject of Chapter 12, which also focuses on liquidity and solvency, as well as on the aftermath of leverage on the investor and his savings – a concept leading to the rethinking of return on equity. Chapter 13 follows up on this frame of reference, introducing and explaining why the computation of return on equity can benefit from fair value accounting.

The theme of Part Five is case studies in investments. These are presented in two chapters. The case studies in Chapter 14 bring to the reader's attention both positive and negative results on equity valuation. Cisco Systems and IBM are examples of the former; Internet stocks, Lucent, Nortel and other entities are examples of the latter. The choice of case studies has been influenced by the fact that an investor can learn much more from failures than from successes. *If* what went wrong teaches us no lesson, *then* we will most likely repeat the same mistakes.

Chapter 15 is a case study on Parmalat, the greatest financial failure and scandal in the history of European equities. On the one hand, Parmalat demonstrated how and why companies crash. On the other, it documented that industrial and commercial entities can hide the true nature of their financial woes from investors for more than a dozen years – often with the complicity of market players.

Parmalat was really a hedge fund with a dairy products line on the side. Its crash had much in common with that of Long-Term Capital Management (LTCM), the Rolls-Royce of hedge funds, in September 1998. Both have been characterized by lack of transparency, murky deals, superleveraging and lack of effective government supervision.

The lesson that should be learned from LTCM, Enron, Global Crossing, Adelphia, WorldCom, Eurotunnel, Vivendi-Universal, Parmalat and so many other equities, is the pain that high leveraging and lack of transparency create for investors, financial markets and society as a whole. The role of rigorous supervision is to ensure that entities lacking business ethics and those with unscrupulous individuals do not tear apart the economic fabric. When the regulatory authorities take it easy, investors are bound to suffer no matter how much homework they have done.

Human nature being what it is, government regulation must always account for lust and greed as well as for the effects of political patronage. 'You don't set a fox to watching the chickens just because he has a lot of experience in the henhouse' Harry

Truman once said. Effective, meaningful regulation of the securities industry is not just a good solution. It is prerequisite to free markets, their proper functioning and their contribution to investor prosperity.

My debts go to a long list of knowledgeable people, and their organizations, who contributed to this research. Without their contributions this book would not have been possible. I am also indebted to several senior executives from financial institutions and to securities experts for constructive criticism during the preparation of the manuscript.

Let me take this opportunity to thank Mike Cash for suggesting this project, Jennifer Wilkinson for seeing it all the way to publication, and to Deena Burgess and Carol Lucas for the editorial work. To Eva-Maria Binder goes the credit for compiling the research results, typing the text and making the camera-ready artwork and index.

Dimitris N. Chorafas
Valmer and Vitznau
October 2004

Abbreviations

3G	third generation (mobile technology)
ADAM	Association de Défense des Actionnaires Minoritaires
ADR	American Depository Receipt
AIMA	Alternative Investment Management Association
AOL	America On-line
ARPU	average revenue per user
ASB	Accounting Standards Board
BIS	Bank for International Settlements
bps	basis points (not to confuse with bits per second)
BU	business unit
CAPM	Capital Asset Pricing Model
CBOE	Chicago Board of Options Exchange
CCPU	cash cost per user
CD	certificate of deposit
CDO	collateralized debt obligation
CEO	chief executive officer
CF/S	cash flow to share
CFO	chief finance officer
CFPS	cash flow per share
CFTC	Commodities Futures Trading Commission
CIBC	Canadian Imperial Bank of Commerce
CIO	chief information officer
CLN	credit-linked note
CMO	collateralized mortgage obligation
COC	cost of capital
COO	chief operations officer
CPA	Certified Public Accountants
CPI	consumer price index
CPM	corporate performance management
CVAR	credit value at risk
DAX	Deutscher Aktienindex (German share price index)
DCF	discounted cash flow
DEPS	diluted earnings per share
DJ	Dow Jones
DJIA	Dow Jones Industrial Average
DP	default point
DPS	debt per share

DTA	deferred tax asset
EBIT	earnings before interest and taxes
EBITDA	earnings before interest, taxes, depreciation and amortization
EC	economic capital
EC	European Commission
ECB	European Central Bank
EIS	executive information system
EPS	earnings per share
ERR	earnings revision ratio
EU	European Union
EVA	economic value added
FAS	Financial Accounting Standards
FASB	Financial Accounting Standards Board
FDEPS	fully diluted earnings per share
FDIC	Federal Deposit Insurance Corporation
forex	foreign exchange
FSA	Financial Services Authority
FTSE 100	Financial Times Stock Exchange 100 Index
G-10	Group of Ten
GAAP	Generally Accepted Accounting Principles
GDP	gross domestic profit
GE	General Electric
GM	General Motors
GMAC	General Motors Acceptance Corporation
GNP	gross national product
HFFD	high frequency financial data
HP	Hewlett-Packard
IAS	International Accounting Standards
IASB	International Accounting Standards Board
IMA	Investment Management Association
IMF	International Monetary Fund
IPO	initial public offering
IRB	internal rating-based
ISO	International Standards Organization
IT	information technology
JIT	just in time
LAN	local-area network
LIBOR	London Interbank Offered Rate
LPC	Loan Pricing Corporation
LSE	London Stock Exchange
LTCM	Long-Term Capital Management
M&A	mergers and acquisitions
MIT	Massachusetts Institute of Technology
NASD	National Association of Securities Dealers
NASDAQ	National Association of Securities Dealers Automated Quotations
NAV	net asset value

ND/E	net debt over equity
NOPAT	net operating profit after taxes
NPV	net present value
NTC	New Trading Company
NYSE	New York Stock Exchange
OC	operating characteristics
OCC	Controller of the Currency
OECD	Organization for Economic Co-operation and Development
OTC	over the counter
P/BV	price to book value
P/CF	price to cash flow
P/E	price to earnings
P&L	profit and loss
PBGC	Pension Benefit Guaranty Corporation
PC	personal computer
PCAOB	Public Company Accounting Oversight Board
PEPS	primary earnings per share
PwC	PricewaterhouseCoopers
R&D	research and development
RAROC	risk-adjusted return on capital
RMO	risk management officer
ROA	return on assets
ROC	return on capital
ROE	return on equity
ROEC	return on economic capital
ROFC	return on funding capital
ROIC	return on invested capital
RORAC	return on risk-adjusted capital
S/IC	sales to invested capital
S&Ls	savings and loans
S&P	Standard & Poor's
S&P 500	Standard & Poor's 500
SBC	Swiss Bank Corporation
SEC	Securities and Exchange Commission
SIPC	Securities Investor Protection Corporation
snafu	situation normal, all fouled up
TMT	technology, media and telecommunications
TSE	Toronto Stock Exchange
UCLA	University of California Los Angeles
UL	unexpected loss
VAR	value at risk
VIX	volatility index
VOC	Verenidge Oost-Indische Compagnie
x	times
Y2K	year 2000

One
The art of investing

1 Golden rules of investing

1.1 Introduction

It has been a deliberate choice to start, so to speak, with the conclusion. This conclusion crystallizes in advice on the management of equity investments based on the views of cognizant people who participated in the research leading to this book, as well as on my own experience as an investor. Some of the references coming from the masters. For instance, quoting Benjamin Graham, Warren Buffett says: 'The first rule of investment is don't lose. And the second rule of investment is don't forget the first rule. And that's all the rules there are.'

Investment means savings, forgoing today's consumption for benefits some time in the future. The high rate of unemployment, virtual bankruptcy of the social security system established seventy years ago and the fact that many institutional investors, from life insurers to pension funds, are under water (see Chapter 2), see to it that a sound policy of investment is cornerstone to everybody's life plan. In all likelihood, individual investments will be the only solution on which he or she will eventually depend for a living.

Down to basics, above and beyond any rule of investment is the need to understand *why* one is investing – including *savings objectives* and *their risks*. This is fundamental for both professional investors and retail investors, the two populations to which this book is addressed (more on this later). Both individual investors and the professionals yearn for future benefits. Both:

- Will be subject to profits and losses (Ps&Ls), and
- May face one or more liquidity crunch.

If Buffett's 'don't lose money' is the conclusion, then there should also be a beginning which introduces, step by step, the more elementary rules characterizing sound management of investments. To document *how* not to lose money, and guide the hand of an investor, such rules should proceed in a clear and crisp manner without being lost in a labyrinth of explanations.

Moreover, given the importance of a methodology for winning in investments, a subject vital to a fast-growing number of people and organizations, it is preferable to provide at the start a holistic picture. This is done through the twenty golden rules shown in Table 1.1, leaving to subsequent chapters the task of documenting the advice provided by each individual rule.

Among themselves, the twenty rules in Table 1.1 encapsulated long experience of how to manage one's portfolio to avoid being awake in the night because of inordinate losses, and to assure that invested money will grow – albeit at reasonable pace.

Retail investors	Professional investors	Rule	
+	+	1	Understand the difference between investing and speculating (*Chapter 1*)
+	−	2	Do not borrow, do not buy on margin, do not leverage yourself and do not sell short (*Chapter 1*)
+	+	3	Decide whether you invest for income or for growth (*Chapter 1*)
+	+	4	Bet on the challenger, but do not buy at peaks (*Chapter 2*)
+	−	5	Invest only in stocks quoted in big boards (*Chapter 2*)
+	+	6	Observe the 5 percent rule about assets at risk (*Chapter 2*)
+	+	7	Look at homework as a better guide than advice by other experts (*Chapter 6*)
+	+	8	Learn how to do fundamental analysis and technical analysis (*Chapter 6*)
−	+	9	Learn how to detect and analyze market trends (*Chapter 6*)
+	+	10	Never chase the return of shares you did not buy (*Chapter 9*)
+	+	11	Always listen to contrarian opinion (*Chapter 9*)
+	+	12	Appreciate the need for rigorous risk management (*Chapter 10*)
+	+	13	Accept responsibility of your own decisions (*Chapter 10*)
+	+	14	Never hesitate to cut losses (*Chapter 10*)
+	+	15	Do damage control through limits and profit targets (*Chapter 10*)
+	+	16	Consider flexibility as one of your best friends (*Chapter 10*)
+	+	17	Use mathematical models, but understand they are not fail-safe[1] (*Chapter 10*)
−	+	18	Factor-in the impact of market liquidity and volatility (*Chapter 12*)
−	+	19	Appreciate the impact of business risk (*Chapter 13*)
+	+	20	Look at conflicts of interest as part of daily life (*Chapter 13*)

Note:

1 D.N. Chorafas (2002). *Modelling the Survival of Financial and Industrial Enterprises: Advantages, Challenges, and Problems with the Internal Rating-Based (IRB) Method.* Palgrave/Macmillan.

Table 1.1 The twenty golden rules of investing

Experienced investors appreciate that the doors of risk and return are adjacent and identical.

A question which immediately comes to mind when one looks at Table 1.1 is 'For whom have these investment management rules been written?' This has been a basic issue discussed with the publisher when the contract for this book was negotiated. The population to which the text should appeal evidently shapes its contents.

- The publisher's choice was *professionals*, but
- As the author, I would have preferred to address *individual investors*.

In the end, the decision was taken to cover, as far as possible, both populations: professionals and retail investors. As the reader will see in this and in subsequent chapters, this is achievable because the majority of sound investment rules and practices, as well as the methodology behind them, applies equally to both populations, though there are a few exceptions.

For instance, the first and third golden rules of investments in Table 1.1, as well as many others, appeal to both professional investment managers and individual investors. By contrast, the second and fifth golden rules fit best the retail population. Alternatively, the rules which should characterize professional investment decisions, because they require more knowledge and skill than that typically available among retail investors, are the ninth, eighteenth and nineteenth. This leaves fifteen golden rules common to both investor populations.

Moreover, apart from the fact that there exist *general guidelines* characterizing investments in equities, as we will see in detail through practical examples, it is appropriate to note that professional investment activities are in no way immune from retail investment objectives and the rules behind them. Institutional investors' such as:

- Life insurance companies,
- Pension funds, and
- Mutual funds (unit trusts) and other asset managers

are in business to satisfy the investment needs of savers, whose money lubricates the wheels of institutional investment activities. In fact, this interaction between professional and retail investors is a two-way street. Since individual investors use the institutional investors' services, they should themselves always be aware of how the latter work, which rules are driving them and on which criteria or conditions their decision-making process is based. This is true both of investing and of risk management. It is therefore right that this book has followed this dual perspective.

In conclusion, the management of investments is the management of money done under a variety of aspects: money as raw material commodity, expression of wealth, and accounting measure which makes it possible to judge obtained results in a factual, documented and objective manner. Subjectiveness is a very bad guide in investments. 'Often when I travel in the crazy world', Siegmund G. Warburg used to say, 'I meet people who have an erotic relation with money ... I find it difficult to understand this relation, but I (also) find it amusing.'[1]

1.2   Asset classes of investing

Investing is for the longer term. Bob Keen, director of Global Private Banking Group at Merrill Lynch, defines the longer term as being a minimum of five years (three years is really medium term), but longer than that in the case of a pension plan. By contrast, speculating (see section 1.3) is very short term. 'Today, one's own investment plan is everybody's responsibility', Gordon Midgley, research director of London-based Investment Management Association (IMA), aptly suggested, adding that *all* individual investors must answer the query: 'Why am I investing?'

- Is it to maximize life consumption?
- To save for old age, enabling the person to be self-supporting?
- To supplement other types of future income, making feasible a higher life standard?

The answers the investor gives to these queries have a significant impact on his or her investment plan. In fact, this impact goes all the way to the role played by professional investors because, as we have seen, they are in business to serve the needs of individual investors entrusting them with their future income – whether they look at it in this way or not.

Keen took as an example the case of his daughter whom he encouraged to start her own pension fund. She is twenty-five years old and has just started in employed work and, like other young people, should be sensitive to the fact that, quite likely, if she does not *now* look after her income at retirement – 40 years hence – nobody else will.

Investing is not just keeping money in a savings account at the bank, even if both private and institutional investors have long regarded banks as pillars of the economy. During the 1970s, 1980s and 1990s many credit institutions got into difficulty, and when this happened investor confidence was greatly undermined. Hence, the need for detailed research about creditworthiness and trends in the banking industry, even if the investor is only a depositor of cash.

- Investors must be sure of the outlook of their counterparty, *before* making an investment decision.
- For investors, ratings by independent rating agencies constitute a frame of reference which tells a story about the counterparty's probability of default.[2]
- For individual companies and their commercial paper (for example, bills of exchange), ratings allow access to the capital markets, a lower interest rate and diversification of funding.

The evaluation of creditworthiness is very important to all investors and all issuers, given the magnitude of new issues brought to market every year. This reference also underlines the fact that investing does not only address equities (the main theme of this book) but also debt instruments. Even if there were only three alternatives – cash at the bank, equities and bonds – their existence would have posed the challenge of making a choice – a process known as *asset allocation*.

Decisions on how an investor, whether retail or professional, should allocate the assets under his or her control, returns the issue of investing to the most basic query: 'Why am I investing?' The answer will vary not only between individual investors and professional investors, but also within each class of investors. For instance, age often makes the difference in the content of the reply:

- A twenty-five year old person is likely to go for *growth* in investments, in the expectation that the right market choices will increase his or her capital.
- Other things being equal, a fifty-five year old person will make an investment plan loaded on the income side, since he or she will be preparing for retirement (more on this, in the discussion on the third golden rule).

Furthermore, a thoroughly studied investment solution should be integrated into one's own employment perspective. If an investor's unemployment risk is high, then he or she should save more than otherwise and should not buy cyclical stocks. Note that up to a point what has just been stated is as valid for pension funds as for annuities managed by insurers.

A valid answer to questions associated with asset allocation must consider a long list of decision factors sensitive to individual requirements. Every investor's personal perspective must be considered to provide responses which assist in fine-tuning the management of savings. By contrast, much more general is the concept of asset allocation by major class. As Figure 1.1 shows, there are several competing assets classes, some of which offer better protection against inflation than cash, bonds or equities.

Each of the major asset classes shown in Figure 1.1 can have subdivisions. Take equities as an example. There is a wide variety of companies issuing stock in the capital market – as well as debt instruments, including senior and subordinated debt, commercial paper, preferred stock and secured bank loans. In alphabetic order, the forty-four most important industry sectors are shown in Table 1.2.

A division into industry sectors is not the only way to categorize different entities and their equity. Another type of clarification addresses issues related to type of currency and country risk. Within this frame of reference, a major distinction

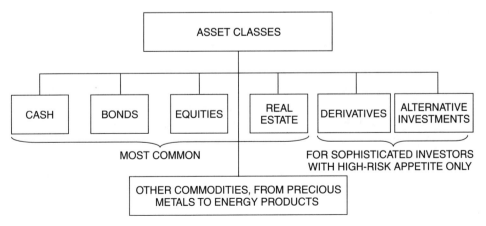

Figure 1.1 Asset allocation decisions must consider a wider spectrum of investments, though some of them will be discarded as incompatible with savings objectives

Aerospace	Investor-owned electric power
Agriculture (retail)	and natural gas
Agriculture (wholesale)	Leisure and lodging
Banking	Machinery
Building products	Media
Chemicals	Merchandising (retail)
Construction	Merchandising (wholesale)
Consulting	Metals and mining
Consumer products and services	Motor vehicles
Defense	Municipalities
Electronics	Mutual funds
Energy	Paper, forest products
Fisheries	Pension funds
Food, beverages, tobacco	Professionals
Forests	Public-owned electric power
Government (municipalities)	Real estate
Government (national or federal)	and gas
Government-guaranteed entities	Securities
Health care	Semiconductors
Hedge funds	Technology
Household appliances	Telecommunications
Industrial products and services	Transnational entities
Insurance	Transportation

Table 1.2 Forty-four industry sectors which are usually addressed individually or in small groups

will be between:

- Home country/home currency, and
- Host countries/host currencies.

In Chapter 9, we discuss this choice and its relation to conservative versus aggressive-type investments. In principle, but only in principle, the better the knowledge an investor has about the country in which the investment lies, the industry sector to which it belongs and the specific company it concerns, the more certain he or she will be about the choice being made.

At the same time, however, the more sophisticated the analysis of creditworthiness and performance, the more other factors enter into the evaluation, such as quality of management, products in the pipeline, market appeal, prevailing economic conditions and the pros and cons of the chosen instrument.

Regarding cash investments, for instance, when market uncertainty is high, cash can be king. However, under normal conditions professionals choose to be invested in securities rather than holding a large amount of cash. Alternatively, for private individuals cash has its attraction.

In several countries, many people who do not trust the government and the banking system hide cash in their mattresses. More to the point, however, private individuals count the cash stream from their entitlements as a 'sure' source of future income – better than investments. The trouble with this line of thinking is that in the twenty-first century that source is far from being 'sure'.

Real estate, another investment box in Figure 1.1, had its time, though opportunities for real estate investments are far from over. In this asset class, a distinction must be made between real estate investments in commercial property and those in housing. Another distinction is real estate for renting or reselling, and for one's own home.

■ The former has the risk associated with the accumulation of excess housing and/or office space, which impacts on market price.
■ The latter is nearly always rational, inasmuch as it fulfils an important personal need with a long time horizon: A person's house is his or her castle.

A similar statement about past investment glories can be made about gold. Gold used to be the commodity of refuge in hard times. Today, however, other commodities hold professional investors' attention. With the equity market still unsettled and interest rates at a forty-five year low, many professional investors have significantly increased the commodities share in their portfolio, particularly in oil and other energy products.

The last two boxes in Figure 1.1 relate to derivative financial instruments, and structured products associated with them. It would be nonsense to suggest professional investors should abstain from gambling in derivative financial instruments. Practically everybody does it, and some of those who do so try to kill two birds with one well-placed stone:

■ Reap extraordinary profits, and
■ Attract money now managed by other professional investors.

On the other hand, very few retail investors, and not necessarily all professionals, truly appreciate the risks to which they are exposed because of their bets through leveraged instruments like derivatives. Neither is the information on risk and return provided to investors factual, documented and impartial.

For instance, one of the banks promoting a fund of funds said to its clients that because it allocated the alternative investments capital among twenty professionals, its exposure to each is a mere 5 percent.[3] Linearly speaking this is true, but it is no less true that the relationship is nonlinear, and the investor has no control of:

■ How his money is invested,
■ To how much leverage it is subjected, and
■ How well his or her assets are being managed.

A serious, responsible answer to the query about investing in derivative products and structured alternative investments, must go all the way back to the investor's *savings objectives* and *risks* associated with them. Why is the retail or institutional investor reaching 'this' rather than 'that' decision on asset allocation is a matter closely related to the:

■ Mission the investor has to accomplish for him or herself or for clients,
■ Risks the investor is willing or allowed to take, and

■ Share of the assets which is subject to exposure well beyond prudential limits, to maximize projected returns.

The difference between investors and speculators rests on these simple premises, as section 1.3 demonstrates. The questions in the preceding paragraphs have to be asked before a decision is made on an investment policy. It is a very poor practice to 'shoot' first and ask questions later. Whether professional or retail, investors who work that way face strong headwinds and have a very difficult landing.

1.3   Investors, speculators, risk and return

To *invest*, says Webster's dictionary, is to cover, furnish with power, privilege or authority; also to put money into business, stocks, bonds, real estate for the purpose of obtaining an income or profit. This income or profit is the *return* on investment. As we have seen, investments also have *risks*, and the reader is by now aware that the doors of risk and return are adjacent and identical.

'*Capitalists* are in business because they expect to prosper', says Dr Edward Yardeni, a New York economist. 'Capitalists that use their own funds are *investors*. Capitalists that use borrowed funds (hence leveraging) are *speculators*. They borrow money because they are speculating that they can achieve a return which exceeds current rate.'

One of the reasons *investors* tend to confuse the doors of risk and return is that, almost by definition, they cannot be pessimists. If they were, they would get out of the business of investing. *Economists* tend to be pessimists, and that is why economics is known as 'the dismal science'. Economists are pessimists because they usually see further than investors and the majority are concerned about the negative aftermath of leveraging.

Speculators buy and sell financial instruments, for instance, futures contracts, with the expectation of profiting from changes in the price of the underlying commodity. A speculator who believes, say, that *cash* gold prices will be higher in the future may buy gold futures now and hold the contract until a time when he or she can sell it at higher price. Most often, however, speculators have a very short time horizon.

Futures are bought in a public exchange and forwards are bought and sold over the counter in bilateral agreements. Counterparties enter into speculative transactions aiming to generate income by taking a particular view of a specific market or instrument. Typically, they are betting on the market's direction, *volatility* (see Chapter 12), or both.

Leveraging (see also Chapter 12), or gearing, means living, trading or investing beyond one's means. Leveraged transactions can generate large gains or losses, and are often constructed with minimal, or no, downside protection. *Derivative* financial instruments are powerful leveraging tools.[4] A more classical tool, however, is borrowing.

Speculation through derivative financial instruments can be particularly dangerous for people and companies that do not have what it takes to gamble in leveraged instruments and/or the financial resources to support significant losses, which means those who do not have financial staying power. Leveraged derivative transactions represent the pinnacle of speculation, and they can be particularly damaging if not properly understood and controlled in terms of exposure.

Speculative transactions of the type discussed in the preceding paragraphs can be profitable if the price a speculator pays is less than the price of the commodity when he or she sells the contract later on. If the speculator's projections are wrong, and the price of the commodity does not rise but falls, then the speculator will lose money all the way to going bankrupt, as the case of LTCM and so many other entities demonstrate.[5]

- Derivatives is a relatively low-cost leveraged way for speculators to make bets on future prices of various commodities, but it is by no means a 'sure bet'.
- Speculators, as well as investors, must therefore have the resources to sustain potential losses and sufficient knowledge to understand the nature of the risks being undertaken.

They must also appreciate the deeper sense of *risk*, looking at it as the chance of injury, damage or loss – a hazard. Risk is omnipresent in all acts of daily life. In finance, it can be expressed quantitatively as the probability or degree of loss. Such probability is not just mathematics. It is a function of:

- The type of loss that is covered, such as counterparty default, interest rate change, exchange rate collapse or type of accident.
- The nature of the counterparty to a transaction – person, company, country – and its ability and willingness to honour its obligations.

Because risk is omnipresent in trading and investing, risk management has as an objective to identify fundamental risk factors; determine linkages between commercial and financial operations; establish metrics; take measurements, test and reach conclusions; elaborate dynamic correction capabilities; and track the execution of orders regarding the control of exposure. All this is part and parcel of risk control (see Chapters 10 and 11).

Risk management is a complex task which must cover the whole spectrum of transactions and positions in an investor's portfolio. This is as true of the individual investor as it is of the professional investor, though the former will exercise risk management at a lower level of sophistication. Figure 1.2 provides a snapshot of two types of exposure: market risk and credit risk. There are also other types of exposure like business risk (see Chapter 13) and operational risk.[6]

All investments are subject to exposure, whether they are done by private individuals, professional investors or by businesses. Theoretically, there is a difference between these classes because businesses primarily invest money in their own research, production, marketing and distribution facilities. They do so to increase market reach and the appeal of their products – hence, their future profits. But during the past ten years businesses also take speculative bets; for instance, selling options on their own stock.

Just as institutional investors and private investors interact with one another, the latter being clients of the former, businesses and individual investors also work in synergy. Individuals depend on business enterprises for their employment, and they also benefit from company-sponsored retirement plans. But businesses fail, people lose their jobs and retirement plans get severely wounded – all reasons why retail investors have every interest to take the proverbial long, hard look at their savings.

Section 1.2 has brought to the reader's attention that acting as private individuals people have different ways of investing their savings: from banking accounts and the money market, to equities and bonds. In a macroeconomic sense, the wealth invested by individuals and households is taken out of immediate consumption. On the other hand, private sector money going into savings in the banking industry assists the investments being made by business – while the private sector's purchase of equities promotes the capital market (see Chapter 3).

In early March 2004, Dr Alan Greenspan, the chairman of the Federal Reserve, identified another important role of savings. He said that the hugely negative current account balance of the USA essentially represents the difference between savings and investments by Americans. Traditionally characterized by a low level of savings, in the last decades of the twentieth century and early years of the twenty-first century the American economy has:

- A negative savings balance, but
- A relatively strong investment policy propelled by the capital market.

While Buffett's 'don't lose' rule essentially says that savings must always be protected, it is no less true that all types of investments must cope with interest rate, foreign currency, equity price, counterparty and other risks. Even if a portion of these risks is hedged, as professional investors usually do, volatility could impact adversely on a portfolio and associated financial position.

For instance, fixed income securities are subject to interest rate risk even if the portfolio is diversified and consists primarily of investment grade securities to minimize credit risk. Moreover, all stocks in an investment portfolio are subject to market risk, which sometimes wipes out the investor's savings. The Eurotunnel provides a relatively recent example.

1.4   Savings down the drain: the Eurotunnel fiasco

Eurotunnel plc, Eurotunnel S.A. and their subsidiaries comprise the Eurotunnel Group which designed, financed and constructed the tunnel that runs under the English Channel. The British and French Eurotunnel companies have shared equally the cost of the project, and they will operate the tunnel until 2086.

The flotation of Eurotunnel has been, arguably, the launch of popular shareholder capitalism in France, like the privatization of Deutsche Telekom has been popular shareholder capitalism German-style. Individual shareholders still own 65 percent of Eurotunnel's equity. They were taken on board, so to speak, following a meeting of Margaret Thatcher and François Mitterrand in the early 1990s, in which Thatcher refused to finance the tunnel through public funds.

In 1986 a myriad of small investors bought Eurotunnel's initial public offering (IPO) at 200 pence, and continued pouring their savings into the equity as its price skyrocketed to 780 pence in 1988, the high-water mark. Subsequently, Eurotunnel's

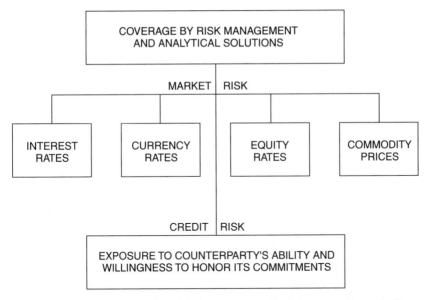

Figure 1.2 Investors are vulnerable because of credit risk and market volatility

equity price dropped to the 300 to 400 pence range up to 1994, when the tunnel opened for business, with a 460 pence spike at the opening of the service.

Investors who read and understood what the risk and reward numbers said, had good reason to be wary of this privately financed European infrastructure project whose total cost has been £9.5 billion, double the initial projection. Such a huge investment has been financed in part by £2.5 billion of share capital raised by six equity issues between May 1986 and May 1994, of which £2.1 billion was used to fund construction. The balance of financing was provided by £7.4 billion of bank loans.

The rise in construction costs, the delays to the start-up of operations and the awful miscalculation of demand for Eurotunnel services, considerably increased the project's vulnerability. Funding requirements zoomed to the point of making a financial restructuring operation necessary at the end of 1995. Implemented in April 1998, the restructuring consisted mainly of:

■ Issuance of more questionable financial obligations, and
■ Converting part of the debt owed to the lending banks into shares.

The restructuring made available an interest-free loan until 2006 (the Stabilization Facility), to cover the interest Eurotunnel would be unable to pay with its available cash flow. As a contribution to this restructuring operation, the French and British governments agreed to extend the Eurotunnel concession from 2052 to 2086.

As this reference documents, since 1998 Eurotunnel has conducted a number of financial operations aimed at reducing its debt (achieved to the tune of £1.2 billion), as well as to downsize its annual interest charges by up to 40 percent. Still at £6.4 billion, the current Eurotunnel's debt remains considerable. If there is a consolation for lenders, it is that, as with all equity, those who paid most dearly for their mistake, with their savings, have been the shareholders.

It is in no way a surprise that within two years of opening for business, with costs skyrocketing and the projected traffic figures failing to materialize, the price of Eurotunnel stock collapsed – all the way to becoming a penny stock. Critics say that this has been a con because to small shareholders the Eurotunnel investment was presented as 'win-win':

- Conservative like 'Ma Bell' (AT&T) in the 1980s, but
- With huge growth prospects, given the terrific traffic projections.

The projected traffic and huge profits that went with it, never materialized. Postmortem, experts are suggesting that Eurotunnel's business opportunity analysis was made to attract investors and their savings, not to provide a realistic estimate of risk and return. Projected traffic figures were overstated and the only thing that skyrocketed was the construction costs which went out of control.

In the aftermath of all these negatives, the Eurotunnel venture required significant capital increases by its investors, who had already burned their fortune with it. No wonder Eurotunnel has been described as the biggest financial scam in Europe – on a par with Parmalat (see Chapter 15). In France, the myriad of small investors who lost their savings with Eurotunnel decided to strike back. Market watchers say that they are a motley crowd ranging:

- From fringe groups such as 'SOS Petits Porteurs',[7]
- To the 'Association de Défense des Actionnaires Minoritaires (ADAM)'.

The most recent shareholder activism succeeded in a way, as Eurotunnel's entire management got sacked at the stakeholder meeting, which took place on 7 April 2004 – precisely for such purpose. This, however, did not help the 'petits porteurs'. Reacting to management instability, the Paris Bourse pushed Eurotunnel's equity down to less than 0.45 euro (30 pence) per share.

In conclusion, a lesson investors should learn from the Eurotunnel debacle is that not everything that shines is gold. The whole business of investment decisions is a process of risk, because there is no beginning and no end to securities selection and deselection, portfolio construction, risk monitoring and the other chores which constitute the framework of asset management. (See also section 1.6 on caveat emptor.)

To protect themselves from a financial precipice, sophisticated investors *hedge*, which is also what companies practise to offset adversity from credit, market and other risks. If hedging is well done and if it is free of speculation, it can provide cover from price changes in a commodity in which one has an interest. This may be stocks, bonds, currencies, metals, wheat or any other commodity.

- True hedgers assume a futures position with the objective of reducing their risk.
- In contrast, speculators willingly take on additional risk with futures positions, with the objective of profiting from price changes.

While futures markets enable the investor to hedge some part of market risk, the element of financial exposure is *always* present because assumed future price might be much lower (or higher) than what one has guessed that it will be. Many things can happen between 'now' and 'then' to change the price dynamics – and, therefore, to turn a hedge on its head.

Alternatively, the investor may transfer the future price risk to someone else, by paying a premium to buy an option. For instance, companies hedge their exposure to interest rate risk with options in the event of a major increase in interest rates. Similarly, because many securities held in the equity portfolio are subject to equity price risk, companies may hedge it with options, but private investors do not have the knowledge to do such hedging – let alone the fact that:

- Hedging is not an exact science, and
- It is always subject to the uncertainty principle which characterizes all investments (see Chapter 10).

In conclusion, precisely because nothing can be certain, investors must appreciate the possibility of both wins and losses in portfolio value, and be ready for them. This is true for one's own property as well as for managed funds. Old hands in asset management suggest that if the account manager does not call the client when he or she is losing money, someone else will. Therefore, an honest policy is to phone the client and explain *what* has happened, *why* it has happened and *which* are the proposed corrective steps.

1.5   Understand the difference between investing, trading and speculating

The *first golden rule* for winning in trading and investing is to appreciate the differences (and some of the similarities) which exist between investing and speculating. A speculator (like a trader) is always concerned about the short-term direction of the market. The speculator would go short or long, according to market trends. By contrast, an investor tends to be long, even if he or she is keeping part of the funds he or she manages in cash because of uncertainty about the market's direction.

The first golden rule applies equally well to individual investors and to professional asset managers. To develop a plan which pays due attention to risk and return, rather than just giving lip service, the professional investor should use as starting point his or her mandate – precisely, the one given by the client. The professional investor should also account for the fact he or she is constrained because of managing *assets*, not liquid money, as used to be the case in the past.

The Eurotunnel example discussed in section 1.4 has dramatized the fact that, in connection with any investment plan, both professional investment managers and the retail investors should fully take into account credit and market risk which may hit their objective. 'Risk should always condition the choice of assets', Gordon Midgley advised. Individual investors might drift into speculation if they believe in promises of high return and low risk – as has been the case with Eurotunnel.

Market debacles cannot only decimate one's savings, but also have political consequences when a large percentage of the population are shareholders. Some '70 percent of voters own stock', says Grover G. Norquist, president of the pro-tax-cut

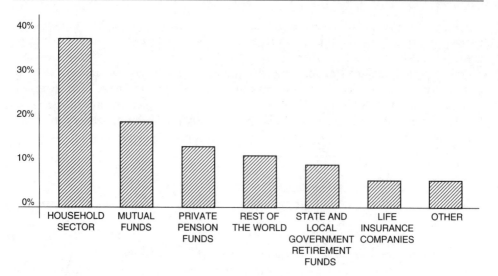

Figure 1.3 Who owns stocks in the USA?

Americans for Tax Reform. 'Bush recognizes that the investor class is the most important demographic group in the country.'[8] Figure 1.3 gives a bird's-eye view of who controls the equity of US companies.

'Investments', a knowledgeable financial adviser said, 'is a mystery item which defies full explanation. We can only judge investments by what is involved in the act of investing as contrasted to speculating.' Under both headings may come government securities, other debt instruments, listed and unlisted equities and other commodities.

The principle with all investment classes is: 'Never forget why you invest.' The next crucial question is: 'How?' One of the important characteristics of institutional investors is that their activity tends to combine in the same person both views inherent in investments:

- The short-term trader/broker viewpoint, and
- The longer-term view of the assets manager.

Some experts are using the concept of a *holding period* as a measure of an investor's steadiness and, in certain cases, of performance. Evaluating gains and losses resulting from investment decisions solely on a calendar year basis is arbitrary. What one really wants to know is what the odds are for profitable performance over a holding period of a chosen length, with both risk and return as part of the picture.

The holding period and the investor's *time horizon* correlate (see Chapter 9). Typically, investors have a longer-term horizon than traders, and therefore their priority is picking stocks which, using current knowledge and some future projections, could be held over a period of time. By contrast, the trader's key phrase is 'fast turnaround'. This difference is not a value judgment, but a reflection of trading and investment dynamics. To make matters more complex:

- In the past, investments were made with a more or less long time horizon, but
- During the past twenty years, the investment world became much more short-term oriented.

This relatively shorter term influences investor choices and calls for answers to focused queries. For instance: 'Will the central bank raise or lower interest rates?' The central bank's move has important implications for both the bond and the equity markets, and thus for asset allocation. As a way of thinking about the relationship between sector performance and asset allocation, some investment advisers advance the paradigm of an *investment clock* which depicts how an economic cycle works.

The investment clock is a paradigm, and paradigms are important to conceptual analysis inasmuch as most activities concerning financial instruments – whether made for trading, speculating or investing reasons – try to develop market perceptions. Even if traders and speculators, in contrast to investors, have a short time horizon, their market perception is not the same.

- Speculators typically work for their own account; they earn the profits for themselves and cover the losses from their own account.
- Traders and investment managers work for their company's and their clients' accounts.
- Their commissions aside, the profits and losses belong to the company.

The trader aims to execute an order to buy or sell at best price available, or at a limit the client specifies. But he or she may also be an arbitrageur, purchasing and selling securities and futures to benefit from an anticipated change in their price relationship. In this particular case, the trader acts as speculator and depends on a fast switch to end in the black.

Counterparties enter into arbitrage transactions to obtain increased earnings, lower funding costs or to capitalize on what is perceived as market inefficiencies. For instance, many derivative transactions are executed to take advantage of discrepancies, the so-called 'anomalies', which from time to time exist in the financial market.

Speculators seem to take comfort from a strategy exploiting anomalies, particularly if they somehow perceive the risk they are assuming as being limited. Yet, many transactions thought of as yield enhancing, such as writing options in order to generate additional premium income, may not be as low risk as they appear. Arbitrage transactions are not generally suitable for non-speculators because the amount of exposure they entail is rarely appropriately judged:

- Whenever speculators, traders or investors thinks they 'know the market', they are engaging in self-delusion.
- Every market player should appreciate the financial universe is totally impersonal: it does not care whether one makes or loses money.

Efficiency in market moves requires a holistic view of market behavior, within a frame of reference like the one presented in Figure 1.4. Notice that a basic prerequisite is

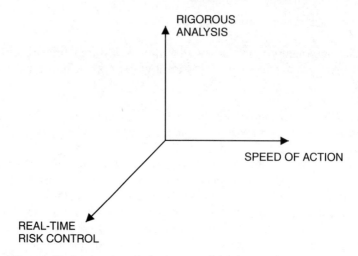

Figure 1.4 Frame of reference for a holistic view of the financial universe and for a better chance to be ahead of the game

rigorous analysis (see Chapter 6) which talks a lot about the homework that needs to be done.

Whether they use fundamental or technical analysis to project equity price movements, traders and investor must develop a strategy which factors in the likelihood of both risk and return. Part of this strategy is to know when to enter and exit the market, as well as how to manage assumed risk. As we have briefly seen in section 1.3, risk control:

■ Is an issue of primary importance, and
■ Is one of the weaknesses of many market professionals.

When money is lost, who is responsible? Speculators have only themselves to blame for their losses. But individual investors, as well as institutional investors who depend on third party advice and/or administration, blame their fund manager not only for losses but also for underperformance. Usually fund managers answer is 'Caveat emptor' (see section 1.6).

In case they outsource fund management, professional investors should never delegate their responsibility for investment strategy to a third party. Success in investments and investment strategy correlate; therefore, an investment strategy should never be outsourced. Moreover, investors should not change their strategy to chase hot sectors of the economy, or high-flying companies whose fortunes depend upon a range of unpredictable factors:

■ From the state of the economy, or
■ To product and market trends that temporarily enhance their competitive positions.

This chasing after a chimera is done by investors either directly or through fund investing. For instance, funds that specialize in technology rose 55.8 percent in 2003, and investors poured \$312 million into them during that same year. This compared with withdrawals of \$6.7 billion the previous year (2002), when technology funds lost 43 percent on average. Even more red ink ran in 2001 and 2000.

But jumping on the bandwagon also has a downside. The Jacob Internet Fund provides an example. It led shareholders into a three-year tunnel, losing 79.1 percent in 2000, 56.4 percent in 2001 and 13 percent in 2002. While the fund gained 101.3 percent in 2003, Jacob's record of volatility suggests the fund is willing to take on a high level of risk in pursuit of big rewards which sometimes prove elusive. This may be acceptable if the investor understands and appreciates the risks he or she is getting into, but it is wrong if he or she believes that high returns are achievable at no risk.

1.6 Caveat emptor and human nature

The unreliability of assumptions as well as of unreasonable expectations from investments are, to a large extent, part of human nature. And as Dr Alan Greenspan aptly stated at an early 2004 lecture: 'I don't know what monetary policy we can implement to alter human nature.'[9] Greenspan's dictum applies hand-in-glove to hypotheses connected to risk and return with equities, interest rates, currency exchange rates and other commodities.

Sometimes our assumptions are no better than guesswork, averages chosen without any proof, correlations picked out of thin air, fancy equations which have no substance and unchallenged acceptance of claims made by brokers and fund managers. Practically, in all these cases, it is the investor who is at fault. Originating in Roman law, the caveat emptor clause is frequently referred to in commercial and financial transactions, and it means 'Let the buyer beware'.

'Buyer or investor beware' is generally considered to be a sound method of operating a market, and not only because it has survived for so many centuries. Investors should be alert to the risks they are taking. The downside of this principle is that the small investor does not have much of an understanding of:

- Risk(s) embedded in transaction, or
- Exposure embedded in his or her portfolio.

As a result, the retail investor who is unaware of assumed risks does not stand any chance in market gyrations, the proof being that many small investors have time and again lost all their savings, as we saw in section 1.4. Neither are the rights of investors always well protected. Therefore, investors are pressuring legislators and regulators to strengthen their rights in publicly quoted companies in the European Union, in a way commensurate with the recent regulations by the Securities and Exchange Commission (SEC) target in the USA.

Since 2001 in the aftermath of Enron, WorldCom, Marconi, Eurotunnel, Vivendi, Parmalat and many other cases, weak supervision and poor corporate governance have been disastrous to investors. This happens at a time when entitlement programs wane because society cannot sustain them anymore, and personal savings through investments, starting when one begins a career, seem to be the only way to provide a reasonable income at retirement.

The answer to the query 'Why do I save?' asked in section 1.2, is different today than ten or twenty years ago. Politicians do not have the courage to openly say so, but most definitely the trend is towards reducing entitlement programs and benefits. On 25 February 2004, testifying about the ballooning US Federal budget deficit, Dr Alan Greenspan demanded reducing Social Security and Medicare benefits for workers at or near retirement age.[10]

There are reasons behind this stance. The Fed chairman said that 'We will eventually have no choice but to make significant structural adjustments in the major retirement programs', adding that this should be done 'as soon as possible' on the grounds that the government was overcommitted to spending on:

- Required benefits, and
- Health insurance.

'I think it is terribly important to make certain that we communicate to the people who are about to retire, what it is they are going to have to live with', Greenspan stated, urging Congress to push up the retirement age for Social Security and Medicare, and to reduce the cost-of-living increases, which are linked to inflation. According to Greenspan the main fiscal problem is Medicare, partly due to the fact that:

- Advances in medical technology allows people to live longer, and
- Longevity as well as higher technology increase the level of spending for retiree health care.

But if savers become investors – either directly or through mutual funds and pension funds – then they want to see that the law is making company executives accountable to their stakeholders. Laws alone, however, would not change the investment landscape, because laws need to be enforced. Even if some codes of corporate behavior have been published, and these are sparse in continental Europe, companies are not rushing to comply with them.

The law enforcement industry has a major job to do, human nature being what it is. Supervisory authorities must have expertise both in regulation and in policing, short of which caveat emptor would be an empty term. By themselves, codes of conduct are making little more than general statements of good intentions. In a survey of thirty-nine different codes existing in European countries, the European Commission's (EC's) lawyers found that:

- Many were outright failures, and
- There were gaping holes in investors' rights.

For instance, one survey documented that only 9 percent of UK-listed companies it reviewed fully comply with all the recommendations of the corporate governance code. In Belgium, which has four different codes on subjects relating to investments, there has been evidence that control over corporate governance activities is slowing.[11] Evidently, this is to the detriment of investors.

Moreover, the caveat emptor principle is being challenged by a 3 June 2002, US Supreme Court ruling in favor of a Securities and Exchange Commission action against a broker. The Supreme Court stated that the securities markets' regulations introduced in the 1930s 'sought to substitute a philosophy of full disclosure for the philosophy of caveat emptor, and this to achieve a high standard of business ethics in the securities industry'.

According to this ruling, analysts may have a legal duty of care for their retail customers, which means, for example, offering them only such advice as they would give to themselves. On this ground, even prior to the aforementioned US Supreme Court decision, countless private lawsuits have been pending against financial services firms, and they seem likely to drag on for years, some of them expecting to result in huge payouts. As a matter of principle, investment advice must be characterized by independence, impartiality and neutrality.

- *Independence* means the absence of any objective link – personal, business, or otherwise – between the analyst and any of the equities which he or she covers.
- *Impartiality* refers to the lack of subjective attitude by the analyst, who should not favor any one of the equities he or she covers, for any reason.
- *Neutrality* is a concept connected to a position of the analyst who should have no interest, and no conflict, resulting from the outcome of the research he or she is doing and the investment advice being given.

Rigorous investor protection rules are vital both for professionals and for retail investors. Their aim must be to provide a shield against malfeasance, not to take care of investors' risks. And because prudential regulation is necessary but not enough, both speculators and investors much be proficient in risk management in regard to every transaction and portfolio position. Risk control is the common core to all types of investments, as Figure 1.5 suggests.

Beyond the understanding of risks assumed with investments, a sound method-ology and first-class technology are instrumental in the control of exposure. Timely and accurate data washes out wishful thinking, which is destructive because it takes attention away from diagnostic processes. Whenever traders or investors gets com-placent or careless they abandon basic principles, and therefore lose their position. Another similarity between good trading and sound investing is the delicate balance between:

- The conviction to follow one's own ideas,
- The ability to recognize when one made a mistake, and
- The courage to correct it without loss of time, though money may be lost.

The policy outlined by these three bullets is of fundamental interest to all investors, since they are bound to be wrong on a number of choices they make. Extensive experi-ence and rapid self-correction of mistakes helps in learning how to gain confidence in one's own investment skills. Big egos destroy self-confidence, because confidence and humility share the same mind.

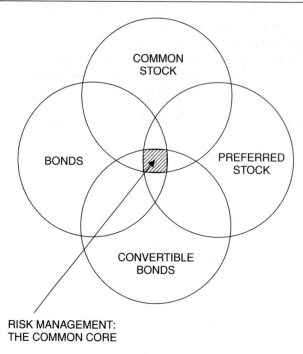

COMMON
STOCK

BONDS

PREFERRED
STOCK

CONVERTIBLE
BONDS

RISK MANAGEMENT:
THE COMMON CORE

Figure 1.5 There is a common core in risk and return valuation with investments

1.7   A golden rule for private investors, but not necessarily for all professionals

The *second golden rule* in investing is to own your assets: stocks, bonds or other commodities. Private investors should not borrow money to buy equities, and they should not take a mortgage on their house to play in the stock market. This is what Amadeo P. Giannini, who built the Bank of America, advised his friends, clients and employees. Giannini's 'own your stock' is excellent advice. *Worry* is the extra interest investors pay when they buy stock on margin or with borrowed money.

This rule 'Do not borrow, do not buy on margin, do not leverage yourself and do not sell short' is golden for retail investors, for whom it should be supplemented by one more clause: 'Do not use your equities as collateral (part of buying on margin), because the market can move against you and you will lose all your savings.' Violating this rule will definitely be against the savings objectives of a serious investor.

- If the investor borrows funds from his broker to purchase securities,
- Then, the broker's collateral for the loan will be securities purchased, and other assets in the investor's margin account as well as assets in any other accounts at that broker.

If the securities in the investor's margin account decline in value, so does the value of the collateral supporting his or her loan. As a result, the broker can take actions – from issuing a margin call, to selling securities or dispose of other assets in any of the investor's accounts held at the brokerage. This is necessary to maintain the required equity in the account, but in the aftermath, the investor can lose far more funds than he or she deposits in the margin account.

While the risks which have been outlined are always present, it does not take two heads to understand that the second golden rule does not apply in its entirety with professional investors. In fact, hedge funds do exactly the contrary of what this rule states, and that is part of their job. To professional investors who know how to be in charge of their risks, leveraging is the way to expand their business opportunity. Up to a point, this is also true of *short selling* which is essentially a one-way bet considered to be:

- A comfortable gamble in the foreign exchange market where macroeconomics and politics dominate, and where governments provide some direction by their policies.
- Much more risky in equity markets where technical research (see Chapter 6) may give the wrong signals and market psychology is king – leading to unexpected turnarounds.

One of the experts who participated in the research leading to this book was to suggest that the second golden rule might be valid even for professional investors, depending on the time frame in which they operate. For instance, this advice might have been good for 2000 to 2004 but it was surely bad for the 1955 to 1999 period. In fact, a lot of the boom and bust of the late 1990s was caused by leveraging and speculation.

This cognizant investment adviser rephrased the second golden rule for professional investors to read in the following way: 'The moment you are uncomfortable with market signals, get out of leveraging.' Immediately thereafter he added that such advice is not always taken by professional investors who try to carry their luck a bet too far. 'You can take your horse to the water, but you cannot make it drink', said the veteran investment counsellor. Pension funds and life insurers should take notice.

To appreciate Giannini's dictum behind the *second golden rule* of investments, it is necessary to remember that in the late nineteenth and early twentieth centuries, as now, there were plenty of opportunities to make and lose a fortune. On 10 October 1907, prices on the New York Stock Exchange dropped sharply. Runs on banks quickly followed, triggering the worst financial panic in US history up to that time.

The crisis started in New York and spread rapidly westward. In a single day both the Pittsburgh and New Orleans stock exchanges suspended operations. There were riots in a dozen different American cities, while more than 130 banks across the country closed their doors. A run by their depositors combined with the failure to keep reserves anywhere near legal limits, pushed many of them into bankruptcy.

On 31 October 1907, in an effort to prevent a depositors' stampede from pushing more credit institutions into the abyss, James Gillette, the governor of California, declared a bank holiday. Soon after, San Francisco's largest banks began issuing *clearing script*, or funny money, to make up for the lack of gold. But Giannini's months of quiet preparations paid off in facing the obligations of his credit institution – and in increased prestige for the Bank of Italy, forerunner of Bank of America.

No sooner had the panic hit San Francisco, than Giannini passed the word among the bank's customers that he was ready to pay gold on demand to depositors who wanted to withdraw their savings. He himself and three of his employees were waiting with the biggest part of the gold he had been accumulating stacked behind the cages of tellers' windows; and everyone could see it. Giannini and his Bank of Italy were the talk of San Francisco.[12]

This is a precious reference the reader will be well advised to keep in mind, because it kills two birds with one well-placed stone. When Giannini advised his friends, clients and employees to own their assets and not to leverage themselves, he meant that individual investors should be very prudent. But the great American banker applied the same policy to his own credit institution. If he had not, he would not have been able to pay with gold his depositors while other banks folded.

'Own your assets and do not gamble' is not just advice for individual investors but for everyone – including institutions. Behind this prudent policy lies the fact that financial markets are volatile and their twists are for any practical purpose unpredictable. If an investor owns his or her equities and bonds and the worst happens, then there is no reason to panic. He or she should not sell the assets but sit on them and wait. Eventually the market will turn around.

Amadeo Giannini's cautions and preparedness in 1907 was no one-off event. The great banker was genuinely concerned about the tens of thousands of small investors who were borrowing money at 'usurious rates' from banks and finance companies to speculate in the Bank of Italy's stock. Just prior to the Great Depression, on 14 March 1928, he issued a press release warning investors to:

- Pay off their debts, and
- Get out of the market.

'The public is attributing to me miracle working powers which I do not have', Giannini said, adding that 'We want them to own their own shares outright. We do not want them held as security for loans. We want our stockholders so firmly entrenched that they cannot be forced to sell out at some unfavorable time.' As the market fever mounted, Giannini sent an open letter to banks and brokerage firms across the US, urging them to refrain from making loans on Bancitaly stock where the obvious intention of borrowers was to use the money to speculate on his institution's equity. Events proved him right.

For individual investors, a logical and important extension of the advice given to private investors by Amadeo Giannini on taking positions only with one's own money is never to sell short.[13] An investor is short on a given equity if he or she sells it without having it inventoried in his or her portfolio. The resulting risk can be huge, because if one misses the switch (or the market does not move in the direction the investor guessed) the next stop may be bankruptcy.

This does not mean that short sales should be outlawed, though some governments tried to do so without success. What it means is that short sales are for speculators *not* for investors. They are made when there is downside in the equities market or a company is greatly wounded, but nobody – particularly the experts – can say for sure when the market would turn around, obliging the short seller to cover his or her position(s) by buying the assets at a much higher price than that at which he or she sold them.

Though it may not be recognized as such, selling short is not only a predatory activity but one that has all the characteristics of a big ego. Respect for the wisdom and ability of other traders, who are our market opponents and are expected to be the losers in *our* shorting of shares, aids in keeping our own ego small. Experienced traders suggest that it is always wise to examine the other party's strengths and weaknesses, asking questions such as:

■ Why is he buying or selling?
■ What does he know that I do not?
■ Is he closer to the truth about the state of the market (or of an entity) than I am?

Several traders and investors said, during the research, that they experienced their biggest losses after they saw their biggest gains. This is not unreasonable, because it is after the biggest gains that one's ego inflates. Therefore, the answers one is giving to the quiz in the above three bullets are part of a sound risk control policy. They are pillars of a winning style in trading and investing. Critical questions which oblige us to think in depth are also instrumental in:

■ Extending winning streaks, and
■ Reducing position size before large losses.

For individual investors, never selling short and not allowing one's stock to be borrowed are two issues which may look different, but they correlate. Speculators borrow equities from brokers to sell them short, and brokers rent out equities of their clients who are on margin – therefore they bet on borrowed money (more on short sales and their aftermath in Chapter 5). A corollary to this is to avoid leaving one's stock with the broker in 'street name'. It is precisely this ability to vote on stock as owner of record that gives stock exchanges and brokers their power over the economy.

1.8   Income, growth and control of exposure

Since, by following the second golden rule, the money one invests is one's own, one has to decide in a factual and documented manner on the objectives of the investment prior to entering into it. This essentially means what the saver wants to do with his or her capital. A basic decision is whether the investor is after *income* or *growth*, also appropriately defining the level of risk he or she is willing to assume.

Typically, though not necessarily always, with *income*, an investor's objective is to maintain capital and also get a good return adjusted for inflation. One should, however, appreciate that investment returns could be very low or, in some years, even negative. With this constraint in mind, the goal is to obtain a continuing income stream from dependable debt (or equity) sources.

Other things being equal, the higher the income objective, the more the investor should be willing to assume risk of principal loss. Risk increases if the goal is to accumulate wealth, over time, rather than bet on current income, and it increases further when the investor is seeking to achieve above average returns.

Precisely because the aims, instruments and risks associated with an income strategy and a growth strategy are different, wise investors do not target both income and growth at the same time. Moreover, for either choice they take care to provide appropriate identification and definition of risk factors, appreciating the fact that:

- Fixed income instruments, therefore bonds, have interest rate risk and credit risk.
- Equities have market risk which can be significantly higher than interest rate risk; but they also have credit risk as the cases of Enron, WorldCom, Marconi, Eurotunnel, Parmalat and many others document.

Based on these premises, the *third golden rule* prompts the investor to decide on income or growth. This decision is strategic. If the investor goes for equities, then it is better to concentrate on growth-oriented stocks rather than income stocks. If income is one's objective, then it is just as good to buy bonds or open an account in a bank if the interest rate is appealing and the bank is a highly rated counterparty.[14]

- With bonds, one can receive higher yields than with income-oriented equities, and
- There are always Group of Ten government bonds with no credit risk, albeit at lower interest rate than with corporate debt.

The opinion expressed in the preceding paragraphs does not find unanimous approval among experts. Gordon Midgley said that this binary type of distinction – income versus growth – is rather arbitrary. What the investor should be looking for is the bigger picture which incorporates not only expected return and associated risks (including inflation) but also an investment solution which is not correlated with his or her work. For instance, if the investor works for an oil company he or she should not buy energy stocks. Look at Enron!

Bob Keen suggested that there is also a totally different way of looking at the third golden rule, that is, from the individual investor's perspective. In his opinion: 'If the investor has enough capital behind him, he may not be concerned about the choice of growth or income; and if he is really for growth, then more often than not, the investor will choose to invest in his own company believing that this will give him the best return for his money.'

What about the income versus growth choices of the professional investor? The experts' opinions converged to answer that he or she should go back to the *mandate*. The professional investor typically represents other people's interests. What precisely are those interests? What are the options available to satisfy them? What is the risk appetite behind each of them? What are the risk control measures and their effectiveness?

Let us take investments in equities as an example. Though they are a better bet for a growth strategy, investors must be aware that many growth-oriented companies, big and small, assume a significant amount of risk. They also have an equity giveaway policy through management options – in many cases a rip-off of investors.[15] Therefore, it is good to examine the options policy of a company before buying its stock, and this is just one of the variables affecting an equity investment choice and its risks.

I would find no difficulty in admitting that what the preceding paragraph stated about executive options is a contrarian opinion, though in 2004 with the new regulations issued by the Financial Accounting Standards Board (FASB) it is becoming the law of the land, at least in the USA. (This book includes many concepts the reader may consider contrarian.)

We will see in Chapter 9 (in connection with the eleventh golden rule) that to become a successful investor it is necessary to be both a pro and a contrarian. Thesis and antithesis can coexist in people who have the appropriate culture, which is gained by increasing one's background knowledge and by learning the twists of financial history. 'Who knows only his own generation remains only a child', George Norline, a former president of the University of Colorado, used to say.

A contrarian view for instance is that while free markets can only operate unmolested in a democracy, they themselves are not at all democratic. Because wealth is concentrated in a few hands, the markets are oligarchic. This fact has not escaped the attention of people who think about such matters. At the end of the nineteenth century, Vilfredo Pareto, a Swiss-Italian professor of economics and mathematics, developed the venerable law which bears his name:

- Pareto observed that 1 percent of the Swiss population controlled 35 percent of Switzerland's wealth.
- A century on, in spite of all the 'isms' which challenged society – socialism, fascism, nazism and communism – Pareto's law is always valid.

In the financial market, and most specifically in stock exchanges, what might appear a democracy operates on the principle of 'one dollar one vote', with voting power highly concentrated among the few who have the dollars, pounds, euros, yens and other currencies. These few are the top traders, major investors and well-known speculators – nearly all motivated by the profit motive.

A few of the successful traders and investors have an innate gift, like that of being a great pianist or violin virtuoso. But for the majority of competent market operators, the secret is *steady learning*. Trading and investing are skills one can learn, provided one is willing to do so and has the right methodology. This is what this book aims to bring to the reader's attention. Knowledgeable traders and investors appreciate that while one may not know what will happen tomorrow, he or she can have a very good idea of what might take place over the longer run, by using powerful analytical tools to:

- Challenge one's own vision, and
- Supplement one's experience.

Other prerequisites are a well-thought-out strategy and a first-class risk control system – both indispensable whether the investor opts for income or for growth. Some of the rules underpinning effective risk management are fairly simple, and can be expressed in one short sentence. For instance, one of the most suicidal things in trading and investing is to keep adding to a losing position to bring down the average – but altogether risk management is no linear enterprise.

Whether the choice is growth or income, in order to create value professional investors and retail investors must be willing to take on risks. Firms practising strategic risk management create value by shaping a dynamic strategy, exploiting market flexibility and using their ability to bear risks without forgetting the need for:

- A concept of comparative advantage in risk bearing,
- A policy for balancing risk with return, while preserving value, and
- A policy for imbedding risk management into core investments, not as a one-off but over their life cycle.

Theoretically, because of having been rattled by uncertainty about companies' finances following the major bankruptcies of the early twenty-first century, investors should need no reminder of the importance of steady risk control. Practically, a timely reminder is always necessary, as proven by 2003 and 2004 events where the high-yield (read junk) bond market had its fastest rally on record. This is surprising, given investors' fears about how ravaged companies' balance sheets had become.

In conclusion, risk is a cost that has to be effectively controlled, and the same is true of other costs. In the late 1960s, John Paul Getty invited Ahmed Zaki Yamani, then Saudi Arabia's mighty oil minister, to Sutton Place for lunch. Arriving at the home of the richest man in the world, Yamani was shown to a payphone and told that any visitors wishing to make a call should use this. Then, before leaving on a tour of Getty's art collection, Yamani was asked if he wanted a coat. To this he replied, 'Is it outside?' and the answer was 'No'. He only realized why it was necessary to have a coat when he discovered that Getty never heated more than a few rooms in his large mansion.[16]

Notes

1 Jacques Attali (1985). *Sir Siegmund G. Warburg. Un Homme d'Influence.* Fayard.
2 D.N. Chorafas (2000). *Managing Credit Risk, Volume 1: Analyzing, Rating and Pricing the Probability of Default.* Euromoney.
3 D.N. Chorafas (2003). *Alternative Investments and the Mismanagement of Risk.* Macmillan/Palgrave.
4 See D.N. Chorafas (1996). *Managing Derivatives Risk.* Irwin Professional.
5 D.N. Chorafas (2001). *Managing Risk in the New Economy.* New York Institute of Finance.
6 D.N. Chorafas (2004). *Operational Risk Control with Basel II: Basic Principles and Capital Requirements.* Butterworth-Heinemann.
7 SOS Small Shareholders.
8 *Business Week*, 20 January 2003.
9 *The Economist*, 6 March 2004.
10 *Executive Intelligence Review*, 5 March 2004.
11 *Financial Times*, 8 April 2002.
12 Felice A. Bonadio (1994). *A.P. Giannini, Banker of America.* University of California Press.

13 D.N. Chorafas (2003). *Alternative Investments and the Mismanagement of Risk.* Macmillan/Palgrave.
14 D.N. Chorafas (2004). *Economic Capital Allocation with Basel II: Cost and Benefit Analysis.* Butterworth-Heinemann.
15 D.N. Chorafas (2004). *Management Risk: The Bottleneck is at the Top of the Bottle.* Macmillan/Palgrave.
16 Jeffrey Robinson (1988). *Yamani: The Inside Story.* Simon and Schuster.

2 The area where professional asset managers and private investors meet

2.1 Introduction

Private banking, pension funds, mutual funds, and (to a lesser degree) hedge funds are the areas where professional asset managers and retail investors meet. At least in the general case, these funds are profitable business which interface between household savings, company treasuries and endowments[1] on the one hand, and capital markets and money markets in the other. Capital markets are the theme of Chapter 3.

Private banking benefits not only those individuals using it and those institutions promoting it, but whole countries as well. For instance, Switzerland's traditional strength has been, and remains, private banking. In today's world, there are sixty to seventy countries whose citizens have surplus money and want to invest in a safer place. In counterpart, there are six or seven major financial centres with expertise in wealth management and with the necessary infrastructure.

The most profitable private banking operations are for high net worth individuals, not for the merely comfortably off. Providing the infrastructure necessary for a tailor-made investment advisory and management service is expensive as well as labor intensive in terms of knowledge and skills. Many banks look at an investment of $1 million or more per client as the minimum to allow a sound return, and many of their 'dear clients' are in the $5 million to $10 million range, or beyond.

It needs no explaining that some institutions are better tooled to do the personal banking job than others. Swiss banks are a good example because they attract a huge share of international wealth, looking after about a third of all private financial assets invested across borders, much more than other financial institutions anywhere. Moreover,

- Personal banking related services contribute about a third of Switzerland's consistently huge current account surplus, and
- They have been generating significant tax revenues, which help to keep down taxation elsewhere in the economy.

Pension funds are a different story. In its beginning, the pension fund industry preceded both private banking and mutual funds as we know them today. In 1927, AT&T funded the first big corporate retirement plan, but it was much later that the big pension fund business arose and the weight of institutional investors in the stock market became felt.

In the USA and the UK, pension funds have been long-term investors for decades. They are not only an accepted but also a welcomed part of social services and of the financial industry, managing the savings of millions of working individuals, and being an engine behind the drive for shareholder value. A similar statement is valid about life insurance companies and their annuities.

This, however, does not mean that there have not been scams and mismanagement associated with the plans which are offered to savers. In July 2000, Britain's Equitable Life, the world's oldest mutually owned life insurer, lost a court case brought by pensioners to force it to meet guaranteed annuities (see also Chapter 8). The insurer said this decision would cost it as much as £1.5 billion ($2.7 billion) – and not being able to afford it, it responded by putting itself up for sale. In March 2004 the release of a report by a government commission made the public aware of the level of mismanagement which brought the venerable insurer to its knees.

In continental Europe, retirees have long relied on pay-as-you-go public pension schemes, theoretically financed by the working population as an independent entity, but practically part of the government's budget. It is no secret that the near bankruptcy of social security is creating tensions. With minor exceptions, there are no private pension funds in continental Europe to take up the slack.

Not only state-run social security but also private pension funds can fail, as we will see in section 2.6. Subsequently, section 2.7 demonstrates that mutual funds, too, have their weaknesses – a case in point is the different types of improprieties whose financial aftermath hit savers and investors. To right the balances, in the week of 4 April 2004, Bank of America announced a new code of ethics for its mutual funds. (Reputational risk is discussed in Chapter 9 and ways and means to measure business risk in Chapter 13.)

What is written in this chapter about pension funds and mutual funds is not a critique of the work they are doing, but an alarm bell. In the general case, their contribution as institutional investors is commendable, because they fulfil an important social need created by changed demographics. The puzzle is why kill the goose which lays the golden eggs through scams which destabilize business confidence.

A pragmatic evaluation of current investments would reveal that, to a very significant extent, the area where professional asset managers and private investors meet is made by the prevailing demographics. Within this area, financial trends work sometimes in synergy and sometimes against one another, having at the center the crucial issue of *future financing* of pensions, health care and other safety nets.

Every individual and every collective investment plan should take notice that the dependency ratio of non-active retirees to the active population erodes rapidly, while other demographic trends like increased life expectancy oblige our ageing populations to make a valid and consistent economic contribution to its own retirement. In most industrialized countries public deficits have risen enormously over the past three decades and this necessarily limits social protection expenditures at both sides of the age and occupation distribution shown in Figure 2.1.

To cope with a rapid increase in expenditures for social services and entitlement programs, in recent years, policy-makers introduced new policies aimed at the inclusion of older workers: Raising the age at which a person becomes eligible to a state pension, drastically reducing early retirement incentives and allowances, curtailing access to disability and unemployment insurance for early retirees, and educating employers about the value of older workers given that early retirement means a considerable loss of experience and expertise – which could be useful to industry.

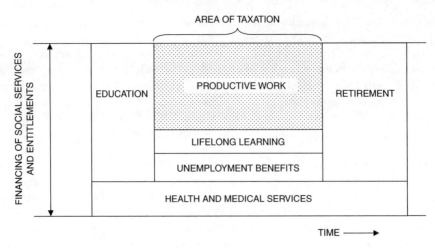

Figure 2.1 Life-cycle support typically financed by the government, through taxation of the working population

But the workforce itself must also be proactive in terms of savings and investments for education, health care and retirement – three domains where savings can be put to work. The best term in this case is *end-of-career management* which should start early in the life of a working person (see the reference by Bob Keen in Chapter 1) and cover his or her occupational life as a whole. This is a dynamic process which must be steadily re-examined in order to adapt its cycle and its mechanics to the abilities and needs of the lifelong worker.

2.2   Investments through private banking

In order of importance to the banking industry as a whole, the now classical big market segments have been corporate, institutional and retail. Regarding goals they are after, corporate and institutional entities have more or less opposite aims.

- Corporate clients search for competitively priced funding.
- Institutional investors are looking for best value and for creditworthiness.

Retail clients combine both patterns, and are influenced by the synergy of shifting demographics, changes in returns obtained through equities and bonds, as well as technological advances allowing better deals in investments. This produces a much larger investing universe which promotes private banking but also poses significant requirements in:

- Human capital,
- Organization, and
- Technology.

Technology plays a key role in planning and controlling modern investments, but it is no substitute for commitment to long-term personal relationships and provision of a full range of products and services specifically designed for the target audience. A private banking organization typically offers comprehensive wealth management services centered on investment advice through:

- The systematic division of the bank's customer base into marketing segments, and
- Provision of services able to meet each customer's individual investment needs.

Because private banking can be a lucrative and steady business, the better-managed credit institutions aim to achieve a noticeably more efficient market presence, with the dual goal of greater market share and further improvement in earnings. The building and sustenance of a private banking unit is a dynamic enterprise in a business environment in full evolution.

Successful personal banking entities use technology to help them focus on customer service excellence, profitability and growth of the investment, while controlling costs and exposure. In many cases, the private banking and corporate banking department co-operate to exploit the synergy of investments which are appealing to both populations. This, however, can lead to conflicts of interest.

A properly run private banking business would see to it that each individual client receives advice tailored to his or her investment objectives and risk appetite. To formulate an independent and consistent investment policy, the private banking adviser draws on research sources within the bank and from third parties. Knowledge artifacts can be of invaluable assistance in flashing our trends in market conditions and/or changes in client requirements.

Institutions with private banking services see to it that their efforts increasingly reflect the changing profile of savers, as well as the fact that competition is causing them to step up their efforts. Moreover, clients are becoming more sophisticated as they are taking a more active role in managing their wealth. Several credit institutions and brokerages have answered demands for extended availability of services through Internet access.

While the majority of private banking clients is still rather passive with its investment, a growing number of credit institutions' clients is demanding more advanced products and a broader geographical range of services. This cannot be provided at competitive prices without high technology. Personal banking clients are also increasingly focused on asset performance and they are watchful over proper allocation coupled with:

- Transparency in wealth management,
- Quality and actuality investment information, and
- Verifiable results of expert advice.

Globalization provided new challenges in terms of investment advice. While a great deal of private wealth is invested in the domestic markets where clients are domiciled, particularly in the form of equity and equity-linked products, as capital markets become more globalized the sources of investment spread worldwide. With this comes the requirement of a unique mix of businesses' intelligence and well-documented investment positions, necessary to maintain customer loyalty.

In their modern incarnation as end-investors, top to medium net worth individuals demand high standards with regard to personal investment advisory and wealth management services – and rightly so. They desire factual and comprehensive financial advice, and they expect specially tailored financial solutions including addressing in an able manner questions regarding:

- Risk and return with each type of investments,
- Issues beyond financing, which include tax optimization,
- The role of personal investments as supplement or substitute to pension(s), and
- Other investment perspectives such as inheritance law and legal issues.

Some private banking organizations proudly announce to their clients that their global product offering is carefully tailored to meet country-specific tax and legal regulations, over and above its ability to respond to different aspirations of clients in different markets. Where local regulations allow, client advisers who serve clients both domestically and internationally report to a single manager,

- Helping to avoid channel conflict, and
- Ensuring that private banking clients receive a consistent high-quality service whether they bank at home or abroad.

In addition, several private banking outfits have established expert global teams which concentrate on the requirements of particular client groups, or private specialized services. Examples are a family office for wealthy families, including family foundations; sports and entertainment group focusing on special life-cycle related needs, real estate investment services and trusts; Islamic banking providing products designed to be Shari'a compliant; art investment, numismatic and other special interest groups.

Many credit institutions are now targeting an improvement of their skills in handling private banking clients, extending the range of their handholding. This is understandable inasmuch as high net worth individuals want to deal with first-class private bankers able to collaborate with them in developing tailored financial strategies, characterized not only by a higher return but also by compliance with the client's risk appetite.

The polyvalence of customer requests sees to it that not only must investment advisers be on call, but also that they should exhibit a comprehensive knowledge of investment matters, including domestic and foreign products. To fulfil such client requirements, a private banking organization must have direct access to traders and third-party providers, as well as to in-house expertise on tax law, estate law and retirement planning. It must also assure nearly real-time customized reporting fine-tuned to the individual client's particular needs, which requires effective interfaces provided by relationship managers who are:

- Dependable,
- Technically educated,
- Easy to work with,
- Sensitive to clients' needs,

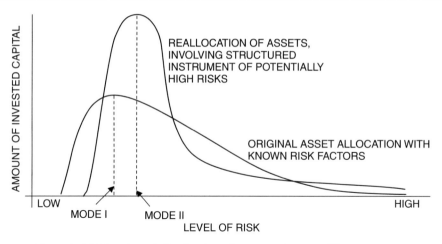

Figure 2.2 Risk-oriented distribution of assets under two different options

- Readily accessible, and
- Highly competent.

Other qualities which distinguish one private bank from another include flexibility, a growing worldwide presence and leadership on the information front. This can be assisted through a network able to access the best services and products of the world's leading investment institutions, and fashioning them into solutions that fit the clients' distinctive goals.

In an effort to take an integrative view of their clients' net worth and acquire more of these clients business, some banks provide asset reallocation services, along the lines of the example given in Figure 2.2. They estimate risk and return factors under the client's current asset allocation, and provide an integrative proposal which, in the bank's judgment, protects in an able manner the client's investment interests. To a substantial extent, this reflects the fact that private clients are discriminating individuals who choose their bank with care.

- They expect personal service from first-rate advisers, and
- Demand solutions that answer all their wealth-related needs.

Private banking clients, however, should be wise enough not to relegate to a third party all the responsibility for managing their wealth. In their effort to protect and build up their assets, high net worth individuals must have round-the-clock access to information concerning markets and industry sectors, and be able to look for clarity in the flood of available information and of investment proposals made to them.

True enough, sometimes private banking clients fall with a trend, as attested by the fact that roughly half the money which is managed by hedge funds comes from high net worth individuals. In other cases, they fail critically to analyze the hidden risks in an investment proposal, by challenging the 'obvious'. For example, in the two distributions of Figure 2.2 the new allocation plan may involve derivative financial instruments whose toxic waste may be far from being apparent.

In conclusion, if the investor truly aims to achieve a lifetime investment goal, such as securing his or her retirement, providing for children's education and assuring the financing of a family health plan, then he or she has no alternative than taking an active part in the management of his or her wealth. Answering investment questions with confidence requires a financial strategy, the first step of which is assessing one's current portfolio to assure it is working to meet established goals. To this are dedicated the three golden rules of investment in sections 2.3 to 2.5.

2.3   Betting on the challenger and learning to diversify

If the decision the investor makes is to invest in equity for growth (see Chapter 1), then the next question which comes up is, should one choose the leader or the challenger in a given industrial sector? Though there may be exceptions, practical experience suggests that, other things being equal, the best is to bet on the challenger – but not at any price.

'Bet on the challenger, but do not buy at peaks', is the *fourth golden rule* of investments. There are reasons for suggesting that the challenger is a preferable investment bet than the leader. First, as far as growth is concerned, the challenger has a better chance because, if successful, it may gain part of the leader's market share. Alternatively, the leader may buy the challenger in which case he will be paying a premium. As an article in *The Economist* had it 'because Bank One is ... being bought [by J.P. Morgan Chase] ... [its] shareholders will receive a takeover premium [of about 14 percent] instead of paying one.'[2]

The two sides of the fourth golden rule: 'Bet on the challenger' and 'Do not buy at peaks' correlate. Since my University of California Los Angeles (UCLA) studies I remember that a free piece of advice usually given in connection with equity investments is, 'Buy low, and sell high'. This is like the saying about apple pie and motherhood, the difference being that buy low/sell high is empty of substance. A sound approach must define what exactly is meant by 'low' and 'high' – a matter addressed in conjunction with the fifth golden rule of investment in section 2.4.

The second reason for betting on the challenger is more esoteric. Some investment experts advise buying only the common stock of companies that are second or third in their respective fields, because further growth will provide specialists (see Chapter 5) with built-in support for a *bull raid* they will conduct on the shares of these companies. Most of these bull raids will occur before the company's potential is publicized in terms of earnings or market share announcements. Wise investors position themselves ahead of market forces.

'This rule makes common sense,' said one of the experts, 'much however depends on what one is expecting in terms of risk and return, and how much risk adverse the investor is.' In the opinion of another specialist in investment research, the difficulty in applying this rule lies in the fact that nobody really knows where the peak is. Therefore the expert suggested splitting the fourth golden rule into two parts, addressed to retail and professional investors respectively:

■ Retail investors should not be entering and exiting the market by relying on peaks and lows.

- But as far as professional investors are concerned, it is their job to judge market trends and guess an equity's peaks, lows and what comes after them.

This advice, however, runs contrary to the opinion of a professional broker who said he doubts anybody can really recognize the peaks and the lows in an equity's longer-term life cycle. 'Experts cannot and will not say where the peak is', the broker commented, adding right after that he liked the first half of this rule: bet on the challenger. Another investment specialist pressed the point that rather than emphasizing peaks, savers should be advised to avoid overpriced stocks.

Analysis provide important help in reaching this and other investment objectives (see Chapter 6 on fundamental and technical analysis). Theoretically at least, the price of financial assets is determined by the present value of the future cash flow that investors expect to derive from holding the asset (see Chapter 9 on intrinsic value). Applied to the valuation of shares, the price of an equity should equal the sum of expected future dividends discounted by:

- A risk-free interest rate, and
- The risk premium which investors require for holding the equity.

Earnings expectations can replace expected future dividends in the valuation, if we assume that a certain percentage of earnings will be paid out as dividends. Such earnings expectations by analysts in financial markets are usually available for quoted companies (which leads to the fifth golden rule in section 2.4). Figure 2.3 provides the pattern of earnings growth and decline in the 1990 to 2003 time frame.

Some principles associated with the use of an approach which takes into account earnings expectations and market trends can be of interest to the investor. For instance, actual earnings growth generally tends to exhibit a more volatile pattern compared with twelve months ahead earnings growth expectations by analysts. Moreover, actual and expected earnings growth figures tend to move in tandem, and upward

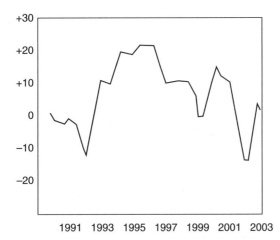

Figure 2.3 Actual earnings growth for the S&P index

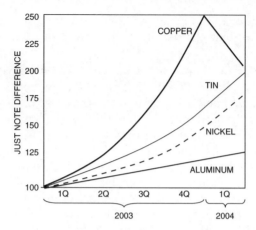

Figure 2.4 Trend lines of base metal prices which reached eight-year and fourteen-year highs in a span of less than one year

and downward changes in earnings expectations are usually followed by similar movements in actual earnings.

What the reader should retain from this discussion is that whether the investment choice is income or growth, the price of entry into equity ownership matters. If the investor pays too much for an equity, the income per invested dollar or pound will be proportionally less, and part of the expected capital growth will be lost in having paid too high a price. The same principle applies with all other investments, including bonds and commodities such as base metals.

From May 2003 to April 2004 (when this text was written) base metal prices soared thanks to strong demand from China. Copper and aluminum, for example, have hit eight-year highs, while tin prices reached fourteen-year highs. The trend lines are shown in Figure 2.4, where the reader will also notice the copper's volatility.

For sophisticated investors, this example dramatizes the interest of diversification. Returning to the third golden rule, which was discussed in Chapter 1, it is likely that up to a certain percentage both income and growth will be in an investor's portfolio. The challenge is to define which proportion of one's wealth should be allocated to bonds and which to equities. This is a shot in the direction of *diversification* which, by choice, must be part of the fourth golden rule.

Like freedom and democracy, diversification is an often used word, but one which is very rarely practised in a documented manner; or for that matter one which is long-lived. Practically all financial institutions and all asset managers, though by no means all individual investors, incorporate into their plans hypotheses about diversification of risk and return across their area(s) of operations. Knowledgeable bankers, however, appreciate that most of the statements concerning diversification are untrue.

■ If and when it is achieved, the diversification of risk and return is bound to be ephemeral because market forces change the rules of the game.
■ Therefore, investors must learn how to diversify dynamically both between debt and equities (and sometimes other instruments) and within the equities traded in the market.

As an initial condition, diversification of risk can be achieved by investing in more than one industry sector, or by investing in markets not correlated with one another – if such markets can still be found. Because of globalization, this policy of market diversification is becoming increasingly more difficult to implement. Even more taxing is how actually to keep such a policy as market forces evolve.

The reader should be careful on this issue of diversification and its sustenance because there is plenty of hype in the investment community around it. There is as well an issue distinguishing theory from practice. Theoretically, diversification is good for an investor; but, practically, holding too many different equities or debt instruments makes it difficult to follow their fortunes. Between these two statements, which contradict one another,

- Every investor has to establish his or her diversification vs. concentration rule, and
- This must be done in a way which best fits the investor's goals and risk profile, in conjunction with the fifth and sixth golden rules (see sections 2.4 and 2.5, respectively).

Looking back to the masters for inspiration and guidelines, Amadeo Giannini used to say: 'I see nothing wrong with a man putting all his eggs in one basket. But watch that basket.' The biggest problem with concentration is that the typical investor does not know how to 'watch that basket' – and the same is true with many of the experts, including several bankers and investment advisers.

'Watch that basket' means plenty of work and responsibility. Giannini did not build a financial empire by going on vacation or taking it easy. He slept, lived and breathed the bank, which he referred to as 'my baby'. This type of hard work is no longer part of the morals of our society. A recent study in France has documented that those who profited the most from the thirty-five hour week (instituted by the socialist government of the late 1990s) are the managers who turned the shortened working week into longer and more frequent vacations.

True enough, the leaders of finance and industry still work sixty- to ninety-hour weeks, but not everybody is a leader, and it is likely that the investors' accounts will not be followed personally by one of the masters of finance. At least theoretically, for the typical investor, diversification is a good policy. Practically, in the average case, four to eight stocks are enough for an individual's portfolio – and a dozen or so bonds.

For diversification reasons, these equities and debt instruments should preferably be in different industries. The investor who knows what he or she is doing needs no more than these positions. If the investor does not, he or she should not be in the stock market in the first place. Even AAA and AA bonds in an investor's portfolio require one to step up to the plate and play the game of investment management and risk control.

2.4 Increasing the visibility of one's investments

One of the most critical advantages investors gain by learning about the market and its gyrations, as well as by being in charge of their investment strategy rather than leveraging themselves and their assets, is that they do not need to run for cover when confronted by adversity. This is significant inasmuch as an investor's great strength is that he or she never panics. Self-control overrides the pain which the investor feels when:

- The paper losses mount, and
- Adverse moves in the market translate into a calamity in one's portfolio.

Clients who appreciate that risk and return are indivisible are most valuable to asset managers, because both in private banking and in the institutional investor's line business the client is king. The best asset management philosophy is one based on the quality of the relationship developed between the fund manager and his or her clients. To reach this objective, the assets business must see to it that the client–adviser relationship becomes increasingly more dependent.

Critics say that this policy has major costs associated with it, but private bankers, investment advisers and asset managers are paid well for the services they offer. Precisely because such services are costly, investors expect to obtain, in return, earnings enhancements commensurate with the best the market can offer. This sets a floor to private banking standards.

High net worth individuals and the best-managed institutional investors, will not fail to test from time to time if the services they currently get compare positively with best-in-class competitors of their present asset manager. The dual objective of earnings enhancement and best personal service is obtainable, and its reward is achieving growth in net new money in the private client and asset management business. There is plenty of profit to be made through a client-driven policy addressing:

- Securities,
- Investment banking, and
- Wealth management.

Several cases demonstrate that this policy thrives through an unrelenting market watch, propelled by means of top-quality research, factual and documented advice, and post-mortems comparing the investor's portfolio contents with alternative scenarios accessible through the world's capital markets.

A couple of experts participating in the research expressed the opinion that, whether we talk of individual or institutional investors, a sound strategy is to look at the performance of both the portfolio of the client and each of the equities contained in it. With such an approach, the experts said, it is advisable to examine the whole company in which an investment is made, not just its financial statement. Also, go beyond the company, examine the state of the industry sector as well as the market or markets within which it operates. How is this industry going forward?

Going beyond the company's financial statements, permits an evaluation of critical industry determinants which may be changing. Can the management of the company in which the investor put some of his or her wealth turn on a dime, when these determinants move fast? Or is the company falling behind its challengers – meaning that the investment violates the fourth golden rule?

- Information on the company, the industry sector and the market is the cornerstone in answering investment queries.
- Therefore, part and parcel of the understanding of how well one is doing as an investor is knowledge about where to buy the equities.

For the individual investor, the open market is the best bet. Private placements are often secretive, hence highly risky for retail investors. Many of the institutional investors have come to the same conclusion in a painful way. Credit institutions, too, are licking their wounds. I know several banks which lost big money with private placements, and only very few who really profited from them.

This leads to the *fifth golden rule*: individual investors should acquire only stocks quoted in big boards (see Chapter 3). For instance, the New York Stock Exchange (NYSE), London Stock Exchange (LSE) and National Association of Securities Dealers Automated Quotations (NASDAQ) fall under this heading (big boards are discussed in Chapter 9). Small local exchanges do not. Moreover, the absence of significant institutional participation on small exchanges makes it possible for speculators to conduct bear or bull raids that can peak out in an hour's time. Other reasons for choosing big boards are:

- A stock's bigger capitalization,
- The presence of institutional investors with deep pockets, and
- The fact that equities in big boards tend to give advance warning of price distribution.

Behind the statement in the third bullet lies the fact institutions begin their selling near the end of a stock's high. A corollary to this advice is never to buy at peak quotation, which constituted the fourth golden rule (see section 2.3). Investors should appreciate that a sure way to get burned is to buy following an upswing just 'to be in the bandwagon'. In fact, some experts suggest restricting purchases to *stocks that have declined at least 35 to 50 percent from their highs* – which lies at the junction of the fourth and fifth golden rules.

Let me repeat this to make sure it is well understood. It is a bad investment policy to wait to buy until stocks are making new highs, or something is announced which is attracting public attention to a given equity. Generally, highs in equity prices tend to make their appearance after the halfway mark in a bull market. Therefore, at that time it is better to begin thinking of selling rather than of acquiring shareholdings.

As should be expected, the fifth golden rule has its contrarians. 'This is too strong a rule', said one of the experts. 'It may be good for retail investors, but not for professionals.' Another expert added that putting all money on the Financial Times Stock Exchange 100 Index (FTSE 100) is not wise. It would be a good idea to have some money in small capitalized companies (small caps), but this poses problems for the individual investor because small companies are not given the same coverage by analysts as big ones. (The difference between small caps and large caps is explained in Chapter 9.)

On the other hand, while the experts whose contribution has been reflected in the preceding paragraph were altogether rather favorable about investing in small caps, they differed in their views about the way to go about it, as well as in the nature of assumed risks. 'You can win with small caps', said the first expert. 'But you have to know what you do. You can invest in a fund of small caps. This, however, brings in the individual fund manager risk.'

The other expert did not consider the latter risk worth talking about if the investor gets a good stockbroker for small caps. 'There exist', he said, 'brokers who understand the small cap industry and can manage the investor's assets. Pension funds go that way.' But other people equally knowledgeable on investments, who took part in the research, did not accept this concept. Their rule was that:

- If they do not understand a company,
- Then they simply do not invest in it.

Two more investment experts suggested that today we are a long way from the 1950s when companies quoted in the major boards were too big to fail. Both said that bankruptcies which have shaken the financial markets during the last few years prove that there is nothing like 'the big company investment is a sure thing'; anything can happen at any time, hence the need for steady vigilance.

More along this line of thought, other experts pressed the point that, for professional investors, concentrating on quoted companies in major boards can lead to downplaying other business opportunities, their rewards and their risks. Among the examples given in the course of these discussions are:

- Venture capital firms,
- Private equity investments, and
- Investments in structured products.

Typically, structured financial instruments are offered by investment banks to their clients. They are not quoted in the capital markets though the bank originating them may have a quotation service for the products it has already sold to investors. Also typically, these are the products of *funds of funds*, which invest in other hedge funds and sell their instruments to retail investors.[3]

Some financial institutions pride themselves by announcing that their clients can access a wide range of alternative investments, from in-house hedge funds to third-party private equity funds and fund of funds services. They also offer their discretionary portfolio management clients the option to include alternative investments in their asset allocation.

Both alternative investments and discretionary portfolio management diminish the investor's visibility of the risks embedded in the way his or her wealth is being managed. For starters, with *discretionary portfolio agreements* investors delegate the management of their assets to one or more of the bank's portfolio managers, according to an investment strategy:

- Worked out with the investor's client adviser, and
- Theoretically reflecting the client's risk appetite and investment goals.

The argument usually presented by institutions promoting discretionary portfolio management is that, through it, clients benefit from the investment expertise of the financial institution and its ability to access and assess a large amount of investment information and experience. Always theoretically, the client should feel secure in the knowledge that his or her portfolio and the risks taken with it are continually monitored. Practically, discretionary portfolio solutions:

- Significantly increase the bank's freedom to act, and
- Limit the investor's information stream, as well as the ability to make his or her own decisions.

It is therefore not surprising that in investment volume terms, the share of discretionary portfolio management accounts is falling. Though the exact amount varies from one institution to the next, available statistics indicate that on average it has shrunk from 30 to 35 percent in the early 1980s to about 25 percent in 2000, and to roughly 20 percent in 2004. This is good news as far as investors' assumption of responsibilities is concerned, but it is bad news for bankers.

2.5 The 5 percent rule about assets at risk

The message section 2.4 has conveyed is that 'savers and investors must be able to fulfil financial planning prerequisites, to help themselves achieve their personal objectives and cope with important life-cycle events': for instance, their retirement plan, educational requirements, health care needs and changes in tax regulation. For all these reasons, they have to develop and execute a customized solution using the expertise they themselves developed (see Chapters 9 and 10) and that of top external consultants.

The financial planning advice investors should provide for themselves and their families must cover every stage of family life, including education funding and gift to children through a business start-up as well as succession planning. This is part of the sense of strategic wealth management and asset protection. A sound financial plan would cover a whole range of business situations.

An integral part of a sound approach is the investor's ability and willingness to put a low ceiling to his or her own lust and greed, the way wise people who are active in trading and investing nearly always do. The *sixth golden rule* of investing says that an investor can risk 1 percent of his or her capital on a single trade, or can risk up to 5 percent in the same equity or other portfolio position. But he or she should be knowledgeable enough to realize that:

- The more he or she risks,
- The more volatile will be the returns, including expected and unexpected losses.

Applying this 1 percent rule to transactions and 5 percent rule to assets at risk is tantamount to learning discipline in money management. Experienced traders advise trying hard not to risk more than 1 percent of the portfolio on any single trade because it is unavoidable that this amount of money is at risk, no matter what the investor thinks or other traders and fund managers might say. However, observance of the rule requires looking not only at the amount of each bet but also at:

- Correlation of trades, and
- The way this correlation may impact exposure.

For instance, if one is taking a given long position in two different but related markets, these are two bets with a strong correlation. When this happens, what might have seemed to be a 1 percent exposure can rise to 2 percent, depending on how much the two correlate. Therefore, never betting more than 1 percent of net worth on any one trade, does not mean that we have to be wrong 100 times to lose all our money. Correlations can significantly reduce the number of wrong bets which lead to bankruptcy.

Investors and traders should also keep in mind that correlations are not necessarily known a priori. They develop as the market moves. In physics the Heisenberg principle provides a good example of analogical thinking in the financial markets.[4] If something is closely observed, the chances are it is going to be altered in the process. There is evidence that the Heisenberg principle is also valid in finance. With this background, let me repeat the premise made in this section as a golden rule of investments:

- Less than 1 percent in any one trade, and
- Less than 5 percent on any commodity, no matter how great its future might look.

'This is a good rule', said Bob Keen. 'Investors should not put all of their eggs in the same basket.' Keen added that the question then becomes one of how many baskets one should have – and the answer must be found by returning once again to one's savers' objective(s). Another investment specialist expert suggested that the exact level of the percentages should be fine-tuned in conjunction with the investment strategy one chooses; namely, how conservative or aggressive it may be.

- A conservative investment strategy may put a ceiling below the 5 percent rule.
- By contrast, one which is aggressive will violate the 5 percent from time to time, or even permanently, but there should *always* be an upper limit.

Still other experts suggested that an upper limit at the level of 10 percent of assets, made sense to them. 'Typically, the 5 percent or a similar rule is for any single company,' said Gordon Midgley, 'but when Vodafone made about 10 percent of capitalization of the London Stock Exchange, UK funds found themselves confronted with a tough choice on how to invest their assets in compliance with regulatory guidelines.'

There is a most fundamental reason behind the 5 percent rule. Successful traders advise that one has to be willing to make mistakes, both because they are inseparable from brilliant market moves and because they can teach good lessons – albeit the hard way. For instance, a company making no errors would not have the troubleshooters when he or she needs them. In fact, there is nothing wrong with making mistakes now and then, provided that:

- They are quickly corrected, and
- Limited bets see to it that they are not devastating.

Down to basics, the 5 percent rule has to do with diversification in investments, said an asset manager, and experience suggests that it its not easy to achieve optimal diversification let alone the fact that this might become very expensive. According to this opinion, there is always a tradeoff between diversification and cost, and this has an impact on the level of the single commodity ceiling – or that of the single transaction.

The counterpart to this argument is that position size can be deadly when one is trading much too big, or his inventory of assets is one-sided in terms of assumed exposure. Another major error in any market is to get attached to the trade one makes, or the commodity one holds in the portfolio. A characteristic of sound trading and investment decisions is that they are taken unemotionally; emotions usually mean trouble.

Can we measure the exposure being taken with any one trade or portfolio position, and with all of the inventoried positions? The answer is not necessarily positive. Several analysts and rocket scientists now believe that value at risk (VAR) models, which have been generalized with the 1996 Market Risk Amendment by the Basel Committee, have massively increased the volatility of financial markets by forcing all traders and investors to make similar moves and/or construct almost identical portfolios.

The concept behind this assertion is that if the model becomes part of the market's mechanism and impacts upon its volatility or liquidity, then it is no more an objective metric. Let alone the fact that VAR models are, by and large, an obsolete measurement of market risk,[5] the fact that they may tell traders and investors to sell at the same time is not at all welcome. Through model-induced herd behavior, market players:

- Change the pattern of market moves, and
- Tend to increase the risk embedded in different portfolios.

Traders with considerable experience in the stock market have suggested another example of the financial application of the Heisenberg principle. If an equity is in tight consolidation and then breaks out on the day financial analysts in known brokerages upgrade this stock to strong buy, then:

- The odds of a price move upwards are high, but
- The likelihood that this break-out will be sustained is small.

Equities may also move in sympathy with other equities in the same industry sector. Semiconductors are a classical example. As the price of a given commodity, for instance, a well-known software stock, moves up (or down), the chances are that other software stocks will move in the same way.

What the reader should retain from the above is that such moves establish correlations which, in a globalized market, are quite often transborder. Their study requires sophisticated models, high frequency financial data (HFFD) and real-time computing – in short, interactive computational finance. Only if research results are based on rigorous analysis, they can be of value to traders and investors.

Another reason why HFFD approaches have become a competitive advantage is that the able implementation of the 1 percent/5 percent rule has, as a prerequisite, the steady, careful analysis of everything that moves and everything that does not move in the market. This cannot be done with paper and pencil, overnight batch processing, or by just talking with experts over the phone and keeping in mind their opinion.

Investors should appreciate that many aspects of HFFD analysis are subtle and require hypotheses that have to be tested. For instance, if an analyst's, trader's or investment adviser's statement is that nobody believes there is reason for this equity to break out, and it suddenly does, then the chances are there exists an important underlying cause; a cause much greater than the analyst thought. In application of the Heisenberg principle,

- The more a price pattern is observed by speculators, the more likely it is its 'typical' signals are false.
- The more a market responds without speculative activity, the greater is the significance of break-outs.

These two bullet points are hypotheses suggested by experience and discussed in the course of the research. Contrarians, however, say that while the Heisenberg principle may fit a physical law, it does not necessarily need to hold in every case in finance. This may be true but, if so, this is another reason justifying observance of the 1 percent rule in transactions and the 5 percent rule in investments.

Another factor which has significantly changed market patterns in a globalized economy is the growing correlation in investments in different equity markets. Prior to the 1970s, the US stock market and that of continental European countries were not highly correlated, but with so many investors rushing to capitalize on this fact, this pattern has radically changed. Now they are correlated, with NYSE and NASDAQ being the leaders.

In the mid-1990s, investors piled into Asian investments both because returns were seen as high and, more importantly, because Asian stock markets were perceived as being uncorrelated with Western markets, making them especially attractive to global portfolio managers. But by 1997, the overcharged Asian markets crashed, investors got burned and the correlation of Asian equities to Western equities somehow increased.

In conclusion, experience and assumptions guiding the hand of the investor, asset manager or finance director, including those concerning correlations, are always tentative because they change over time. What we know from science is that everything has to be tested. Hence the need for powerful tools and for a methodology. Also needed are rules which make it possible to exercise damage control if the hypotheses we create about future market behavior turn on their heads.

*   *   *

It is appropriate to include a contrarian opinion to the 5 percent rule. As mentioned on page 39 while warning investors to pay off their debts and avoid speculating in the market, Amadeo P. Giannini, the founder of Bank of America, also said that he sees nothing wrong about putting many of one's eggs in the same basket – provided one is willing, able and knowledgeable enough to closely watch that basket.

Several decades prior to Giannini, something similar was stated by Andrew Carnegie, the king of the steel industry, author, and philanthropist, who has also been in his early career a bonds salesman. However, Peter Krass, Carnegie's biographer who quotes him on this statement of putting all of one's eggs in the same basket, notes that Carnegie himself was well diversified in his holdings. He had equity in twenty different companies – and major ones for that matter.

Moreover, Andrew Carnegie closely followed the Darwinian principle of business survival advising, who would hear, that when you go by survival of the fittest rules 'you have no reason to fear the future'. Another one of Carnegie's principles in choosing people with great business futures was: 'Look out for the boy who has to plunge into work direct from the common school, and who begins by sweeping out the office. He is the probable dark horse that you better watch.'[6] Carnegie knew a great deal about dark horses. He had been one of them.

2.6   Challenges faced by pension funds

Up to the early 1990s pension funds were content to put their assets with top quartile fund managers. Even if the fund managers lost money, the trustees consoled themselves with the thought that they had, at least, hired the best available investment consultants in the equities market. Behind this policy was the need to preserve the assets set aside to provide people's pensions coupled with the fact that pension funds had, at that time:

- No investment management expertise, and
- No risk control system worth talking about.

This policy of outsourcing investment management presented no major hiccups in the 1990s, but when the stock market bubble burst, the pension funds' relatively prudent attitude in their equity bets changed. In 2001, Calpers, the giant Californian public employees pension fund, moved into hedge funds trying to gain higher returns. The guideline adopted by its management seems to have been that it can pay a lot of 'benefits' with just $1 billion in hedge funds – which is less than 1 percent of its $150 billion assets under management.

- The 1 percent rule was upheld, but
- At the same time this meant $1 billion was at high risk.

Critics say that there is no way to characterize the use of hedge funds and funds of funds by pension fund managers as a wise move. They also point to the fact that investment decisions by pension fund managers are often wanting, and even the pensioners are not making the right decisions in connection with their savings and their financial future after retirement by holding the stock of the company they work for.

For instance in the USA, more than half of 401 000 savers put nearly all their money into stocks. Hardly any rebalance their portfolios to safer bonds as they get older and can ill afford pension plan misfortunes. Worse yet, some studies indicate that between a fifth and a quarter of American employees hold more than 20 percent of their pension assets in their own companies and if their company goes bust, as with Enron, WorldCom, Global Crossing and so many others, they lose both their job and their nest egg.

More to the point, even without the mass of bankruptcies, stock holdings are good as long as the market goes well. But then comes a bear market and the value of funds drops dramatically. Beyond this, as we have seen, investing in the stock of one's own company is not a brilliant idea, because it maximizes the saver's exposure. Is it then better to believe the storytellers of funds of funds?

The answer is not positive. One of the misleading slogans of hedge funds and funds of funds is that 'your money is actively managed around the world'. Actively in what? And how much is this costing the investor in terms of fees and assumed risk? Heavy charges, the merchandisers of risk say, are largely to reward investment skills. In the 2000 to 2002 time frame, however, investors have lost heavily.

- The average UK equity retail fund has been down some 40 percent over that period, and
- The typical UK company pension fund has suffered a cumulative negative return of about 25 percent.[7]

For their part, corporate pension funds are subject to the ups and downs of the firm itself and of the industry sector to which it belongs. Mid-January 2003 Fitch Ratings warned that US domestic airlines had a funding gap for pension obligations of $18 billion, a steep change from 1999 when they were overfunded by about $1 billion. Shortly thereafter American Airlines, the largest US carrier, underlined the sorry state of the sector's underfunded pensions when it said it would take a $1.1 billion charge to equity to cover its pension liabilities.

American's pension problems came alongside its worst annual loss of $3.5 billion, with losses of $529 million in the fourth quarter of 2002 alone. Don Carty, its chief executive, admitted it remained a treacherous time for the company and emphasized the need for a quick reduction in labor costs to put the airline on a sustainable footing aimed at its continued survival. The call for deep cuts, of 20 percent or more in wages and other benefits, came a couple of weeks later, on 4 February 2003.

For its part, to cut its huge pension fund deficit, estimated at $18 billion, in the last week of June 2003 General Motors (GM) sold $10 billion of debt in the unsecured and convertible debt markets. Its fully owned auto financing subsidiary, General Motors Acceptance Corporation (GMAC), planned to sell an additional $3 billion.

In London, several investment experts were surprised that GM's bond issue has been oversubscribed, raising more than $16.5 billion in the bond market. While GM's bond sales seemed to satisfy yield-hungry investors, others remained worried about the financial outlook for auto manufacturers. 'Do we in our heart of hearts, want to lend to GM for 15 years? I don't think so. Pricing may affect that, but there are a lot of risks', said Dennis Gould, head of UK fixed-income at Axa Investment Managers in the UK.[8]

The bonds issued by GM to plug the huge hole in the treasury of its pension plan had also the distinction of being the biggest corporate debt-raising exercise up to that date. To attract investors GM had priced the issue at an attractive level. Contrary to most companies that had issued debt in 2003, and had done so at market prices, GM offered about 100 basis points above the yield on similar bonds, in multiple tranches of debt denominated in dollars, euros and pounds sterling.

For instance, in the sterling market GM raised £350 million ($630 million) through a twelve-year bond that yielded almost 4 percentage points above benchmark gilts. With this and other offerings, the value of auto debt, which fell sharply in 2002 because of the problems of the motor vehicle industry, rose in 2003 as investors sought higher-yielding securities. Pricing several hundred basis points above government securities has been helped by the fact that interest rates for dollar-denominated instruments have dropped to forty-five year lows.

Given that in America the largest part of pensions is covered by company pension plans, what happens when these firms go bust? The answer is that the retirees are taken care of by the Pension Benefit Guaranty Corporation (PBGC), albeit at cut rates. This is a quasi-governmental agency that insures America's private, defined-benefit company pension plans, but PBGC, too, faces financial problems. As 2003 came to a close, massive costs saw to it that the pension plans insurer fell $7.6 billion deeper into the red, to a new record low.

The PBGC reckons that another $85 billion in pension deficits can be found in the books of the country's most shaky companies, while Corporate America, as a whole, has a pensions deficit of some $350 billion. This is worrisome because, technically, the US government does not stand behind PBGC with ironclad guarantees. Yet, nobody believes that the PBGC, which insures the pensions of 44 million voting Americans, would be allowed to collapse.

According to some experts, particularly worrisome is the fact that because pension accounting is complex, it is very difficult to determine whether or not a firm's pension fund is solvent. 'Creative accounting' practices, too, enter the picture, with incentives for firms to invest in assets that make their bottom lines look good at the expense of longer term stability.

Perhaps the most damaging and urgent problem, is a mismatch between corporate pension plans' heavy investment in equities versus risk-free sovereign debt of Group of Ten countries, to the tune of almost 60 percent of pension plan assets in 2002. During the 1990s, bond investments by pension funds were minor. To right the balances, on 29 January 2004, the PBGC announced that it would shift more of its assets from equities to bonds[9] – a very much delayed measure.

Can the problems facing public and private pension plans be fixed? On 30 March 2004, a group of leading pensions experts were summoned to 11 Downing Street and asked to improve the standards for governing the £800 billion ($1.5 trillion) held in UK pension funds. At the core of this meeting was the Myners review carried out by the former Gartmore chairman, Paul Myners. In 2000, this was set up principally to examine why pension funds were not investing in small businesses.

Myners reported his findings in 2001 and said the knowledge and expertise of the trustees that were appointed to look after company pension funds and make decisions on how funds were invested needed to increase. Behind this suggestion has been the facts that:

- Most pension funds are invested heavily in equities, and
- As stock markets have collapsed in recent years, this policy has left them with deficits running into billions of pounds.

At the aforementioned meeting, the British government spelled out which areas the industry must work on. Its main concern seems to have been that not enough progress is being made in educating trustees on where to invest the assets which they supervise and for which they are responsible.

■ Trustees have a hefty responsibility as every penny counts in the pension fund.

Where pension funds invest their assets is the biggest decision they will make, and it has to take appropriate account of the liabilities of the pension management industry. This is the problem faced by every saver and investor. Another concern is that many pension fund trustees are highly reliant on consulting actuaries and employee benefits companies, which earn huge fees from advising trustees on how to run their schemes. Still another concern has been that:

■ Trustees assess investment performance on a short-term basis, which can lead to wrong longer-term decisions.

As we will see in Chapter 9, the investment horizon is one of the challenging problems faced by all managers of assets – from retail investors to professionals. The retirees' and potential retirees' time horizon defines the pension fund's cash outflow, and its trustees should appreciate that the sure way to kill any business is for it to run out of cash.

One of the themes which seems to have concerned the participants of the Downing Street meeting is that many companies today are battling against the rising costs of their pension funds. They are closing down pension schemes and cutting back on the retirement promises they have made to staff. In the UK alone, up to 60 000 workers, some having contributed to their company pension plans for decades, are already facing penury in retirement:

■ After their companies became insolvent, and
■ The pension plans were unable to meet pension commitments.

This is, indeed, a universal problem and, as such, it underlines the need for a personal investment plan, or at least one which is closely supervised by the interested person. Governments, companies and the working population should appreciate that the years of complacency about pensions – classically seen as part of entitlements – are gone.

As the Geneva Association aptly suggests, the burden an increasing old-age dependency places upon societies is heavy. A smaller and smaller proportion of the working-age population has not only to generate the goods and services to be consumed by retirees but also to pay for them, and the weight of this task is all too real.

One only needs to look at the widely available tables on forecasts of old-age dependency ratios in the most developed countries to get some idea of the magnitude of this issue. The situation is likely to become even worse since, according to the experts, several of the less developed countries may be underestimating the fiscal and economic consequences of population ageing, given that their official population projections assume that current trends in longevity and fertility will substantially reverse.

It is not that the world is running out of money. To use an allegory, the Stone Age did not end because of a lack of stone, but because there was a phase shift in society. In the same way, there is a phase shift in the financing of retirements, of which individual investors, institutional investors and governments must be fully aware.

2.7 Are mutual funds a good alternative?

It has been a deliberate choice to present to the reader what has gone wrong, or can go wrong, with pension funds because this is far more important than what has gone right. The same principle guides the writing in this section, the reason being that only in this way can savers be aware of the risks which they confront with their investments before adversity hits, which it may.

Starting with the issue of market risk, there has been little refuge for equity mutual fund investors during 2000, 2001, 2002 and first quarter of 2003. Precious metals, base metals, and real estate funds were the only ones to profit. According to Morninstar, in the USA the average domestic stock mutual fund fell 11.6 percent in the second quarter of 2003, and the pain was widespread, with declines in value hitting both large cap and small cap funds. At the same time, there was a steady decrease in stock fund inflows going:

- From just over $17 billion in April 2003,
- To $6.5 billion in May, while June saw an outflow of $10.4 billion.

Indeed, while 2003 was generally considered a year of recovery in equity values, the uncertainty surrounding the stock market, reinforced by these statistics, is far more than a question of consumer sentiment. Consumer spending has helped the US economy weather the recession, but consumer spending slowed and, as investors shun stocks, companies have a much harder time raising the capital they need to expand operations and improve revenues and profits.

Neither has the mutual funds industry been helped by scams. First came the September and October 2003 revelations by Eliot Spitzer, New York State's attorney general, about mutual funds scandals. Spitzer had launched an investigation into this industry, which oversees $7 trillion of America's assets, and in the aftermath the mutual funds industry has been fighting for its reputation.

- Several dozen class-action lawsuits have been filed in a matter of a few months, and
- More were expected to come from the attorney general's probe, as well as another from the SEC.

Like investment banks, with which Eliot Spitzer and the SEC reached a settlement in April 2003, mutual funds have long been known to have potential conflicts of interest. This is not surprising since the earnings of fund managers are related to how much money they manage, while their quest for size and performance can clash with the financial interests of their investors.

In September 2003, the New York State attorney general's office said that it had obtained evidence of widespread illegal trading schemes that potentially cost mutual fund shareholders billions of dollars annually. This is in addition to the corporate accounting scandals which, since 2001, have rocked the confidence of investors. At the same time, mutual funds scams have the potential of being even more devastating, because such funds are fiduciaries and their mission is to manage and safeguard clients' money. By taking payoffs, they are:

- Breaching their fiduciary duty,
- Shaking investor confidence, and
- Creating a situation whereby everybody can be a loser.

Spitzer's charges were leveled at four big fund companies that till now were well regarded and trusted by millions of investors. The major funds initially cited have been: Nations Funds, owned by Bank of America, Strong Capital Management, Janus Capital Group and Bank One's One Fund Group.[10] The aforementioned companies said they were co-operating with Spitzer's investigation, which could trigger criminal as well as civil charges.

Experts suggested that Spitzer's revelations are serious and the existing evidence compelling. If this continues, let alone spreads, it can break the mutual funds industry which has been around for about eight decades. Indeed, as more revelations of improprieties come to the public eye, America's $6.8 trillion mutual fund industry finds itself in a position which:

- Further alienates small investors, and
- Stalls a nascent stock market recovery.

Even if, strictly speaking, what has happened is not entirely illegal, it is unethical that mutual fund companies, including major ones, pump up profits using dubious trading schemes that cost small investors billions of dollars annually. 'The full extent of this complicated fraud is not yet known,' Spitzer said, 'but one thing is clear: The mutual fund industry operates on a double standard. Certain companies and individuals have been given the opportunity to manipulate the system.'

At least sixteen mutual fund companies, twelve brokerage firms, four banks and dozens of individuals have been implicated so far, and analysts predict the scandal will continue to spread. With the mutual fund industry under intense scrutiny by regulators and legislators, a significant overhaul of the way funds do business is in sight – including new rules on trading, redemptions, fees, disclosure and boards of directors.

Experts suggest that such sweeping changes could have a profound impact on companies' bottom lines. 'We could see some margin compression in 2004 due to changes in regulation and legislation for the industry', suggested Kenneth Worthington, a financial services analyst at CIBC Oppenheimer.[11] We can also see some well-deserved prison sentences as Eliot Spitzer revived the Martin Act, New York's once dormant 1921 Blue Sky law, which was originally passed to combat fraudulent stock schemes. On 17 December, James P. Connelly Jr, the forty-year-old former vice-chairman of Fred Alger & Co., became the first mutual fund executive to be sentenced to jail, for one to three years.

As a prosecutor, the Attorney General has the ability to both subpoena and indict, something the SEC can do only through referral to the Justice Department. These charges sent shock waves through the industry, which had been, till then, one of the few financial places not tarnished by scandals in the 2000 to 2003 time frame. There is also the case of collusion with hedge funds, as evidenced by a $40 million settlement announced in early September 2003, with Canary Capital Partners, a little-known hedge fund.

Spitzer said Canary gave four mutual fund companies banking business in exchange for the ability to engage in illegal after-hours trading and market exploitation. For instance, Canary had a deal with Bank of America that let the hedge fund buy mutual funds after 4 p.m. ET but get the fund's share price for that day. 'This is another example of the little guy being told to play by the rules, while the big player gets the breaks', said Jim Cramer, a former hedge fund manager. 'I never thought mutual funds would jeopardize their business by compromising individual investors.'[12]

- The after-hours agreement gave Canary the advantage of being able to buy at the 4 p.m. price with knowledge of post-close developments.
- By contrast, an investor must buy before 4 p.m. to get that day's price, while a purchase after 7 p.m. gets the next day's price.

Market timing has been another gimmick. Janus and Strong allegedly allowed Canary to buy several of their funds one day, then sell them the next. In return, Canary allegedly made big investments in those firms' other funds. With all this now in the public domain, the key question is: 'How were investors hurt?' If the charges are true, Canary enjoyed advantages that small investors did not. Moreover, big movements of money in and out of a fund can force it to sell stocks the manager would prefer to keep. This:

- Hurts returns, and
- Has a negative market impact.

In early April 2004, Eliot Spitzer fired another shot at America's mutual fund industry. Theodore Sihpol, formerly a low-level executive at Bank of America, was charged with forty counts related to improper trading. Sihpol said he would plead not guilty in a case that will test the legality of 'late trading'.[13]

In the past, problems have included stock manipulation charges against manager Ron Baron of Baron Asset fund, and the collapse of Heartland High-Yield Bond fund, which is in receivership. But those were not enough to trigger fund reforms. The industry was strong enough to lobby hard against the Mutual Funds Integrity and Fee Transparency Act, which cleared the House Financial Services Committee in 2003 but was not introduced in the Senate.

The new scandals now bring the investigators' focus on scams such as soft-dollar arrangements in which many funds steer trading business to particular brokers in return for research and other services. Soft-dollar arrangements can mean that the fund pays more for trades than it would otherwise and also buries some expenses, reducing by so much transparency of information to end-investors.

For its part, the SEC moved to join the growing investigation into the mutual fund trading scandal. Stephen Cutlet, SEC's enforcement chief, said the commission was requesting documents from dozens of mutual fund companies following allegations by the New York attorney general's office that the industry is rigged against small investors.

Meanwhile, Spitzer continued to issue subpoenas to major mutual funds and their larger clients, such as hedge funds, with the loosely regulated investment pools for wealthy investors at the center of the trading probe. People close to the situation suggested that Millennium Partners, a large hedge fund run by prominent investor Israel Englander, emerged as a primary focus.[14] Among large mutual funds, Invesco Funds Group and Putnam Investments, a unit of Marsh & McLenna, confirmed they had been contacted by Spitzer's office.

Scandals also underline some latent responsibilities. Critics say that, basically, this whole business is an indictment of the SEC and the paternalistic attitude the industry has taken to shareholders which can be phrased in a short sentence: 'We are taking care of you, and don't you worry about independent directors.' Rationally speaking, the mutual funds industry itself should be eager to regain investors' trust, by working closely with regulators and by being transparent in its wheeling and dealing.

This will not be easy, because what has been written in this section is not the only critique hitting mutual funds. In a 2003 book, Maggie Mahar suggests that the role mutual funds played in fuelling share-price momentum during the mid to late 1990s cycle, sheds new light on what a surprisingly large number of fund managers did which contributed to the bubble in the market. As Mahar writes, 'fund managers looking for momentum did not care so much about actual earnings as the rate of quarterly earnings growth, the percent by which earnings grew – or were projected to grow – every three months. Their focus was short-term, their object: speed.'[15]

The message the reader should retain from this is that the investor has no alternative than being in charge of his or her savings and wealth. Even if one uses the services of professional asset managers, which is likely, he or she should definitely be able to personally assert the trustee's ethical standards, and follow how well his or her personal investments are managed. Part 2 and Part 3 are dedicated to this end.

Notes

1 D.N. Chorafas (2002). *The Management of Philanthropy in the 21st Century*. Institutional Investor.
2 *The Economist*, 17 January 2004.
3 D.N. Chorafas (2003). *Alternative Investments and the Mismanagement of Risk*. Macmillan/Palgrave.
4 Named after Dr Werner Heisenberg, the physicist who developed it.
5 D.N. Chorafas (2002). *Modelling the Survival of Financial and Industrial Enterprises: Advantages, Challenges, and Problems with the Internal Rating-Based (IRB) Method*. Palgrave/Macmillan.
6 Peter Krass, *Carnegie*, Wiley, New York, 2002.
7 *Financial Times*, 18 November 2002.

8 *Financial Times*, 23 June 2003.
9 *The Economist*, 7 February 2004.
10 *International Herald Tribune*, 4–5 October 2003.
11 *BusinessWeek*, 12 January 2004.
12 *USA Today*, 4 September 2003.
13 *The Economist*, 10 April 2004.
14 *USA Today*, 5 September 2003.
15 Maggie Mahar (2003). *Bull! A History of the Boom 1982–1999*. HarperBusiness.

Two
Capital markets and their players

3 Capital markets and the securities industry

3.1 Introduction

'We spend all morning, and no one mentioned the stock market, which I find interesting in itself', said Alan Greenspan to the twelve members of the Federal Open Markets Committee, in one of the first meetings he attended as chairman of the Federal Reserve.[1] Implicit, if not explicit, in this statement has been the notion that capitalism rests on four markets, whose interaction is shown in Figure 3.1:

■ Loans,
■ Bonds,
■ Equities, and
■ Foreign exchange.

Bonds and equities are securities (more on this in section 3.2) traded in the capital market. The same is true of securitized loans. The capital market is pivot point of

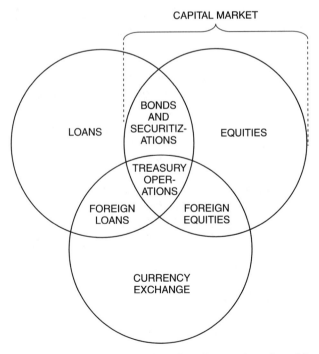

Figure 3.1 Principal financial markets for creation of wealth

capitalization, and Dr Greenspan's comment was quite relevant. According to expert opinion, during the past fifty years the US Federal Reserve (Fed) has probably been the most influential global institutional factor for capital markets.[2]

To appreciate the breadth and impact of capital markets, it is necessary to recall that the foregoing list of four markets includes the principal financial commodities which, either by themselves or through their derivatives, are traded in the exchanges and over the counter. All of them are sensitive to the Fed's decisions. The value of other commodities, such as real estate, usually also follow the interest rates, currency exchange rates and creation or destruction of wealth by these four principal markets.

The markets identified by the above four bullets interact with and influence one another. High interest rates mean higher returns on bonds for investors, which sees to it that fixed interest instruments eventually attract money from the stock market. Higher interest rates also mean more expensive borrowing for business which depresses business earnings and profits, leading investors to expect less return from equities.

We will see in Chapter 4 that equities were first traded in Amsterdam in 1602, but the polyvalent capital market, the way we know it today, was born in the USA in the late nineteenth century propelled by capital needs that credit institutions alone could not satisfy. Its time had come because of the largest project the US had undertaken till then: the building of coast-to-coast railroads network which required vast sums of money.

With the growth of the modern capital market nearly fourteen decades ago, came investment banking houses (see section 3.3) which made it relatively easy for industrialists and for magnets of the transport industry to tap a wide pool of American and European capital. It comes as no surprise that the largest US industrial and transport enterprises, which were the main beneficiaries of the early years of the capital market, accumulated huge financial resources in the years between the 1880s and World War II.

To a substantial extent, capital market financing has been a self-feeding cycle. Railroads transported ore to the furnaces, and the mills produced steel for the rails. The construction of railroads and rapid urban growth gave work to unskilled immigrants, and the new workforce:

- Provided labor for growing industrial enterprises, and
- Increased the demand for their products.

Buyers and sellers of securities traded in the capital markets came together to accomplish something that none of them could achieve alone. This is a simple concept, but one that has been forgotten by many in the boom years of the market when speculators called the tune and investors who trusted their capital to equities, and debt instruments, were taken for a ride.

The principle behind the growth of capital markets has been that scale, scope and structure all depend on what an organization is trying to do – and on how well it can do it. Organizations are the means to ends, not ends in themselves. They exist to serve the needs of the economy, as well as of people both and outside these organizations, and part of the larger social structure.

Contrary to Chapters 1 and 2, which concentrated on six of the twenty golden rules of equity investments, the present chapter presents to the reader the *gros plan* of capital markets and their *correlation*, including the risk of contagion because of synergy which exists between *capital* and *markets*. The term 'correlation' is preferable to that of 'synthesis', 'interpretation' or 'analogy' because it implicitly contains them while also adding to them the notion of a common relation and complementarity.

3.2 Securities and their legal protection

The term 'securities' denotes stocks, bonds, debentures, notes and certificates of deposit (CDs). In addition, it includes certain investment contracts and certificates of participation, or interest in a profit-sharing agreement, as well as in oil, gas or mineral royalty or lease. Typically, though not necessarily always, securities are traded in exchanges.

In some countries, investment in publicly traded contracts or interests are protected, up to a certain amount per owner, by a government-sponsored authority – if, and only if, they are registered as securities. For instance, in the USA the Securities Investor Protection Corporation (SIPC) is registered with the SEC under the Securities Act of 1933 (see Chapter 4). This protection amounts to $500 000 per securities depositor, of which $100 000 is cash.

Though often thought by investors as being liquid like cash, shares of money market funds are also securities when such entities are organized as mutual funds. In the USA, warrants or rights to purchase, sell or subscribe to the above mentioned securities are also protected by the Securities Act.

There are however exceptions. Shares of mutual funds are securities protected in the same way by the Act if they exist in securities accounts with SIPC members. To the contrary, broker-dealers who trade exclusively in mutual funds are not SIPC members, and claims against such firms are not protected by the SIPC. In the globalized market, the legal aspects concerning securities and their protection (or lack of it) are a maze. There are no simple answers.

- No investor should ever think the securities in his or her portfolio are protected because the person or company who sold them said so.
- Painstaking research and legal advice are necessary, and even then some risks remain because what is true in one jurisdiction is not necessarily valid in another.

Beyond the fine print of legal protection there exists a common ground as well as rules which characterize the *securities industry* – which includes all the players in the capital market. One of these concerns its competitiveness. As the securities industry gets more competitive, ingenious marketing as well as new product development become vital, and the same is true of productivity, cost control and risk management to enhance the financial staying power of companies operating in the capital market.

In order to gain market leadership, *investment banks* (see section 3.3) and *brokerage houses* drive innovation in financial instruments, expand their range of services beyond trading to include, for instance, asset management, try to gain a better market focus and develop an information infrastructure for the masses of paperwork associated with trading and administering stocks and bonds.

- Some of the brokerages specialize in debt; others focus on equities; still others trade in both.
- Some of the brokerages limit themselves to their home market, others have an international perspective in their operations.

Among securities, *debt* is easier to trade on a global scale than equity and, as far as companies using debt instruments are concerned, taxation favors corporate debt.[3] The fact, however, is that nobody can control the worldwide debt market – whose behavior depends on expected, anticipated *liquidity* (see Chapter 12) and other vital factors.

Typically, the securities industry is paper-intensive. High technology is an important competitive advantage not only in swamping paperwork, but also – if not primarily so – in trading. In the race to *buy low/sell high*, securities houses that do not master *interactive computational finance* are frozen out at the switch, or jump into the market with incomplete knowledge and get burned. In Wall Street, the City of London, and other major financial markets, computers and communications are not only seen as the tools which help in

- Gaining a market edge, and
- Holding one's leadership,

but also as a means for attracting *brainpower*, which is an important competitive advantage because organizations comprise people. Market leadership is more than ever crucial to investment bankers as the clients who matter tend to deal with a smaller number of banks and securities houses, than in the 1980s and 1990s, retaining only those which can offer:

- Greater ingenuity, and
- Higher quality of service.

In 1980, AAA American companies had on average thirty-six banks to deal with. Today, this number has been reduced to seven and is still falling. Alternative means of financing, particularly the better terms and lower cost of capital markets, further underline this reduction in the number of intermediaries. One result of high technology in securities and in banking is that the financial institution becomes its client's assistant treasurer, but it can hold this position only as long as it is:

- Inventive in the type of products which it offers to its clients, and
- Able to keep ahead in market know-how, so that its clients continue to need its services.

This requires both innovation in financial investments and virtuosity in the management of change, two domains in which many of the larger financial institutions are weak. To a substantial extent, such weakness is an aftermath of the Big Company syndrome which leads to widespread conformity.

A good way to appreciate where conformity leads is to look back to the twentieth century's communist regimes. One of their common characteristics is that conformity led to the clogging of organizations' arteries. Another aspect is the almost total intellectual stagnation – two negative qualities which go hand in hand, and distinguish the dying species from bankers and brokers who:

- Move ahead in their profession, and
- Contribute to the profitability of the institution for which they work, and which pays their wages and premiums.

Profitability in the securities business, however, is not a one-way street. Like investors, securities houses that trade on their own account experience both gains and losses. Therefore, beyond the more classical aspects of organization and structure, they must have in place a rigorous risk management system, one able to cope with the aftermath of globalization along the three-dimensional frame of reference shown in Figure 3.2.

Within the globalized securities market, risk management cannot be seen independently from the jurisdiction within which the company operates, the prevailing legislation and the role played by regulatory authorities. In Chapter 5, we will take as an example the US Securities Act of 1934 and the functions of the SEC.

Finally, like any other human enterprise, the securities industry at large, and most particularly investment banking, needs brains and lots of thinking. If high technology is a precondition for success in securitization and other financial products, the other

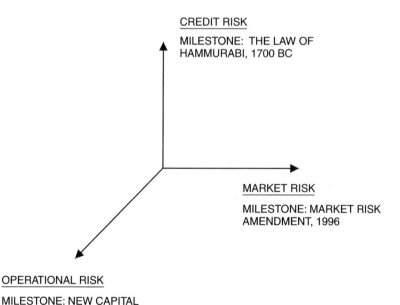

Figure 3.2 A framework for integrated risk management on a global scale

pillar on which market leadership rests is *brains*. They are necessary for coping with novelty in the financial industry, which requires:

- New thinking, and
- New departures.

The people employed by the securities industry should use their brains every day; whatever becomes routine must be handled by computers. Not everybody agrees that new thinking and new departures are beneficial. When King Ferdinand of Spain visited the conservative University of Cervera, the rector proudly reassured the monarch with the words: 'Far be from us, Sire, the dangerous novelty of thinking.'

3.3 Investment banking and underwriting

Both in literature and in daily practice, investment banking has no unique definition. Often it is confused with brokerage and with merchant banking. Therefore, the definition given in this section is the one I myself follow and, up to a point, it also has to do with personal characteristics. According to Anthony Sampson, there are two types of bankers who can sometimes be distinguished by their look and the pace of their walk and talk:[4]

- The men and women from *deposit banks*.

These are mainly commercial banks or clearers, responsible for millions of bank accounts in hundreds of branches. To attract deposits, they have to look very dependable, otherwise people would not trust them with their money. Commercial banks have made most of their profits from interest. Investment banks profit the most from fees.

- The investment bankers (or merchant bankers).

Their speciality is to make deals between rich individuals or companies, which do not involve the small saver. According to Sampson, given the nature of their job, they are allowed to look more aggressive. A better way to say this is that investment bankers have greater freedom and enterprise than commercial bankers.

The distinction just made is consistent with Sampson's approach of focusing on the personality of people in different sectors of the banking business. Other authors may have different viewpoints and opinions. But there are no doubt differences in the personality of people involved in distinct areas of banking – which is both influenced by and has an impact on the type of business itself. The two issues are interrelated.

- The man makes the job, and
- The job helps in shaping up the person doing it.

Since investment bankers and brokers make much of their money from fees, a salient problem for them is whether the advice they are giving can justify the fee. This is also the consultant's salient problem. On the other hand, both the investment banker and the high-paid consultant are aware that top management nearly always respects independence:

- Of mind, and
- Of income.

In a modern banking frame of reference after the repeal of the Glass-Steagal Act, which separated investment banking from commercial banking, this interest versus fee distinction in the business of financial institutions is no longer as clear-cut as it used to be. Many commercial banks also try to make more (if not most) of their income from fees, as the traditional profits center – the spread between interest expense and loan rates – shrinks.

Commercial banks feel the need to branch into investment banking because their more important and lucrative clients, among industrial companies and high net worth individuals, need expertise so far provided by investment banks. Moreover, AAA- and AA-rated companies do not need to ask a bank for a loan; they go directly to the capital market with:

- Commercial paper,
- Corporate bonds, and
- Money market instruments.

To address the capital market, industrial companies hire the services of an investment bank. The financial intermediary is no longer the commercial bank, but the investment bank. In the post-World War II years, 85 percent of all publicly offered securities were distributed by investment bankers. Of this 85 percent, about 70 percent were handled by purchase and sale, and 15 percent on a best efforts basis. To succeed, this activity requires:

- Cultural background,
- Investment expertise,
- Client and investor base,
- Financial staying power, and
- High technology.

In contrast to what has been said about the line dividing investment banking and commercial banking, the difference due to greater enterprise and business dynamism dividing merchant from commercial banks still exists. As such, it constitutes one of the landmarks in the line separating more classical commercial banks from merchant and investment banks, even if this is only a thin line. Investment bankers are:

- Investing their firm's capital in restructuring established companies,
- Advising in mergers and acquisitions,
- Providing bridging loans,
- Funnelling seed money to venture-capital firms, and
- In many but not in all cases, acting as brokers and asset managers.

Goldman Sachs, Morgan Stanley and Crédit Suisse First Boston are examples of investment banks. Merrill Lynch is an investment bank and a broker. All of these institutions
are going well beyond the traditional risk-taking of:

■ Market-making, and
■ Underwriting.

It needs no explaining that *underwriting* a certain issue, whether securities offered to
the capital market, insurance policies or any other financial instrument, involves risks.
Therefore, underwriting is normally preceded by an analytical study to document risk
and return. This helps to provide a factual basis on whether to go ahead with the
underwriting.

If the investigation concerning, for instance, a new security proves favorable, one
of two types of contracts is signed between the issuer and the underwriter(s). One
involves a firm commitment by the underwriter(s) to purchase the entire issue outright
for resale to the public. The firm *contract*, however, contains a *market-out* clause
which permits the bank to cancel this contract if certain specified events take place.

The second type of contract entails an undertaking without financial obligation by
the underwriter(s) to use his or her (or their) best efforts to sell the issue. This type
of contract is typically used for very strong or very weak issues. No matter the type
of contract, investment banking like any other enterprise has *risks*. Its rapid pace and
global nature require constant vigilance to monitor:

■ Overall position risk,
■ Counterparty risk,
■ Interest rate risk,
■ Exchange rate risk, and
■ Omnipresent liquidity risk.

The overall position risk concerns concentration and diversification of underwriting,
investments and different types of loans. Also there are time horizon issues. To keep
risk in control aggressive banks must steadily focus on a three-dimensional system
which considers the business environment, each instrument traded or inventoried and
each individual customer – as shown in Figure 3.3.

Since the investment bank operates on a relatively narrow margin of gross profit
and because security prices are highly sensitive to market changes, the risk in carrying
inventories of securities is extraordinarily high. This speaks volumes for the level
of detail and sophistication necessary to control exposure, with great emphasis on
market risk.

Merchant banking assumes different types of risks, which have to do with its origin,
as it developed from the beginning in connection with trade. Early merchants conducted trade by barter; a direct aftermath has been the bill of exchange. In lending
activities, merchants were preceded by pawnbrokers and moneychangers in Florence.
In that sense, banking activities in Europe can be traced to the twelfth century, when
money exchange was born.

In the twentieth century the merchant bank has been, in effect, a private bank with
partners who among themselves define the orientation of the institution's business.

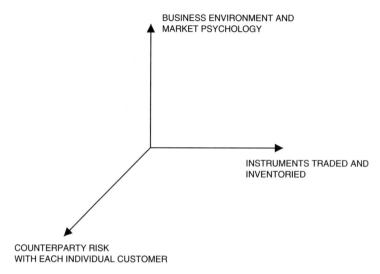

Figure 3.3 Investment banks must manage their risk along a three-dimensional frame of reference

This definition often contrasts with the old definition whereby the nearest equivalent to a merchant bank was one who undertook lending connected to a commercial activity. In American-style merchant banking the foundation is advising corporations on mergers and acquisitions. At times a merchant bank takes positions in the acquisitions activity it conducts for its clients, making it difficult to distinguish it from an investment bank.

3.4   Investment bankers and primary dealers

The relationship characterizing the different types of banking is not necessarily linear. In money terms, merchandising activities come in all possible sizes, but unlike some of the merchant banks' endeavors, in investment banking the average unit transaction is large.

From the size of individual transactions to overall position risk, when it comes to underwriting, the originating house ordinarily joins other banks in an underwriting or purchase syndicate, of which it acts as the manager. An agreement among the parties in this purchasing or underwriting syndicate defines the terms of the venture (see also the discussion on correspondent banking, in section 3.5). Current practice generally limits the liability of each member of the syndicate to the amount of its participation. The manager's powers include:

- Borrowing to carry the inventory of securities in process of sale, and
- Stabilizing the market price of the new issue by purchases and sales, for the syndicated account.

The investment banker attempts to achieve rapid, widely profitable and permanent placement of the underwritten securities in the *primary market*. The selling group is the principal vehicle for the actual distribution of new issues to investors, organized and managed by the manager of the underwriting syndicate, with which it usually enters into a contract. Participants in the selling group comprise some or all of the underwriters as well as additional dealers.

In fact, a more common, term than primary market is that of *primary dealers*. Primary US government securities dealers are reporting to the Market Reports division of the Federal Reserve Bank of New York. Examples (in alphabetic order) are Bank of America, Bear, Citigroup, Goldman Sachs, Merrill Lynch, J.P. Morgan Securities, Morgan Stanley, Stearns; and so on.

The *secondary market* of US Treasury securities is conducted through these primary dealers, who provide bids and offers (see Chapter 4) on a continuous basis on all out-standing Treasuries. These market-makers in Treasury securities are entities approved by the Fed. In addition, on behalf of the Board of Governors of Federal Reserve Systems, the Federal Reserve Bank of New York conducts, through actions involving the primary dealers:

- Its open market operations, and
- Its repo and reverse repo transactions.

In the overall underwriting business, stand-by is a special type of agreement, fairly common when an established company offers additional stock direct to its own stockholders, or when a corporation which is recapitalizing (or is in the process of restructuring) offers new securities in change for its outstanding issues.

In such cases, an underwriting group may be formed which, for a commission, guarantees the disposal of the entire issue. Such a group is typically obliged to take up any portion of this entire issue, particularly any portion not absorbed or exchanged by existing holders. In this manner, the issuer is certain to obtain the needed cash for corporate purposes, including the case of paying off the non-assenting security holders. To perform these activities in an able manner, investment bankers must have:

- The ability to *spot opportunities instantly*.

Quite often, business opportunities are a by-product of mismatched market conditions which are short-lived, and must be exploited on the fly. For this reason, successful underwriters are characterized by:

- A fast reaction time, once the opportunity is identified.

Mismatched conditions which create business opportunities tend to reach equilibrium quickly. Then, they disappear, and while they might reappear, it is likely that this will happen under totally different aspects. Therefore, to be on firm ground investment bankers:

- Need to test new and old products for embedded risks.

As we have already seen, the bank must be ready to innovate, in order to retain its most valuable customers, attract new ones and keep up with expanding market demand. But it simply cannot afford to do so at any risk level. Control of exposure requires:

- Know-how and preparation to capitalize on the cutting edge of the market.

A bank should be ready to try new instruments and marketing approaches, but should also be ready to withdraw if the product does not meet with market acceptance. In banking, as in practically any other business, there is an enormous difference between:

- A process whose purpose is equilibrium of supply and demand, and
- One in which supply or demand has a selection and promotion function, rather than equilibrium.

Selection and promotion are processes characterizing many aspects of investment banking. Acting as high-power (and highly paid) advisers, investment bankers have been brought increasingly into the merger loop, as takeover transactions escalate from millions to billions of dollars and pounds.

'The traditional banks are like the British Empire. There is nothing more to gain, and quite a lot to lose', said Jack Hambro to Anthony Sampson, which the latter reported in his book, *The Money Lenders*. But this does not mean that commercial banks have no role to play in the present financial markets – provided they develop a clear strategy and establish precise goals.

The careful researcher finds no difficulty in establishing that there is significant correspondence between the eighteenth and early twenty-first centuries regarding the 'Who is Who' in banking as well as the strategy followed by the most successful financial operators. Johann Baring has in all likelihood been the first *modern* banker, one who represented what many investment bankers stand for today.

At the beginning of the nineteenth century, together with the emerging house of Rothchilds, the Barings were seen as the behind-the-scene controllers of nations. But while the Rothchilds focused their attention and financial power in Europe, the Barings became both interested and involved in the USA, contributing a great deal to the industrial power which was about to emerge.

- The Barings were making a fortune out of their investments,
- But they were also suffering great losses in a series of unprecedented defaults.

This situation of overleveraging, which in the late nineteenth century characterized American municipalities on and off the edge of bankruptcy, is today representative of the exposure taken by capital markets in regard to company debt and sovereign debt. As the twentieth century came to a close, both corporate and sovereign borrowing far exceeded the pace of economic growth, leaving the different entities vulnerable to a slowdown. Eventually this led to a wave of big bankruptcies.

This can be devastating to investment bankers because those who are active in the global market are not necessarily big companies. To protect themselves from oversized exposure, many City of London bankers, Lazards, N.M. Rothchild, Barings, Schroders (when the latter two were independent entities) – which in American terminology would be called 'boutiques' – ignored pre-Big Bang theories of integration and synergy, preferring to specialize in just a few areas.[5]

For instance, in its years of glory Barings never made markets in British equities. It dealt mainly in the sterling part of the fixed-interest and floating-rate Euromarkets, as well as in private placements of sterling bonds and in derivatives. Eventually, however, this prudent policy was abandoned, in favor of the big game. In 1995, huge losses in derivatives deals, double books, absence of internal control and a lack of rigorous risk management blew Barings to pieces.

3.5 Correspondent banks

An important institution in the financial industry is that of correspondent banks. *Correspondent* relationships among commercial bankers have been instituted to facilitate cooperative action. Over the years, since the end of World War II, they have been adapted to serve more effectively the business financing activities of commercial banks as well as a variety of other purposes to do with the institutions' daily business.

Correspondent banking is an arrangement under which one bank (correspondent) holds deposits owned by other banks (respondents). The correspondent provides payment and other services to respondent banks.

Correspondent banking has dominated the post World War II years. During the 1990s, however, globalization, deregulation, technology, rapid innovation of financial instruments, and the introduction of a cross border currency, the euro (in the first years of the twenty-first century), saw to it that correspondent banking arrangements are no longer considered as vital as they used to be. In the euroland, for example, central banks have favored the establishment of an efficient and robust payments system for the euro area.

This adaptation of correspondent banking arrangements to serve the evolving goals of credit institutions has taken several forms. One of these, which dates back to the early 1960s, is the wider use of participatory arrangements to provide financing facilities for large enterprises in industry and trade. Arrangements of this type:

- May be carried on within a given network of correspondent banks, or
- May involve the joint participation of several correspondent systems.

In such participations, the lead is taken by one of the institutions, usually but not always the larger one. Of special interest in correspondent relationships are participations in which the loan originates in a small institution and, because of its size, complexity or other reasons, is turned over in part to another institution active in the larger money market.

In some cases, by virtue of its experience and specialized personnel, the lead co-operating bank may play an important part in formulating the loan agreement. On the positive side, participatory arrangements make it possible for the banking system to operate as a unit, where such joint operation is essential. An example is the provision of financing facilities for small and medium-sized enterprises requiring specialized types of credit because of the relatively high risks involved. There is also, however, a downside, as we will see later in this section.

In many cases, correspondent relationships are useful in making available to associated banks, especially those of small size, the skills and techniques developed in the specialized departments of big banks. Sharing with correspondent institutions the experience of specialized lending operations is, for many credit institutions, an excellent training ground. While these participations often consist primarily of sharing information on:

- Procedures,
- Practices,
- Experience, and
- Credit risk ratings,

they are sometimes extended to the co-operative assumption of risks on loans which, for various reasons, an individual bank wishes to share with other lenders. Another line along which correspondent banking relationships develop is that in which a given bank makes arrangements with a manufacturer of consumer durable goods, or of commercial and industrial equipment, for the financing of sales, usually on instalment terms. This may take place within a given region through a system of specially selected associated banks.

The case mentioned in the preceding paragraph resembles merchant banking (see section 3.4) but extends the underlying notion to a large circle of credit institutions. Such extension helps in creating a system of independent banks, providing them with advantages of a regional or national organization. There is, however, a downside when one of these banks exploits to its own advantage the goodwill of its correspondent banks, as well as what kind of criteria should be used in selecting a correspondent bank.

One of the better examples of the downside is provided by Banco Ambrosiano and its bankruptcy. This example also poses an interesting question on how large could, or should, the number of correspondent banks be, as well as what kind of criteria should be used in selecting a correspondent bank.

When in mid-1982 Italy's Banco Ambrosiano was approaching default, the correspondent banks of the parent company and of its subsidiaries abroad numbered 250. All of these were desperate to recover the money they had lent directly or indirectly to the network of financial entities created over the years by Ambrosiano and exploited at the expense of its business partners.

There is no magic number for how many correspondent banks are too few or too many. The answer is a function of the business a credit institution is doing, the countries in which it is active but has no own affiliates, the amount of cross-border transactions taking place and their value, as well as other factors. Among these are the marketing activities undertaken by banks looking for correspondents – activities which often forget that there are risks associated with correspondent banking.

On 29 July 1982, at the eleventh hour prior to the Italian bank's default, representatives of 200 creditors participated in a meeting held in London where Ambrosiano's permanent commissioners, appointed by the Bank of Italy, explained how nearly $1.29 billion had vanished through a trap door in Panama.[6] (Note that in 2003, twenty-one years later, Parmalat's failure revealed an even bigger magnitude black hole – to the tune of more than 14 billion euros disappearing through the trapdoors of Cayman Islands and other offshores. See Chapter 15.)

One of the issues raised by Ambrosiano's bankruptcy has been credit insurance. Banks who had lent to Banco Ambrosiano in Milano, the parent company, were protected under the 1975 Basel agreement which made the national bank responsible for credits damaged by default of one of the institutions it supervised. But there was no cover for the debts Ambrosiano's foreign offshore affiliates had contracted.

Under these circumstances, are there any rules banks should follow when choosing their correspondents? My research did not provide much help. The most frequent reference has been creditworthiness. In this connection an AA rating, or better, by independent rating agencies is appreciated. A couple of banks mentioned more specific criteria they apply in connection with their correspondents:

- Network and growth rate,
- Balance-sheet strength, and
- P/E ratio (see Chapter 7) and dividend policy.

One of the cognizant executives participating in the study which led to this book said that among the indicators he considers in rethinking correspondent banking relationships are business expectations, the profile of funds deposited by the correspondent, frequency of notation of these funds, momentum, killer-product stories and level of derivatives exposure. Also worthy of consideration is the economic pain a prospective correspondent bank has suffered in the aftermath of penalties or other action by regulators.

In conclusion, a credit institution should go beyond creditworthiness criteria in judging a correspondent bank. The nature of such criteria vary from one institution to the next, and tends to be rather subjective. Even so, decision-making guidelines help to focus senior management's mind on risk and return from a correspondent relationship, and lead to a calibration which may be fairly dependable.

3.6   The globalized securities market

From the point of view of liquidity alone, it may make sense to trade individual equities on just one exchange. Other things being equal, the greater the trading volume of a share at a particular exchange, the narrower the bid-ask spread (see Chapter 5). Moreover, the larger the exchange and its trading volume, the less individual transactions can trigger particularly strong price fluctuations. Two other positive aspects are:

- Higher trading liquidity tends to reduce transaction cost for investors, and
- Exchanges with very efficient trading can take orders away from less liquid exchanges.

In practice, however, a high level of concentration has many drawbacks. In a globalized market, companies are listed on several stock exchanges because they want to take advantage of resources available in more than one capital market.

And it is an illusion to think that a regional superexchange – for instance, for all EU countries – would answer in each country the investors concerns about creditworthiness and efficiency.

Capital markets have locality, and locality helps in building up *trust*, which underpins every business. Beyond this, an overconcentrated exchange 'solution' would lead to a bureaucracy that would have made any Soviet executive proud. Bureaucracy is another major downside, and the European Union in Brussels provides an example.

Alternatively, if there is a superexchange and local exchanges continue to operate, then sooner rather than later there will develop vicious cycles of decreasing trading volumes at the locals. In this case, the example is NYSE and the different local exchanges (Philadelphia, San Francisco, and so on) in the USA. To survive the latter had to specialize in equities they trade.

In fact, some experts suggest that the creation of a single stock exchange for the whole of Europe, or even more so for the whole world, would be very bad for competition. While consolidating the landscape of European stock exchanges might make sense from the viewpoint of costs, other factors would turn negative. Most damaged of all would be a reduction at level of competition necessary:

- To keep trading fees low, and
- To create pressure for innovation.

Aside from the issue of competition and issues associated with trust and creditworthiness, a single European stock exchange would also be a problem from a regulatory perspective, given legal differences prevailing by jurisdiction. Assigning control of all capital markets to a single authority would be the nearest to a supervisory nightmare. It would also lead to turf wars without ending.

Based on current evidence, in all likelihood, the solution of listing global companies at more than one exchange is the best. However, this means that in the absence of truly international accounting standards, companies listed on more than one exchange have to follow and present to:

- National supervisors, and
- The investing public

different versions of their financial accounting according to rules prevailing within the jurisdiction. This is necessary even if the lion's share of trading of an equity listed on more than one exchange is done in the company's domestic (home) market.

Take as an example German and Swiss firms listed on their home exchanges and on the NYSE. In September 2001, in the middle of stock market doldrums worldwide, eleven German stocks listed in Frankfurt and eight Swiss stocks listed in Zurich were also listed on the NYSE. With few exceptions, however, trading volumes at the NYSE were below 10 percent of those on the home exchange, as shown in the sample of seven German and seven Swiss companies in Figure 3.4.

At the German companies' side, the relatively high trading in Deutsche Telekom and DaimlerChrysler can be attributed, respectively, to the VoiceStream takeover and the merger between Daimler and Chrysler. Apart from these two references, only one Swiss company exceed the 10 percent ratio, while two German and two Swiss

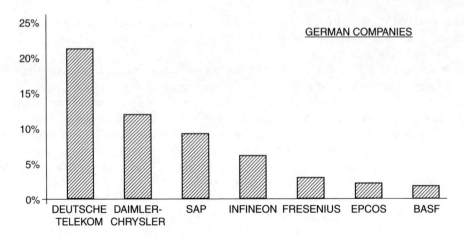

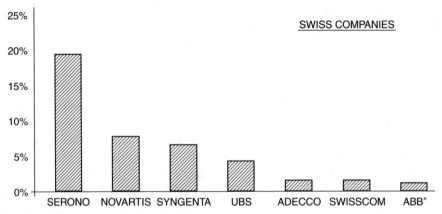

Notes: * ONLY FROM THE DATE LISTED ON THE NYSE, 6 APRIL 2001
       ** STATISTICS BY CREDIT SWISS

Figure 3.4 January to July 2001: the trading volumes of seven German and seven Swiss
equities listed on NYSE, compared with their home market stock exchange**

companies found themselves in the 5 percent to 10 percent bracket. The balance of
equity trading was done in each company's home country exchange.

Statistics on trading in equities listed in both home and host countries is a good
example of globalization of stock markets. It is also, in a way, an example of the
prophet (company) going to the mountain (stock exchange), because the mountain
would not come to the prophet. The NASDAQ tried to do so through an investment
in Europe, but it was not profitable.

It is therefore not surprising that during the past three decades capital markets
globalized through a multipolar solution, which has led to a high degree of cross-
border interdependence. On the other hand, globalization has raised the risk of global
contagion, making it more difficult for economic policy-makers to stop a snowball
effect, let alone reverse it after it gets going (see section 3.7).

To any company, the real cost of multiple listings in capital markets is keeping the books – including reconciliation, valuation and income recognition – under more than one standard. Take as an example a company listed in Switzerland as home market – under International Accounting Standards (IAS) – and as host country the USA, where the books must comply with Generally Accepted Accounting Principles (GAAP).

In several respects, the financial reporting principles of IAS are different from those of GAAP, including valuation differences. An example is purchase accounting. The merger of Union Bank of Switzerland and Swiss Bank Corporation, as reported to the UBS Annual Report post-merger, is an example.

Under IAS, the group accounted for the 1998 merger of the two Swiss credit institutions under the uniting of interests method. The balance sheets and income statements of the banks were combined, and no adjustments were made to the carrying values of the assets and liabilities. On the contrary, under GAAP the business combination creating UBS AG has been accounted for under the purchase method, with Union Bank of Switzerland the acquirer. Under the purchase method:

■ The cost of acquisition is measured at fair value, and
■ The acquirer's interests in identifiable tangible assets and liabilities of the acquiree are restated to fair values at the date of acquisition.

With this method, any excess consideration paid over the fair value of net tangible assets acquired is allocated first to identifiable intangible assets based on their fair values (if determinable). The remainder is allocated to goodwill.

With IAS, the business combination of the two banks was accounted for under the uniting of interests approach, under this method of accounting, a single uniform set of policies was adopted and applied to all periods presented, resulting in a restatement of 1997 shareholders' equity and net loss. By contrast, GAAP required that accounting changes be recorded in the income statement in the period the change was made. Therefore,

■ The accounting policy harmonization recorded under IAS for 1997 was reversed, and
■ The impact of the accounting changes was recorded in 1998.

Another unwanted consequence of multiple listings is the need still present in some countries to face the supervisors' corruption. An article in *The Economist* is illuminating on this account:

The governing coalition in Thailand has learned how to maximize its say on the panels that select members of the country's various watchdog agencies, which have become much less meddlesome as a result. Indonesia's parliament, which just set up a similar agency called the Corruption Eradication Commission, declined to appoint the most crusading candidates as commissioners.[7]

The Economist article went on to say that in Indonesia the courts can also undermine counter-corruption efforts, as 'all courts are for sale', according to one Supreme Court justice. In the Philippines, legal cases can be drawn out for so long, through so many appeals, that the risk of prosecution does not provide an effective deterrent to corruption.

The same article pointed out that, apart from Singapore and Malaysia, practically all the countries in South East Asia, still rank in the bottom half of the most recent 'Corruption Perceptions Index' (which should be viewed as one of the important equity indices, in a globalized economy). At least in part, this poor showing comes from a lack of laws, personnel and money to combat corruption – which talks volumes for one of globalization's dark sides.

3.7   Risk of global contagion

According to expert opinions, global contagion has been a major reason why the economic slowdown that began in 2000 in the technology and manufacturing sectors of the USA has spread around the world – resulting in a synchronized downturn for the first time in a decade. The downturn in the USA hit like a hammer the Asian economies. After a decade-long slump, to mid-2001, Japan has been slipping back into recession while the export-oriented companies of South East Asia found they have few places to which to sell their goods.

'This is a serious contagion that, left to its own dynamics, would become a vicious cycle that feeds on itself', suggested Allen Sinai of Decision Economics. In mid-2001, Sinai put the odds of a global recession at 40 percent.[8] 'We don't yet fully understand all the elements in the international area which are affecting the industrial countries', Alan Greenspan acknowledged in congressional testimony in June 2001.

During this testimony, the Federal Reserve chairman told the Senate Banking Committee that the banking industry faced deterioration in asset quality, requiring bank supervisors to step up their scrutiny. Then, he added that 'fortunately our banking system entered this period of weak economic performance in a strong position'.

One of the reasons for Greenspan's optimism – which with hindsight has not been corroborated by the facts – was that banks had improved their risk control systems, which should lead to a better reaction to cyclical weakness. By contrast, at about the same time outgoing Federal Deposit Insurance Corporation (FDIC) chair Donna Tanoue told the same Senate Banking Committee that while banks continued to exhibit strong financial results, they were seeing signs of stress. In particular, vulnerabilities existed in the areas of:

- Subprime lending,
- Agricultural lending, and
- Deposit insurance reform.

Tanoue added, in her testimony, that all these areas merited attention before reaching a crisis stage. Comptroller of the Currency, John Hawke Jr, told the Senate Banking Committee that while the banking industry was far better prepared to deal with a slowing economy than it was ten years ago, loan underwriting standards were still a reason for concern. 'By responding when we first detect weak banking practices, supervisors can avoid the need to take more stringent actions during times of weakness', Hawke suggested.

What Tanoue and Hawke stated in their testimonies proved true not only in the USA but also in Europe and Asia – as if these were one market together with America. In the 1990s, the banking industry had positioned itself in a way that could greatly benefit from advanced globalization, but could also hurt itself when the global financial health deteriorated.

One of the negative statistics at the time of the aforementioned testimonies, which preceded the early twenty-first century low in the global banking and investments markets, concerned the drop in world trade. This was serious because by late July 2001 world trade accounted for 25 percent of the world's economic output. That was double the percentage in 1970, but much less than the 2000 figures.

In retrospect what has happened since 2001 documents that globalization of banking and investment induces markets to behave in tandem to indicators of economic acceleration or slowdown. This is not difficult to understand, if we bear in mind that:

- The same investors now participate in all the major stock and bond markets, and
- The same global banking and securities firms make loans and trade in all the major economies.

As a result of relatively strong financial links what happens in one capital market affects the way investors and lenders behave elsewhere. The rise of multinational corporations has contributed to the connectivity in the global economy. When a multinational company is doing well, it boosts investment and employment everywhere; both its home and its host countries are benefiting. The reverse is also true: when a multinational firm begins to feel the slowdown pinch because several of its divisions are in trouble, there is a tendency to:

- Pull back, and
- Be much more prudent.

Prudence in regard to investment and other expenditures may also be advisable because of major events whose nature is not financial, but which have a financial impact. An example is provided by the 11 September (9/11) 2001 terrorist attacks and their effect on the globalized markets. One of the big issues which followed the tragic events in New York and Washington has been the extent to which 9/11 was an attack not only on innocent civilians, but also on globalization.

In retrospect, 11 September did not have a significant and lasting impact on trade flows, cross-border movements of capital, global supply chains and foreign direct investments. This was not at all evident in the weeks after the event, particularly so as stock markets nose-dived prior to turning around. Indeed, over a period of time, the disruption created by the terrorist attack at the World Trade Center and the Pentagon left its footprint on global emerging markets, particularly those running big current account deficits that rendered them more dependent on foreign capital. Also 9/11 prompted the Federal Reserve, European central banks and the Bank of Japan to injecting a great amount of liquidity into the market. Investors, too, went more liquid and more defensive as a result of the terrorist attacks.

Notes

1 Bob Woordward (2000). *Maestro*. Simon & Schuster.
2 Merrill Lynch (2004). *2004 – the Year Ahead*. January. Merrill Lynch.
3 D.N. Chorafas (2004). *Economic Capital Allocation with Basel II: Cost and Benefit Analysis*. Butterworth-Heinemann.
4 A. Sampson (1982). *The Money Lenders*. Coronet Books/Hodder & Stoughton.
5 In 1986, Margaret Thatcher's 'Big Bang' blew away the enforced separation of banks, brokers and traders.
6 Rupert Cornwell (1983). *God's Banker*. Victor Gollancz.
7 *The Economist*, 21 February 2004.
8 *Philadelphia Inquirer*, 22 July 2001.

4 The trading of equities

4.1 Introduction

Financial history says that, four centuries ago, Dirck Pietsersz Staetmaker, a Dutch citizen, was the first person to receive a formal share certificate. This confirmed he was the owner of 60 guilders (about $900 in today's money) of shares in Verenidge Oost-Indische Compagnie (VOC) – the United Dutch East India Company. By all accounts, this was the first initial public offering on record.

The equity certificate made Staetmaker part owner of a company which issued shares to the public, and had them publicly traded. The concept of *shareholder equity* has significantly evolved since that time, to include – on the financial side – common stock, preferred stock, convertible bonds; concepts associated with ordinary capital, reserves and general provisions; profits and losses; market capitalization; subordinated liabilities; net unrealized securities; the impact of interest rate risk and foreign currency risk; and exposures associated with derivative financial instruments.

To better appreciate the common equities early beginnings, as well as its risks, it is helpful to recall that VOC was formed in 1602 through the merger of six charter companies based in Amsterdam, which had sprung up during the 1590s in an attempt to wrest away from Portugal the lucrative world monopoly in spices. At first, each voyage was separately funded, with investors collecting all the proceeds from the sale of spices and other wares. This changed with the creation of United Dutch East India Company, which was given an initial ten-year monopoly to trade between the Cape of Good Hope and the straits of Magellan. Notice that:

- Staetmaker's 60 guilders denomination of equity in VOC was for small investors,
- Big investors bought an equity of as much as 85 000 guilders each, and
- Through big and small investors VOC raised 6.5 million guilders ($98 million) in August 1602, which was an impressive amount at that time.

According to financial history books, shareholders of the Dutch East India Company collected a good income in dividends, which over the first fifty years of VOC's life averaged a respectable 25 percent return on capital (ROC). That yield diminished over time and it dropped to about 12 percent in the early eighteenth century. Later on, the company's fortunes waned, and investors were forced to accept their dividends in kind.

The financial history of the Dutch East India Company is interesting not only for equity issuance and ROC reasons, but also because it has some parallels with the late 1990s' excesses of the corporate world. Floated on a wave of investor enthusiasm, secondary trading in the shares on Amsterdam's Merchant Exchange took off. Not just VOC's shareholders but also investors in other entities prospered; but then came a downturn.

A bubble economy, which also financed the tulip mania till its crash, saw to it that between flotation and 1650, the United Dutch East India Company shares rose, on average, 27 percent a year. This pace slackened, but not before an on-and-off speculation pushed them to fifteen times their issue price. Toward the end of the eighteenth century, VOC became:

- Overladen with debt, and
- Riddled with corruption.

The crash came when, in 1780, a trade war began with England and, in the aftermath, trade with Dutch East India dried up, leaving VOC with no income to service its near 100 million guilders of debt; a leverage which had risen to fifteen times its original equity. The fans of the Franco Modigliani-Merton Miller hypothesis on the advantages of debt finance, should take notice.[1] As VOC went down the pan, the Dutch government:

- Revoked its monopoly,
- Nationalized it,[2] and
- In 1799, it was declared bankrupt.

What had started as a success story, and stayed so for more than a century by creating wealth for its shareholders, became an entity unable to manage itself and riddled with debt. Mismanagement rather than lack of business opportunity was the cause of its downfall. Over nearly 200 years, United Dutch East India ships made 4800 voyages, carrying almost a million people to the colonies. The VOC's nearest rival had been the English East India Company which sent 2700 ships, but they carried only 20 percent of the Dutch entity's 2.5 million tons of Asian cargo.

This is history. In a modern equity market, there are different measures of underlying health. The four most important are breadth, volume, new-highs/new-lows and annual rate-of-change. Experts believe that if those measures are in gear with the market, investors could bet that new recovery highs in the indexes should be confirmed by similar highs in the indicators. This is a popular hypothesis, but the market has its own mind and its own dynamics.

4.2 Equities, stock exchanges and over-the-counter operations

Chapter 3 has introduced to the reader the concept of a capital market. It has also explained the role of investment bankers who act as *underwriters* as well as *primary dealers*, for instance in US government securities. A brief reference has also been made to the *secondary market*. A secondary market provides a means whereby the owners of existing securities can dispose of them. Such market has two parts:

1 The recognized and organized *stock exchanges*, which provide central market places for the purchase and sale of securities.

Companies are registered and listed in the exchanges according to rules established by supervisory authorities – for instance, in the USA, by the SEC (see Chapter 5). Securities are bought and sold through public auction characterized by bids and offers co-ordinated by means of a well-developed trading system: the two-stitched auction.

Shares, or equities, traded in an exchange are financial assets which represent property rights on companies. These generally entitle holders to a share in the corporation's profits and, in the event of liquidation, in the remains of its net assets after other stakeholders are satisfied.

- Shares generally provide holders with a part in the ownership of the corporation whereas, in the case of debt securities, holders are creditors.
- The class *quoted or listed shares* covers all shares with prices quoted on a recognized stock exchange or other forms of regulated market.

Trading in an exchange involves only listed securities. There are conditions which lead a stock exchange to *delist* one or more of the securities on which trading has been taking place. For instance, early in 2000 the American Stock Exchange advised Echo Bay Mines that its listing eligibility was under review. The review was undertaken because the company had fallen below two of the exchange's continued listing guidelines:

- It had sustained net losses in its five most recent fiscal years (1995–99), and
- In the exchange's view, its shareholders' equity under US generally accepted accounting principles (GAAP, see Chapter 3) was inadequate.

All companies listed in an exchange have to look out for reasons which might lead to their delisting. When any reason is found, it has to be addressed through immediate damage control action and periodic progress reviews. Being listed in one or more exchanges is not a *right*. It is a *privilege* for which a listed company may no longer qualify.

2 The off-board, or unorganized, *over-the-counter* (OTC) market, in which prices are determined by negotiation by two willing counterparties.

In a broad sense the OTC market includes distribution of new securities to investors through underwriting operations, as well as through other means: the making of a direct, off-exchange market for securities that are already outstanding; trading in derivative financial instruments, many of which are designed to fit a counterparty's trading or investment requirements; and so on.

A big difference between organized exchanges and the OTC market is that the latter is informal and, to a large extent, unregulated. Traders and brokers effect transactions chiefly over the telephone with other traders and brokers. Unlike the recognized exchanges:

- Most OTC participants do not act as brokers who execute orders as agents for customers, receiving a commission for their work.
- Instead, they operate as dealers who buy and sell on their own account – essentially, that of their institution for which they work – in the expectation of a profit.

Some of the OTC dealers try to avoid taking a position in the instruments they trade, by keeping the volume of buying and selling in balance. The majority, however, is willing to buy more than it sells (or vice versa), thus taking a long or short position with whatever this means in risk and return.

Contrary to established exchanges, in the OTC market transactions are not the result of a double auction, with its open bids and offers. Deals are made through *private negotiation* between buyers and sellers, who seek out one another. In this wholesale or *inside market*, between the dealers themselves, the spread between bid and ask is much smaller than in the retail or *outside market* of established exchanges – where dealers negotiate on behalf of their customers.[3]

Participants in the OTC market include investment banks, commercial banks, stock exchange houses, so-called 'dealer banks' active in government and municipal securities, and treasurers of industrial and commercial entities. Specialized government and municipal bond houses and specialized OTC entities are other participants. Moreover:

- Much business is done with institutional investors and owners of large blocks of securities.
- Secondary distribution is provided, in contrast to the primary distribution afforded by investment bankers.

There are several reasons why the OTC market is flourishing. Derivatives is one of them, but not only derivatives. In the 1980s and 1990s, for instance, the syndication of loans evolved to the point where their buying and selling became a regular practice in the banking industry: Loans of all sorts from mortgages to credit card receivables can be *securitized* and sold in an exchange or placed OTC.

- Money center banks which are usually asset-long and liquidity-short serve as both originators and sellers in this market.
- The buyers are other banks, including retail and savings and loans (S&Ls) as well as institutional investors, who are asset-short but liquidity-long.

Credit institutions and investment banks securitizing loans and other products, typically ask an independent rating agency to grade them.[4] This helps in selling them, provided they can obtain an investment-level grade. Rating is so important because, typically, a stock exchange is a voluntary unincorporated membership association which:

- Provides facilities for its members, and
- Regulates their operations, in a way to safeguard both their interests and those of the investing public.

But it is the members of the exchange, and not its governing authority, which decide what to buy, what to sell and at what price. There are plenty of examples of stock exchanges around the globe. Two are the London Stock Exchange and New York Stock Exchange. The latter dates back to 1792, when it started as an outdoor market.

Sound exchange governance is most important. The board of governors of the NYSE comprises persons whose terms of service are staggered in order to ensure consistency in policy. They represent various interests, including active brokers and traders, partners of members (allied members), and some people selected to represent the general public.

Scandals can occur, however, either among the members of the exchange or some of its managers. The latest scandal regarding the governance of an exchange, which happened in late 2003, concerned the golden parachute of $140 million awarded by the board of NYSE to its retiring president. The aftermath has been a public outcry, as well as action by supervisory authorities.

Some of the members of the exchange are partners in *commission houses* executing orders for purchase or sale of securities received from non-member customers. They are the connecting link between the floor of the exchange, and investors and traders. In their offices are registered representatives who deal with customers. Many commission houses operate branches.

Other members of the exchange act as *floor brokers*. They have no direct contact with the public, their mission being to execute orders on the floor for other brokers. Still other members of the exchange are the *specialists* who concentrate their activity on one or a few stocks at a single trading post on the floor (see Chapter 5). Their primary responsibility is that of fostering an orderly and continuous market, absorbing a temporary excess of demand or supply. The specialists act as floor brokers and *floor traders*.

■ As brokers, they receive from other brokers, mainly commission houses, orders in issues unsuitable for immediate execution.
■ As floor traders, they buy and sell for their own account, subject to certain restrictions aimed at protection of outside customers.

At any moment, the specialists *book*, which is available on the exchange, shows the prospective demand and supply for the stock or stocks in which they specialize. There is, however, a certain controversy concerning the specialists book (more on this in Chapter 5). One of the services provided by specialists is that they make it possible for brokers to leave orders with them at prices above or below the current market price of an equity. Such orders are subsequently executed if and when the stock touches the specified price level.

4.3   Basic facts about equities: common and preferred stock

Prior to examining the role of different players in stock exchanges, as well as that of regulators, it is appropriate to establish what the role of equities is and, with this, what might be the shareholder's risk and return. Equities, as we will see in this section, is a form of financing, and shareholder value depends a great deal on how good the company's management is.[5]

The stock a company issues can be *common* or *preferred*. Textbooks say that common corporate stock represents ownership. In reality, it represents residual claims on assets, after the parties with priority claims have been satisfied. Preferred stock pays a fixed dividend and has priority over common stock. Some preferred stock is convertible to common stock; hence, it has a similarity with convertible bonds (see section 4.4); and there are also *deeply subordinated bonds*.[6]

On the upside, preferred stock offers protection against dividend cuts. Much of its attraction comes from the fact that the cash-strapped issuer is required to cut the dividend on its common stock before it cuts the preferred payout. This provides not only a cushion but also a forewarning sign to preferred stockholders; however, they may have problems unloading their assets since common and preferred stock prices tend to correlate.

Common stock offered in exchanges may come from new companies perhaps with a great future but a weak current base and more or less precarious financial conditions, or it may belong to well-established companies whose future may be better secured but less brilliant. The latter are known as *blue chips*, a term which has its origin in the color of the most expensive chip in the casino in Monte Carlo.

Note that the advantage from purchasing company shares as a commodity can also be a disadvantage. Common shares are a familiar investment tool, but the commodity nature of a share can be diluted by a variety of factors including the company's poor management.[7] 'They don't know their ass from their elbow about running companies', said an analyst about the top management of a given listed firm, adding that when the board finally decided to fire the chief executive officer (CEO), 'It was like taking candy from a baby.'

High leveraging is one of the signs of poor management, and it is also a high risk on its own. Leveraging is not only the assumption of an inordinate amount of debt. Typically, high marginal cost companies offer a high leverage to commodity price movement, but also represent a fragile structure which cannot afford to meet with adversity.

Each company's ability or inability to control costs and translate conditions into profits, affects its performance in a significant manner. The same is true of the company's consistent and well-directed efforts to innovate products, and be ahead of the game in terms of:

- Market appeal,
- Cash flow, and
- Profit margins.

The market appeal of a company's equity may slide when investors find out how leveraged this entity is. If we leave aside for a moment the risk associated with leverage, there is no simple trade-off in choosing between debt- and equity-financing. Theoretically, debt-finance is cheaper than equity-financing, because investors take on less risk when purchasing debt, and this requires a lower return. Practically, this argument forgets that a debt-laden company is a weak counterpart:

- Its equity has a volatility, and
- Its debt is more generally seen as a burden.

When the firm becomes too heavily indebted, equity-holders and debt-holders alike will start demanding higher returns to compensate them for the risk they are assuming. This reaction means that the firm's cost of capital will rise – a fact some economists tend to forget.

In their original paper, and in a later one, Dr Franco Modigliani and Dr Merton Miller favored debt over equity, to a large extent because of tax laws. Generally, a company that issues debt can deduct interest from profits before paying taxes, while it cannot deduct dividend payments or the capital appreciation of shares from profits. It can also play with creative accounting like pro forma reporting, giving shareholders a biased view of earnings before interest.[8] Debt, however, is by no means void of other risks, particularly so when the company:

- Becomes overleveraged, or
- Operates in a market which make it difficult to service its debt out of current cash flow and profits.

Because indebtedness and quality of management affect in a significant way a company's financial staying power, and they correlate with the market's response to the company's equity and debt, let us look a little more carefully into this theme. When a company needs cash, it issues equity or debt, or obtains bank loans. In this connection, investors need to remember some basic facts:

- Common stock pays a variable dividend,
- Preferred stock pays a fixed dividend,
- Bonds pay a fixed interest,
- Convertible bonds can be converted into stock,
- Warrants give rights to buy stocks at a given price,
- Bank debt, usually pays a fixed interest,
- Senior debt is served first, and
- Preferred stocks are senior to common stocks.

When a firm issues new equity, the price tends to fall for two reasons. New equity as well as options given to managers and employees are a dilution of old equity. Moreover, investors appreciate that the company's managers, who (usually) are also shareholders, have better information than the common shareholders, and are likely to sell when stock is overvalued.

A listed entity's share price may also fall for other reasons: too much debt, loss of market share, obsolete products or a decrease in dividends. Dividends are a barometer because they affect shareholders' bottom line and, generally, they are smoother than earnings as management does not like to increase dividends if it must decrease them later on (and vice versa).

In conclusion, equity is like an *option* on a company and its assets. Acting on behalf of equity-holders, management may undertake very risky projects which turn these assets into ashes; look at Enron, Global Crossing, WorldCom and Parmalat, among many other firms, for how supposed success stories were like castles built on sand.

Buying a company's debt instruments looks as if it is less risky than buying its equity, but it involves credit exposure and does not have a great deal of market upside. Moreover, because management cares mainly about the shareholders' response, some projects regarding bondholders may be neglected, creating debt overhang problems. Also, generally but not always, debt imposes more discipline on managers than equity does.

4.4 Convertible bonds defined

Convertible bonds, or simply *convertibles*, are hybrids of bonds and stocks. They have been among the early debt equity instruments, used by issuers to raise capital. In standard form, a convertible is a bond offering the investor the right to convert the debt instrument of which he or she is a holder into a specified number of shares, if a certain conversion price is reached. When this happens the equity generated by the issuer and given to the investor extinguishes the latter's claim on the debt.

■ Convertibles are derivative instruments in the borderline between stocks and bonds.
■ Originally issued as bonds, they are convertible to equity but with a catch.

If the price of the common stock rises, the value of the investor's conversion rights rises too; hence the market price of his or her convertible security is likely to go up. But in a down market the price drops, often in percentage terms more than twice as much as the norm (more about risks associated with convertibles later). In a general sense, and in line with the general principle just outlined, features of convertibles may include:

■ A call provision permitting the issuer to buy back the bonds at specified prices.
■ A sinking fund requirement, obliging the issuer to redeem the bonds over a given time period.
■ A put option giving the investor the right to sell the bond back to the firm at a predetermined price.

These and other features greatly affect the bond's market value and its behavior, as well as its risks. Precisely, because the convertibles represent a spectrum of characteristics, these are different securities than the more classical type of bonds. Another major difference is due clauses leading to complexities between the derivative and underlying instrument affecting the market's response.

For instance, a convertible which has not been converted into equity is effectively a bond with an option or warrant attached to it. The level at which the bond may be exchanged for equity is similar to the strike price of an option. But, though the convertible contains an embedded instrument which acts like a call option, conversion of the debt instrument into equity results in the issuer actually generating new equity, which is different from the case of a pure call option.

Convertible bonds are not the only instruments giving the holder the privilege of exchanging them for securities of a different type, usually common stock. Such a feature may be attached to any type of security, but typically characterizes preferred stock and debenture bonds. Convertible bonds are a means of raising new capital, and their appeal, or lack of it, depends on:

■ Market conditions,
■ The issuing company, and
■ Their special features.

Debentures are also debt instruments. Etymologically, the sense of debenture is debt, but financial practice has restricted its meaning to include only those bonds not secured by any specific pledge of property. Issuing debentures appeals to companies because the absence of a specific lien:

- Gives greater freedom to management, and
- Preserves the issuance of secured obligations in periods of emergency.

Nevertheless, this is not a *carte blanche*. Convertible bonds and debentures are subject to rules which are often written in fine print, escaping the investor's attention, but rules do exist. For instance, the instruments may be redeemable at the issuer's option, as specified in the applicable pricing supplement, or be otherwise subject to mandatory redemption.

In the case of optional redemption, the issuer may, and in the case of mandatory redemption the issuer must, redeem certain bonds at times when prevailing interest rates may be relatively low. Accordingly, the holder may not be able to reinvest the redemption proceeds in a comparable security at reasonably high interest rate.

The issuer's redemption right may also have an impact on the investor's ability to sell his or her bonds as the redemption date approaches. Moreover, the credit ratings of convertible bonds and debentures may not reflect the potential impact of all risks related to structure and other factors on the value of these debt instruments. And at the same time, real or anticipated changes in the issuer's credit ratings will generally affect the market value of convertible bonds and debentures.

The message these paragraphs aim to convey is that whether we talk of equities or debt instruments, investors should always keep in mind that there may be an uncertain trading market, with many factors affecting the trading value of assets in one's portfolio. No issuer can assure that a trading market for equities or bonds is maintained, while reasons independent of his or her creditworthiness have an impact on the trading and market value of assets and liabilities sold to investors. In regard to bonds, such factors include the:

- Method of calculating principal, premium and interest,
- Time remaining to the maturity of the debt instrument,
- Outstanding amount of this and similar debt instruments,
- Associated redemption or repayment features, and
- General level, direction and volatility of market interest rates generally.

In addition, for any specific issuer or issue, as well as for the market as a whole, there may be a limited number of buyers if and when the holder decides to sell at all. Therefore, no investor should purchase convertible bonds, or other debt instruments, unless he or she understands what they stand for, and is sure of his or her ability to bear the related investment risk.

The statements made in the preceding paragraphs are valid for all debt instruments. This is a direct reflection of the fact that the convertible bond market is part of the fixed-income sector, even if in reality it lies at the junction of fixed income and stock markets.

Risks associated with convertibles arise from the fact that only a few investors really appreciate the merits and demerits of convertible bonds – and what these mean to the value of their holdings. Most investors are either ill informed or too trusting when deciding to invest in an instrument they do not understand. Yet, every investor:

- Should have an adequate comprehension of the limitations inherent in an issue, and
- Should not accept that information concerning a given instrument is esoteric and reserved for the selected few, such as issuers, traders and brokers.

When somebody relegates his or her basic responsibilities as an investor, he or she should not be surprised if his or her money is subjected to the worst of risks. As cannot be repeated too often, investing is an unforgiving business where joining the bandwagon of issuers and other investors means putting one's wealth in peril because of:

- Non-appreciated risks, or
- Miscalculation of risk and return.

As one of the experts suggested, precisely because risks associated with convertible bonds are not clear to the average investor, convertibles are finding their way into portfolios in increasing numbers – including portfolios generally considered to be conservative, where they do not fit. Few of their holders understand that convertibles are special debt contracts generated by a company for public sale through brokers as direct placements, or by competitive bids, and their pricing does not necessarily reflect all their risks.

A direct placement may, for instance, be negotiated with an institutional investor such as an insurance company or pension fund. Usually, the broker presents the convertible as a safe senior security, saying that in the event of liquidation the holder of the convertible would be paid off first. In reality, convertibles are negotiable bearer instruments that give the investor a long-term call on the common shares of the company.

Because convertibles involve both credit risk and market risk connected to the equity, if the common stock is attractive there is no need to purchase a convertible. It may be to a company's advantage to issue convertible bonds instead of common ones, but the company's and the investor's interests are far from being the same.

Investors should also appreciate that if the company is really interested in selling convertible bonds, it will gild them to make them seem as attractive as possible, in order to attract investors' interest. But it may also be that the common equity is held in disfavor by the market. Therefore, more common equity cannot be sold in the exchange and the company is offering common equity disguised as a convertible. Investors beware!

4.5   The funding competition between capital markets and commercial banks

The discussion about business funding through stocks, bonds and convertibles is more relevant today than ever before, because in many countries the classical commercial bank intermediation is on its way out. For instance, in America, the early 1990s saw two different populations – technology start-ups and established AAA companies – moving away from traditional bank borrowing.

These enterprises approach their funding by raising capital through the issuance of equity and debt instruments in the capital market. So far, this process has not achieved much momentum in continental Europe or in Asia but several experts believe this is going to happen. Table 4.1 shows the percentage of company financing by the banking sector in the USA, Germany, France, Italy and Japan.

One of the key reasons why in the First World's financial environment companies tend to go for capital market's financing, is that market's are much more efficient than commercial banks in terms of cost of transactions. High-rated industrial and commercial enterprises, particularly, are able to obtain better terms.

There is documentation suggesting that, today, company financing through the banking system is highest in less developed countries. Many economists, however, believe that overdependence on intermediation by domestic credit institutions is a basic reason why a financial system is unable efficiently to allocate available monetary resources. Statistics tend to support this hypothesis:

■ In East Asia (including Japan) bank assets are larger than those of stock markets and bond markets combined.
■ By contrast, in the USA this relationship is reversed. Stock and bond markets are four times larger than bank assets.

The catch is that capital markets would not grow, the public would not trust them and the markets themselves would not trust the companies – their equity and their obligations – unless there is a proven amount of transparency (see Chapter 8) as well as evidence of senior management accountability throughout the financial system. Transparency has been the goal of the 2002 Sabanes-Oxley Act in the USA. But transparency is in short supply in most of the world's capital markets, where banks are still locked into intermediation.

Country	Percentage
USA	30
Germany, France, Italy	70
Japan	80

Table 4.1 Percentage of company financing by commercial banks

The call for accountability, transparency and prudence made by clear-thinking economists, regulators, regional development boards and what Ben Graham called Mr. Market, has consistently met with resistance by domestic players who profit from secrecy; double books and crony capitalism. Resistance also comes from foreign investors who hope for a quick buck followed by an eleventh-hour bailout by the International Monetary Fund (IMF) – a bailout which creates moral hazard.

Governments as well as regulators should be aware that this state of affairs leads to a dysfunctional economy. Serious investors are put off by inflexible and/or ineffectual government regulations, different sorts of management malfeasance, high walls raised by embedded interests, inadequate or non-existent transparency, and disregard for:

■ Shareholder value, and
■ Bondholder interests.

By contrast, foreign investors, particularly speculators and hedge funds, are attracted by the possibility of obtaining big profits, and obtaining them fast. These, however, are unstable investments. Contrary to most commercial banks who have a longer-term horizon in their investments, hedge funds and speculators go into a foreign country in a big way when there is the opportunity for fat profits, but get out of it fast at the first sign of trouble. The problem exactly lies in:

■ 'Getting out' of a market takes place from the same door, and
■ There is not enough time and money for everybody to recover his or her assets and profits intact.

When capitalists (see Chapter 1) mistrust those who are in charge of the economy, their instinct is to favor the relative security of Group of Ten (G-10) treasury bonds rather than the greater risk and return found in so-called developing countries. If capital markets trust the issuers of equity and debt, then prevailing interest rates play an important role in the overall economic funding process. These are also instrumental in the management of monetary policy. The US Federal Reserve, for instance, now concentrates more on interest rates than on money supply.

■ Over the longer term, domestic interest rate movements, and therefore a capital market's rate, are determined by domestic factors.
■ But in the shorter term, the movement of interest rates in Western nations generally follows US market trends – in a way emulating the behavior in equity markets.

A basic principle today is that only in a closed economy, which is completely cut off from external influence (a practical impossibility), are capital market rates determined by domestic factors alone. By contrast, in the globalized financial environment, external influences can be transmitted to the domestic market through a number of direct and indirect ways.

International influences traditionally have been imported indirectly through physical goods markets, but currently this occurs, increasingly, through the financial market. A domestic capital market is also exposed to direct external influences, because of cross-border portfolio management, and monetary policies by central banks which add weight to investors' decisions. Unavoidably, direct and indirect foreign influences affect the term structure between domestic and foreign capital markets.

■ Empirical evidence,
■ Macroeconomic factors, and
■ Currency exchange rates provide suitable reference.

Another critical variable which has not yet been appropriately recognized by economic theory is that, since 1996, money supply and debt are closely linked, while profits by the corporate sector have decoupled from both of these. Based on American statistics, this trend is clearly shown in Figure 4.1. As 2003 came to a close, money supply, expressed in M3 stood at 14 percent of gross domestic profit (GDP) – double the traditional ratio.

For starters, money supply measured by M0 is currency in circulation; M1 is equal to M0 plus overnight deposits; M2 exceeds M1 by deposits redeemable at notice up to 3 months, plus deposits with agreed maturity of up to two years. Adding marketable instruments to M2 gives M3. These are:

■ Repurchase agreements,
■ Money market fund shares and units, and
■ Debt securities issued with a maturity of up to two years.

Theoretically GDP and M3 correlate, because M3 growth contributes to a liquid economy. In practice, this is not always true. Based on statistics from the European

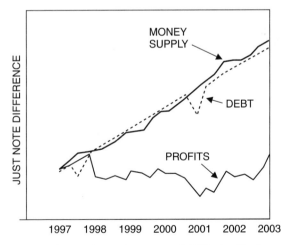

Figure 4.1 Money supply stands at 14 percent of GDP, double the traditional ratio

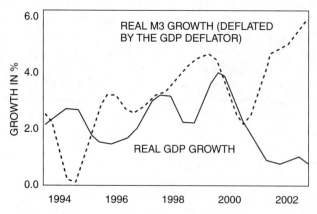

Figure 4.2 Real M3 and real GDP growth in Euroland, in the 1994 to 2002 time frame (*Source*: ECB, *Monthly Bulletin*, September 2003, Euro Area Statistics, Table 2.9, own calculation. Reproduced with permission)

Central Bank, Figure 4.2 shows that in Euroland there has been a diversion, during the 2000 to 2002 severe stock market downturn. The extra liquidity created by a rapid growth in M3 has not been picked up by the productive sectors of the economy, in a way commensurate with increase in profits.

■ The decoupling of debt and profits suggests that debt cannot be effectively served.

The acceleration of money supply is due both to an inordinate increase of monetary base and faster circulation of money, with the result that:

■ Inflation and interest rates will eventually come up from under, escaping monetary policy control.

Both bullets are of great interest to investors. Mathematical models developed to study the direct and indirect effects of money supply, as well as of international capital mobility, on interest rates, assume that the impact depends on institutionally imposed restrictions on the extent to which market players may invest or raise financial assets without hindrance. The term 'without hindrance', however, is neither easily attainable nor wanted.

In terms of global capital movements, government controls and tax regulations may impede cross-border capital transfers. But capital mobility is also determined by the readiness of market players to conduct international financial transactions – as well by their preferences and their propensity to take risks. A similar statement applies in terms of:

■ Internal capital market debt, and
■ Market-defined interest rates.

In the case of unrestricted capital movements, interest rate parity helps in determining market equilibrium. If there are major deviations from interest rate parity, this implies a low degree of integration between financial market segments at home and abroad. Such lack of integration may be due to government interference, transaction costs, differing default likelihood and current or expected capital controls.

4.6   Stock markets and equity prices

At the level of commercial banking and retail banking, the financial system performs the essential function of channeling household savings to the corporate sector, as well as allocating investment funds among firms. This is the classical sense of intermediation. The efficiency of allocation of financial means and implied risks determines (1) the ability of the population to shift between consumption and savings, over time and (2) the industrial and commercial firms' capacity to build up and renew the capital stock. Such allocation is effected in either of two ways:

■ Through contact between borrowers and lenders on capital markets, via the issuance of securities like stocks or bonds.
■ By means of financial intermediaries like commercial banks, pension funds or insurance companies.

Within the realm of the first bullet point comes the general importance of the stock market – as has been discussed in Chapter 3. In the specific case of stock markets, this largely rests on how widely the corporate sector, households and institutional investors typically use equity as a financing and investment instrument – usually determined by a complex network involving:

■ Market forces,
■ Economic policy,
■ Tax laws,
■ Slowly changing traditions and conventions, and
■ Legal and regulatory framework of the financial system.

In the economic and financial environment described by these bullet points, companies issue stocks and sell them either to the general public by means of shares quoted and traded on stock exchanges, or to other companies, institutional investors and high net worth individuals, through private placements. The latter are unquoted shares used to raise external funds and finance their activities. Companies may also repurchase their own stocks to adjust their capital structure (buybacks).

In all these activities equity competes with other sources of corporate finance. Tax laws and the relative cost of capital – the difference between the return on equity capital demanded by the market and the interest rate on loans or bonds – often determine the supply of stocks and, to some degree, their pricing. From the investor's perspective:

■ Through dividends, stocks usually pay a periodic stream of income to their holders.
■ But stock returns also, if not most importantly, comprise capital gains or losses stemming from market price changes.

Differences in the taxation of equity and debt, inflation or deflation, market certainty or uncertainty, the degree of government involvement in the pension system, insurance regulation, as well as money supply and interest rate policies, determine trends in stock market developments. By contrast, swings in stock prices, which change the relative cost of equity and investors' expectations of stock returns, cause short-term cyclical variations in the stock market for issuers and holders.

The stock market plays a role in economic development through building up (or destroying) business confidence, reducing the cost of capital and recycling wealth. It also has certain balance sheet effects. Rising stock prices affect not just investment but also consumption, through wealth and confidence effects. A decline in stock prices may signal increased downward risks to future economic activity and employment, which:

- Hurts consumer confidence, and
- Impacts on actual consumption spending.

This, incidentally, is true even of households that do not own stocks. Moreover, a general fall in stock prices, and in consumption, may lead companies to revise downwards their profit expectations and investment plans. By contrast, an increase in stock prices may signal good opportunities for investment, because this investment can be financed at lower cost by new issues of stock.

Other things being equal, when stock prices rise, the market value of the firm relative to the replacement cost of its stock of capital tends to increase. This is the so-called 'Tobin's Q-ratio' (see the appendix to Chapter 7). Management can therefore decide that it would be profitable for the firm to expand its capital stock,

- Motivated by forecasted greater aggregate demand, and
- Leading to increased investment spending.

Stock prices affect consumption and investment through a balance sheet effect. The relationship between wealth and consumption is based on the permanent income hypothesis, which states that household consumption is driven by wealth that is perceived through the present value of future income. Future real and financial assets are equal to current non-consumed labor income remunerated at a given rate, and current assets. The current value of planned future consumption equals:

- The consumer's total assets, real and financial,
- Plus current value of his or her expected future labor income.

Even if paper profits would not turn into real ones unless the equities are sold, there is an undeniable impact of wealth on consumption. A long enough increase in stock prices implies an increase in households' financial wealth, which leads to higher, hence stimulating, aggregate demand and output.

As far as consumption is concerned (and for companies the capital budget and operating budget), another crucial factor in decision-making is the party's ability to borrow. Whether firms and households are able to borrow depends on the value of collateral they can offer. As the value of stocks increases the collateral given to a bank increases too – and hence the ability to borrow and invest increases.

This is known as the financial accelerator. But the reader must be aware there is risk attached to the value of stock used as collateral. Such risk is essential in determining the magnitude and duration of the effects of equity price changes on investment and consumption. It should be added that, precisely because market prices change using equities as collateral, this has very negative effects on the stock market in a downturn.

As these examples document, the aftermath of equity prices defined by the market should not be taken lightly. Its impact can be widespread. On the other hand, changes in stock prices do not occur at random. Under other than fire sale conditions, they reflect a reassessment by market participants of short-term prospects for:

- Economic growth,
- Corporate earnings, and
- Overall economic activity.

If market expectations tend to be confirmed by economic developments, stock prices firm up. Under the opposite conditions, they cave in. Many economists believe that equity prices can be used as a predictor, or leading indicator, of real economic growth.

Contrarians to this concept note that equity prices may also rise if investors apply lower discount rates, which can result from lower expected real interest rates – a case which has characterized the 2002–04 time frame. Alternatively, stock prices may rise because of an increased appetite for risk or lower perceived equity risks. The model reflecting equity prices is fairly complex and, as such, it suggests that it is not easy at any given moment in time to identify which precise factor is driving the change in equity prices.

To further appreciate the complexity of equity pricing, it is appropriate to recall that at any given moment there is a number of other critical features, which among themselves help in defining a market. These include:

- Trading rules and regulations,
- Efficiency of market access,
- Types of interaction by intermediaries,
- Continuity for price formation,
- Anonymity (or lack of it), and
- Transparency (or its absence).

Markets differ according to the type of orders allowed. Trading protocols include buy/sell on limit, at market, off market, stop order and so on. Among rules regarding trading are opening and closing, minimum tick size, trading halls and the like. Such rules are not the same in all jurisdictions. Transparency of financial transactions often leaves much to be desired (see Chapter 12).

Market access includes several issues one of them being intermediaries. In most markets, investors do not trade directly with each other, but do so through brokers, while the brokers have to go through specialists (see Chapter 5). Many markets feature *segmentation* between the inter-dealer and the dealer-to-customer relationships. Execution may also involve specified market-makers.

Types of interaction by intermediaries are *bilateral or multilateral order flows.* Bilateral interaction typically permits price negotiation and the establishment of relationships. Multilateral interaction refers to the pooling of trading, which can be continuous or periodic. In a periodic trading system, orders are batched and cleared at given intervals. Effective continuous execution requires real-time solutions and, therefore, advanced technology.

With regard to *price formation,* prices can be determined within the system which provides a mechanism for price discovery. Alternatively, they may be taken from outside the system. All these differences play a significant role on how markets work, how sensitive they are to events and how dynamic they are in their behavior. Price formation can be:

- Order driven, where prices follow orders, or
- Quote driven, where orders follow prices.

Under order-driven price formation, orders are sent to a central location and prices are derived from the interaction of order flows. Under quote-driven price formation, market-makers quote prices at which they are willing to buy and sell securities. However, prices for larger trades are usually negotiated bilaterally (see in Chapter 5 the discussion on big blocks).

Anonymity means whether the identity of the counterparty is disclosed, either pre- or post-trade. *Transparency* refers to the amount and extent of information being disseminated, both pre-trade, such as bid/ask, and post-trade. For example, with last trade price and volume, trading systems offer various degrees of transparency which characterize their operation. As has been stated on several occasions, market transparency helps to build investor confidence, and the same is true of financial transparency.

4.7 Stock market indices: Dow Jones, S&P and NASDAQ

One capital market in the world accounts for about 56.6 percent of global equity capitalization. This is the USA, followed by the capital market of the UK which accounts for 10.4 percent. As shown in Figure 4.3, taken together, the capital markets of the USA and the UK represent two-thirds of global capitalization, followed at distance by Japan. The largest exchanges in the USA are:

- The New York Stock Exchange, and
- The National Association of Securities Dealers Automatic Quotation system.

In terms of capitalization, the former is bigger than the latter, though in the first quarter of 2000, prior to the collapse of technology and Internet stocks, NASDAQ was on its way to overtaking NYSE.

As the histogram in Figure 4.3 indicates, among themselves the top contintental European exchanges in France, Switzerland, Germany and Holland (in that order) represent 11.6 percent of global capitalization – about 10 percent ahead of Britain. Turnover as a percentage of capitalization is also an interesting statistic. Between them, the aforementioned four exchanges had, in 2003, a combined turnover of

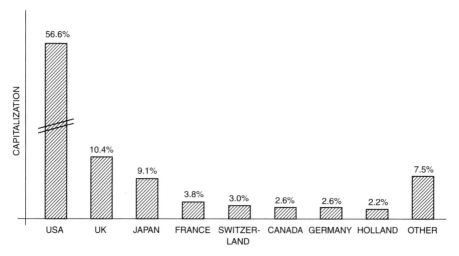

Figure 4.3 Capitalization of the global stock market among major exchanges

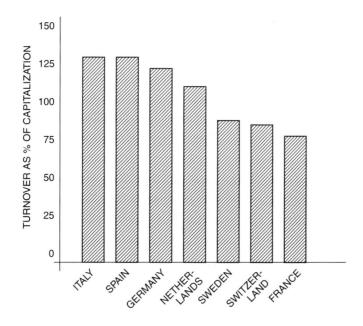

Figure 4.4 Stock market turnover at continental European exchanges as a percentage of capitalization

3.11 trillion euros ($3.73 trillion) the bigger share being in Germany and France, followed by Switzerland and Holland (in that order).

Still another important statistic concerning activity taking place in exchanges, is turnover as a percentage of capitalization. In Europe, on this count, the highest ranking is the British capital market, with a 2003 turnover of nearly 140 percent of capitalization. The corresponding figures for the continental exchanges are shown in Figure 4.4, but the reader will notice that Italy and Spain have higher turnovers than the other four aforementioned continental exchanges.

How do the American exchanges compare with European exchanges in terms of turnover as a percentage of capitalization? The answer is that though US turnover is significant, the sheer size of US capital markets sees to it that this statistic is low. In fact, in 2003 it stood at about 65 percent which, is less than half that of the British.

An important statistic which demonstrates the stock market's domination by a few companies, is the capitalization of the top ten firms quoted in an exchange, as percent of total market capitalization. According to information published in *The Economist* on 17 April 2004, at the end of March 2004 this represented:

■ Less than 20 percent in the United States and Japanese exchanges,
■ About 40 percent in the exchanges of United Kingdom, France and Germany, and
■ More than 60 percent in the exchanges of Holland, Belgium and Switzerland.

Even less than 20 percent, however, is a big number because at the end of March 2004, stock market capitalization in the US stood at $15 trillion. Capitalization in Japan was $3.7 trillion, the UK $2.5 trillion, France $1.5 trillion, and Germany $1 trillion. Compared to these statistics, Swiss stock market capitalization was $0.7 trillion and that of Belgium only 180 billion.

Another interesting statistic is stock market capitalization as a percent of GDP, because it tells something about leverage in the economy. Based on statistics from *The Economist*, in 2003 the highest stock market capitalization as a percentage of GDP was in Hong Kong, to the tune of 440 percent followed by Singapore at 260 percent. China featured as one of the lowest, at about 30 percent, among the G-10 countries.

■ Britain's stock market capitalization stood at 140 percent,
■ The NYSE in the USA represented a capitalization of 110 percent, and
■ Japan followed with 70 percent, which is higher than China's but a fraction of the two Asian tigers.[9]

The barometer of highs and lows of capital markets is their indices. The NASDAQ index is a statistic based on 100 stocks traded in its exchange. Like NASDAQ, the Dow Jones Index, or more precisely the Dow Jones Industrial Average (DJIA), is the statistic index probably most widely used by investors.[10] It is also nearly 110 years old, having celebrated its centenary at the end of May 1996 – after completing fourteen years with an almost uninterrupted race to higher prices (with the exception of the October 1987 crash and August 1990 mini-crash, when Iraq invaded Kuwait).

During these fourteen years, Dow Jones has grown 614 percent, which is a quarter more than its increase in the 1920s (468 percent) and the post-World War II boom (487 percent from 1949 to 1966). But none of these market trends compares with the sharp bull market of the mid to late 1990s. For optimists, the comparison with the 1920s is biased. Critics of this rapid Dow rise of the 1990s, however, point out that the way to interpret it is inflation of financial instruments. In fact, it is an inflation not of any financial instrument, but of the most popular of them.

The DJIA reflects the composite of the market value of thirty selected equities, among the biggest and the best in the US stock market. This *group of thirty* common stocks comprising the Dow Jones Industrial Average is chosen by the editors of the *Wall Street Journal* as representative of the broad market and America industry. Its composition has not remained static over the years. This would have been an impossibility in the first place, since of the 100 largest US companies prior to World War I only one still remains in that class – General Electric.

New companies are continually brought into the Dow Jones index, and old ones which no longer qualify are dropped. The steady renewal sees to it that the thirty stocks comprising the DJIA index belong to companies which, in a number of different industries, continue to accumulate profits and conquer markets. For these reasons, as well as its wide acceptance,

- Dow Jones is of a major psychological value, both inside and outside the USA, and
- Both investors and economists regard it as the health bulletin of the American economy.

News releases inform the whole world about the DJIA, and many people follow it, even if the companies in it represent only a small part of the global economy. Note, as well, that even the method by which it is computed – a simple arithmetic mean adjusted by a coefficient – is nothing sophisticated.

Over the years, the Dow Jones index has given rise to an investment theory focusing on market trend. Known as the *Dow theory*, it states that the existence of a primary bull market is confirmed when the DJIA closes at a new high, in conjunction with the string of new closing high in the Dow Jones Transportation Average.

When the NYSE advance/decline line breaks to the upside, reinstituting its major up trend, it reflects a broadening-out within the internal structure of the market. This is considered to be bullish, as we will see in Chapter 7 in relation to the discussion on quantitative criteria for judging equity performance.

Often criticized as being narrowly based, the DJIA is not the only important index in the American equity market. Another widely followed index is the Standard & Poor's 500 (S&P 500), which reflects a wider population of equities by far than the DJIA, being a broad-based capitalization-weighted index. Theoretically, there exists no relation between the DJIA and the S&P 500. Practically, there is an empirical ratio with a mean value around 7.

- When the mean value shrinks below 7, then it is likely that large caps lag below the run of their smaller counterparts.
- When this mean value increases, the message is that the thirty large caps advance faster than smaller companies which are not in the DJIA but are in the S&P 500.

These are empirical observations which have nothing to do with theory. Moreover, Standard & Poor's (S&P) has not one but many indices. Next to the S&P 500, the more popular are the S&P Midcap 400 and the S&P Smallcap 600. As their label implies, they are weighted indices of 400 and 600 stocks, respectively, each providing a broad indicator of price movement.

Standard and Poor's Midcap 400 index is capitalization weighted and measures performance of the mid-range sector of the US stock market. The index was developed with a base level of 100 as of 31 December 1990. The S&P Smallcap 600 index is an International Standards Organization (ISO) capitalization-weighted, measuring performance of selected US stocks with a small market capitalization – developed with a based value of 100 as of 31 December 1993.

Both the Dow Jones and the S&P have subdivisions. Those of Dow Jones are shown in Table 4.2; those of the S&P, in Table 4.3. Subdivisions of the NASDAQ index are shown in Table 4.4.

As shown in Table 4.3, the S&P's has a more narrowly based large capitalization index known as the S&P Composite. This consists of the twenty-five biggest US companies, which are nearly indispensable components of big investors' portfolio. Institutional investors are sensitive to S&P Composite's weighting.

Investors who want to compare the behavior of the DJIA versus the S&P Composite should note that the composition of each index is different enough to make such comparisons less meaningful – unless one targets exactly the difference in *index composition*. The DJIA and the S&P Composite differ in:

Dow Jones Industrial Average
Dow Jones Transportation Average
Dow Jones Utilities Average
Dow Jones Computer Average
NYSE Healthcare Index
NYSE Financial Index
NYSE Energy Index
NYSE Composite Index
NYSE US 100 Index
NYSE International 100
NYSE TMT Index
NYSE World Leaders Index

Table 4.2 Subdivisions of the Dow Jones index and other NYSE stock market indices

S&P Composite
S&P 100 Index
S&P 500 Index
S&P 400 Midcap Index
S&P 600 Smallcap Index
S&P 1500 Supercomposite

Table 4.3 Subdivisions of the Standard & Poor's index

NASDAQ 100 Stock
NASDAQ Composite Index
NASDAQ Financial
NYSE Energy Index
NASDAQ Industrial Index
NASDAQ Telecom Index
NASDAQ Computer Index
NASDAQ Biotech Index
NASDAQ Insurance Index
NASDAQ Bank Index
NASDAQ National Market Industrial Index
NASDAQ Financial Index
NASDAQ 100 Pre-Market Index
NASDAQ 100 After Hour Index

Table 4.4 Subdivisions of the NASDAQ
index

1 Their manufacturing/services representations.

The DJIA is almost 50 percent manufacturing industries, while manufacturing represents about a quarter of the S&P Composite. The reverse is true for services, as the
services component of the S&P Composite is almost half of that index.

2 Their technology component, too, is quite different, with the S&P Composite being
a better technology barometer.

Technology is weighting about 17 percent of the S&P Composite, whereas it is about
10 percent of the DJIA's. This has an impact on the S&P Composite in both technology
boom and bust. As a result it is reasonable to expect divergent performances for the
DJIA and the S&P Composite. The upside of such differences in index composition is
that it gives a measure of sector volatility. Being in the right sector at the right time
may matter more than the company names an investor keeps.

Moreover, when comparing the DJIA to the S&P 500, investors should appreciate
that the Dow Jones is a price-sensitive barometer, not a capitalization-weighted index.
By contrast, the S&P 500 is capitalization weighted. Therefore, the price of individual
components and the average's divisor have a big impact on the daily calculation of an
arithmetic index like the DJIA.

Normally, one would add up the thirty components and divide by thirty. But
because the Dow Jones is 110 years old, there have been many stocks splits among its
thirty components, so that the divisor shrinks, and the index is subject to more daily
volatility.

Still other US stock market indices are those of the American Stock Exchange (owned
by National Association of Securities Dealers), Russell 2000 and its variations, and
more. The Russell 2000 comprises 2000 of the smaller stocks of US-based companies.

American Stock Exchange
AMEX Major Market Index
AMEX Composite Index
AMEX Institutional Index
AMEX Computer tech Index
AMEX Oil Index

Others
Russell 1000 Index
Russell 2000 Index
Russell 3000 Index
Wilshire 5000
Value Line Index
Inter@active, an Internet index
Philadelphia Gold & Silver Index
Philadelphia Semiconductor Index
Oil Service Sector Index, and so on

Table 4.5 Other stock indices in
the USA

Table 4.5 Other US indices, some of which, like the Wilshire 5000, are becoming popular.

4.8   European market indices

The most popular index in the UK is the FTSE 100. As Table 4.6 shows, it has a number of subdivisions. The leading indices in France are CAC 40, Nouveau Marché and Second Marché, plus some others. In Germany, the leading indices are DAX, CDAX Performance, and Neuer Markt. Others are shown in Table 4.7. The leading indices in Switzerland are Swiss Market Index, SPI Swiss Performance and DJ Swiss Titans 30. The Swiss Market Index was developed with a base value of 1500 as at 30 June 1988. It is a capitalization-weighted index of the largest and most liquid stocks traded on the Electronic Bourse System.

In Italy, MIB 30 and others shown in Table 4.8; in Spain IBEX 35, as well as the DJ Spain Titans 30; in the Netherlands, the Amsterdam Exchange Index.

For European stock exchanges altogether, there is the Bloomberg European 500 index, as well as several Dow Jones (DJ) indices, S&P indices, FTSE indices, MSCI indices, Euronext and others. These are shown in Table 4.9. The DJ Euro Stoxx 50 Price Index is a capitalization-weighted, involving fifty blue-chip stocks from Euroland countries, using free float shares in its calculation. This index was developed with a base value of 1000 as at 31 December 1991.

The DJ Stoxx Price Index is a broad-based capitalization-weighted European stocks' index, which duplicates the DJ Global Indexes Europe Index. It has been developed with a value base of 100 as of December 31, 1991, also using free float shares in its calculation.

FTSE 100 Index
FTSE 100 for EurOpts
FTSE 250 Index
FTSE 350 Index
FTSE 250 for Inv Trst
FTSE Fledgling Index
FTSE Lower Yield Index
FTSE Higher Yield Index
FTSE Smallcap Index
FTSE Aim Index
FTSE All-Share Index
FTSE TechMark 100 Index

Table 4.6 Subdivisions of
the FTSE index in the UK

DAX 100 Index Price
DAX MidCap Index
DAX Price Index
CDAX Performance
DAX 100 Constr Index XETRA
EUR Neu Mkt Blu Chip
HDAX Index
NEMAX All-Share Price
SDAX Perfm Index
SMAX All Share Prf

Table 4.7 German stock
exchange indices

Italian Small-Cap Index
Italian Stk Ex IPOS
Milan MIB Telematico
Milan Index (Historic)
Milan Mid-Cap Index
Milan MIB-R Index
Milan Numtel Index

Table 4.8 Italian stock
exchange indices

As it is to be expected, there is a significant number of indices associated with the Japanese stock market. These are shown in Table 4.10. The Nikkei 225 Stock Average is a price-weighted average of 225 top-rated Japanese companies listed in the First Section of the Tokyo Stock Exchange. The Nikkei Stock Average was first published on 16 May 1949. The average price was 176.21 yen with a divisor of 225.

Bloomberg European 500
Bloomberg Eur New Mkt 50
DJ Euro Stoxx 50 Price Index
DJ Stoxx 50 Price Index
DJ Euro Stoxx Price Index
DJ Stoxx 600 Price IX Euro
FTSE Eurotop 100 Index
FTSE Eurotop 300 Index
FTSE Eurofirst 80 Index
FTSE Eurofirst 100 Index
FTSE Med 100 Index
FTSE EuroStars Index
MSCI Euro
MSCI Pan-Euro
Euronext Top 100 Index
Euronext Top 150 Index

Table 4.9 The rich crop of European stock market indices

NIKKEI 225
NIKKEI 300 Index
TOPIX Index (Tokyo)
TOPIX Core 30 (TSE)
TOPIX Large 70 (TSE)
TOPIX Mid 400 (TSE)
TOPIX 500 (TSE)
AMEX Japan Index
Bloomberg Japanese IPO
Japan-Tokyo Index
TOKYO Large Lot Index
TOKYO Medium Lot Index
TOKYP Small Lot Index
JASDAQ Stock Index
JASDAQ-BBG MK VL MID 400
JASDAQ-BBG MK VL TOP 100
JASDAQ-BBG MK VAL TOP 50
OSE High Tech Index
OSE Consumer Index
OSE Financial Index

Table 4.10 Subdivisions of Japanese stock market indices

4.9   Appendix: The Paper Ships Index[11]

Indices are not cast in stone. New ones develop all the time. In September 2003, the London-based Baltic Exchange launched a *Paper Ships Index*, which trades on the future cost of ships themselves, rather than future freight rates. Another index in-the-making (for late 2004) is the *Demolition Assessment Index*, which will trade on future scrap value of ships.

In Oslo, the International Maritime Exchange, a competitor to the Baltic Exchange, estimates that the futures market for cost of shipping will grow most rapidly, by up to 80 percent per year. If so, it may well follow a growth curve not too different than that of oil futures.

According to *TradeWinds*, the Norwegian Futures and Options Clearinghouse (NOS) claims that two dozen companies have expressed interest in applying for clearance to trade shipping derivatives. Several reasons may be in the background. The way a recent article had it, Japan faces an exodus of private shipowners looking for new homes to escape punishing domestic taxes. Indeed, in several lines of business, derivatives have proven to be the instruments of excellence in tax evasion – or 'tax optimization', according to your lights.

Available information indicates that not only shipping companies, but also financial institutions, and other businesses, are in the process of entering the Paper Ships Index and generally futures instruments related to shipping. Heavyweights such as Goldman Sachs and Morgan Stanley have already moved into these deals.[12] At NOS:

- Cleared members can trade forward freight agreements (FFAs) on the International Maritime Exchange (Imarex), and
- The Norwegian Futures and Options Clearinghouse members are said to be able to trade without the risk of their counterparties defaulting on payments.

Estimates made by Imarex indicate that the shipping derivatives market more than doubled to $8 billion in the first half of 2004 as banks, oil companies, shipowners, and industrial groups sought to exploit booming markets. HSBC Shipping Services is reported to have predicted this new derivatives market could grow to $30 billion by the end of 2004 – which is a high multiple of 2003.

As one of the experts in ship insurance was to comment, shipping industry futures have been more or less in existence since the early 1990s, and they have caused various casualties already, albeit with cargo traders rather than with shipowners. The first victim of freight 'hedging' instrument was a Belgian charterer highly specialized in Brazil/Europe trade. Five years ago a substantial Lausanne trader collapsed, and estimates are that there exist other casualties covered by profits in different business lines.

There are several new financial instruments related to shipping as underlier. According to Lloyd's *Shipping Economist*, new financial instruments in the class of asset-backed securities (ABS) now account for 60 percent of global ship financing. Even more dramatic growth has been in shipping futures, which allow shipping companies to lay off risks.

Forward freight agreements (FFAs) to deliver goods on a particular route at some point in the future are a popular derivative instrument in the shipping business.

In 2003, FFAs have grown to be roughly the size of the physical market – according to Bill Lines of the Baltic Exchange, who sells these forward freight agreements. This, too, is a rise which, in a way, parallels that of oil futures in years past.[13]

Notes

1 D.N. Chorafas (2004). *Economic Capital Allocation with Basel II: Cost and Benefit Analysis*. Butterworth-Heinemann.
2 This works in tandem with the socialist dogma of the twentieth century that 'When companies are nearly bankrupt we nationalize them, and when they are profitable we privatize them.'
3 See also, in Chapter 4, the role played by specialists.
4 D.N. Chorafas (2000). *Managing Credit Risk, Volume 1: Analyzing, Rating and Pricing the Probability of Default*. Euromoney.
5 D.N. Chorafas (2004). *Management Risk: The Bottleneck is at the Top of the Bottle*. Macmillan/Palgrave.
6 *Deeply subordinated bonds* are a new invention. Because of the doldrums of the equity market, regulators permitted banks to add to their core capital (eligible Tier 1 regulatory capital) by means of perpetual deeply subordinated notes callable 10 years down the line. These pay the investor a higher interest rate, usually indexed to EURSwap but capped to a maximum coupon. Compagnie Financière of Crédit Mutuel issued such bonds in June 2004 on a nominal amount of Euro 100 million, subsequently increased because of market demand. The Anglo Irish Bank followed up in September 2004 with Euro 200 million, increased to Euro 600 million. Investor in deeply subordinated bonds are at par with equity holders in capital at risk, without benefiting from equity's upside.
7 D.N. Chorafas (2004). *Rating Management's Effectiveness with Case Studies in Telecommunications*. Macmillan/Palgrave.
8 For tricks played with EBITDA see D.N. Chorafas (2004). *Management Risk: The Bottleneck is at the Top of the Bottle*. Macmillan/Palgrave.
9 *The Economist*, 20 March 2004.
10 The Dow Jones Average was created by *Wall Street Journal* founder Charles Dow. Its first major test as a barometer of market psychology came in May-to-August 1896, when it fell from 40.94 on May 26 to 28.28 at the end of August – a more than 30 percent drop.
11 The author is indebted to Alain Bernard, an expert in shipping insurance, for his contribution to this text.
12 *TradeWinds*, 6 August 2004.
13 *The Economist*, 24 July 2004.

5 Regulation and operation of the exchanges

5.1 Introduction

Theoretically, regulators are in business to protect investors. Practically, while investor protection is one of their goals, it is not at the top of their priorities. Moreover, regulators, shareholders and bondholders do not have the same perspective, even if they all look at performance, current and future, and would like to see the exchanges run like clockwork.

At the top of *regulators'* priorities is to keep capital requirements on a par with evolution of the banking system and its risks. For reasons of creditworthiness, and control of systemic risk, regulators would like banks to have an AA rating or better. Regulators also want to avoid pouring taxpayers' money into saving big banks from going broke. The orderly operation of exchanges and investor protections is the next priority in the regulators' list.

Investors, too, appreciate dealing with institutions rated AA or better. But they also have other requirements which are heterogeneous by investor class. For instance, *bondholders* want good credit rating, protection of principal, regular interest payments and relatively low risk. On the other hand, *shareholders* look for:

- Quality of profits,
- Amount of profits,
- Dividends,
- Increasing capitalization, and
- Sound risk and reward trade-offs.

If this is what shareholders are after, it is not necessarily what makes an exchange run well. Exchange regulation has more goals, which can be best demonstrated through a practical example such as the Securities Exchange Act of 1934 in the USA. The exchanges themselves have other aims, the topmost being increased capitalization of listed securities because this attracts more companies to list in the exchange, and more dealers and investors to trade in it.

There is no way to ensure that capitalization of listed companies will increase, and the collapse in the securities markets that began in the USA in 1929 had more than one aftermath. It not only led to the Great Depression, but also promoted federal regulation of trading in already issued securities. This regulation was provided by the Securities Exchange Act of 1934, with the purpose of:

- Eliminating abuses that had developed over a period of time, and
- Ending different ways and means of bypassing existing rules and regulations.

The 1934 Act aimed to secure a free and open market, in which stock and bond prices reflect, at least to some degree, demand and supply based on informed judgment, not influenced by artificial manipulation or deceptive practices. Another of its objectives was that of supporting a securities market in which the volume of trading is contained, so that it serves investment rather than speculation which destabilizes the economy.

Human nature being what it is, it would not come as a surprise that the Act's goals have been only partially fulfilled. To modernize its clauses and to plug loopholes, the 1934 Act has been amended on various occasions, but it basically still employs a mechanism of control, enforced by civil and criminal sanctions, which includes:

- Directly regulating the operations of brokers and dealers,
- Seeking full and fair disclosure of facts regarding listed securities,
- Aiming to maintain just and equitable principles of trade, and
- Forbidding manipulation, and banning practices which are judged detrimental to the public interest.

It is, for instance, *prohibited* to match orders, where transactions occur between two or more persons acting in concert without actual change of ownership; to wash sales, where one person sells something and buys it back at about the same time; to pool operations, where a series of transactions is undertaken to influence the price of a registered security, and so on.

There are practical reasons why such activities are forbidden. For instance, pools usually try to raise the price of a security by concerted activity on the part of the members of an exchange. Or, they attempt to unload at a profit on the public, attracted by bets which have nothing to do with a free exchange. Information disseminated about a stock based upon false financial statements is another punishable activity.

The Securities Exchange Act of 1934 has also prohibited bear raiding, which involves short sales of stock in volume, but this prohibition has been totally forgotten. As the 2000 to 2003 events have shown, short sales are *en vogue*. For instance, in the aftermath of 11 September 2001 there has been a torrent of short sales. The 1934 Act prohibition did not bother the many short sellers and hedge funds behind them. Moreover, several other prohibited acts have since become common practice, often in covert ways.

Investor protection is therefore an elastic concept. Certain practices which have been outlawed after being judged harmful to investors reappear under new guides, and political lobbying sees to it that past laws are reinterpreted in much milder ways – or simply fade into oblivion. Investors therefore should be on alert and should protect themselves through their own prudent investment management policies (see Chapters 1 and 2) and steady risk control practices (see Chapters 10 to 13).

5.2   Role of a regulatory authority

Topmost in the list of functions of a regulatory authority is that it: establishes guidelines and rules of prudential supervision based on existing laws; licenses the different players who operate in the environment under its jurisdiction and revokes their licenses when they misbehave; and ensures that all operations in the securities exchange business comply with laws and rules and applies penalties when they do not. A regulatory authority does this in order to:

- Ensure an orderly market,
- Indirectly protect the investors, and
- Avoid systemic risk due to big financial failures.

A regulatory authority does not necessarily decide whether or not a company is financially sound. It simply ensures that everything is disclosed in the proper manner, and that financial statements are reliable. Also, it ensures that there is transparency in the exchange, thereby permitting investors to make learned decisions. This is the meaning of indirect protection previously referred to.

A critical issue connected with regulation and supervision is whether the entity to which this responsibility has been assigned has the authority necessary to take immediate corrective action. A case in point is *Regulation T*. Theoretically, US law does not allow bankers to lend money that will be used for purchase of stock. Regulation T deals with this issue. However, this is one of the laws that are not being enforced – even if its enforcement is important for reasons of:

- Curtailing equity speculation,
- Avoiding booms and busts, and
- Assuring better control of the expansion of credit.

In terms of law enforcement, the penalization of insider trading has been more successful. Board members, executive directors and other insiders have been prosecuted by the SEC for this reason. The financial press publishes lots of information on *corporate insider activity*, which essentially profits some people who buy or sell shares at the expense of the other investors.

When we talk of the role of a regulatory authority it is important to keep in mind that several players in stock exchanges are not inclined to respect the law, particularly when major market events take place. In July 2001, for example, insider sales have exceeded purchases by a four-to-one ratio. Such a preponderance of selling was influenced by the bear market and it is presumed to have had negative implications for:

- The performance of listed companies, and
- The fortune of all types of investors who trusted them by purchasing their stock.

Moreover, while insider buying is typically done because insiders have information which provides them with an optimistic outlook for the company and its stock, insider selling can be done for reasons other than just a negative outlook. Reasons other than negative outlook are diversification by purchasing non-financial assets, end of a lock-up period on an IPO, and so on.

One way for regulatory authorities to establish a level ground for market players is to look whether investors have been oversold risky issue, because they do not understand the risks they are assuming. As an example, in late August 1998 Merrill Lynch agreed to pay a $2 million penalty for its part in the 1994 bankruptcy of Orange County. This specific penalty has been over and above a prior $400 million settlement by Merrill Lynch to Orange County in compensation for huge losses suffered by collateralized mortgage obligations (CMOs) sold to it by the broker:

■ The SEC accused the broker of negligence for failing to warn the investor of the risks.
■ Merrill Lynch agreed to both payments while denied wrongdoing.[1]

Since 1995, the SEC has imposed billions in fines on different parties, but half of this money has never been collected. The better managed firms and speculators who care to clear their name usually pay up. Michael Milken paid $450 million in fines, the largest bill paid by any person so far. Others, however, chose to go bankrupt, exploiting loopholes in the law.

The largest ever Wall Street settlement, at least so far, came on 28 April 2003, in the aftermath of findings of fraud with associated penalties and disgorgements to the tune of nearly $1.4 billion. Announcing the settlement, William Donaldson, chairman of the SEC, himself a former investment banker, said 'I am profoundly saddened – and angry – about the conduct that's alleged in our complaints. There is absolutely no place for it in our markets, and it cannot be tolerated.'[2]

That behavior which made Donaldson saddened and angry was widely tolerated during the boom years of the late 1990s and beyond, and such tolerance allowed banks and hedge funds to behave as if they were unaware of legal risk involved in their acts. Table 5.1, which shows the parties in this settlement, shows how wide the misbehavior of well-known financial institutions has been.

Usually, the SEC does a fairly good job within the confines of its charter, but its charter does not include the supervision of all US financial institutions. Neither is it like that of the Federal Reserve and of the Controller of the Currency (OCC) in

	Penalty	Disgorgement	Independent research	Inventor education	Total
Citigroup	150.0	150.0	75.0	25.0	400.0
Crédit Suisse First Boston	75.0	75.0	50.0	0.0	200.0
Merrill Lynch	100.0[1]	0.0	75.0	25.0	200.0
Morgan Stanley	25.0	25.0	75.0	0.0	125.0
Goldman Sachs	25.0	25.0	50.0	10.0	110.0
Bear Stearns	25.0	25.0	25.0	5.0	80.0
JP Morgan	25.0	25.0	25.0	5.0	80.0
Lehman Brothers	25.0	25.0	25.0	5.0	80.0
UBS Warburg	25.0	25.0	25.0	5.0	80.0
Piper Jaffray	12.5	12.5	7.5	0.0	32.5
Total	487.5	387.5	432.5	80.0	1387.5

Note:
1 Payment made prior to April 2003 settlement.

Table 5.1 The 28 April 2003 settlement with Wall Street firms (in $ millions, in order of importance)

terms of power of inspection of credit institutions. There is a gap in the US regulatory armory because the Fed's and the OCC's examiners have no mandate for inspecting non-banks, like hedge funds. The Commodities Futures Trading Commission (CFTC) might have had such a mandate if Congress had not clipped its wings.[3]

One of the regulatory domains where LTCM, Enron, Global Crossing, Adelphia, WorldCom and their like have much in common is the lack of a safety net to compensate the financially weak victims of hedge funds and credit institutions, or even industrial companies (see Chapter 15 on Parmalat) acting as hedge funds. The best example of what I mean is the FDIC, which guarantees deposits of up to $100 000 per person, thereby providing a safety net.

Small investors and employees who were victims of CEO malfeasance were right when they said that they would like to see former Enron chairman Kenneth L. Lay, former CEO Jeffrey Skilling, former CFO Andrew Fastow, members of Enron's Audit Committee, other top officials of Enron, and the partners at Arthur Andersen and Vinson & Elkins, personally repay the financial losses they had created. But this type of action regarding investor compensation because of senior management malfeasance,

- Is not part of the charter of regulators and supervisors,
- Yet there are stakeholders of failed companies who received a triple hit as employees, investors and pensioners.

Deprived of direct protection under the Securities Exchange Act of 1934, investors suffering from senior management malfeasance resort to class actions. On 8 April 2002, four months after the fall of Enron, nine big banks and two law firms were added to a class-action lawsuit against Enron that alleged that they had helped Enron defraud shareholders.

This 485-page complaint named J.P. Morgan Chase, Citigroup, Merrill Lynch, CSFB, Canadian Imperial Bank of Commerce (CIBC), Bank of America, Barclays Bank, Deutsche Bank and Lehman Brothers as key defendants. The target of this class action was a series of allegedly fraudulent transactions, creating a 'mythical picture' of Enron's profitability.

Through information from Congressional hearings and press reports, investors participating in these actions established that several of the aforementioned banks took stakes in off balance sheet partnerships created by the energy company's chief finance officer (CFO), that helped Enron to hide debt. In the aftermath, Enron produced underwriting files on debt issues sold to the public, showing that its finances were sound, while senior management seemed to know otherwise.[4] In the ensuing years, these methods and tools of creative accounting and investor deception have been 'improved', as we will see in Chapter 15 with the case study on Parmalat.

5.3   Self-regulation by the exchanges and conflicts of interest

Beyond the action taken by the government's regulatory authority, capital markets are supposed to exercise their own self-regulatory action. This is fundamental to the proper functioning of an exchange, as well as for investor protection purposes. Moreover, exchange regulations should see to it that listed companies obey a code of ethics and comply with sound principles of corporate governance.

Even in a globalized financial market, there is no universal code of ethics. Every exchange puts together its own rules. For instance, in December 1995, the Committee on Corporate Governance of the Toronto Stock Exchange (TSE) issued a report containing guidelines for effective corporate governance regarding Canadian corporations listed on the exchange. As a result of TSE guidelines, listed companies are required to disclose:

- Their corporate governance practices, and
- Where those practices vary significantly from the TSE guidelines, as well as why.

In the aftermath, critics said that this is the sort of regulation the different players, including listed companies, take as a joke. Who would say that its practices vary significantly from the 'guidelines'? Paper tigers are a laughing matter; they do not promote better ethics.

Apart from the listed companies, stock exchanges should regulate and supervise their own *members*, including their assets and liabilities, as well as the way in which they manage their clients' relations. A stockbroker's assets include: cash and equivalents; cash and securities segregated according to prevailing rules; securities purchased under agreements to resell; deposits paid for securities borrowed; receivables from other brokers and dealers; receivables from clients; securities owned; and other assets.

Liabilities, including investors' equity with the broker, are: drafts payable; loans payable; securities sold under agreements to repurchase; deposits received for securities loaned; amounts payable to other brokers and dealers; amounts payable to clients; securities sold but not yet purchased; accounts payable; accrued expenses; and other liabilities. An integral part of brokers' liabilities are subordinated debt and investors' equity.

Investor's equity in safekeeping of the broker is a very important issue, subject to regulation. The client's account may or may not be on *margin* (see section 5.6). If it is not, that is, it is *cash*, the client may exercise his or her own voting rights, or the account may be on *street name*. Holding shares in street name means that the investor holds them through a brokerage, bank or other nominee. Therefore, the shares are not held in the investor's individual name. Few investors truly appreciate the street name aftermath.

Stock exchange members have the right to vote for, or are able to control the votes of the proxies of stock left in their custody by their customers. This equity is typically registered in *street name*, which means in the broker's name as the *owner of record*. Normally such stock should be held in a segregated account for the broker's customer known as the *beneficial owner*, but existing rules give the broker, not the customer, the right to vote this stock.

Brokers benefit handsomely from such arrangement, and therefore they are eager to advertise that they hold billions of dollars worth of customers' stock in street name. Another, less well-known, aspect connected with this issue is that hedge funds and specialists can borrow from the brokers their inventory of equity belonging to beneficiary owners, who have signed margin agreements. The latter allow the broker, as owner of record, to lend the stock at his or her discretion.

Sometimes banks and brokers also lend to speculators their clients' equities held in cash accounts, which in the majority of jurisdictions is illegal. Investors should watch out for this practice because it is to their disfavor. When caught, the wrongdoers find an excuse to avoid penalties and they call it 'changes in securities lending'. Here, as an example, is copy of a letter I received from one of the banks where I have an investment account:

Dear client,

In December 2001, when opened your safekeeping account with us, you received a copy of the new general conditions which included the safe custody regulations. The latter contained provisions relating to securities lending, and came into force on 1 January 2002. These allowed you to take part in securities lending *automatically*.[5]

A number of different client reactions, together with a changed market environment, have led us to reconsider this policy. In future, participation in securities lending in line with the safe custody regulations will not be an option; instead, this will only be possible on an individual, contractual basis.

As a client you may continue to benefit from the securities lending service we offer. By signing a separate securities lending agreement you will once again be able to participate in the securities lending programme.

If you require any further information, your relationship manager will be only to glad to assist.

Yours sincerely

There is a conflict of interest in this and many other similar cases. Internal stock exchange regulations, as well as the action taken by supervisory authorities, should address all instances of conflict of interest and their sources. It is also important to recognize the possibility of conflicts inherent in brokers acting as directors of stock exchanges, because this works against the principle that:

■ Every investor must be treated equally, and
■ Stock exchange members should be accorded no privileges, in terms of information, commissions or otherwise, that are not available to the public.

Behind equal rights lies the fact that exchanges are operating a facility that is like a public utility. One of the reasons for eventual conflicts of interest lies in the fact that brokers not only act as intermediaries, but also operate asset management services. Advising on investments, managing wealth and doing day-to-day trading, all in one, tends to lead to at least some speculation – or, at least, the use of one of these functions to promote the other, thereby generating commissions.

In fact, the easiest way for third parties to profit from equity price volatility lies in exploitation of stockholders in a variety of ways: from rumors spreading in the market, to lending and selling short their equity held in street name. This can have alarming implications, because there are ways for doing these things without contradicting, or conflicting with, existing legislation.

Weeding out conflicts of interest is most important because investors should be able to believe without reservation in the integrity of free markets. If, as happened with the scams of 2000 to 2004, investors see that corporate officers and directors – or for that matter directors of stock exchanges – are indifferent to ethical values, and interested solely in their own ability to profit, then the fabric of the market economy is destroyed.

The people responsible for capital markets should appreciate that their business rests on investor confidence. Denting that confidence has inevitable consequences in terms of the relationship between stockholders, the companies' management and stock exchanges. Therefore, rigorous rules guaranteeing reliable regulation of stock exchanges is by no means a theoretical issue, but a practical one at the core of a free market.

An ideal regulatory structure, and one which can give most dependable results, would rest on four pillars: the governmental regulatory and supervisory authority, like SEC in the USA and the Financial Services Authority (FSA) in the UK; the stock exchange's own regulatory and disciplinary action; every company's able and honest governance, supervised by the audit committee and certified public accountants; and the investors skill for self-control and for risk management decisions.

5.4   Role of specialists in a stock exchange

At the NYSE the *specialist* is a person who directly handles the functions of buying, selling and inventorying specific equities. The Securities Exchange Act of 1934 recognized the specialist as a person who should work only as a broker, and be prohibited from trading on his or her own account. This provision, however, has been subsequently eliminated – a reason why some people say there is conflict of interest in the specialist's functions.

The specialist has a book in which are written the buy orders on one side and sell orders on the other side. In this book, he or she records the transactions that are desired by another broker representing investors, doing so at different prices away from the last market price. In that sense, at the NYSE the specialist's function is to maintain fair and orderly markets in the stocks which he handles. The problem comes from the fact that to do so he or she must buy and sell on his own account:

■ When there is a temporary disparity between supply and demand, and
■ When an investor's request to buy a given equity has no competing public offer.

Precisely, because buying and selling orders from the general public may be disconnected, specialists help in price continuity; through their action they also affect the liquidity of the market. Thus, on the one hand they are enabling investors' orders to be executed but, on the other hand, human nature being what it is, specialists might use the information to their own advantage.

There are some 400 NYSE members registered as specialists. These are organized into specialist units, each handling between one and nine persons or entities. Such specialist units may operate as individuals, partnerships, corporations, joint accounts or combined books – with partnerships being the favored method.

Contrarians do not accept the argument that the sole goal of the specialist is to protect and maintain the continuity of the market. They say that the theory is fine, but one must look at the exceptions to understand how it works in practice; for instance, to appreciate why some events occurred which look close to being insider trading. What these contrarians are specifically asking is:

- What is the responsibility of the specialist to his or her book and its contents?
- What part does the specialist and his or her book play in the activities of the stock market?

Theoretically, the book itself is only the vehicle in which the public's orders are recorded. Typically, such orders are given by investors to stockbrokers who submit them to specialists; hence, they come from investors who are away from the market. This remoteness sees to it that, in practice, the public can never compete with the specialists. At least, that is how contrarians look at this issue.

At the basis of the argument on the role of the specialist and the market advantages he or she may be gaining, lies the fact that the specialist's book has an importance beyond that of a mere repository, of not yet executed agency orders. Properly exploited as a database, it can also serve as an indicator of investors' interest in a particular security.

- If a book contains many orders close to the market, this indicates that the stock is an active one of wide interest.
- By contrast, if the book on a given equity is light, this may indicate that this stock is less active, or that if active it may be volatile.

This case is fairly complex, since the argument behind it is whether the number of buy and sell orders contained on the specialist's book is an indicator of forthcoming market trends. Many specialists say that the book is almost valueless from this particular viewpoint. Contrarians, however, insist that this is not so and that there should be a rule requiring complete disclosure of the book, which is not currently the case.

Evidence on the need to rethink the role specialists play at the NYSE, as well as the exchange's internal control activities, is provided by a recent settlement between specialists and the SEC. On 18 February 2004, five NYSE specialist firms tentatively agreed to pay $240 million in a settlement with the SEC for allegedly:

- Mishandling trades, and
- Skimming profits on the floor of the Big Board.[6]

The five firms – LaBranche; Van Der Moolen; FleetBoston's financial subsidiary Fleet Specialist; Bear, Stearns subsidiary Bear Wagner Specialists; and Goldman Sachs subsidiary Spear, Leeds & Kellogg – received notices from the SEC in January 2004 that they could face civil charges for their activities. Subsequently, they agreed to pay $155 million to disgorge their allegedly illegal profits, and another $85 million in fines. LaBranche's part of the deal stood at $64 million.[7]

In the background of the need for rethinking and revamping specialist activities, lies the fact that the best way to look for a trend in the market is through a database of firm buy and sell orders. For every stock these can be found in the specialist's book. Therefore, a book which contains many sell orders or many buy orders contains valuable information for investors. This issue has greater validity when:

- Limit orders to sell are filled in after a stock has reached a low, or
- Limit orders to buy are entered at a level which a stock has just gone through because of a sharp rally.

It is not certain, of course, that all of the specialists are fully exploiting the information in their books by way of deriving trends and patterns. Neither is it certain how much time and attention each specialist gives to each order, and whether he or she will use the book to benefit the customer or him or herself.

What some people object to with the current system, and on this there is a general convergence of opinions, is that the specialist has immunity and he or she is subject to exceptionally poor controls. He or she never has to meet an irate investor who has lost money in the market, and most investors probably do not even know who the specialist is who is handling their buy and sell orders – or the person or entity connected with equities that they deal with.

Moreover, specialists do not confine their transactions to the trading accounts to which reference has been made. They also have and use two other types of accounts. One is known as a *segregated investment account* or a long-term investment account. This is used by the specialist in different ways, but most particularly for tax purposes.

Some experts suggest, particularly in connection with long-term investment accounts, that specialists' dealings may be motivated by considerations of tax optimization rather than by the needs of the market. For instance, segregated investment accounts might be used to hide profits which would otherwise be taxed as ordinary income. This is achieved by turning such accounts into long-term capital gains.

In fact, a 1963 special study group of the SEC made some biting comments about segregation:

it seems clear that the segregation of specialty securities into long-term investment accounts is subject to strong possibilities of abuse without any corresponding public benefit or reason of effective regulation, and in addition represents an unfair use of the specialist's exemption from margin requirements. On both grounds, the practice should be prohibited.

The other segregated account, known as *omnibus*, has all orders for buying or selling stock placed in the name of a bank or a broker. Some experts make critical comments regarding the use of omnibus accounts, as well as of pooling operations, by specialists. They say that such accounts serve to accumulate stock for the specialists themselves, their friends and their big-block customers (see section 5.5). The contrarians' opinion is that omnibus accounts must be outlawed.

There is one more controversial subject to be brought to the reader's attention, and it concerns *margin requirements* for specialists. Following a Federal Reserve decision, presumably taken to raise stock exchange morale, not only are specialists exempt from margin requirements, but also all members of the exchange have been included under the same umbrella, under Rule 325 from the NYSE Constitution and Rules. Many people consider this to be a highly controversial practice.

Note that Rule 325 is curiously phrased:

No member or member organization doing any business with others than members or member organizations, or doing a general business with the public, except a member or member organization subject to supervision by State or Federal banking authorities, shall permit, in the ordinary course of business as a broker, his or its Aggregate Indebtedness to exceed 2,000 per centrum of his or its Net Capital ...[8]

This is a very curious 'limit' indeed, as it is tantamount to 2000 percent leverage; a huge amount. Exchange members can leverage their capital at that high rate, while non-members are granted credit of only 20 percent according to the rules laid down by the Fed – and rightly so. Moreover, specialists can seek credit on 'any mutually satisfactory terms', which seems to further extend the elastic 'limits' to leverage.

5.5 Bid, ask, large blocks and the third market

A *bid* is an invitation; an offer to pay or accept a price; an effort to acquire, a win, or to attain a proposition. A bid also indicates the amount offered. *Ask* is to inquire; put a question; solicit; make the price of an asset. Between this brief description of terms lies the whole game of a bid/ask system in stock exchanges, as well as the way the auction market works. Equities are usually quoted in a stock exchange through a bid offered by a buyer and an ask quoted by a seller. Between the two there is a spread.

Under a bid arrangement, the proposed security is offered for sale to competing investors, and is sold to the one making the most advantageous bid. Taken together, the competitive bids create the pattern for the sale of a security. Bidding is a feature not only of stock exchanges but also of federal, state and municipal bond issues, as well as of other commodities markets.

A bid plan is not conducive to the establishment of permanent relationships between buyers and sellers of securities in an exchange. Neither is a bid plan favoring a security of lower standards by emphasizing the price or a given security rather than its qualitative features. Instead, competitive bidding underpins free-market operations, which are essential to sound investment.

Bids, however, may reveal important information about a security rather than price alone. For instance, bid/ask spreads of Treasuries is a measure of their liquidity. Such spreads vary among issues. In market terminology, the most recent issues on the auction cycle – the 91-day, 182-day, 364-day, two-year, three-year, four-year, five-year, ten-year and thirty-year – are called *on-the-run*, and they typically have narrower bid/ask spreads than the older, *off-the-run* issues. As issues become older, that is, more off-the-run,

- Their liquidity usually decreases, and
- Their bid offer spread widens.

The bid/ask spread increases when liquidity disappears or the market becomes more hectic. This change in behavior is very significant in terms of risk and return. To capture the message conveyed by bid/ask spreads, traders and investors must refine their tools, use high frequency financial data and undertake data-mining. Otherwise they miss the market switches, making difficult if not impossible a sustained profit.

Market information is recorded in *ticks*. A tick, up or down, is the minimum possible price movement in a market. Different commodities have different ticks. A one point move in Treasury bond futures is equal to $1000 per contract and it corresponds to thirty-two ticks. An *uptick* rule by regulators says that short sales can only be implemented at a price above the preceding transaction.

Bids, asks, spreads and ticks are valid metrics for normal exchange transactions, characterized by open bids and lots of reasonable sizes. Sometimes, however, investors' buy or sell orders are outside what is considered to be normal size limits. As such they require special procedures for handling them.

Large blocks are oversize equity orders, often in the range of 5000 to 300 000 or more shares, bought and sold through a transaction. The background to large blocks may be market speculation, but there are also other reasons like underwriting, different bonuses, or special motivations. Society at large enjoys no particular advantages from the existence of large blocks, but the financial industry likes them.

Such block trades have risks. Experts suggest that everyone bidding for business in the hypercompetitive market of larger blocks seems to get in trouble at some point. For instance, the market thinks Goldman Sachs suffered a sizeable loss in a transaction involving a block of Vivendi shares that it bought in the opening years of the twenty-first century.

As another example, on 29 March 29, Goldman bought 9.4 percent of Telenor, the Norwegian telecommunications operator, from that country's government. The price at which it bought the stock was not disclosed, but according to at least one report the bank paid 48.60 Norwegian kroner (5.77 euros) a share, for a total outlay of 8.2 billion kroner (980 million euros). Telenor's stock, however, fell 5.4 percent after the market was shaken by the arrest of terror suspects in London. Goldman, which had been selling stock at 48.90 kroner a share before markets opened, had to reprice its deal at 48.50 kroner a share.

On the price Goldman reportedly paid, it would have taken a loss of about 2 million euros had it sold all its stock. However, the bank was left with a stake on its books. The investment bank did not disclose its holding. What is known is that Telenor's stock sank. This may be bad luck. But it also reflects the razor-thin margins that banks leave themselves when they bid to win big deals. The lesson for long-term investors is:

■ Do not try to second-guess the market, and
■ Do not deal in block trades, but focus on normal quantities.

Large blocks of securities may be offered for sale by institutions or individuals, and their handling requires a well-tuned machinery because the auction market is not broad enough to do so unaided. Formerly, some sort of manipulation was employed to raise the price and stimulate sufficient activity to absorb large blocks of securities on offer. After the 1934 Act, however, *secondary distributions* have been used.

- Large blocks are offered by the board, immediately after the close of the stock exchange at about the closing quotation of the day.
- To channel large blocks in the market and find a counterparty, brokers and dealers receive either a commission or a price concession from the seller.

In 1942, the NYSE developed a plan of *special offerings* whereby members acting as brokers for public buyers, who pay the public offering price without extra commission, receive their commission from the seller. Ordinarily, this special commission is greater than the regular brokerage commission for securities.

This plan by NYSE has substituted a negotiated settlement for an auction market, and it is known as the *third market*. There are brokerages that specialize in such transactions. While members of NYSE must, according to the rules, execute all listed stocks on the exchange, non-members can trade OTC in NYSE-listed stocks. Critics say big blocks are planned efforts by an individual, group of individuals or entity, to make the market price of a security behave in a way irrelevant to underlying supply and demand.

- On the buy side, big blocks are traded through special bids beyond the normal exchange acquisition.
- On the sell side, they are handled through special offering, secondary distribution and specialist purchasing procedures.

These are common practices in the USA. In Europe, legislation and regulation varies significantly from one country to the other, though in the European Union (EU) there is on-and-off talk about a harmonizing regime accompanied by some half-baked measures. For instance, in late 2003 the EC wanted to replace the current, ten-year-old, ineffective law on investment services with a new version which would harmonize regulatory regimes across all member states of the EU.

The aim is to break down barriers to cross-border trading, in pursuit of a single financial market across the EU. For this reason, the Commission is anxious to get the European Parliament to pass the law before the next elections. But opinions diverge. France and Italy are its staunchest supporters; Britain and other countries oppose it (see also, in Chapter 3, the downside of a single pan-European exchange and capital market).

The City of London generally supports the aim of harmonizing regulatory regimes, but it is balking at greater regulation of *off-market* (third market) transactions. This is the price that apparently must be paid for creating a common European regulatory regime. In the EU, off-market trades are fairly common:

- In London, where investment banks do deals for professional clients, matching buy and sell order without going through the stock exchange, and
- In Frankfurt where big banks conduct similar transactions, and risk losing a lucrative business.

This is not a problem in France, Italy, Spain and Greece where such deals have up to now been forbidden. To allay concerns in Mediterranean states with less developed financial markets, that investors who trade off-exchange might be vulnerable to being ripped off, the European Commission is proposing that there should be pre-trade transparency:

- Investment banks would have to make firm quotes public ahead of a trade,[9] and
- This requirement will only be lifted for transactions above a certain size, as parties to it could be assumed to be sufficiently knowledgeable.

This EU proposal is not liked by investment banks, which protest that it constitutes too great a regulatory burden. In their opinion, the obligation to honor pre-trade prices runs counter to the need to adapt to market circumstances. Contrarians think that the big banks' reaction is not based on a strong argument, because, no matter which may be the specific regulatory regime for fair trading purposes, a facility must be provided that records up-to-the-minute information for investors on price and volume of all big-block transactions in a given equity or other commodity,

- Whether these trades are on an exchange or in the third market, and
- Whether they concern purchases or sales of large blocks of securities.

Moreover, if corporate insiders are buying or selling equity, then this company's shareholders have the right to know immediately how their management teams are exercising the power vested in them by their stakeholders. Big-block trading can dearly affect a company's capitalization and, in a way, its fortunes. They can also be a covert way to bypass regulations, as well as to provide a basis for switches in ownership of an entity which may be against its shareholders' interests.

5.6 Cash and margin accounts

Transactions executed in the exchanges, specifically purchases, are either outright for *cash* or on *margin*. The margin buyer puts up a certain fraction of the purchase price to protect the broker against loss. This is, of course, leveraging, since by doing so the investor hopes that with the same capital he or she can magnify his or her gains – doing so at the risk of increasing his or her losses. As the reader will recall, in Chapter 1 golden rule number 2 advised the typical investor not to buy on margin.

The way margin accounts work is that the balance of the purchase price is loaned by the broker to the customer, but the buyer must keep the margin good by depositing additional cash or acceptable securities in the event of a decline in price below the minimum margin requirement. This poses additional risks as we will see later on in this section.

The broker finances the margin accounts of his or her customers from several sources. In addition to his or her own capital, a member of an organized stock exchange can use free cash credit balances which the customers deposit with him or her to finance the margin purchases. Also, quite often, under a general loan agreement which does not specify the amount of the loan, the broker obtains a demand or call loan from his or her own bank,

- This loan is renewed daily, and
- It is secured by collateral consisting of diversified stocks and bonds carried for the customers who are on margin.

The margin required of the broker by the bank must be distinguished from the margin required by the broker of his customers. A similar statement is valid regarding the initial margin at the time the stock is bought, from that subsequently maintained. In the USA the Securities Exchange Act of 1934 empowered the Federal Reserve to set initial margins on registered securities, while the stock exchange fixes minimum margins that must be maintained in the account.

The Fed authorities also regulate margins on loans to brokers and dealers, except when secured by customers' collateral. With such facilities in place, stockbrokers inform their customers that they can lawfully borrow funds to purchase securities. The broker's collateral for the loan will be the securities purchased, other assets the customer has in his or her margin account and other assets in any other accounts at the broker.

- If the securities in an investor's margin account decline in value, so does the value of the collateral supporting the loans,
- Then, the broker is empowered to take action, such as issue a margin call and/or sell securities or other assets in any of the client's accounts held.

This is reasonable enough, since the broker has to maintain the required balance of risk in each of his or her customers' accounts. What is important, however, but is not self-evident, is that the customer fully understands the exposure involved in trading securities on margin. Such exposure includes a number of issues summarized in the following list:

- The client can lose more funds than he or she deposits in the margin account.
- The broker can force the sale of securities or other assets in the investor's account(s) without contacting him or her.
- The investor is not entitled to choose which securities, or other assets, in his or her account(s) are liquidated or sold to meet a margin call.
- The broker can increase his or her *house* maintenance margin requirements at any time, and is not required to provide advance written notice to the client.
- The client is *not* entitled to an extension of time on a margin call, even if he or she asks for one because he or she faces financial problems.

As can be seen from this list, no matter if margin accounts are legal under the 1934 Act, they are a danger to the investor's assets. Beyond what these five items have indicated, margin accounts give the broker not only the right to borrow cash from the customer's cash account, but also to borrow stock from it. This is implicit in the signing of a margin agreement by the customer.

As a result of outstanding and not cancelled margin agreements, when they receive their statement many investors find that their account was switched from a cash to a margin account as a routine course without their knowledge or consent. For instance, if there has been a small debit balance in a customer's cash account, instead of requesting payment, the broker:

■ Can use the opportunity to lend this customer money, and
■ Then switch to margin the customer's account.

This permits the broker to kill two birds with one well-placed stone, given the advantages margin accounts provide to brokers. Neither is it an unusual practice that sales people are offered a bonus for opening margin accounts, allowing the broker to borrow any securities which he or she may be carrying for the customer to securities 'loaned' to the broker or dealer. These will be used by the broker or dealer as part of his or her capital, subject to the risks of the business the broker or dealer takes.

The freedom to use the customers' securities as his or her own, has often led to the curious phenomenon known as *failure to deliver* by brokerage firms. For instance, when the margin customer sells stock, this has already been sold by a short seller, who has borrowed such security from the broker, and the broker does not have the equity to deliver to the buyer. Investors should therefore always remember the second golden rule: 'Do not borrow, do not buy on margin, do not leverage yourself and do not sell short.' Always remember that:

■ Fully paid investors' securities cannot be legally sold by the broker,
■ But those that were in margin accounts can be pledged and handled as the broker wishes.

Once a customer signs a margin agreement, whether or not he or she makes use of it, he or she consents to the use of the cash and equities. Beyond this, the customer leaves his or her securities with the broker in street name, and the broker uses them the way that best fits his or her business interests – from lending them to hedge funds and speculators, to voting as he or she chooses on the owner's behalf.

It is appropriate to note in this connection that the restrictions imposed for paid securities on brokers and exchanges are valid under US law because of the 1934 Act. They are not necessarily representative of European, Asian or Latin American jurisdictions. Every state has its own laws, and investors will be well advised to study these laws *before* opening an account with a local broker.

The reader would also want to take note of another fact. A portfolio of equities can and often has been used as collateral. The problem, however, is that equities are too volatile for this role, and using them as collateral makes them even more volatile. This is true in the general case, not only in connection with accounts with brokers and dealers.

When a bank makes a non-purpose loan and the collateral used is stock, the stock is put in the bank's custody. That is the way the system works. Although, technically, banks are obliged to contact their borrower before they sell his or her stock, they often sell it without notice when the price falls below a certain level – in exactly the same way as described in the preceding paragraphs in connection with margin accounts.

This is not totally unreasonable because banks have to protect themselves. To do so, they often enter stop orders in the specialist's book if they think the market might drop. Such practice is even more common among *unregulated lenders*, that is, lenders other than banks and brokers, who take stocks as collateral but are not subject to Federal Reserve controls.

Since they lend a high percentage of equities left with them as collateral, and they have as a result less of a cushion than regulated lenders, entities working as unregulated lenders tend frequently to enter stop orders. There is also another important difference:

- With regulated lenders, the amount of collateral must be a specified percentage of money borrowed.
- By contrast, unregulated lenders decide for themselves what percentage of the loan they want as collateral.

In conclusion, non-purpose loans principally used as collateral for stocks which could be carried at loan margin are easily subject to an unfavorable sale of the collateral by custodians during deteriorating markets conditions. This constitutes a potential threat to the borrower's wealth but also to market stability, as the fact that price volatility causes the lender to sell out the collateral if the maintenance limit is passed when prices decline, leads to a vicious cycle.

5.7   Short sales and reverse/forward splits

This section contains two issues theoretically different from one other, but practically in synergy because they share the query: *What price per share?* The first issue, short selling, has been mentioned several times but as yet has not been technically defined (see later in this section). The other issue, reverse/forward split, is undertaken by some companies because it results in cost savings by reducing the number of shareholders with small holdings.

As an example of how an investor's account can be hit by the professionals (and speculators) through short sales, let us take the example of a bank or broker acting as custodian. This entity has rented out the client's shares to a hedge fund, and such equities have been sold short by the hedge fund that borrowed them. In the aftermath, the custodian is no longer able to deliver these equities when the investor (who owned them) sells them.

This, as previously mentioned, is known as 'failure to deliver'. Because such cases do exist, safekeeping contracts typically stipulate that the custodian will pay the investor cash for the assets that no longer exist. The big question is, what is a fair cash-out prize? As the reverse/forward split, in the second half of this section will demonstrate, the cash-out may hurt the investor very much – for no other reason that, unknown to him or her, a speculator borrowed his or her shares from the custodian and sold them short.

Investors are therefore well advised to be aware of the damage which can be caused to their assets through other peoples' short sales. For instance, Luxembourg banks have a clause stipulating that the custodian has the right to redeem the investor's shares in cash – but without stipulating at what price per share. For fully paid investments, this is a very unfavorable clause to the investor, and he or she will be well advised never to sign the contract.

Basically, short selling is a very dangerous exercise to the owners of the stock borrowed and sold short, and to the market as a whole, not only to the speculator or trader who is doing the short selling.[10] A hedge fund often takes a short position on the basis of negative market psychology, earnings warnings, other unfavorable news and rumors, as well as extreme events like the 11 September 2001 attacks on the World Trade Center and the Pentagon.

Short sales may take place as a purely speculative action or as part of a long/short strategy. In contrast to the more traditional type of investing by taking long positions in assets, in a long/short strategy portfolio managers take long *and* short positions to gain quick advantage of market fluctuations. Theoretically, this helps to reduce market risk. In practice, the results are at best uncertain and at worse dramatic. Hence the ongoing joke that to make a small fortune on Wall Street you had better start with a big one.

As a standalone exercise, the more speculative, short selling has features molded around the broker's/bank's hope that it would buy back the borrowed and sold stock at a lower price, and therefore making a hefty profit. Contrarians to short selling say: 'Eliminate this practice and you eliminate the speculators' ability to quietly lay the groundwork for the market's downfall, if not outright chaos, by establishing accounts from which they upset market pricing.'

For instance, the market may turn against the short seller, who might be obliged to buy the stock he or she borrowed and sold, at much higher price than the one he got by selling it. This is behind the view which holds short selling as a major instrument of equity price volatility – if not outright manipulation, which has no place in a free market. The truth is that short selling:

- Is usually done with other peoples' borrowed assets,
- Destabilizes the market, making a negative sentiment worse, and
- Is a predatory activity which engenders major risks to more than just one party.

Precisely because of the risks associated with this practice, some countries have tried to ban short selling, but without much success. Richard Ney mentions Holland as an example. Three hundred years ago, according to the records, a major decline in Dutch stock prices was caused by short selling. In an effort to eliminate this practice, the government first banned short selling and, when this was not successful because the law was ignored, it levied a tax on all short sales. This, too, ineffective. Eventually, the Dutch government repealed the law.[11] England and France have experienced similar regulatory problems.

Ney makes the point that, as the history of speculation shows, a major reason for controlling run-away wheeling and dealing should be not to keep prices from declining once they have risen, but to eliminate pooling operations and other practices of insiders that push prices up not down. Then, after they achieve their profits, let them fall. Behind this thesis lie the facts of major investors' losses and eventually depressions caused by bull raids, 1929 and 2000 being examples.

Here is an example of what can happen with speculation through short selling on a scale much more limited than that implied in the previous paragraph. Edge is a young Japanese Internet company, until recently called 'Livin' on the Edge'. In late 2003/early 2004 its equity saw a spectacular rise. Its shares zoomed to the daily limit allowed by the Tokyo Stock Exchange for fifteen consecutive days, before falling on 21 January 2004.

At its peak, Edge's market capitalization was almost 1 trillion yen ($9.5 billion), which is way out of proportion for a company with only 11 billion yen (a little over $100 million) in sales in 2003, and 359 employees. Even after the fall, Edge's market capitalization was still bigger than that of Japan Airlines which made 2 trillion yen ($18.6 billion) in sales in 2003.

Edge's rise started after its stock split in December 2003. Shortly thereafter it was said that delivery of the new shares would be delayed and would not be completed until 20 February 2004. This created a temporary imbalance between supply and demand, made worse when a securities house accidentally:

- Sold short some 10 000 old Edge shares, and
- Was left scrambling to buy them back.

Seeing an easy profit, speculators placed huge orders for Edge stock in the hope of buying any old shares left in the market. What followed is reminiscent of the Internet bubble. Another Japanese version of a one-company market bubble has been New Deal, a scandal-ridden company with a dud music-distribution business, which took the market for a ride with a planned 1000-for-one stock split.[12]

Let us now look at problems facing investors in connection with reverse/forward splits, which are, Avaya, the electrical equipment manufacturer which is a spin-off from Lucent Technologies. Avaya had a large number of shareholders that owned relatively few shares.

From 1 October 2002, of Avaya's more than 1 million registered shareholders, approximately 858 000 held fewer than thirty shares of common stock, and the next 50 000 held fewer than fifty shares in their accounts. The cost to Avaya for continuing to maintain accounts for these shareholders, including that associated with required shareholder mailings, was more than $3.7 million per year. Company management, therefore, looked for a way to do away with or minimize this cost.

In addition, of Avaya's nearly 2 million shareholders keeping their stock in street name, through a nominee bank or broker, approximately 1.4 million were holding fewer than thirty shares of common stock, 135 000 fewer than forty shares, and 80 000 fewer than fifty shares in their accounts. The cost of continuing to distribute required mailings to these shareholders was an additional $2.5 million per year.

Based on these statistics, the company's board of directors authorized and recommended for shareholders' approval three *alternative* reverse/forward stock split transactions at the thirty-, forty- and fifty-shares level. The example given in the following paragraphs describes a reverse one-for-thirty stock split followed immediately by a forward thirty-for-one stock split of the common stock. The forty- and fifty-share actions were similar.

With a reverse stock split, each minimum number of common stock shares registered in the name of a shareholder is converted into one share of common stock, followed immediately by a forward split, after which each share of common stock outstanding (upon consummation of reverse split), will be converted into the minimum number of shares of common stock.

As permitted under Delaware law, shares of common stock converted into less than one share in the reverse split are instead converted into the right to receive a cash payment. However, if a registered shareholder holds the minimum number, or more, of common shares in his or her account at the effective time of the reverse split, any fractional share in such account resulting from the reverse split will not be cashed out and the total number of shares held by such a holder will not change as a result of the reverse/forward split.

In Avaya's case, with thirty shares taken as a threshold, 858 000 registered shareholders and 1.4 million in street name, were to be paid in cash for their equity. After this, they would no longer be equity owners of this firm. Correspondingly, with forty shares as the threshold, the respective numbers would stand at 934 000 registered shareholders and 1.6 million in street name – leaving the company with 120 000 registered shareholders and 390 000 in street name.

As in the case of inability to deliver because of short sales, the trick in a reverse/forward split is the proper definition of the *cash-out price*. At Avaya, the board suggested the stock price prevailing when the aforementioned proposal was made, which stood at about $3 per share. An equity holder with twenty-five shares would have received $75. It may sound reasonable, but . . .

The 'but' is that between proposal date and effective date, should the stockholders approve the transaction, the share price can change significantly. In Avaya's case, it went up to $10, which means that the shares bought back by the company would have been worth $250 for their holder, rather than $75.

Notice that this transaction is legal. As was written in the Avaya prospectus: 'In order to avoid the expense and inconvenience of issuing fractional shares to shareholders who hold less than one share of common stock after the reverse split, under Delaware state law Avaya may either arrange for the sale of these fractional shares or pay cash for their fair value.' The question is: what price per share is a fair price to the shareholder?

Notes

1 *The Economist*, 29 August 1998.
2 *Financial Times*, 29 April 2003.
3 D.N. Chorafas (2004). *Management Risk: The Bottleneck is at the Top of the Bottle*. Macmillan/Palgrave.
4 *USA Today*, 6 March 2002.
5 In spite of the fact that I had explicitly asked my equities should not be lent to any party, under any condition, at any price.
6 *Miami Herald*, 19 February 2004.
7 *The Economist*, 21 February 2004.

8 Richard Ney (1970). *The Wall Street Jungle*. Grove Press.
9 *The Economist*, 11 October 2003.
10 D.N. Chorafas (2003). *Alternative Investments and the Mismanagement of Risk*. Macmillan/Palgrave.
11 Richard Ney (1970). *The Wall Street Jungle*. Grove Press.
12 *The Economist*, 24 January 2004.

Three

Performance criteria and quoted equities

6 Technical and fundamental analysis

6.1 Introduction

Management is responsible for a company's success or failure, and the same is true of investment performance. Most often, investors and asset managers act according to certain guidelines which, however, are not universal and they change over time. For instance, many experts now believe that the 'buy and hold' time of equities which prevailed in the decades after World War II is past. Therefore, a portfolio of securities has to be dynamically controlled.

- Technical and fundamental analysis is a way of providing the needed control information.
- But analysis also requires an inquisitive mind, lots of skill pertinent to investment and a great deal of homework.

Doing one's homework as an investor is a better guide than taking wholesale advice from experts. Still, the experts do matter (more on this later). The *seventh golden rule* for traders and investors is that they should always do their homework in a way which is meticulous but not arrogant. When people get a big ego, they acquire a one-track mind, forsake risk control and eventually pay dearly for this failure.

'Your homework helps you to avoid the herd', said Gordon Midgley, adding that today there are plenty of investment research services to which individual investors can subscribe. The larger mutual funds, too, have Internet sites providing research advice to individual investors – including charting. Moreover, the LSE has a question-and-answer course one can do via a personal computer.

Eventually, the user of such services can graduate to his or her own research environment, but to graduate he or she must learn to use what is already publicly available. While subscribing to the need of doing one's homework, Bob Keen questioned whether the growing number of retail investors in Europe have what it takes for fundamental and technical analysis. In his opinion, Americans are better positioned for this type of work, because:

- They have had for some time the investors' culture, and
- More information on securities is generally available in the USA than in Europe.

Keen further suggested that while it is a good idea to use experts as part of one's homework, investors should learn to make their own decision for which they assume responsibility. Because no investment plan is perfect, the best investors are those who:

- Understand their own limitations, and
- Appreciate that, to get a better insight, one has to challenge the 'obvious'.

Can a consensus of investment analysts' opinions be of help to the retail investor? 'No', answered one of the experts, adding that this 'no' is valid whether in relation to individual accounts or institutional investors. Consensus is not really a good approach to asset management. Experience teaches us that there is no way to get out of one's daily homework unless one wants to be clobbered by the market.

Some sound advice is not to be too complacent after making profits. Short of taking such profits home, it is tough holding on to paper profits in the stock market since nobody really has the secret of the market's future behavior. Analytical approaches, simulations[1] and stress tests[2] will help in deciding when to exit a certain equity, or the market altogether – but they are not fail-safe. Wise people do not switch in and out until their homework shows that a change in positions is really necessary.

■ An investment strategy has to be flexible enough to change when the market changes.
■ Knowing when to stay out of the market is as important for an investor as knowing when to be in.

The mistake most people make is that they stick to the same investment strategy all the time or, alternatively, they make too many switches. The way financial blunders go, the inability to adapt to changing market conditions can lead to a torrent of red ink – and the same is true of changing too often and too fast without adequate study and preparation.

Doing one's homework has many aspects. One of these is to consider alternative scenarios, from the most likely to the most unlikely outcomes. Not everybody does this. Most traders who make a deal that works do not think: 'Why did it work?' or 'What did I do here that I might be able to repeat in another market, at another time?' The win seems to them to be something obvious, forgetting that it is always necessary to challenge the strategy one has used.

Also part of the homework is the fact that a lot of reflection is needed in the processes of investing and trading. Wise investors not only study their alternatives prior to commitments, but also do post-mortems. An after-the-fact evaluation is truly being analytical about the work one has done and keeps on doing. Investors and traders must think about everything they do, keeping track of:

■ What was done right,
■ What was done wrong, and
■ What was done right but over time went wrong.

This is every investor's personal responsibility and he or she should not rely on experts who work for other companies and other interests to help out. Successful traders consider this reliance on third parties to be the leading cause of financial disablement. Brokers and their analysts rarely, if ever, give a 'sell' signal. Therefore, a great deal of money can be lost by listening to brokers and other advisers.

This does not mean, however, that investors should reject wholesale the brokers' advice. They should use it as one of their inputs because, to a significant extent, it represents the outcome of a professional *securities analysis*. The function of securities analysis is to assist the investor in recognizing undervalued and overvalued stocks, as well as market trends. While they also aim to provide the investor with advice that tells him or her when a given stock should be bought and sold, this advice should be most carefully scrutinized.

A factual, timely and honest securities analysis is important because fashions in stocks and bonds, and the percentages of each that one should include in his portfolio, are continuously changing. However, as the scams in securities analysis of the late 1990s have demonstrated, quite often opinions expressed by brokers may be subject to conflicts of interest with investment banking activities. Or, the broker may have large inventories of certain shares on his shelves that he or she must get rid of in one way or another.

Biased investment advice is not the subject of this chapter. What may lie behind it will be discussed in Chapter 11 in connection with risks being assumed. The present text addresses itself to technical and fundamental analyses – their concepts, their tools and their output. It has been a deliberate choice to dissociate fundamental and technical securities analysis from the different metrics used for measurement purposes. These are presented in Chapter 7.

6.2　Fundamental analysis defined

The distinction between fundamental and technical analysis is not yesterday's subject. Still, most investors do not get the right signals about what each of them is and is not, or what each can deliver. Part of the difficulty associated with the appropriate definition is the fact that the concepts underpinning each type of analysis evolve over time.

In the early 1950s my professors at UCLA taught their students that there are two types of equity analysis: fundamental and technical. Today this is not a generally acceptable division because, in the mean time, quantitative analysis has become a self-standing discipline – and significant enough, for that matter, to make it a separate branch of analysis. Or is it not quite so?

Opinions are divided, as Figure 6.1 shows. In the upper half of this figure, fundamental and technical analysis constitute the main division. Under 'technical' there are two subdivisions: charting and quantitative analysis. Nearly half the experts I interviewed opted for this model. The other half said that it is not so, because nowadays there are three main disciplines:

- Fundamental,
- Technical, and
- Quantitative.

All three stand practically on equal terms. Under quantitative, come the better known ratios like earnings per share (EPS), price to earnings (P/E) and return on equity (ROE) (see Chapter 6) but also new ones like debt per share (DPS). Also included in the quantitative category is, most importantly, all the work rocket scientists are doing (see Chapter 9). In fact, as we will see, the seventeenth golden rule of investing says: 'Use mathematical models, but understand they are not fail-safe.'

In a way, it is good news that the opinion of experts is divided not only on the classification of types of analysis but also on each type's relative merits and demerits.

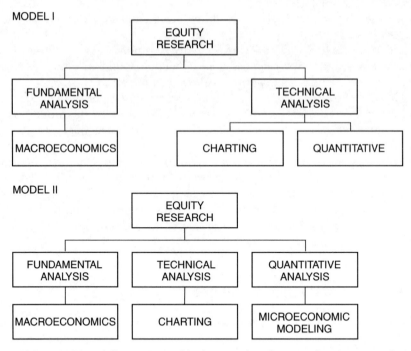

Figure 6.1 Two different ways of looking at classification of equity research

Differences of opinion are what really make the market. 'People who really care for their money make decisions based on fundamentals', said one of the experts, adding that investors who know their trade:

- Monitor their decisions frequently, but
- They do not trade frequently

In the opinion of this expert, part of the downside of technical analysis is that it tends to push investors towards frequent trading. 'This is not so,' said another expert, who chose the classification model in the lower half of Figure 6.1, 'what quantitative analysis is doing is to torture the market data till they confess their secrets.'

The same expert explained that while in the past most quantitative work was under technical analysis, a growing number of applications have demonstrated that modeling through numerical analysis how the price of an equity, or index, might evolve is not at all the same with charting. And as a proof that technical analysis and quantitative analysis have developed into distinct disciplines, the pros bring in evidence the fact that, today, advertisements in journals and newspapers ask for quantitative analysts in a separate advertisement from those searching for technical analysts.

'There are borderline issues which lead to this difference in opinion on how to classify analytical work', suggested Eugen Buck, managing director of Rabobank. 'As a banker I want to serve my customers and give them research advice. Essentially the customers would dictate which type of research they want to have.' Moreover, Buck said that this issue of equity research classification, and of analytical results, is in full evolution, adding that: 'At Rabo, we had to change our view of what we do as equity research and what we research for.'

Integrated within the perspective of the references in the previous paragraphs is the *eighth golden rule* of investing. Not only one should undertake fundamental and technical analysis (or fundamental, technical and quantitative analysis), but also one should appreciate the differences among them – including the fact that the results each provides can contradict those of the other methods (more on this later).

This brings up the issue of *defending* research results when the outputs of different methods of equity analysis do not converge. 'Somebody must stand at top of this and say: "This is the view of Merrill Lynch",' said Bob Keen, 'or maybe convey the message why different analysts have reached different conclusions.'

The reason why different methods may end in different, and sometimes contradictory, output has to do with both their goals and their tools. The object of *fundamental analysis* is to identify basic economic and political factors that help to determine a commodity's price (see section 6.6). Fundamental research focuses on macroeconomic factors, including current and future supply and demand particularly for a given equity or other commodity which is the subject of analysis, to determine:

- If a price change is likely,
- If such price change is imminent,
- In which direction it may go, and
- By how much the price could be expected to change.

In connection with equities, investment decisions based on fundamentals look at earnings ratios (see Chapter 7), the announcement of a merger, a new product, a stock split and so on. An analyst following the fundamental approach essentially asks: 'What makes investors pay $80 a share for a stock that at one time sold for $30?' Or, 'for $120'?

In 2004, the Deutsche Bundesbank commissioned a study at the University of Regensburg on correlation coefficients. Though its object has been conditioned by capital adequacy requirements under Basel II,[3] its results are significant for the present discussion. The study focused on obligor default rates, and it demonstrated that the inclusion of variables connected to macroeconomics and the business cycle improves the forecast of default probabilities.[4]

It might be that a valid answer to the queries expressed by the previous bullet list items is well enough provided by market fundamentals, but one should not forget that several factors underpinning stock price fundamentals are not directly observable. This implies that any evaluation of whether stocks are efficiently priced requires a *judgment* about investors' expectations regarding:

- Intrinsic value,
- Future dividends,
- Interest rates, and
- Stock market risks.

The critical query is whether these factors, and their evaluation, are justifiable and correctly reflected in stock prices. What sort of arguments may be put forward to arrive at such a conclusion? In general, an assessment based on fundamentals has to reflect empirical and theoretical considerations, since both are instrumental in shaping the outcome of a fundamental analysis.

Critics say fundamental analyses do not achieve great returns, given that prices reflect most (though not all) publicly available data – past and present. This includes macroeconomic variables, political news, product announcements, annual reports of corporations, investors' newsletters, public databases and other data streams from information providers. This argument comprises two issues:

- The efficient market hypothesis, which is utterly undocumented (see section 6.3), and
- The ability of some people to print tomorrow's newspaper today.

On the one hand, even tomorrow's weather reports are not necessarily reliable – but we still use them. On the other hand, it is a fact that the 'news in the future', which is sometimes the theme of some fundamental research, is largely guesswork. It should be kept in mind, however, that serious fundamental analysts do not aim to be gurus but, rather, to:

- Correct lags or distortions in information transmission, and
- Better comprehend available data, to capitalize on market inefficiencies.

After all, what are our alternatives? To the query 'What is a given equity worth?', the general and superficial kind of answer is, 'A stock is worth what the market is willing to pay for it.' This is nonsense because it leads to situations of hype and overvaluation which may well bankrupt the investor. It is therefore important to find out *why*, *what* and *how much* an equity kicks, as well as *when* and *where* might be the limits.

Sometimes better answers are provided in conjunction with technical analysis (more on this later) even if, quite often, fundamental and technical views of given stock markets differ. Notice that such differences, too, can be proactive as they challenge the expert – while convergence leads analysts to say they have reason to believe that 'by the second half of the year, the technical read and the fundamental view will justify an uptrend'.

It needs no explaining that fundamental analysis has prerequisites which need to be fulfilled, such as gathering substantial amounts of economic data. Fundamental research also needs political intelligence, as well as assessing the expectations of market participants and analyzing this information to predict future price movements. Altogether, this is a time-consuming and tedious process, but it might be rewarding.

Fundamental analysts look into factors affecting supply and demand for a commodity, including general economic conditions, price levels, prices of substitute commodities, government policies, international tensions and the like. Sometimes economic models are employed, but more frequently analysts use relatively simpler forecasting approaches which help them to:

- Evaluate and interpret basic economic and market conditions, and
- Understand how futures prices relate to underlying cash prices, and which way they might be going.

A long list of factors comes into play in this work, with several among them regarding financial assets, like stocks and bonds. Governmental and central bank policies, both in the home country and in foreign (host) countries of the equity under examination can be of critical importance. Expectations about future policy changes, including current and projected inflation rates, are also important. For foreign currency rates, crucial issues are international trade, capital flows and government policies.

In conclusion, fundamental analysis requires that the major determinants of a commodity's demand and supply are properly identified and evaluated. This information must be updated constantly, on a daily, weekly and monthly basis, to unearth shifts in demand or supply that may indicate coming price changes. Though much of the important fundamental information is publicly available through government and privately published reports, other more esoteric sources also need to be used in order to get a better insight.

6.3   Technical analysis defined

Technical analysis is a different entity. It is the study of historical prices aimed at the prediction of equity or other commodity prices in the future. Technical analysts frequently use charts of past prices to identify historical patterns which can help to forecast future price trends (more on this in section 6.4). That is why technical analysts are often referred to as *chartists*.

By and large, technical analysis works better when relatively simple trend-following gives commendable results, also, ironically, when the majority of traders and investors do not have access to charting tools. This used to be the case in the 1960s and 1970s, but is no longer true today because technical trading systems have become popular, with the result they kill themselves off.

Critics say that technical analysis cannot achieve abnormal returns because market prices already reflect past prices and events, as well as a fair amount of risk and return information. At the core of this argument is the fact that no investor can hit the jackpot by using trading rules based on historical information alone. This, however, is not necessarily the fault of technical analysis – and it is unfair to look at it that way.

To critics like Burton G. Malkiel, of Princeton University (see a more detailed discussion in Chapter 13), as well other economists, technical analysis is about as scientific as palm-reading, calling it anathema to the academic world.[5] Other economists, however, and plenty of equity analysts, keenly study patterns in price charts like head and shoulders formations and resistance levels (see section 6.4).

Believers in technical analysis are actively developing computer software that identifies some of the chartists' favorite formations in a consistent way. They are also determining whether these patterns have any predictive value, given that technical analysis summarizes in a compact way the influences of supply and demand on the market's pricing of financial instruments.

Precisely because the behavior of both natural and human-made systems leaves a footprint which has certain predictive characteristics on future behavior, the study of patterns can be revealing. Hence, it comes as no surprise that technical analysis has grown in popularity, particularly so since the development of models and of facilities for on-line data-mining:

- Permit rapid retrieval of information elements from large databases, and
- Enable complex, sophisticated study of historical prices and their trends.

Technological advancements have seen to it that during the past twenty years technical analysis has changed radically. The catalyst, and vehicle, of this transformation has been the computer, which made superfluous laborious and time-consuming manual plotting of commodity prices and indicators on graph paper.

- Models and computers also increased the degree of abstraction in technical analysis, as well as the researcher's sensitivity to an equity's performance.
- Specific indicators can be quickly tested over chosen periods of time, to explore a web of relationships within a stock's price structure.

Technical analysts look for a pattern in this web that, seen through charting criteria (see section 4), may tell what is going on in that stock. This is most valuable information to the analyst, and by extension the investor. Major accumulations or distributions that are in progress can be detailed – and sometimes they can be anticipated – but the method is *not* fail-proof.

Technical analysts believe that fundamental analysis does not provide sufficient information for successful trading. They argue that the study of supply and demand, though interesting, is not timely enough to be useful – particularly so as fundamental analysis relies on data that is available only on a weekly, monthly or, even, quarterly basis. For example, consumer price index (CPI) figures are not released by the Department of Commerce until a month or so later.

The technical analysts argument is that such delays can be deadly in a market performance sense, because futures traders must always be sensitive to short-run price movements, and market prices themselves contain this sort of useful and timely data. An extension of this argument is that market prices quickly reflect all available fundamental hindsight, as well as other information, like market:

- The market's psychology, and
- Market participants' expectations.

Critics of technical analysis answer these arguments by saying that there is no reason why historical price patterns will be repeated in the future. New information, they add, arrives in the market randomly so that repetitive price patterns are unlikely. In their judgment, it is also unclear:

- What other data is contained in prices, and
- Why the inclusion of noise in price information should result in orderly price patterns.

To a significant extent, these criticisms are biased. Serious technical analysts do not say that past performance repeats itself, which would have been a silly statement. What they say is that price patterns are formed, and study of these can be revealing. Such study is effectively done through charting, but the reader should be aware that charting, too, can be subject to errors and misinterpretations.

One of the misinterpretations which is more prominent in fundamental analysis but also biases technical analysis, concerns the rationality often ascribed to market behavior. In theory, the hypothesis of *market efficiency* rests on the assumption that investors have an incentive to use all available information when deciding at which price to sell or buy stocks.

This is a half-baked assumption. Investors and traders make (and lose) fortunes in the market precisely because the market is *inefficient* by definition, and they know how to exploit its inefficiencies. If the markets are efficient, then the performance of equities, and other commodities, would have been flattened over long periods of time – which evidently is not the case.

Proponents of the efficient-market theory answer that even if investors do not all use the available information in a rational way, an effective arbitrage mechanism might ensure that rational investors push securities' prices sufficiently close to their fundamental values. Such a hypothesis, however, demands too much from the average investor in terms of patience and skills.

Arbitrage might work perfectly when, for example, skillful rational and technically equipped investors can sell overpriced securities in one market and simultaneously buy the same assets, or securities, with the same pay-off structure, as a hedge in another market where it is correctly priced or underpriced. The effect of such theoretical arbitrageurs' trades would cause the prices on the two different markets quickly to balance out at a 'fundamentally justified level', whatever this might happen to be.

This is, however, a theoretical mechanism for eggheads which is totally unrealistic. While it might have been able to bring about efficient prices, even if investors do not all behave rationally, it is too far-fetched to even approach such an objective. The assumptions on which it rests are on 'cloud 9'.

- Arbitrageurs are in business to make a quick buck.
- Their self-imposed mission is not to guide the markets into being efficient.

In real-life stock markets, no such ideal mechanisms exist, and no such perfect substitutes for market-based inefficient stocks pricing are available. As a consequence, fundamental analysis and technical analysis have a role to play, even if the price for using them is the risk investors take in believing in their output, which might be right or wrong. Only real life would tell which has been the case.

6.4   Theory behind the art of charting

Properly studied and interpreted, charts – onto which is mapped the market's pricing of a given equity – can provide analysts and investors with an insight into the changing outlook of market participants in regard to that equity. *Chartists* plot historical prices to identify their pattern, which could then be used to predict a future direction of an equity's price. Charting is the basic tool of technical analysis and chartists rely primarily on three bodies of data:

- Prices, intraday, daily, weekly, monthly,
- Trading volumes, and
- Interest rate levels.

Analysts who, through technical analysis, follow an equity's fortune and its prospects often look at charts as a means to capture shifts in market sentiment and market psychology. At times, this can be a rewarding enterprise, its downside being that using technology as a facilitator, a growing number of chartists is now after:

- The same trends, and
- The same changes in direction of price movements.

This can be misleading. Alert traders know that their colleagues, who collaborate with chartists, can be counted on to buy and sell as a group, in case the fluctuations in 'this' or 'that' stock's price describe what chartists refer to as a 'buy' or 'sell' signal. It is always possible that some market players manipulate a given equity to provide false buy or sell signals.

While the preceding paragraph mentioned some of the negatives, on the positive side the more skilled chartists have developed techniques that make it difficult for other market participants to trap them. These are typically value-added improvements over the rather traditional charts, based on:

- Investment theory,
- Interactive computational finance, and
- Fairly sophisticated mathematical models.

Investment theory says that after a stock has been declining for several months, it tends eventually to lose downside momentum and starts to move sideways. With downside pressure wearing off, buyers and sellers tend to go into equilibrium. The stock has plummeted because sellers were far stronger. When the 200-day moving average loses its downside slope and begins to flatten out, it is said that it is searching for a base. This is the *basing area* hypothesis.

There is no clear rule on how long an equity stays in the basing area; the answer depends on the market. If it breaks out of it fast, the decline and rise resemble a 'V'-type curve. If it stays long in it, they resemble a 'U'-type curve. Similarly, there may be 'inverted V'-type curve, if after reaching the top the stock has a reversal. This action is sometimes accompanied by:

- A price gap, and/or
- An event that changes the perception of an equity in a matter of a few days or weeks.

This is a time when investors try to exit all at once. Unless there are serious reasons why an equity or a stock market index (see Chapter 4) is destabilized, it is likely that after it stays for some time in the basing area it will start moving out of it. However, in this move it may encounter resistance. Breaking out above the top of the resistance zone, the 200-day moving average might master an impressive volume, which is the start of an uptrend.

The 200-day moving average usually starts turning up shortly after the breakout. Experts usually bet on a trend characterized by two steps forward and one sharp step back. As long as all these swings and shakeouts take place above the stock's rising forty-week moving average, this stage generally ends with a stock pausing or consolidating.

A top or consolidation area is formed as the upward advance loses momentum and starts to move sideways. Buyers and sellers are once again about equal in strength, while at the previous stage, buyers were stronger and overwhelmed the sellers. Eventually, the stock's price advance ends, and the equity price is in equilibrium.

Something similar to the basing area starts to take shape at the equity's higher price level, till sellers get the upper hand and there are signals of deteriorating technical characteristics. Examples are:

- Light volume on rallies, and
- Heavy volume on declines.

Within the confines of a top area, the stock (or index) begins breaking the 200-day moving average and at times trades at, or below, this temporary benchmark. Oscillators which work best in horizontal trading ranges, become very useful at this stage, as they start to show divergence in price and momentum, and possibly other signs of impending reversal.

The declining phase follows a period of moving back and forth in a neutral trading range. A stock eventually breaks below the bottom of its support zone, and volume increases – while a breakdown is often followed by a volume decrease on a pullback to the breakdown point. To chartists, this signals that the downward stage in a stock's behavior is starting to unfold.

Once the stock breaks into the declining phase, the upside potential is very small; on the contrary, downside risk is considerable. There may be one or more rallies back to the breakdown point, as bargain hunters feel that the stock is cheap compared with its recent price. Eventually, however, the downtrend becomes evident, bargain-hunters pull back, and the moving average declines. From a risk/reward point of view, this is a dangerous situation because at that stage:

- Each decline drops to a new low,
- While each oversold rally falls short of the prior peak.

Technical analysts consider this behavior of a stock's market price as a textbook example of a downtrend. More or less all of this negative action takes place below the declining moving average of the equity; that is, the exact opposite of a stock's uptrend which we examined earlier in this section. How to distinguish uptrends and downtrends is one of the issues addressed in section 6.5.

Many financial analysts have their own criteria for picking out the most technically attractive stocks. For instance, they cross-index chosen equities by using both their technical and fundamental ratings. They call a stock *twice-blessed* when both the technical and the fundamental analyses rate it positively.

The reader will recall that technical and fundamental analysis may well diverge in their signals. For instance, during 2003 there has been a divergence between the technical trend of the market and the fundamental valuation picture, though by the end of 2003 the two were in the process of converging.

Sometimes technical analysts focus their attention on market behavior, beyond the use of quantitative tools (see also section 6.5). When all three methods: fundamental, technical and behavioral are used rather than only the first two, a *thrice-blessed equity* is said to be one with a 'buy' by all of these three disciplines. Among technical indicators of market behavior are momentum, sentiment, speculative activity and historical cycle/patterns.

Momentum analysis has two aspects: one is longer-term rate of change which measures variables, such as annual rate of change of the S&P 500 index (see Chapter 4). The other is persistent broadness of the advance, as measured by the cumulative daily advance-decline (breadth) index or the percentage of NYSE common stocks' prices above their 200-day moving averages.

6.5   The bolts and nuts of charting

Because analysts who develop advanced approaches keep these close to their chest, this section describes the basic technical analysis methods, while section 6.6 will look into how technical analysis can assist the investment process by computing the future price of a commodity; or, more precisely, by looking after price changes which tend to establish a trend, and might be depended on to continue that trend.

Starting with the fundamentals, chartists try to establish the trend they are looking for within the confines of parallels that form a channel. An example is shown in Figure 6.2, which shows a downtrend, a 'v'-type reversal and an uptrend. A *trendline* on a price chart is frequently identified by a straight line connecting periodic highs and lows.

Figure 6.2 An example of reversal and channel characterizing the price of equity X

- A *downtrend* is a sequence of either falling lows or falling highs.
- A *reversal* identifies a change in market sentiment about an equity.
- An *uptrend* consists of a sequence of either rising price highs or rising price lows.

Upturn or downturn is a trendline that runs through at least three points, for example higher prices on a certain day. The better identified trendline is able to link price swings with each other. The more points on which this single line is based, the more relevant and the more credible it will be.

Usually, a trend is confirmed by the *volume* of transactions taking place in connection with a given equity, and eventually to the market at a given point in time. A different way of putting this is that there should be evidence that the volume follows the trend. A trend is broken when the closing market price:

- Falls below the upward trendline, or
- Rises above the downward trendline *and* volumes temporarily rise as the breakthrough occurs.

The existence of a *resistance level* (see also section 6.4) is significant here. In an uptrend, this is a price level at which there appears to be substantial selling pressure, which keeps prices from rising further. By contrast, a *support level* is that at which there appears to be substantial latent buying power to keep prices from falling further.

Support and resistance levels are intrinsically linked with the concept of trends in an equity's (or index) price. Technically speaking, a *reversal chart* is one in which a price trend is reversed by a predetermined minimum price change in the opposite direction.

- There is said to be resistance if, after a rise, the price is at least temporarily unable to exceed a certain level.

This may be due to technical, fundamental or purely psychological factors, which analysts aim to unearth through their research.

- There is said to be support if the price is, also at least temporarily, unable to fall below a certain threshold.

Technical analysis makes use of certain relationships between support and resistance levels. An example is the so-called Fibonacci ratio, named after the Italian mathematician who developed it. It largely corresponds to the ratios of the Golden Mean: 0.382 to 0.618 and 0.618 to 1.0.

According to the Fibonacci hypothesis, if following a price rise there is a consolidation or a temporary deterioration in the price, the first significant support may be expected at 61.8 percent of the preceding rise. By contrast, the first significant resistance threshold may well be at 38.2 percent of the total preceding decline. Many technical analysts refer, rather imprecisely, to a one-third or 38-percent retracement.

Apart from the arithmetic milestones, charting analysts look after not only trendlines and channels, but also *geometric formations* which help them to predict market tops,

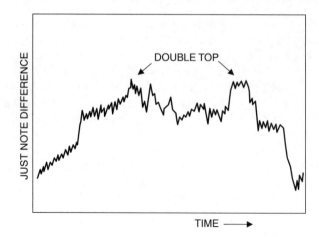

Figure 6.3 An example of tops characterizing price movements of equity Y

bottoms and – up to a point – future price movements. Some of the criteria used in connection with support and resistance are double tops, and double bottoms, as well as heads and shoulders.

■ *Double tops*, or bottoms, are frequently used to identify a price reversal.

In an uptrend, the failure of prices to exceed a previous price peak, on two consecutive occasions is considered a double top. Chartists look at this as a warning signal, telling them that the uptrend may be about to end and a downtrend is about to begin. A double-top formation is shown as an example in Figure 6.3.

The double bottom is practically the mirror image of this double-top price pattern, but the first leg is a downtrend. Also, after the reversal comes an uptrend. The double bottom occurs when falling prices fail to penetrate previous support levels on two occasions, and it is often followed by the upside penetration of the previous price high.

■ *Head-and-shoulders* formations are among the most frequently employed technical templates for identifying a price reversal.

A head-and-shoulders pattern consists of four phases: the left shoulder, the head, the right shoulder and the penetration of the neckline. A head-and-shoulders reversal pattern is complete only when the neckline is penetrated, either in an upward or downward direction connected to an equity's price trend. Other terms with which the reader should be familiar are:

■ Congestion areas,
■ Blow-off and breakout,
■ Momentum and oscillator indices,
■ Twice- and thrice-blessed, and
■ The general context of Dow theory (see section 4.7).

A *congestion area* occurs when prices move sideways, fluctuating up and down within a well-defined range, with no clear-cut movement in either direction. Congestions are not created overnight; they develop over a considerable period of time. When prices break out of a congestion area, either by penetrating support or resistance levels, it is a signal to sell or buy, respectively.

A *blow-off* is the climax of a stock's price development. When it is taking place, prices break above existing resistance levels, signaling that the bull on the stock's price structure has entered its final phase. A blow-off materializes at the end of a long, accelerated rise in price. By contrast, a *breakout* occurs in the early stages of a strong market advance.

Momentum and oscillator indices are rate-of-change metrics, used as leading indicators of price changes. Both trend and momentum are key elements in technical analyses, but note that in conjunction with momentum a trend is not seen as a trendline in the sense of a straight line. It is defined as a moving average over a certain period of time whose employment serves to smooth the price curve in order to:

- Recognize more easily underlying price performance, and
- Identify changes in direction that may be occurring.

In technical analysis, an *oscillator index* is a normalized form of a momentum index. One problem with these indices is that they lack a predetermined upper and lower boundary, whose existence is quite helpful when applying statistical techniques.

Moving averages are another technical indicator used as decision support in determining price trends and trend changes. For example, moving average is a statistical technique for smoothing price movements in order to identify more easily developing trends.

Section 6.4 referred to market behavior within this perspective; *market sentiment* is judged through indicators based on opinion surveys, such as the investors' intelligence tabulation and other advisory services based on opinions of market players. Other sentiment indicators are computed by means of transactions analysis, like the Chicago Board of Options Exchange's (CBOE's) put/call ratio.

A metric for *speculative activity* is the increase, or decrease, in the NASDAQ/NYSE volume ratio and IPO activity. An example of *historical cycle/patterns* is the US Presidential election cycle. Looking back to 1900, the DJIA registered an average annual price return of 9.2 percent during election years. In addition, eleven of the last fifteen election years, prior to 2004, have produced positive returns for the Dow.

Other notions pertaining to a technical analysis, of which the reader ought to be aware, relate to *volume* and *open interest*. Both have to do with the movement of an equity or index. In a way, they are lagging indicators because official volume and open interest figures are reported a day later than futures prices. However, they are important, as technical analysts believe that volume and open interest provide information about whether a price move is strong or weak.

Theoretically at least, if prices are rising and open interest and volumes are increasing, then new money may be flowing into the equity market, reflecting new buying. This is considered bullish. By contrast, if prices are rising but open interest and volume are declining, the rally is thought to be caused primarily by short covering. Money leaves rather than enters the market. This is considered to be bearish. These are the general rules characterizing technical analysis.

6.6 Financial analysis and future price of a commodity

The question regarding the right price of a commodity, whether this is an equity or any other commodity, has always been important to investors. The current price is a statistic; what investors want to know is the price which can be expected or achieved in future. At the bottom line, this is the object of analysis – technical or fundamental.

Some experts say that in principle there is hardly any difference between the factors which determine prices on the capital markets and those in other areas of the economy. This is not necessarily true. Neither is a price computation based solely on the abstract concept of supply and demand a 'sure thing'. If one asks a fundamental analyst about the price development of a particular stock or bond, his or her inclination would be to:

■ Start by eliciting the future costs and earnings structure of a company,
■ Merge them with macroeconomic factors, and
■ From this basis deduce a valuation for the underlying security.

This valuation procedure seems fairly linear, but it is usually full of analytical stumbling blocks, which make forecasting price movements rather difficult. Problems range from necessary assumptions about general economic and sector data, to unavoidably subjective assessments which are the essence of an analyst's trade and put his or her personal stamp on the price inference being made.

By contrast, a technical analyst would study through graphical representations price changes which take place over a given period of time, without much reference to the fundamentals. But he or she, too, would have to interpret trends, draw channels, judge reversals and, above all, work on the supposition that historical prices and volumes determine future price developments. Chartists, typically make explicit assumptions that:

■ Stock prices move in trends, and
■ Certain known behavioral structures, as expressed in particular patterns and formations, repeat themselves.

Without this hypothesis, technical analysis is not able to interpret the trendline of a commodity's price movements, whether these are short, medium or long term. Nor can it find clues as to whether an emerging change is merely a technical correction, a technical reaction or an early expression of a trend shift, without the support of hypotheses leading to that choice.

Moreover, whether we talk of fundamental or technical analysis, little or no account is taken of greed and fear in stock markets. Yet, both are human traits encouraging a sort of exaggeration which tends to undermine rational judgment. It is no secret that several aspects of the underlying market characteristics are based on emotions.

One of the issues where opinions are divided is whether emotional trend tends to follow the price trend or vice versa. Was the massive rise in technology stocks in the 1990s, and their dramatic reversal, an emotional trend following a price trend; or did the market psychology push up technology stock prices in the first place? I have asked several experts about this, but did not get a consistent answer.

Fundamental, technical and quantitative criteria (see Chapter 7) used in obtaining a view of an equity's future price are so important because they work as proxy to traditional means of evaluating worth. Note that some of the criteria used in the past do not really mean much. An example of a relatively meaningless indicator of a company's assets is *book value*, based on the accruals method applied to its assets.

Book value means nothing unless the company is going to liquidate, and even then it is not sure it represents a real value of assets. Book value is largely based on past investments, laws governing depreciation and amortization, and some accounting conventions. All this means very little, except as a very approximate guide, because there certainly is no guarantee that:

- Next year will be like last year, or
- The assets carried at book value would be worth something a willing buyer would be ready to pay.

More significant than book value in terms of what a company is worth is its *debt equity ratio*. Entities with a high debt equity ratio are vulnerable to shocks that dry their cash flow or disturb the supply of bank capital. The higher the debt ratio, the more likely that any adversity will cause illiquidity, default and bankruptcy. Hong Kong's Peregrine Securities which folded in mid-January 1998 is an example. This criterion has two corollaries which start showing up in analysts' evaluation sheets:

- Debt per share, and
- Debt capital, in percent.

It is not the objective of this book to elaborate on the very negative contribution of high debt capital on the company's valuation, and its long term survival; this subject has been treated in another book in contrast to the well-known (but unstable) Modigiliani-Miller hypothesis.[6] Suffice to say that a high debt to equity ratio means senior management must be extremely careful to control exposure. The need for prudent debt to equity and cash flow management can be served by:

- Prudent policies avoiding high debt at all cost,
- A quantum leap in technology to track changes in assumed risk, and
- Rigorous mathematical analysis that surpasses competitors in keeping risk under lock and key.

Moreover, policies, procedures and tools regarding both technical and fundamental analysis, as described in preceding sections, must be in place to help in the search for facts behind figures. This is part of the investor's homework, and it is not devoid of subjective factors. As with all scientific work relating to analysis, an element of interpretation is necessary to understand figures and the pattern.[7] For instance, prices reflect what market participants believe. In the analysis of price movement, one tries to appreciate what the market is thinking. A good deal is contributed to understanding this by:

- References to past experience,
- Interpretation based on theories, and
- Intermediate conclusions produced by each practitioner's own viewpoint.

Experience helps, but as Confucius said some twenty-five centuries ago, experience is like a lantern each one of us carries on his back. As such, it illuminates the past rather than the future. This explains why analytical work does not always benefit from experience. And the reader should also note that in real life, things and conditions never behave exactly as we expect.

What has just been said does not diminish in any way the importance of fundamental and technical analysis. It just puts them in perspective. The real cost of analysis is the risk of inaccuracy because of:

- Deficient skills,
- Possible bias, and
- Insufficient data, and other reasons.

Skills can be improved through training. The problem is that it takes years to develop a skillful analyst, and current demand greatly exceeds supply. Bias may be personal, but most frequently behind this are the conflicting goals of the brokerage or investment bank. Conflicts of interest come from overlaps with mergers and acquisitions, underwriting, bridging loans and so on. Hence the call for independent research (see Chapter 12).

Data insufficiency is due to two problems. One is that, at least for some equities, the conents of both the analyst's database and public databases are weak. The other challenge is that greater accuracy, as well as discovery of hidden patterns, requires HFFD. Figure 6.4 presents an example on three levels of frequency in data collection, storage and retrieval. High frequency financial data, of course, needs data collection tick by tick.

Moreover, while performance pressures are increasingly forcing analysts, investors and portfolio managers to shorten their time frames, company fundamentals do not change frequently enough to satisfy this growing need for higher frequency data. Because the highest frequency data within the stock market are stock prices themselves, fundamental analysis has taken a back seat to technical analysis.

This is a changing trend in equity studies, as well as in money management, that has caused a shift in the emphasis of many investment variables. Minima and maxima of an equity's price can develop intraday, but be hidden from the traditional opening/closing price considerations. Yet such minima and maxima may be excellent indicators of future price of a commodity.

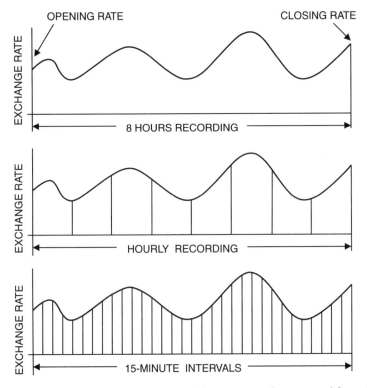

Figure 6.4 The amount of information provided by increasing frequency of financial data is striking, and requires high technology to reveal its secrets

6.7   Learning how to detect and analyze market trends

The discussion on fundamental and technical analysis has provided evidence that doing one's own homework is tantamount to being research oriented. But which type of research? As we have seen, some analysts, traders and investors put more emphasis on fundamentals; others are chartists, depending a great deal on technicals to appreciate underlying market trend.

While we are all subject to personal opinions and choices which condition our minds, the best approach is to tune the homework we do in a way that addresses benefits from all three main lines of equity research: fundamental, technical and quantitative (the latter is discussed in Chapter 7). When well done, a polyvalent approach would be better positioned to satisfy the *ninth golden rule*: 'Detect and analyze market trends before committing yourself to an investment.'

Contrarians may say that even a rigorous research effort can produce results which are in limbo: neither confirming nor rejecting a current or contemplated investment. The answer to this is that the state of a limbo is tantamount to rejection. A serious investor never allows him or herself to be pushed for time. It is far better to forgo what might have been a wonderful opportunity, than to jump blind on an investment bandwagon and lose a leg in the process.

A limbo may, for instance, result when fundamentals suggest that there is an imbalance in supply and demand, with the former outpacing the latter – while the technical analysis shows an uptrend. When this happens and the fundamentals are negative, the technical trend may be simply temporary, the result of factors such as the coverage of short positions, the aftermath of a stock split or of a buyback announcement.

Management quality and ethics are not necessarily taken into account in current equity analysis, which is wrong. The only exception to this statement that I know is rating by independent agencies, which consider quality of management.[8] Company rating is part of the new capital adequacy regulation known as Basel II. It is not yet one of the key variables of financial analysis, and this is a shortcoming. I strongly suggest that investors integrate company ratings into their homework, for two reasons:

- Equity holders are the first in line to lose their capital if the company goes bankrupt, and
- If a company has low rating, let alone being of non-investment level, it makes no sense to invest in it, no matter what fundamental and technical analysis may say.

Beyond this, doing one's proper homework also means considering the shortcomings of each method being used. For instance, the methodology of a fundamental analysis starts with the assumption that the price set by the market, for any commodity on any given day, is the correct price. Then, it tries to find out what changes are occurring that would alter that price. We have spoken of the absurdities connected to the efficient market theory and there is no point in returning to this issue.

It is also appropriate to note that the stock market has many short-term countertrends. After it has gone up, it always wants to come down. It is part of the job of a good trader and of a sound investor to examine his or her alternatives. One of the indicators that may be helpful is that a bull market:

- Would shrug off bearish news, and
- Respond vigorously to positive news.

In principle, a bear market would act precisely the other way around, which is a hypothesis that needs to be put to the test. Models and interactive experimental finance are the analysts', traders' and investors' partners in looking forward through technical analysis indicators, as well as for testing some of the hypotheses being made, and/or correlation of different variables. The other partner is scenarios.

Scenarios are mental pictures of what the market would be like. They are never final, since they are awaiting real-life confirmation. Invariably, most of these scenarios would turn out to be wrong. But a few elements of one of the scenarios uncovered or provoked by a thorough analysis may prove to be correct and become a reality. Financial analysis is not done to prove that one is 'right'. Its purpose is to provide:

- Insight, and
- Foresight.

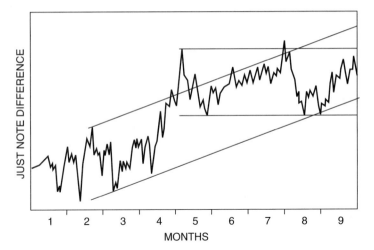

Figure 6.5 A lateral equity price movement within an uptrend is open to misinterpretations

Moreover a technical analysis may come up with contradictory trends. As can be seen in Figure 6.5, the equity under examination is characterized by an uptrend and a lateral movement. The latter has been created over a period of five months, and it indicates a resistance. Whether this resistance will be broken and the uptrend would prevail in the longer run, is a matter of personal (hence subjective) judgment.

- Objective analysts would most likely suggest a neutral approach to this equity.
- Others, however, may well have a different opinion, and find reasons to document it.

To help themselves to come up with an opinion which can stand the test of time, analysts may look into the equity's price/performance relative to that of the general stock market, the equity's recent price behavior in regard to its performance during a particular period in the past, and the volume of trading in this stock. For instance, a relative strength indicator reflects the percentage change in a commodity's price relative to a percentage change in a stock market index, like the S&P 500.

The foregoing examples are among those most frequently encountered in financial analysis. Readers will, however, appreciate that there is a great deal of hype attached to some claims that 'this' or 'that' method predicts the future. A similar statement is valid about a popular saying among traders; for instance that a down Friday is followed by a down Monday. It might happen, but also it might not. Another hype about trends is their continuity, which supposedly permits better documented projections.

Contrary to what several traders and investors tend to believe, economic activity, and certainly the markets as a system, are characterized by discontinuity rather than continuity. Linearity of behavior is still another oversimplification to which reference has been already made. Most frequently, market behavior is non-linear, and therefore simple analytical tools would not do.

- It is a fallacy to think that markets are supposed to make sense.
- In some cases they might, but this lasts only a very limited time.

Over a limited time frame it is possible to detect, even to document, that there is in a market something resembling an up or down wave. When this is found, sharp traders try to capitalize on it, leading to its extinction. Another example is offered by expert traders when they suggest that tight congestions are likely to lead to a breakout – but when exactly such a breakout occurs is something nobody really understands – everyone being mainly interested in good risk/reward deals.

Note also that in a variety of cases opinions are divided, which is good because this is essentially what makes the market. 'The market being in a trend is the main thing that eventually gets us in a trade', said one of the experts. But other experts do not believe that trading in a trend constitutes a fail-safe rule whose application provides good opportunity for profits.

By contrast, opinions are more convergent when it comes to learning from the aftermath of a trend. For instance, trading in a trend can be instrumental in teaching a trader how to let profits run while cutting losses short. Trend-following is a discipline of patience, because it obliges us to:

- Think thoroughly about a trade before putting it on, and
- Develop a plan for different contingencies as the trend evolves.

Therefore, market trends should not be looked at superficially. They must be properly examined and tested to the point of confessing their secrets. A good piece of advice is to stay in markets with major trends, but not to take a position unless one understands the reasons why the market should move, and whether moving in a specific direction is sustainable over a given time frame. All this may be beyond the average investor, but if this is the case then the investor should not be in the stock market.

6.8 The role of rocket scientists

It is likely that those analysts who perform best have a questioning mind and benefit from both a financial and a mathematical background. Since the mid-1980s, as the process of analysis got more complex, investment banks, brokers, commercial banks, but also central banks and other regulators, employ rocket scientists. Their skills are largely use in:

- New product development,
- Risk management, and
- Prognostication of market trends.

The term 'rocket scientist' comes from the fact that these are engineers, physicists and mathematicians who have worked in the past in aerospace, weapons systems and nuclear engineering. Their recycling in finance had as a goal to enrich the process of analysis with the experience of an engineer and a physicist, thereby providing cross-fertilization in different disciplines.

For instance, in their effort to keep risk under lock and key, risk managers seek the assistance of rocket scientists by capitalizing on their brains, their tools and their method. The scientist's method is that of using powerful metaphors describing thought as a process of traveling, and mapping it into models. The image pictures of man-the-thinker come from the greatest empire of all: the empire of the mind.[9]

People with scientific experience appreciate the idea of a road to be traveled which culminates in the *method*. To the scientist, and I am speaking from experience, theory is nothing but a technical product; and so is scientific truth. No matter what some people say, we cannot make even the simplest mathematical model of a real-life situation, unless we:

- Have previously made a small theory about it, and
- Set a course to discover the 'truth', or at least the elemental ideas underpinning it.

To a substantial extent, this explains some of the conceptual qualities a product planner, financial analyst or risk manager needs, beyond those which are traditionally considered to be 'analytical'. A rocket scientist is expected to know that his or her perception and conception should not fight the ambiguity embedded in analytics, or in risk control. Instead, they should use such analytics as raw material to:

- Develop and test alternative hypotheses about, say, assumed exposure, and
- Establish ways and means to keep the impact and extend of hypothesis being made within established limits.

To a significant extent, though by no means exclusively, rocket scientists work with models and computers. In this connection, they should definitely appreciate that the main objects of computing are foresight, insight, analysis and design. It is neither the automation of numerical calculation, nor the development of a better way for data processing.

Another important fallacy to be brought to the reader's attention is that, in the minds of many data processing people and many computer experts, the process is more important than the end result. This is not true of the process of analysis whose end result, which is insight, correlates very much with the twists of the process – the two feeding upon one another. Insight requires:

- Conceptualization and identification of crucial factors,
- Rigorous analytical processes,
- Perception of a framework of results, and
- The ability to make predictions at given level of confidence.

In any science, rigorous analysis must focus on both past data and current information – which are quantitative and qualitative – as well as the context of such information which impacts on its characteristics. Insight is not just looking at last year's, month's, week's or day's data to discover trends. The challenge is establishing:

- Which are the fine mechanics of an actionable business process, and
- How a scientific investigation can provide a greater degree of confidence in understanding these mechanics.

Common ground shared by equity studies and engineering studies is that – other things being equal – the older the process, machine or system under investigation, the fewer unknowns there will be. At the same time, however, expected benefits will also be more reduced than those that might be attained with investigations focusing on new instruments, systems or solutions.

There is a correspondence between the statement made in the preceding paragraph and the fact companies in stock exchanges which are mature and seasoned enjoy the security of a well-financed middle age. By contrast, the newer companies have less capital and less experience – but may also have brighter prospects as they are young and dynamic. Their downside is that they suffer from teething troubles.

Based on their research within this broader picture, rocket scientists come up with different viewpoints, which they must document. Some of the research results they provide may be conceptual. For instance as a January 2004 Merrill Lynch document brought to its readers' attention, the company's chief US strategists belief that:

- US earnings growth will decelerate,
- US bond yields will rise sharply, and
- The dollar will continue to weaken against the euro.[10]

Even if they look at the same market and its particulars, viewpoints by equities, fixed income and foreign exchange (forex) strategists, as well as by rocket scientists, may differ because they examine the situation under different perspectives. For instance, there is a difference in the viewpoints of equity analysts and debt analysts expressed by the way they look at ROE (see Chapter 7).

- Taking the shareholder's perspective, equity analysts concentrate on return, the 'R' part of the term.
- To protect bondholder interest, debt analysts concentrate on dependability of equity; hence the 'E' part.

Bondholder and shareholder interests are not necessarily convergent. Moreover, as we will see in Chapter 11, both investment opinions and investment promotions are not free of operational risk, and legal risk is part of daily life.[11]

6.9 Appendix: Microsoft's 2004 Huge Dividend

Management may reserve surprises which neither technical nor fundamental analysis can reveal. In the week of 19 July 2004, Microsoft decided to return some of its huge cash war chest of about $60 billion to shareholders. Investors will get a special dividend of $32 billion, to the tune of $3 per share. The software company also plans share buy-backs of $30 billion over the next four years, as well as a doubling of regular dividends to $3.5 billion.

Some $3.3 billion of the one-time windfall payment in December 2004 goes directly to Bill Gates, the firm's largest shareholder. Gates promptly pledged to give this entire amount to his charitable foundation – the largest in the world. Microsoft can afford this windfall decision, since it will leave the company with plenty of cash, while at the same time the company keeps on accumulating cash at the rate of $1 billion a month.

The dividend Microsoft is paying its shareholders is worth more than the entire market cap of all but the largest 71 companies in the S&P 500. In the average, this payment comes to roughly $300 for every US household, and it also poses to the Internal Revenue Service (IRS), a crucial question on tax treatment given the most recent American legislation for avoidance of double taxation of dividends.

As some experts at Wall Street see it, an interesting aftermath of Microsoft's shareholder-friendly decision, of its staggering cash flow, and of the fact that software is by now a settled business, is that these days Microsoft is much more like Ma Bell (the old, reliable AT&T) of the immediate post-World War II years, than the go-go firm which it used to be. Achieving the status of a most dependable enterprise is not at all bad for a company that has not even turned 30 yet, and that only declared its first dividend in January 2003.

Notes

1 D.N. Chorafas (2002). *Modelling the Survival of Financial and Industrial Enterprises: Advantages, Challenges, and Problems with the Internal Rating-Based (IRB) Method*. Palgrave/Macmillan.

2 D.N. Chorafas (2003). *Stress Testing: Risk Management Strategies for Extreme Events*. Euromoney.

3 D.N. Chorafas (2004). *Economic Capital Allocation with Basel II: Cost and Benefit Analysis*. Butterworth-Heinemann.

4 A. Hamerle, T. Liebig and H. Scheule (2004). *Forecasting Credit Portfolio Risk*. Deutsche Bundesbank, Discussion Paper 01/2004.

5 *Business Week*, 31 May 1999.

6 D.N. Chorafas (2004). *Economic Capital Allocation with Basel II: Cost and Benefit Analysis*. Butterworth-Heinemann.

7 D.N. Chorafas (2002). *Modelling the Survival of Financial and Industrial Enterprises: Advantages, Challenges, and Problems with the Internal Rating-Based (IRB) Method*. Palgrave/Macmillan.

8 D.N. Chorafas (2004). *Rating Management's Effectiveness with Case Studies in Telecommunications*. Macmillan/Palgrave.

9 D.N. Chorafas (2002). *Modelling the Survival of Financial and Industrial Enterprises: Advantages, Challenges, and Problems with the Internal Rating-Based (IRB) Method*. Palgrave/Macmillan.

10 Merrill Lynch (2004). *2004 – the Year Ahead*. Merrill Lynch, January.

11 D.N. Chorafas (2004). *Operational Risk Control with Basel II: Basic Principles and Capital Requirements*. Butterworth-Heinemann.

7 Quantitative criteria for equity performance

7.1 Introduction

Practically every financial analyst worth his or her salt has developed one or more of his or her own metrics to judge the health of a company, or of an industry sector, and its prospects. But there are as well common standards, such as *price to earnings* ratio, which help in differentiating among companies through what has become by now traditional measurements investors can understand (see section 7.6).

A reason why 'times earnings' is held in esteem is that in it is reflected the effect of a number of factors which have an impact on the price of stocks. As a criterion P/E is elastic, and it can also be quite imprecise as the 'right' multiplier of P/E changes over time. In the 1950s, my professors at UCLA taught their students that a P/E ratio of 8 to 10 is pretty good, while 12 to 14 is rather high. Today, a typical P/E ratio of the S&P 500 (see Chapter 4) is 18 – and many growth stocks trade at high multiples, like 60x (times) earnings or 80x earnings.

- When this high gear occurs, it indicates that the market loses track of reality in regard to an equity's worth.
- By changing an equity's growth rate estimate, analysts and traders seem to justify almost any P/E multiple with a 'Wow!'

On 10 March 2004, four years after the technology bubble's peak, NASDAQ was at a prospective P/E above its trough in 2002. Notice that a prospective profit is not necessarily a sustainable profit, and taxes play a major role in what the prospective profit will be. Some experts suggest that without the Bush tax cuts, earnings of US companies in 2003 would have been 30 percent lower, with an evident after-effect on equity prices.

High P/E ratios embed risks for the investor. Inversely, a common mistake made by many investors is to buy a stock only because its P/E looks cheap. There is often a good reason why the P/E multiplier is a low one-digit number. It is utter nonsense to think a stock is undervalued because it sells at a low multiple. A sound policy with both high and low multiples is to:

- Examine the company's peers, and
- Query what makes that firm so much more (or less) valuable than its industry's average.

For instance, an 18x price to earnings tells what kind of multiple the market attaches to an entity's twelve-month forward earnings. At the same time, the multiplier of P/E indicates how much more (or less) expensive this equity is than its peers. A high

P/E ratio gives a message of investor preference. At book value, the P/E ratio often stands as low as 2x to 3x.

For an industry, the prevailing P/E ratio among companies in its sector indicates how much more this industry as a whole, for instance motors or media is attractive to investors. In the late 1990s, equity in companies in technology, media and tele-communications (TMT) had very high P/E ratios because they were in great demand by investors. When the bubble burst, these P/E ratios crashed (more on this in section 7.6).

Another popular measurement, which is also an input to the P/E ratio, is *earning per share* (see section 7.4). Its calculation takes into account net profit and net operating profit both real and diluted, as well as weighted average shares outstanding, and diluted impact, to produce:

- Basic earnings per share,
- Basic earnings per share, operating,
- Diluted earnings per share, and
- Diluted earnings per share, operating.

Earnings per share are usually estimated for the next three years, and are sometimes accompanied by an estimate of five-year EPS growth. A good measure of EPS is that provided before goodwill and adjustments for significant financial events.

Still another popular metric is the *yield*, which takes the latest twelve-months' dividends per share as a percentage of a given closing price of the equity listed in an exchange. Since the board does, or at least should, declare dividends on the basis of profits, profits and yield correlate. It needs no explaining that *profits* is an important indicator reflecting the after-tax earnings available to common shareholders. Declared profits should come from the company's continuing operations before extraordinary or special items. Earnings and profits from abroad need to be translated at prevailing currency rates, and this involves foreign exchange risk.

Profits come from revenue from sales after subtraction of all costs. *Net sales* reported by a company, also translated at prevailing exchange rates, are an important metric. This is particularly true in manufacturing and merchandising, while revenue for banks and other financial institutions are not comparable to those of industrial companies. A metric used by some banks, and reported in their annual statement, is *net new money*, particularly in connection with private client units.

In their annual statements, cost-conscious companies emphasize the *cost to income ratio*. This is reported at two levels: net basis, and before goodwill and adjustment for significant events. Very important, as well, is the *cash flow to share* (CF/S) – before and after write-offs and funny money credits, like deferred tax assets (DTAs). The reader will also recall two quantitative criteria presented in Chapter 6:

- Debt capital, in percent, and
- Debt per share.

An important family of ratios, used in connection to investment decisions, concen-trates on *return*. This includes *return on equity* and *return on capital*. We will discuss return on equity in section 7.7, as well as in Chapter 13 in relation to business risk.

Some companies report both a net ROE, and one before goodwill and adjustments for significant financial events.

Typically, in the ROE algorithm, return concerns the latest twelve-months' earnings per share as percentage of most recent book value per share. Other important return ratios are *return on investment* and *risk adjusted return on capital* (RAROC). One of the interesting metrics is Tobin's Q-ratio, which the reader will find in the appendix to this chapter.

In spite of the fact Chapter 6 made the statement that book value is practically irrelevant in judging the value of an enterprise, the reader should note that the more traditional ratios are based on book value. An example other than ROE is the *price to book value ratio*, which considers closing price at the end of a given period to the latest available net worth per share or common shareholders' equity.

All told, however, in modern managerial accounting and, increasingly so, in general accounting, the *value of assets* is a better indicator than book value. Note that market value may include more than one class of the entity's stock traded on an exchange, while price and yield data is usually based on the company's most widely held issue which is the common stock.

Moreover, both *share price* and annual (monthly, weekly, daily) *change* in share price are important. The same is true of *capitalization*, or market value equal to share price on a given date multiplied by latest available number of shares outstanding. Capitalization can be used as a proxy to asset value, since it represents what investors are willing to pay for the company. Section 7.3 addresses the subject of treating equity as an option.

7.2   An equity's valuation and need for stress tests

Most of the metrics outlined in section 7.1 are in place to address an issue at the heart of every analyst, trader and investor: what is the value of the company under study (see also section 6.6). If book value is not a relevant figure, then what other *quantitative metrics*, or at least reliable indicators, can or should be used?

A sound way of looking at financial assets, as well as at physical assets which are examined in financial terms, is to value them according to the discounted *present value* of future cash flow that investors expect to derive from holding the asset. This discounted rate applied to future cash flows is known as *intrinsic value*, and it represents the expected rate of return investors demand for the asset in their portfolio, or for an asset they are contemplating to buy.

Applied to the valuation of equities quoted in an exchange, the discounted cash flow method corresponds to the dividend discount model. If stock prices are efficient, then they will equal the discounted present value of rationally expected future dividends. The big question is, *if.* One way to get around this *if* is to break down the discounted rate into a measure of *opportunity costs*, which means:

■ Returns expected on investing in assets other than stocks, and
■ A corresponding equity-specific risk premium the investor would demand for the exposure he or she is assuming.

If investors did not care about differences in risk between the various assets – and this is another big if which has little to do with reality, except for those investors who are worth their salt – then all assets could be expected, in equilibrium, to earn the same rate of return. In this particular case, the discount rate for equities would equal the uniform rate of interest.

However, rationally thinking investors who care about the risks they are assuming, demand higher rates of return for holding riskier assets. The difference between the expected rates of return on a *riskier* and a *safer* asset thus constitutes a *risk premium.* Risk premiums should reflect both:

- Investors' risk preferences, and
- Perceived risk properties of asset returns.

As stocks tend to be riskier than, say, G-10 government bonds, it is only reasonable that investors demand a correspondingly higher expected rate of return for holding equities. The equity risk premium, empirically approximated by the long-term average of the margins by which observed returns on stocks exceeded those on risk-free (G-10 government) bonds, is generally found to be positive.

This is, however, an average figure, and average figures do not signify much. Investors who know how to exercise risk control in regard to their portfolio positions, demand a higher return commensurate with risk being assumed (see Chapter 10). Those who do not know this include no risk margin when choosing their equities and eventually find out the hard way that stock prices do not only rise.

In fact, as shown in Figure 7.1, for a portfolio invested in different markets, not one but three dimensions are important for valuation of an equity and its impact on portfolio risk and return. Section 7.1 explained the reason why foreign exchange risk is important to a company operating in home and foreign (host) countries, and we will discuss the impact of interest rates on equity prices later.

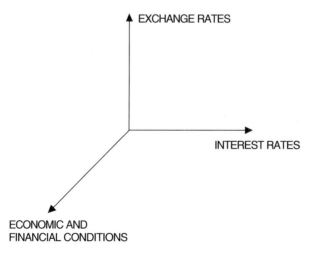

Figure 7.1 Valuation procedures for equities must consider a three-dimensional space

Moreover, astute investors should bear in mind that the pricing of any commodity assures normal markets, not nervous markets and even less so worst cases. Because, however, worst cases do happen, stress tests are necessary to tell how bad things can get in terms of assumed risk. Based on this premise, a sound equities pricing procedure should rest on:

- Normal market valuation, and
- Worst case test as a benchmark.[1]

The normal market valuation methodology should reflect, and be documented by, the premise that a share's price will be determined by its fundamental and technical analysis factors presented in Chapter 6, as well as the quantitative metrics discussed in this chapter. While in the short term all these metrics have their deficiencies, they are particularly important in the longer term. Apart from this, the model's own approximations in the short-term markets are often driven by psychological factors.

- Positive or negative swings on a stock market disconnect the share price from the real value of the company.
- Such distortions represent risks, but also create opportunities for an investor or, more precisely, for a trader.

Apart from the model's approximations and the psychological facts, there is also the problem that, quite often, the advice that investment advisers and other experts give is so general as to be nearly worthless. An example is the advice of 'acquiring first-class quality at low prices and selling as soon as the market has recognized the value potential'; that is, buy at low prices and sell at high prices. A more meaningful advice for an investor is that of doing his or her homework prior to making a commitment, and exercising steady vigilance. The implementation of such an approach requires:

- Careful investment procedures,
- Disciplined equity analysis,
- Expertise in every aspect of corporate valuation, and
- Focused risk management.

The worst case valuation is integral part of the risk management procedure. It helps in knowing one's strengths and weaknesses. As Sun Tzu, the great Chinese general said twenty-five centuries ago: 'If you know yourself and know your opponents, you don't have to be worried of the outcome of 100 battles.'[2]

Sophisticated analysts and investors use cash flows rather than EPS (briefly explained in section 7.1); base their valuation on market prices, assumed debt and its servicing, computation of cash flows, and weighted average cost of capital; and look at the entity's quality of management, including management decisions, product planning, market thrust, cost control and capital budget efficiency.

There are limitations and caveats associated with the use of every method – both the modern ones discussed in this section and in section 7.3, and the older ones briefly outlined section 7.1 and further detailed in sections 7.4 to 7.7. In a way it is more challenging, and may eventually prove more accurate, to capitalize on the best features of both approaches.

- Valuing a firm by using discounted cash flow models,
- Arriving at the value of this firm through a proxy of its assets,
- Making peer-to-peer tests with comparable firms, and using valuation done by a third party such rating agencies.

Some of the challenges relating to this approach have to do with the proper definition of the notion of what is and is not *comparable*. What makes companies comparable to one another? How do we adjust for differences in growth, risk and cash flow across entities when estimating multiples? What kind of special difficulties are associated with comparisons across time and across markets?

One way to answer these questions is through stress testing, using adverse conditions which can be simulated on the basis of historical information, and by means of assumptions. As shown in Table 7.1, such conditions should address all items in the balance sheet and in the income statement (P&L).

It is only reasonable that different industry sectors have different stress testing requirements, because the type of their exposure is by no means the same. For instance,

Balance sheet	Income statement	Ratios
Assets and liabilities	Revenue, sales	Sales/invested capital (S/IC) Price/book value (P/BV)
Shareholders' equity	Net profit Earnings per share (EPS)	Price/earnings (P/E) EPS growth Return on equity (ROE) Return on assets (ROA)
Invested capital	Net operating profit after taxes (NOPAT)	Return on invested capital (ROIC) Risk-adjusted return on capital (RAROC)
Pro forma[1]	EBIT[2] EBITDA[2]	Value/EBIT Value/EBITDA

Notes:

1 Technology companies and startups like very much pro forma reporting, because they beef-up their financial image. However, such reporting is not regulated and it can mislead investors.

2 Earnings before interest and taxes (EBIT); earnings before interest, taxes, depreciation and amortization (EBITDA, see section 7.4). Both are pro forma, neither is part of Generally Accepted Accounting Principles (GAAP) (see section 7.5).

Table 7.1 Basic valuation metrics with equities

banks and leveraged manufacturing, merchandising or service companies with floating rate loans are highly exposed to interest rate risk.

■ For this type of entity, inventoried in the portfolio, the test should be ±100, ±200, ±300, ±400 basis points – with the stress test made at ±400 basis points stress test.
■ For all inventoried *equities*, a good test is, by equity, a price change of ±5 percent, ±10 percent, ±20 percent and ±30 percent – with the stress test at ±30%.
■ For inventoried derivatives, the normal exposure is computed through a demodulation of notional principal amount[3] by 25, with tests done through demodulators by 20, 15, 10 – and 5 as the stress test.

Demodulation by 5 means that 20 percent of inventoried derivatives positions face significant risk, and this provides evidence of irreducible waste. This amount of exposure will hit the company in an adverse market environment, all the way to bankruptcy.

Interactive computational finance helps in obtaining exposure estimates on normal markets and under stress condition, both at the end of a period and through intermediate values. While normal tests can be revealing, lack of stress testing can, most charitably, be interpreted as a mistake. In reality, however, it is a deep miscalculation which identifies ineffective management, absence of risk control and a company exposed to the worse perils.

7.3   Equity as an option and dividend discount model

Some years ago, New York's Loan Pricing Corporation (LPC) accumulated a ratings transition and default database of around 20 000 performing loans and 1400 defaulted loans. This database included proprietary information from some thirty banks, as well as public information. Among the important factors in the LPC data collection have been borrower data such as:

■ Geographic location,
■ Industry sector,
■ Financial profile, and
■ The loan's characteristics and purpose.

Also in the data collection is where relevant information on causative factors determining the amount recovered after default can be found. Among other services which have been provided by this database is that it has helped to confirm some long-accepted concepts, like the positive relationship between the likelihood of default and a decrease in the ratio of a company's total equity value to its total debt. This relationship was first suggested in 1974 by Dr Robert Merton.

■ Merton's hypothesis considers *equity* to be *a call option* on the value of a company's business.

- The background concept is based on the premise that a company defaults when its equity value drops below its obligations.

Simulation based on Merton's approach capitalizes on the information embedded in the equity' market price taken as proxy on its assets. This provides a good enough picture of credit risk, which can be combined with an estimate of the market value's volatility, leading to a default probability. Such approach is instrumental in giving an insight into a company's creditworthiness, and it has been effectively used by Moody's KMV model for credit analysis.[4]

Critics say that while Merton's hypothesis is innovative, it also presents problems, some of which come from the fact that it rests on equity market valuations. This argument forgets that debt markets are just too thin to be a good source of information, while the equity markets are continuous. Moreover, that sort of criticism might have had a basis prior to the new capital adequacy framework (Basel II) by the Basel Committee on Banking Supervision. Today, it does not because the IRB risk method requires:

- Rich databases focused on markets, and
- Plenty of information on defaults and bankruptcies.

Other critics say that, because it is based on asset values, Merton's model leads to high correlations among exposures with the aftermath of requiring much more in terms of capital for unexpected losses (ULs). By contrast, default-based models lead to low correlations. This argument forgets that any statistical test must be based on significant samples – and default data does not fulfill this requirement.

What are our alternatives? The two main models available today for credit risk analysis, which help as prognosticators of default, are Merton's and the RAROC. They are based on different premises, but both are helpful. Therefore, a well-managed institution would want to put them in competition and, over a period of time, compare the result given by each against real-life data. Fundamentally, Merton's method starts with the observation that the payoff to capital comprises three components:

- A risk-free position,
- A long call, and
- A short put.

The put position corresponds with an insurance policy guaranteeing a risk-free return. Its option premium represents the risk cost chargeable to the entire entity. Merton and his colleagues have shown that we can approximate the Black-Scholes cost of such an annual insurance policy with the formula:

$$PR = 0.4\sigma \qquad (7.1)$$

Where PR standard for *premium* and σ is the standard deviation in overall net asset value. An incremental change in one activity results in variation in the premium, the formula being:

$$\frac{\theta\mathrm{PR}}{\theta\alpha} = 0.4\beta\sigma \tag{7.2}$$

where $\theta\mathrm{PR}/\theta\alpha$ is the partial derivative of the premium, α represents the asset volatility of the activity and β the volatility with respect to the institution's portfolio (more on this later). Like the Modigliani-Miller hypothesis on equity and debt, this approach quantifies cost and value without specifying a capital allocation or solvency goal.

Miller's hypothesis is a way of measuring risk-adjusted profits, using the above formulas in determining risk costs. The downside of this approach is that it says nothing about returns and spreads. It starts with asset values, which already embody returns; therefore, required returns are an input not an output. In spite of this shortcoming, Miller's method of treating equity as a call option is recommended because it:

- Has a good potential,
- Can provide commendable results as a predictor, and
- Helps to get away from EPS, P/E and other quantitative factors outlined in section 7.1, which have increasingly become subject to manipulation.

That said, it is no less true that, because the Miller hypothesis uses market value of an equity as its pivot point, a rigorous analysis should also test whether market price properly reflect the value of that equity, or whether such price is riding a wave. This can be effectively done through a dividend discount model (see also the reference to this in section 7.2).

Under the *dividend discount model* for evaluating equities, the value of shares is calculated by discounting the future cash flows to investors by bond yields, *plus* a risk premium associated with the greater exposure taken with equities. As bond yields fall, the present value of such cash flows rises and so does the present value of shares.

The rationale behind the approach followed by the dividend discount model rests on the fact that investors have to do something with their money and they face a practical choice between buying bonds or equities. As bond yields fall, fixed rate instruments become less attractive, prompting investors to buy shares. The opposite is true as bond yields rise. This relationship is nicely reflected in Figures 7.2 and 7.3 which represent the scatter diagrams of ten-year Treasuries versus twelve-month forward P/E ratios.

Another approach is that of *risk-based pricing* of equities, comparing them to credit risk-free Treasuries. As an example, some analysts and investors are gauging the cost of a given equity by comparing its extra riskiness with a practically riskless investment, such as the aforementioned US Treasury bonds. This extra riskiness is captured through the equity risk premium known as the *beta* of an individual share.

Other things being equal, risk-based pricing sees to it that an equity that offers higher returns than the risks' investors are willing to take is cheaper, while one with lower risks but higher returns is expensive. This is consistent with defining cost of equity as risk-free rate, plus the share's beta multiplied by the projected equity risk premium.

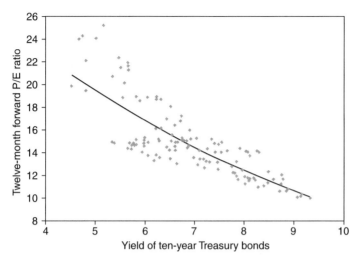

Figure 7.2 Ten-Year Treasury bond yields versus twelve-month forward P/E ratios
(*Source*: Prudential Securities. Reproduced with permission)

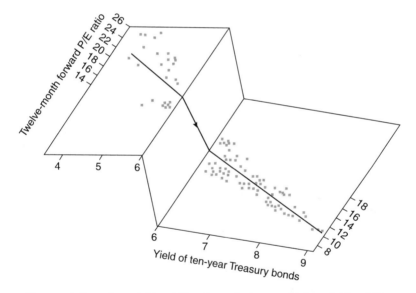

Figure 7.3 From low yield stability through chaos to higher yield stability
(*Source*: Prudential Securities. Reproduced with permission)

The Capital Asset Pricing Model (CAPM) works along these lines. The problem, however, is that CAPM and similar artifacts are static. They also mainly account for past performance, hence they look backwards. Critics add that they also do not properly take into account market volatility. By contrast, a sound risk-based pricing approach must be dynamic, with volatility being part of the equation.

There exists as well another equity valuation model based on the earnings yield/bond yield relationship. This is known as the 'Fed model' because it was developed by economists from the Federal Reserve. This particular model tracks a timing signal; when earnings yields rise sharply above bond yields, that proves a good time to buy shares. But as the markets showed in 2002 when US interest rates were at a forty-five year low, the stock market also has other criteria not reflected in the Fed model.

The reader will note that models are never perfect. By being based on hypotheses, they are only as good as the assumptions being made and the algorithms being used. Models are not supposed to be foolproof, but tying equity prices to bonds is an assumption fairly widespread in the market, though it has been attacked by some economists. Contrarians point out that bond yields have two components:

- A return that investors require to compensate them for expected inflation, and
- A real yield which goes beyond compensation for loss of value of the money.

If real bond yields fall, this is presumably because of a fall in demand for capital, due most likely to lower economic growth expectations, which is bad news for equities. At the same time, the increase in inflation is bad for the equity, and in the bond market it is not always compensated for by the expected inflation component. All these observations provide a sound ground for investment decisions, and they should be reflected in the making of a model.

7.4   Earnings per share and creative accounting solutions

Earnings per share traditionally has been used as metrics for stock valuation. More recent value-added metrics are *EPS change* (year-to-year), *estimated five-year EPS growth* and *consensus EPS*. Earnings per share and its improvements are calculated not only on an annual basis but also quarterly, based on the company's financial reporting, or at shorter intervals as relevant information becomes available.

Because growth companies typically pay no dividends, two other metrics – *dividend rate* and *dividend yield* – are not important to them, though they are used with old economy companies. Since the majority of entities have a cash flow, two metrics applicable in this connection are:

- Cash flow to share (CF/S), and
- Price to cash flow (P/CF).[5]

Note that these two metrics are complementary. Their product gives the price per share. As an example, Microsoft's CF/S was $1.90 in 2000, $2.20 in 2001 and $2.38 in 2002. Microsoft's P/CF was 31.3x in 2000, with an average of 27.1x in 2001 and 25.0x in 2002.

As investor information, CF/S and P/CF go beyond the traditional earnings per share ratio which is often manipulated, particularly when financial information is not as transparent as it should be (see Chapter 8). Still, EPS is a relevant metric because quite often analysts look at the price of a stock as 10x, 20x or 30x the earnings per share. In an effort to take the hype out of EPS, the FASB and International Accounting Standards Board (IASB) have issued new standards for computing EPS. These new rules primarily deal with the earnings estimates used in calculating EPS, since in the denominator is the number of shares, while the amount of earnings is often subject to massaging.

Under Financial Accounting Standards (FAS) 128, the US computation of earnings per share becomes simpler and fairly comparable to the international framework for EPS, by the IASB. This is a welcome convergence, but FAS 128 still requires two EPS statistics and the spread between these two figures could be wide: FAS 128 substitutes basic earnings per share (BEPS) for primary earnings per share (PEPS)

Basic earnings per share is net income available to common shareholders divided by the weighted average number of common shares outstanding. The other statistic is fully diluted earnings per share (FDEPS), which will generally be the same or higher than that currently calculated and referred to as diluted earnings per share (DEPS). Diluted earnings per share tends to be higher than FDEPS when stock prices rise at the end of period, and it will continue to be calculated by:

- The *if converted* method for convertible securities, and
- The Treasury stock method for options and warrants.

Note that the specifics of the calculation diverge between the standards promoted by the FASB and the IASB. Theoretically, it should not have been difficult to have a global standard valid for all companies no matter which are their home and host countries. In practice, this is not easy because standards are established by different bodies like the FASB in the USA, the Accounting Standards Board (ASB) in the UK and the IASB.

Accounting standards are not written in the abstract. They start as discussion papers, and are influenced by the companies participating in their setting. As a result, they have locality, and follow certain traditions. Also contributing to a divergence of opinions, and therefore of standards, is the fact that there exists more than one approach to the calculation of a company's profits. Here are a few examples:

- *Ordinary profit* is the operating profit, computed as: operating profit = operating incomes – operating expenses.
- *Current profit* is the net income, calculated through the algorithm: net income = operating profits + (extraordinary profits – extraordinary losses) – income taxes.
- *Profit from operations*, whose computation is based on the calculation: profit from operations = net income + (fees and commissions income – fees and commission expenses) + (other operating income – other operating expenses) + (interest income – interest expenses).
- *Earnings before interest, taxes, depreciation and amortization* (EBITDA), a pro forma reporting method dating back to the 1990s.

Apart from being the nearest thing to creative accounting, which is bad enough, the downside of EBITDA used as an investment criterion is that: the stocks of companies likely to beat expectations rise fast; rising earnings estimates which have lost touch with reality lure more buyers, and the equity zooms even more. In turn,

- Rising stock prices attract fund managers who do not want to be left behind, and
- Dazzling products that might 'change the world' make stocks seem priceless, leading to even more price leverage.

The net result of using different metrics which provide incompatible earnings estimates is confused investors. While the measurements presented by the different versions of ordinary, current and operations profits have a basis reflected in established accounting practice, and have been integrated into the FASB-regulated GAAP, this is not the case with EBITDA.

One of key problems with the 'before' and 'except' twists in accounting and in financial reporting is that they have no limits. If interest and taxes are exempt from reported profits, then why not depreciation; if depreciation, why not amortization; and in the final analysis why not all costs. In this way, companies can make their income equal to their revenue, even if they are swimming in a sea of red ink.

7.5   Earnings before interest, taxes, depreciation, and amortization

Section 7.2 has already brought to the reader's attention the fact that EBITDA does not answer GAAP's regulatory requirements for financial reporting. Section 7.4 has added to this the fact that elastic pro forma reports serve to misguide investors, and lead to poor decisions concerning their wealth. Serious investors should always remember that:

- Pro forma and 'earnings excluding certain charges', like EBIT and EBITDA, are not made to provide an honest accounting view of a company's financial results.
- If pro forma and EBITDA were rigorous earnings statements, then they should not have been so different from regulatory earnings standards.
- Since pro formas are usually massaged at the reporting company's discretion to sugar-coat the results, they mislead investors and harm market confidence.

Here is what Warren Buffett has to say about EBITDA: 'We do *not* think so-called EBITDA is a meaningful measure of performance. Managements that dismiss the importance of depreciation – and emphasize 'cash flow' or EBITDA – are apt to make faulty decisions, and you should keep that in mind as you make your own investment decisions.'[6]

While in early 2001 a growing number of companies have been forced by real-life events to announce negative profit figures for 2001, some thought it wiser to cover the extent of their financial problems by putting a great deal of emphasis on pro forma financial announcements, with EBITDA the most prominent among them. A company can prove nearly everything through pro forma. Money-losing entities can demonstrate that once all these costs are subtracted, including all the costs for takeovers and debt service, they actually make good profits. AOL Time Warner:

- Came up with a first quarter 2001 EBITDA of $2.1 billion, but
- Under regulatory reporting standards, the firm actually lost $1.4 billion.

If this trend of misinforming the investor is allowed to continue, it is not inconceivable companies will eventually invent the 'earnings only reporting concept', before not only the damage assessment but also before labor costs, material costs, money cost with derivatives, and all other costs and risks the company has assumed. With this, every single entity in the world will always prove to be profitable!

Transparency is at its lowest with EBITDA and this has important consequences. One of the key reasons for Vodafone's long decline in 2001 has been the loss of market confidence in pro forma reporting. Vodafone was reporting a 'terrific' EBITDA but its cash flow was meager. Indeed, for a communications company, average revenue per user (ARPU) is more significant as a benchmark, with cash flow acting as proxy.

- In the case of Vodafone, in 2001 ARPU has been declining, and
- A declining ARPU is a very bad sign for a cash-hungry communications firm, where a healthy stream of cash is king.

As the AOL Time Warner, Vodafone and plenty of other examples demonstrate, pro formas are types of statement promoting what management wants others to hear about the company's self-valuation. From this can come a range of massaged P/E, and disfunctional value estimates. When dealing with numbers which are 'cooked' to sales multiples – revenue/sales, price/sales and so on – because some of the numbers may be massaged, it is always prudent to test the relationship between multiples and discounted cash flows. (More on multiples in section 7.6.)

There are reasons for being on the alert. When in July 2002 the news about World-Com's $3.8 billion fraud hit the market – a fraud which eventually grew to $12 billion – few people truly remembered that this company and its top financial officials were pioneers of pro forma, which soon became a controversial method of financial presentation – even if it was hailed during the takeover boom of the 1990s as a sort of financial messiah. Pro forma accounting involved stripping all post-merger charges and other one-time expenses, out of the company's results.

- The goal of this creative accounting practice has been to show what was claimed to be a 'clearer picture' of the firm's underlying performance.
- As financial accounting gimmicks, this and similar practices in pro forma reporting are, invariably, manipulations intended to show 'steady improvement' in earnings.

In their heydays, WorldCom, Enron and many other companies, several of them by now defunct, profited handsomely from the lack of transparency which came with pro forma reporting. But by depriving investors and analysts of financial detail, pro forma left them dependent on the company's own interpretation of its financial results, which very often proved to be one-sided, biased and misleading.

This does not mean that pro forma practices did not become popular. Curiously enough, for several years nobody truly objected to pro forma as long as the usual suspect companies' stocks continued to rise. These were the 'Wow!' firms enjoying a strong following among analysts, and this shaped financial markets' opinion. But:

- After the easier tricks became widespread,
- Holding the higher ground meant bolder misrepresentation of financial data, all the way to bankruptcy.

The unreliability of a cooked-up EBITDA has been demonstrated on many occasions. A case in point is KPNQwest. In 2001, Jack McMaster, its chief executive, proudly told *Communications Week International* that his company was EBITDA-positive[7] – one of the first of the pan-European new carriers to be able to say that it looked as though the firm was starting to generate enough cash to fund its operations. A year later, in May 2002, the crash of KPNQwest raised serious doubts over whether EBITDA is of any use at all in measuring:

■ The financial performance of businesses, and
■ Their financial staying power and creditworthiness.

A further irony is that by relying on EBITDA firms are effectively reducing *their own* chances of survival, because the sheer weight of decision and moves made in supporting supposedly high earnings outruns the company's ability to turn up the corresponding volume of cash. Also, pro forma reporting masks the facts about financial solvency. All too often, investors have to wait until companies go into administration to find out the truth about:

■ The extent of their liabilities, and
■ The liabilities' excess over assets.

The transition from lack of transparency, and one-sided financial reporting, to outright swindle did not happen overnight. It transited through the earnings before interest, and taxes (EBIT) and went all the way EBITDAO, the 'O' standing for fat and unreasonable executive options. Indeed, it is surprising that otherwise intelligent people at the helm did not appreciate that 'earnings before something' is a totally inadequate guide because:

■ It does not give an indication of how much profit is actually turned into cash, or is tied up in receivables,
■ Nor does it tell how much money banks and capital markets are willing to lend to the firm, and under which conditions.

Yet, for evident reasons, not only startups but also many established companies are enthusiastic users of EBITDA. It gives an enhanced picture of their performance, thereby allowing them to be 'transparent' in their own terms, which often are quite remote from financial reality.

'We are transparent enough that market and analysts can make their calculations the way they want to', said the chief financial officer of Vivendi, which even based its bonus schemes for top management on EBITDA.[8] This unrealistic (if not outright surrealistic) reporting explains why Jean-Marie Messier, Vivendi's ousted CEO, received in 2001 impressive pay (for a French company) of 5.12 million euros ($5.12 million) despite the fact that Vivendi announced France's biggest-ever corporate loss of 13.6 billion euros ($13.6 billion).

'Do you really have to be so tough on EBITDA?' asked one of the reviewers. Allow me to answer this question by means of an allegory. On 17 October 1917, violinist Jascha Heifetz – then only sixteen years old – played for the first time in the New York

Carnegie Hall. In the audience were violinist Misha Elman and the pianist Leopold Godowsky. During the break Elman wiped the perspiration off his forehead and commented to his neighbor: 'I don't know – it is insupportably hot here today.' To which Godowsky responded with a smile: 'Not for pianists!' Thus, EBITDA is a poisonous gift for investors; not for others.

7.6 Price to earnings ratio and its challenges

It has been briefly stated in section 7.1 that the P/E ratio compares a company's share price with its latest earnings per share. What this ratio basically shows is how many years it would take for earnings to match the share price. Typically, if P/E is high, investors expect profits to rise. Differences in accounting rules, however, make comparisons of P/Es on a global scale quite difficult.

The reader will remember the comment made in section 7.1 that P/E ratios vary considerably by company, market and market psychology – as well as, that at liquidation at book value the P/E ratio may be between 2 and 3. Everything above that can be seen as the premium paid by investors for a going concern.

- In the 1950s, a P/E ratio of 12x was considered to be pretty good, the average being about 8x.
- When in the 1960s IBM was the high-flying company, its P/E ratio varied between 30x and 60x.[9]
- In July 1998, AOL has been selling for more than 200x expected twelve-month forward earnings – a failure for which investors have paid dearly.

These are among the reasons why contrarians say that the P/E ratio is flawed. Another fact is that during the 1950s, when the economy was relatively functional, most of the reported earnings were real, derived from productive output in manufacturing, mining, construction and agriculture. During the 1960s, stocks had a higher P/E ratio, partly because of speculation.

Still in spite of equity speculation which had started to come into equity pricing in different G-10 stock markets, in the 1970s and 1980s the P/E ratio averaged something above 12x. In fact, some experts suggested at the time that if P/E gets much above 18x, there is no way that the earnings stream of the company can support such a high price. All this was forgotten in the 1990s.

Some experts say that using a numerical multiplier of P/E, in a straightforward way, is simplistic. In 1934, Benjamin Graham and David Dodd suggested (in their book *Security Analysis*) that investors use a ten-year moving average of profits. This smooths out business cycles. On the other hand, it is quite likely that the ten years include a major market downturn like that of 1987 and 2000–02.

Of course, a company may boost its earnings by creative accounting, downsizing, selling off divisions, playing the derivatives markets and other gimmicks, as some of the bigger companies and practically all of the startups do. Add to this the nearly meaningless (in terms of longer-term stability and solvency) EBITDA, and you see why the critics of P/E ratios, as an investment measure, have a point. What is particularly weakened is the notion behind the multiplier 'x', and the range within which it should vary.

A good way of looking at this 'x' factor is that market P/E is equal to the inverse of a proxy for the pure time value of money. In theory, at least, this constitutes a reasonable limit for a sustainable P/E. When equity markets improve some experts suggest that the range for the maximum sustainable forward P/E is 25x to 29x *next* twelve-months expected earnings. But for any practical purpose, there is nothing really that limits P/Es, and therefore there is no obvious limit for the P/E of a particular stock. It all depends on:

- Expected earnings growth,
- Expected assumed risk, and
- Amount of prevailing speculation.

During the late 1990s some Internet stocks sold at what seemed to be infinite P/Es, because of a lack of earnings likely anytime soon by the companies whose stock was characterized by these infinite ratios. In fact, two analysts argued in the *Wall Street Journal* that P/Es could be 100x and that the Dow should be at 36 000. The first part of this argument saw the light (happily), but not the second.

- In 1990 the Tokyo Stock Exchange index reached this landmark 36 000.
- Then, it fell to the 9000–12 000 range and stayed there for thirteen years.

The fact that in the new economy TMT and Internet companies were in high demand in the capital markets, even if they had no earnings, indicates that something was wrong with their valuation. Some people said the market had radically changed and therefore the old, traditional metrics should be up for a revision. Indeed, in terms of capital market valuation and performance, at least some of the emphasis has been shifting to the ratio of upgrades and downgrades. As investors vote with their money and their preferences for certain equities over others, upgrades and downgrades by independent rating agencies show the direction of credit risk. Along a similar line, this time connected to earnings, an interesting metric is the earnings revision ratio (ERR).

- Small positive values of ERR, between 1.01 and 1.05, are implying marginally more upgrades than downgrades.
- A switch to positive ERR value is significant because it comes in the aftermath of net EPS upgrades.

This trend connection is based on the fact that, in most markets, P/E ratios are rising in good times as increases in share prices outpace profits. The opposite happens in a downturn. Based on a research project of the mid-1990s, Figure 7.4 shows P/E ratios in 1996 and 1997 in selected countries.

It is always wise to keep in mind the trend characterizing a P/E. According to an old rule of thumb, a stock is fairly valued when its P/E divided by its growth rate is 1. Some investors buy when a stock has a ratio of less than 0.5, sell when it is at the level of 1.0 to 1.3, and go short when it rises higher still. This seems to have paid off for a number of investors.

Another criterion connected to P/E ratio is earnings growth. Many stocks are selling at an average P/E that is 50 percent to 200 percent of their growth rate in earnings.

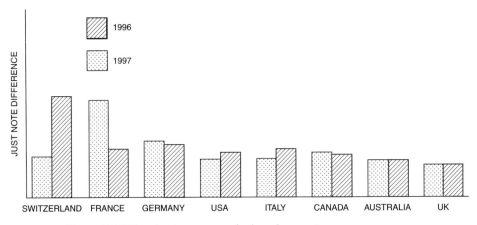

Figure 7.4 P/E ratios in a group of selected countries over two years

A rule of thumb – which tends to apply with small caps and medium caps, but not with large caps which have P/Es far higher than their growth – is that:

- A stock is a good value if its P/E is 100 percent of its growth rate.
- Hence, a stock with a P/E of 20 should be increasing its profits at 20 percent a year.

A serious investor should also consider P/E from the perspective of an equity issuer; that is, a company that sells a share of its ownership to the public. Companies raise capital to finance expansion of their business or to enter new markets by internal growth or by acquisition. Either can be seen as a management project. Every entity always has a range of potential projects under consideration.

- Companies can increase their wealth by investing in projects with a positive net present value (NPV).
- This NPV must be calculated using accurate cash flow projections, and an appropriate risk-adjusted discount rate.

Choices companies make from the projects available to them ultimately determine both their success or failure and their ultimate valuation. A firm that consistently chooses low-risk, low-return projects may ensure its survival, but it will get a lower valuation. A company that chooses risky, potentially high-return projects may fail, but it may also be rewarded with a higher multiple P/E.

To move this argument one notch further, and provide a basis for comparison, let us assume a company with a market cap of $20 billion, and a beta equal to 1. If the average P/E is 40x, then such a company has $500 million in projected earnings. Let us also assume 100 million shares outstanding selling at $60 each, and hence earnings of $5 per share.

Say then that because the economic conditions are depressed, management does not expect future earnings to improve, but estimates that current earnings will be

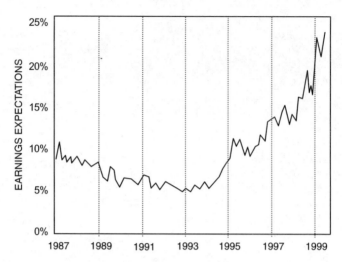

Figure 7.5 Earnings expectations in the aftermath of the 1987 crash and the late 1990s

maintained. Analysts seem to agree with this projection. On this basis, there are reasons to believe the current equity price of $60 will be maintained, and the equity will continue selling at about $60 with a 12x P/E.

Does this sound reasonable? If yes, then this is a mistaken impression. In this and similar examples, the hypothesis that next year's earnings will be at the level of this year's earnings is weak. Historically, stocks have not held lofty P/E ratios for extended periods of time. One of two things tends to happen:

- Earnings rise dramatically to justify the equity's price, or
- The equity's price declines to fall in line with earnings.

Timing can alter this statement. Figure 7.5 presents a graph of earnings expectations from 1987 to 1999. If the time frame of the example which you were given was 1987 to 1992 then, in the typical case, management's supposition that 'next year's earnings' will match those of this year was overoptimistic. But it might have been right, or even pessimistic, if the 'next year' was between 1994 and 1999.

Investors should also be very careful about possible abuses of multiples in valuation through: P/E multiples, price/book multiples, or price/sales multiples. It is always appropriate to ask the questions: what are the fundamentals that drive differences in multiples? How do we control for these differences when comparing multiples across companies? How do we compare multiples across time and across countries?

Precisely because there exist many opportunities for errors and abuses in valuation, shrewd investors do not follow just one method. They choose a double or triple track, and then compare the results. The following three basic approaches to valuation should be kept in mind:

- Cash flows and discount rates in discounted cashflow valuation,
- Multiples and comparables in what can be called a relative valuation, and
- Option pricing techniques, to value certain types of stocks and businesses.

Last, but not least, is the important inverse correlation which exists between P/E multiples and interest rates. As we have already seen in Figures 7.2 and 7.3, P/E ratios and interest rates are inversely related. When interest rates go up, P/E ratios go down and vice versa. If the yield on bonds drops, say from 6 percent to 5 percent, the P/E increase balloons from 15 to 18 or more.

All this is, of course, relative because P/E ratios relate not only with interest rates but also to business prospects and inflation. But since the early 1990s, inflation has remained in check because of increasing global competition that forces companies to become leaner and more productive. The fact that many firms lost their pricing power had a positive effect on inflation, hence on interest rates, and a negative one on earnings.

7.7   Using return on equity as a guide

The metric of *return on equity*, briefly covered in section 7.1, typically has a polyvalent use. The market uses it to measure management's effectiveness in operating an entity and, therefore, as a proxy for obtained results. The companies themselves use ROE as a way of mapping the performance of their divisions and subsidiaries.

A third domain where ROE is important, particularly in the financial industry, is as a means for capital allocation among a bank's business units (BUs).[10] The capital to be allocated to BUs is finite, and the BUs compete for capital. Therefore, it is important to have a measure of performance which helps to make capital allocation more objective. Banks with experience in capital allocation say that, established:

- Capital allotted to branch offices,
- Equity capital of the subsidiaries, distributed for fiscal and legal reasons, and
- Capital by channel, for instance, for legal requirements,

should be decided in conjunction with risk management criteria, even if risk control does not constitute the sole basis for capital allocation. In other words, exposure must be consistently taken into account because, among other reasons, risk has a major impact on ROE. In fact, credit institutions with experience of ROE's role distinguish between:

- A risk-free, and
- A risk-related part.

Usually, the risk-free part of ROE is centrally generated by the risk-free investment of the equity capital, independent of the business activities of operating units. Therefore this part is not included in targets for BUs. By contrast, the risk-related part must be distributed according to risks involved in individual business sectors, along the axes shown in Figure 7.6.

It is advisable that the business risk-related contribution is determined at corporate management level on the basis of the loss potential per risk class, in accordance with *return on risk* criteria. A higher risk-related contribution to the ROE will be expected if

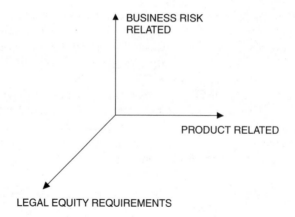

Figure 7.6 The risk-related part of capital allocation to business units must be presented in a three-dimensional frame of reference

the acceptable loss potential – essentially risk capital – of the exposure class in question is set higher at general management level.

- The expected return on risk represents the long-term target for the return on risk capital in connection with a given class.
- This target must take into consideration market conditions and counterparties beyond expected losses.

Along the same frame of reference, the product-related contribution to ROE should be allotted to the products on the basis of both projected risk and income volatility. In principle, the larger the fluctuations in income, the higher should be the long-term contribution of a product to ROE. Volatility of results is determined primarily by volatility of income, since costs might be considered essentially as fixed from the standpoint of a given operational time horizon.

The proper calculation of capital contribution related to legal requirements, determined according to assumed legal risk, is also important. Some companies think this is not so vital because, as a policy, they promote transactions with 'smaller legal equity requirements'. Such a statement is nonsense because legal risk exists everywhere and is increasing.[11] Neither is it true that corporate management knows in advance what sort of legal risk a BU will be assuming.

With all this in mind, the next milestone is that of a methodology for calculating each side's contribution to ROE. The best approach, in my experience, is to take as a basis the cost of capital using as proxy interest in risk-free bonds like US Treasuries or British gilts (chosen according to the base currency). Then, one should add to it the risk factors.

- Risk-based ROE sees to it that every add-on representing exposure, increases the required return on equity.

■ Beyond this, come business-related factors ranging from external credit rating risk to corporate performance measurement.

External credit rating risk is a new concept derived from the implementation of Basel II, but rapidly generalized throughout business and industry. In a nutshell, it means that companies with AAA and AA+ratings by independent rating agencies pay a prime rate, while the cost of money to companies with, say, BBB ratings is much higher. Today banks aim for an AA rating, at least, because below that:

■ The cost of borrowed money significantly increases,
■ They are less able to attract deposits, and
■ Are not considered worthy counterparties in interbank trading.

As this discussion shows, ROE is not an abstract concept; neither is it a number established through a lottery. It has to be studied very carefully, and it must be computed on the premise of adequately covering assumed risks. A similar statement is valid in connection to the concept of *return on assets*.

Ratios of return on equity vary significantly among countries. Morgan Stanley estimates that European companies lag behind their US counterparts in ROE targets, and this is regrettable because ROE is an important measure of shareholder value. Among well-managed firms:

■ The range of ROE for European companies tends to be 10 to 15 percent, with 12 percent as an average.
■ This compares poorly against 20 percent, or better, for American firms taken from a comparable sample in terms of line of business and management quality.

Judgments made on shareholder value are served by ROE because ROE reveals how well a company is using the money at its disposal. Investors should compare a company's ROE to that of its peers and the industry average. But they must also remember that a high ROE can disguise a heavy debt load and, therefore, ROE ratios should be used with great care.

Indeed, one of the ironies of a low equity base, is that the lower the equity to assets ratio, the higher the ROC. This gives a bias to the results of analytical approaches that use equities as a benchmark without considering leveraging and debt level (see Chapter 12). Overleveraged companies may have an impressive ROE, but their base is weak and their survival is in doubt.

Taking account of rating by independent agencies also helps in closing this loophole. The same is true of momentum evaluation. To see whether a company is gaining or losing momentum, investors compare performance over five years or more. This includes both financial results and market impact. Sales growth is not relevant alone. Certain companies could have very high sales growth and make no money. Sales and profitability should be always contrasted over a five-year and ten-year time frame to see if they match.

7.8   Appendix: the Tobin Q-ratio

The Q-ratio has been developed by Professor James Tobin, of Yale University, who won a Nobel prize for his work. Its objective is to compare, for non-farm and non-financial corporations, the value of their plant, equipment and inventories. The latter are valued at their replacement cost while market value is taken as reference for plant structures.

This computation is helped by the fact that, since World War II, when the Federal Reserve Board began calculating such numbers on an annual basis, there is fairly good information on the aforementioned factors. An interesting statistic is that on average up to the 1990s, stocks and bonds sold for about a 30 percent discount to what it would cost to replace corporate assets.

The Q-ratio helps to demonstrate how the stock of a company is valued relative to the plant and equipment that this equity is supposed to represent. Statistics from 1950 through to 1999, show that prior to the 1990s there has been only one period, the 1960s, when the Q-ratio rose above the level of 0.6 and no period when it rose above 1.2.

After the 1960s, which were also active years characterized by a rising stock market and intensive mergers and acquisitions activity, the flare-up subsided and the Q-ratio went down. It started lifting again in the mid-1980 and, ten years later, the Q-ratio had shot up past 1.0 to over 1.4 – the highest level in post-World War II years.

In the aftermath of this blow-out of the Q-ratio, securities sold for at least 70 percent more than their replacement cost, which has been a warning of excessive valuation. One of the problems in estimating overvaluation has been that when the Q-ratio zoomed up in 1995 there was no way of knowing just when the bubble might burst, because – as a metric – Tobin's algorithm provides no facility to *time* the stock market.

Essentially, what James Tobin has shown is that profits on invested capital, measured by its current value, should eventually return to normal levels, because figures far away from normal will produce an imbalance. Eventually higher investment will create competition, eroding whatever factors have been producing impressive rates of return.

Critics say that one of the Q-ratio's limitations is that its figure is exaggerated because replacement costs are underestimated. It is also true that while many companies are selling stock to the public, as would be expected if the price of their equity were high, some are also buying stock back because of management options or other reasons – making acquisitions for cash.

Another of the Q-ratio's limitations – indeed, precisely the opposite to the one just stated – is that it understates the high level of the stock market because of using an oversized denominator owing to the inflation of real estate which represents the market value of plant structure. Also, current replacement cost of equipment may be inflated and, this too, is in the denominator.

If these reservations are left aside, the Q-ratio can be a useful metric. For instance, if in the late 1990s one assumed that the stock market will eventually fall back to an average of about 70 percent of replacement value, which corresponds to a ratio of 0.70, then this would have implied a stock market drop of about 60 percent. And though investor psychology is always an important consideration not included in Tobin's formula, betting only on the euphoric sentiment of investors is not something wise investors should do.

Notes

1 D.N. Chorafas (2003). *Stress Testing: Risk Management Strategies for Extreme Events*. Euromoney.
2 Sun Tzu (1983). *The Art of War*. Delacorte Press.
3 D.N. Chorafas (2000). *Managing Credit Risk, Volume 2: The Lessons of VAR Failures and Imprudent Exposure*. Euromoney.
4 D.N. Chorafas (2004). *Economic Capital Allocation with Basel II: Cost and Benefit Analysis*. Butterworth-Heinemann.
5 Cash flow per share can be increased through the massaging of financial statements through EBITDA and other means. See section 7.5.
6 Berkshire Hathaway, Inc. (1996). *An Owner's Manual*. June.
7 *Communications Week International*, 3 June 2002.
8 *The Economist*, 8 June 2002.
9 In 1929, just before the US stock market's dive, the S&P 500 P/E ratio was 31.
10 D.N. Chorafas (2004). *Economic Capital Allocation with Basel II: Cost and Benefit Analysis*. Butterworth-Heinemann.
11 D.N. Chorafas (2004). *Operational Risk Control with Basel II: Basic Principles and Capital Requirements*. Butterworth-Heinemann.

8 Transparency in financial statements and reputational risk

8.1 Introduction

The biggest risk any company faces is the loss of its name in the market. A reputation takes a lifetime to build, but it can be destroyed in a few days or even in a few hours. Therefore, management should take very seriously decisions and acts which lead to reputational risk, including anything that could harm the image or brand name of its firm. The opportunities for doing so are many, ranging:

- From accounting irregularities,
- To marketing situations normal, all fouled up (snafus) and product recalls, and
- The behavior of the entity's chief executive and his or her immediate assistants.

The well-known corporate scandals of 2000–04, have brought calls for both better corporate governance,[1] and greater transparency. Investors are fed up with scams. Aon, the insurance company, recently surveyed 2000 public and private entities, and found that they viewed reputational risk as their single biggest business hazard.[2]

Neither every board nor every CEO appreciates that if a company for which they are responsible suffers a blow to its reputation, it can collapse with astonishing speed. It is therefore wise to adopt a policy of full transparency in financial statements, rather than trying to hide, or even worse fiddle, the accounts.

This is written in full appreciation that the majority of recent scandals have been the result of conflicts of interest – and human nature being what it is, the ongoing wave of scandal is likely to continue into the coming years. Not least among the reasons for this is the fact that legal proceedings in current cases are far from over. Neither is it difficult to conclude that, to regain investor confidence, standards of corporate behavior must make a great leap forward from their current status. Transparency can help in reaching this goal.

The good news is that there are signs of improvement, even if some corporate crooks may be busy at this very moment fiddling financial figures. Particularly in America, in the aftermath of the Sarbanes-Oxley Act of 2002 chief executives are learning the hard way that, to avoid humiliation and prison sentences,

- They need to be on their best behavior, and
- They must spend what it takes to 'clean the house'.

The focus not only of managers, but also of investors, regulators and politicians must be on improving corporate governance. Hopefully, scams like Enron, WorldCom and Parmalat (see Chapter 15) – among so many others – give the reform process a further nudge in the right direction. On the other hand, unless corporate watchdogs catch most miscreants,

- As far as investors are concerned, the dependability of financial statements will remain in doubt, and
- Everything Chapter 7 said about EPS, P/E and other metrics, as well as a good part of the chartists efforts outlined in Chapter 6, will rest on shaky grounds.

A key advantage of public capital markets is that they are characterized by greater transparency than other deals, like OTC, thanks to the action of regulators – and, increasingly, to market discipline. Other things being equal, transparency allows a larger group of investors than would otherwise have been the case to bear a given risk. The capital market's transparency disappears when books are fiddled. This is a pity, because it can kill the goose which lays the golden egg.

Experienced investors can detect when certain types of transactions start becoming fraudulent, and they pull out of the market. They also appreciate that capital market instruments compete with other forms of investments and they prove superior only when they are:

- Mature,
- Standardized,
- Measurable, and
- Reliable means of risk transfer.

Financial statements are widely accepted in the marketplace when their dependability is uncontested, and their contents are relatively easy to comprehend. Fed by legislation and regulation, the capital market in the G-10 countries is well established and possesses the expertise needed to underwrite a wide range of risk. Still, for market action to succeed, the benefits of transparency must outweigh the information advantage and the skills of the professionals distinguish them from other mortals.

The requirements the foregoing paragraphs have outlined suggest that the business products that can be traded most efficiently are those for which the risks are transparent to, and understood by, potential investors. Listed equities are standardized structures, but they must also abide by the rules of an open society which, among other benefits, help in broadening the range of potential investors and in gaining their confidence.

8.2   Goals of transparent financial reporting

Starting with first principles, the more transparent a financial reporting structure is, the easier it is to understand and the better it helps to explain the nature of transactions. In turn, this is instrumental in calculating the net worth of the banking book and of a trading book, and the gains and losses on the bottom line. That is what investor protection is all about.

Transparency makes it possible to access the right information for factual and documented investment decisions, developing a well-founded navigation plan. It needs no explaining that this is preferable to depending on rumors, doubtful information coming from personal connections and other data which cannot be verified. For this reason, practically no one would disagree on the benefits of disclosure which:

■ Is timely and reliable in respect to its financial contents, and
■ Provides plenty of controllable evidence not only on risks being taken, but also on management of exposure.

This is true of all entities appealing to the capital market – from companies to nations. Thailand, South Korea, Indonesia, Argentina, Brazil, Mexico and other countries, might have avoided sudden exchange-rate crises and panics if investors had had a more accurate idea of the country's foreign reserves. They might also have steered clear of the abyss, if their home companies had been forced to disclose the size of their inland *and* foreign liabilities, as well as their financial staying power.

Lack of transparency encourages governments, companies and people to indulge in reckless behavior, or to use second-rate criteria, compared with rigorous metrics and measurements of risk. An example from the 1990s is that of lending short term to Asian borrowers, promoted by the fact that, following a regulatory loophole, such loans carried a lower risk weighting. Another example is lending to Mexico, in the early 1980s, at prime rate, after the central American country became a member of the Organization for Economic Co-operation and Development (OECD). A short time after this membership became effective, Mexico went bankrupt.

As for the aforementioned regulatory loophole, it had its origin in the fact that at the end of 1997, of the $380 billion in international bank lending outstanding to Asia, 60 percent had a maturity of less than one year. One of the Basel Committee's standards has been that short-term lending requires less provisioning than long-term loans. This proved to have catastrophic effects, as short-term lending has been one of the major reasons behind the:

■ 1997 meltdown in East Asia, and
■ 1998 debacle in Russia.

In Russia investors had bought lots of lucrative but very risky short-term government debt, thinking (incorrectly) that the party would go on forever.

Such blunders by bankers and investors have been surprising, in the sense that years of day-to-day and longer-term practice in loans and in investing should have led to the resolution of prevailing regulatory, accounting, and tax ambiguities.

As cannot be repeated too often, reliable accounting and dependable supervision heavily influence the degree to which market confidence develops, and financial innovation is adopted. Both are also cornerstones to the process of securitizing and transferring assumed risks.

The foundation on which dependable management supervision rests is *internal control*,[3] which is both a concept and a system at the same time. As Figure 8.1 shows, internal control involves the personal responsibility of the chairperson, all members of the board, audit committee, legal counsel, chief executive officer *and* senior management. (There is more on accountability of audit committee in section 8.3). Auditing should not focus only on errors in traditional financial statements. It should also reflect on the company's internal control and its dependability.

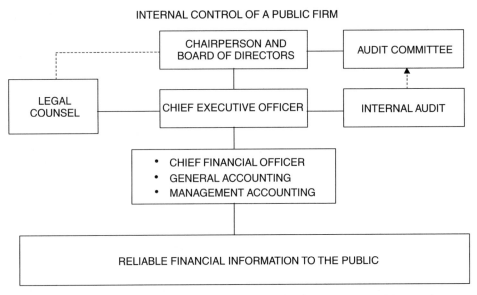

Figure 8.1 The new lines of accountability drawn by the Committee of Sponsoring Organizations of the Treadway Commission, for financial reporting by public companies

It is relevant to recall in this connection that the standards of accounting have been established, and are from time to time revised, with the aim of promoting disclosure. Creative accounting sees to it that the true risks are being hidden. In Parmalat's and so many others' cases, shareholders were cheated not only because they received no information about profits and losses of the company (see Chapter 15), but because they received disguised financial data:

- Ballooning the assets, and
- Keeping away from public view the liabilities.

In this connection, it should be noted that transparency is not a one-off affair which, once established, would always be the guiding light. Transparency is always at the mercy of lust and greed, as well as of conflicts of interest and other reasons leading it to decay. This section makes the point that it is senior management's responsibility to assure transparency is steadily upheld.

Tuning up the accounting standards, and making sure this whole process is transparent, is made even more important by the fact that accounting must capture, record and report big-picture and small-picture changes which occur. An example of a big-picture change occurred in March–April 2000 when the 18 percent drop in the NASDAQ Composite Index wiped $1 trillion from investors' portfolios.

While that major correction was the result of overvalued equities in a technology sector that suddenly confronted reality, there is a clear connection between the bursting of the bubble and creative accounting, the way financial information is reported. Both extremes: pro forma reporting (see Chapter 7) and the backward-looking financial statements which are used today, do not capture the crucial changes in assets and liabilities resulting from:

- A steadily greater leveraging,
- Innovative products and processes, and
- Rapid accumulation of waste through derivative financial instruments.

The result is that investors looking for tomorrow's sources of wealth are flying blind. They are condemned to use unsubstantiated information and suffer wild market mood swings. While first-class accounting cannot cure the market's volatility (see Chapter 12), it can provide investors with a better picture of a company's true worth.

Moreover, to avoid giving their students a near-sighted view of the work they should be doing in reporting financial information, business schools should teach *ethics*, and courses in industrial history should cover the last 150 years of life cycles of corporations – relating the data to what has actually happened in terms of their survival or disappearance. Case studies should:

- Focus on major events like the rise and fall of railroads, automobile companies, computers and telecommunications 'giants', and
- Elaborate on background reasons for the rise in dominance of corporation and their fall from dominance.

Examples of case studies are provided in summary in Chapter 14 and in detail in Chapter 15. Business schools should base their case studies on actual financial data – not only the companies' annual reports but also the footnotes about accounting treatment, and presence or absence of transparency. Management students must definitely learn at first hand the negative effects of creative accounting and other dirty tricks people and companies play by:

- Changing basic financial information,
- Facelifting data on sales orders,
- Manipulating profit and loss statements, and
- Playing illegal games through misuse of statistics.

Students of finance, business administration and management should be taught that both good news and bad news are important in appreciating a company's survivability and, therefore, in analysis. It should be explained to them in no uncertain terms that when one reads an annual report, he or she must look not only for things one wants to see, but also, if not primarily, for those that one does not want to know but which are present.

Both good news and bad news are virtual inputs. It is very hard to deal with information, if one does not put it in context. And it is nearly impossible to understand the impact of information one is reading without the will and know-how to challenge the 'obvious', torturing this information and making it confess its secrets. This is precisely what the analysis of transparent statements is all about.

8.3 Transparency role of an audit committee

Supreme Court Justice Louis Brandeis once said that sunshine is the best disinfectant. What Brandeis essentially meant was *transparency*. Whether we talk of regulatory financial reporting, internal control information or the results of management control tests, including stress tests,[4] the information must be present in a clear, comprehensive way.

■ Every transaction or position on assets and liabilities, and the test(s) applied to each, should be transparent because in a free market this increases business confidence.

One of the problems with transparency, as with so many other activities which are people's direct responsibility, is that it takes time to build up and, after reaching maturity, it is always at the risk of decaying because of different perversities like creative accounting, reinvention of secrecy, fiddling the books because of targeting higher and higher equity prices, overleveraging or some other reason. Figure 8.2 presents in a nutshell this growth and decay curve.

■ The internal control system must be activated when transparent information is not instantly available to all executives – including board members – so that corrective action can be taken immediately.

The CEOs and senior management are directly accountable both for transparent information and for corrective action. Right after the Enron scam, *Business Week* came up with an interesting article, 'Costly lessons', in which it outlined the issue where the audit committee of the Enron board fell short of its responsibilities.[5] Three topics headed the list of shortcomings, which can be generally found in business

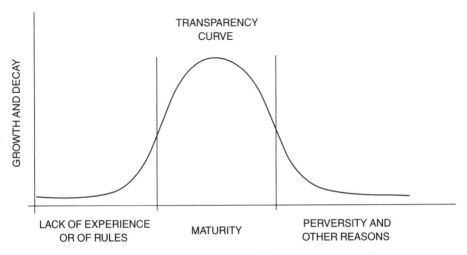

Figure 8.2 Once established, transparency is always at the mercy of some reason leading it to decay

and industry:

1 *Disclosure.* Companies are required to disclose some, but not all, financial ties with
   directors.

Critics have cited conflicts of interest at Enron, which disclosed its consulting contract
with one audit committee member, but not the charitable contributions made to affili-
ated organizations of two others. Transparency requires that companies disclose all
financial ties.

2 *Know-how.* Audit committee members must demonstrate basic financial literacy
   and expertise.

Enron's committee included an accounting professor, an economist and two businessmen, but they apparently did not understand the risks in some of the company's
complex limited partnerships. Audit committee members should undergo both
financial- and industry-specific financial training, including risk control.

3 *Compensation.* Most companies pay directors largely in stock to align their interests
   with those of shareholders.

The principle is not bad, but it can lead to conflicts. At Enron, where some directors
sold shares near the August 2000 high water mark in equity valuation, large holdings
may have made board members less willing to ask tough questions. A good solution
is to ban stock sales as long as directors are on the board.

   Besides, there is a need to clearly define the responsibilities of audit committee
members at large, and more specifically in connection with financial transparency. As
an example, in the execution of their functions audit committee members should be
focused on three areas. The first is adequacy of the company's:

■ Internal controls,
■ Financial reporting processes, and
■ Reliability of financial statements.

The second vital area of audit committee responsibilities concerns independence of
opinion, including assurance that the company's internal auditors and external auditors are performing in an adequate and dependable manner. We will return to this
issue in the appendix to this chapter, which discusses the most likely equivalent of
America's Sarbanes-Oxley Act, in the EU.

   The third important area, in terms of the audit committee's attention, is the company's compliance with legal and regulatory requirements. Figure 8.3 suggests a
framework which can help audit committee members in their mission.

   To get a feel for operations and associated operational risk, audit committee members should meet periodically with senior management to consider the adequacy of
internal controls and the objectivity of financial reporting. They should also discuss
these matters with the company's independent auditors, internal auditors, accountants and other appropriate company financial personnel. In addition, audit committee

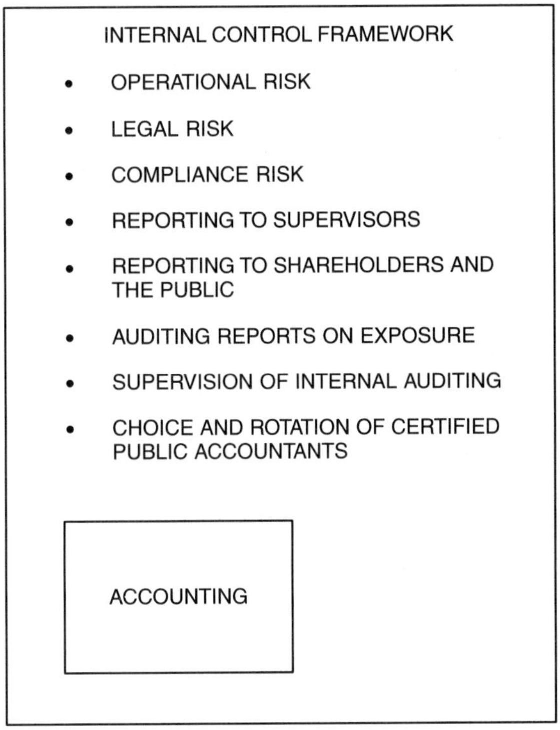

```
┌─────────────────────────────────────────────────┐
│                                                   │
│           INTERNAL CONTROL FRAMEWORK              │
│                                                   │
│       •   OPERATIONAL RISK                        │
│                                                   │
│       •   LEGAL RISK                              │
│                                                   │
│       •   COMPLIANCE RISK                         │
│                                                   │
│       •   REPORTING TO SUPERVISORS                │
│                                                   │
│       •   REPORTING TO SHAREHOLDERS AND           │
│           THE PUBLIC                              │
│                                                   │
│       •   AUDITING REPORTS ON EXPOSURE            │
│                                                   │
│       •   SUPERVISION OF INTERNAL AUDITING        │
│                                                   │
│       •   CHOICE AND ROTATION OF CERTIFIED        │
│           PUBLIC ACCOUNTANTS                      │
│                                                   │
│        ┌──────────────────────────────┐          │
│        │                              │          │
│        │   ACCOUNTING                 │          │
│        │                              │          │
│        └──────────────────────────────┘          │
│                                                   │
└─────────────────────────────────────────────────┘
```

Figure 8.3 The audit committee needs a framework which enables better control

members should review the company's financing plans from an auditing standpoint, and make recommendations to the full board for approval, including the need to authorize corrective action. Needless to say:

■ The audit committee must comprise entirely of independent directors, and
■ The board should adopt a written charter setting out the audit-related functions the committee is to perform.

Appropriate training of audit committee members is important because, even if they have knowledge of financial processes and their control, they may not be up to speed on the complex financing strategies that today have become an integral part of operations in some companies. In other words, meeting the textbook definition of financial literacy is not a guarantee that directors understand:

■ Sophisticated financial instruments, and
■ Their risks, including possible manipulations of financial reporting.

Large global companies, in particular, are so complex that insiders are often the only people who truly understand them, and even this is not certain. Furthermore, as recent scandals have demonstrated, many boards do not exercise the diligent oversight companies need and, invariably, this works to the detriment of the companies.

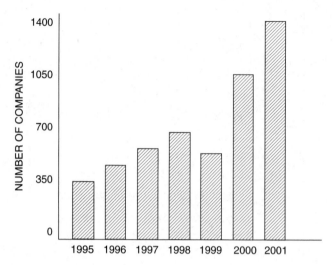

Figure 8.4 The growing number of company financial reports that contain pro forma earnings (*Source:* BIS, *72nd Annual Report*, Basel, 2002)

During my research I have been told of cases where board members joined the pro forma bandwagon of financial misrepresentation by approving these accounts. Whether this occurs actively or silently, it is a bad habit. As the Bank for International Settlements (BIS) has demonstrated, companies with pro forma practices are making investors' understanding of the net worth of the entity so much more complex. In spite of this, and against all logic, there is a growing number of pro forma reports, as Figure 8.4 documents.

Pro forma accounting tactics have been discussed in Chapter 7. What must be added at this point is that they come up every quarter when the company directs shareholders to its *unaudited* pro forma earnings numbers, as the best gauge of its profitability. As the reader will remember, with EBITDA and other gimmicks companies arrive at very positive tallies by excluding ordinary and important costs beyond interest, depreciation and amortization. For instance,

- Acquisition expenses, and
- Payroll taxes on stock options.

Nothing seems to have been learned from the fact EBITDA was the very embodiment of the age of the interest frenzy. Even today, only serious investors pay attention to inflated and inaccurate financial figures; to others, everything seems to be faster, bigger and better. When the sales and earnings growth of some fast-growing companies are second to none, investors simply run for them, and there is no evidence that boards of directors and audit committee members question those unrealistic figures.

The message these paragraphs aim to bring to the reader is that he or she should exercise the greatest amount of prudence. Not only are policy decisions vital, and this is also true of financial information, but so are the results of stress tests. Critical queries on the issue of stress tests and a transparency policy are:

- How should business hypotheses be made and how they should be tested?
- Which tools should be used to promote transparency of *all* exposures?
- What additional risk control programs should be seen in action? And which capabilities interlinking different types of risk?

An integral part of a risk control program is the institution of a real-time, highly accurate and reliable risk management information system. Timely reporting on exposure is by no means a matter of curiosity, though curiosity too has a role to play because it rolls back the barriers of the unknown. A different way of looking at transparency is that the history of the human race is a continuous struggle from darkness toward light. Clear-thinking people *want* to know and to investigate because this casts light on their environment and their investments. When they cease doing so, they lose their professionalism.

8.4 Transparency and corporate governance

Sections 8.2 and 8.3 have explained why transparency and reliable financial reporting are a prerequisite to good governance of any institution. They are also instrumental in the implementation of an effective market discipline. Sometimes, however, the company's reporting system is clogged and what transpires is a sort of *secretive totalitarianism*. In many jurisdictions, and in a number of firms, the motto is: 'As few as possible to know as little as possible, as late as possible.' This is the road to mismanagement, and it is paved with corporate corpses.

To say the least, secrecy in financial accounts is counterproductive, as it is now recognized by a growing number of regulators. During the last twenty years, the Basel Committee on Banking Supervision, and supervisory authorities of G-10 countries, have made plenty of headway in improving transparency in financial reporting. But the Basel Committee's rules are not universal, and different jurisdictions are very defensive about their privileges.

A growing number of experts now say that in a globalized economy jurisdictional heterogeneity is an anomaly, resulting in too little, too late, in terms of supervisory control. The aftermath is that companies find ways to hide losses and keep away from public eyes positions which turned sour. This is the wrong type of corporate governance, which can topple a financial institution or industrial firm. Eventually:

- What has been hidden becomes a rumor, and
- Rumors have a nasty habit of spreading like wild fire.

In early 2000, Nomura Securities published an interesting comparison of American firms in the 1990s with Japanese firms in the 1980s. This pointed out that Japanese companies and banks had tried to conceal their financial problems through shady accounting practices – till the bubble burst. Also, during the bubble, Japanese firms depended almost entirely on banks which, in turn, relied on shares and property as collateral for lending. That left banks completely exposed to falling asset prices in Japan's capital markets.

On the contrary, the Nomura study said, American firms are less dependent on banks for credit. They tap the capital markets, so their losses are less concentrated in the economy. The capital markets, however, have two characteristics which are neither at the top of the list in bank lending, nor are they so influenced by politicians:

- While they may be taken for a ride, as happened in the late 1990s, they subsequently retract and go into hibernation, and
- Because the big investors are in for a quick profit, their time horizon is short. As lenders, they lack the longer-term patience of commercial banks.

In their way, both bullets point to the need for greater transparency, rather than less. Even if global companies are able to capitalize on differences in legislation and regulation among the countries in which they operate, it is in their own interest to sharpen up their internal control structure and conduct stress tests for good governance reasons. This helps their board and the CEO to exercise better management planning and supervision. It also gives them a means to constantly judge the company's effectiveness and performance.

Those regulators who are able to perceive some of the risk that globalization causes to corporate governance, try to ensure that institutions do not capitalize on differences in local legislation by taking inordinate risks. Though global regulation is still wanting, it is slowly falling into place. Establishing a homogeneous global regulation is an urgent matter because, in a service economy, regulatory diversity impedes the continued internationalization of financial services by:

- Reducing transparency in a significant way,
- Magnifying the negative effects of market failures,
- Provoking restrictive domestic trade-related rules, and
- Increasing transactional costs, as well as operational risks.

Barriers to markets exist when governments restrict the number of competitors, limit the operation of a free price-setting system, micromanage the regulations, make it impossible to compute fair value and stiffen innovation. Another instance is when governments try to swamp competitive advantages through restrictive practices such as weeding out potential entrants. Unreliable financial statements eventually discredit a company – and a market. Therefore, all sectors of the economy should be supportive of effective regulation and supervision in:

- Ethical behavior,
- Reliable financial statements,
- Transparency of accounts,
- Financial solvency, and
- Consumer protection.

The right sort of competition law regulates the nature of competition in the market rather than that of individual competitors, giving supervisors the authority to prevent collusive price setting, market sharing arrangements and excessive exposure which lessens the financial staying power of entities in a given market or markets.

In principle, the more dynamic and more competitive a market, the more important is sound corporate governance and prudential regulation – but also the more complex and difficult are the issues to be addressed. Models at large, and more specifically stress testing,[6] contribute to patterning by providing an estimate of the situation, respectively under current and worst-case conditions. The more an economy is leveraged, the more it needs experimentation and tests to:

- Flush out the level of risk assumed by its institutions, and
- Make feasible the taking of appropriate measures to bring exposure under control.

It is the duty of governments, regulators and the institutions themselves to ensure that business and consumer confidence in a global economy is neither misplaced nor undermined, that asset quality and quantity are sufficient to satisfy capital requirements, that needed policy provisions are in place, that internal control is exercised at all times and that corrective action will be taken whenever something occurs which might lead to loss of confidence. Timely corrective action is one of the hallmarks of corporate governance.

In ancient Greece, Demosthenes (384–322 BC) made the dictum that business is built on confidence, and this has been the principle guiding industrial and financial operations ever since. As this book has explained, in the complex society in which we live, and its sophisticated financial operations, reliable corporate governance must be instrumental in promoting the degree of confidence with which we look at counterparties – and their financial statements. Crucial questions are:

- What is the worst case scenario if adversity hits?
- What happens to the firm's treasury if extreme events take place?
- How should financial statements be interpreted under stress conditions?
- What sort of measures are needed to redress a situation before it is too late?

The answer to these type of questions is fundamental to both corporate governance and *market discipline*, one of the three goals of the new capital adequacy framework (Basel II) of the Basel Committee on Banking Supervision.[7] Market discipline is not possible without transparency, which should be extended from internal control at headquarters to everywhere the company operates. Market discipline basically means that business partners and competitors exercise a sort of supervisory control over one another – which cannot be effectively done without transparency and stress tests.

8.5 Forward-looking statements

The thesis this chapter has supported is that markets must be characterized by a continuing increase in transparency. This is achievable if financial institutions carry out more comprehensive accounting practices and senior management is in charge of timeliness and accuracy of financial reports. This is also necessary for compliance reasons. For instance, because of new regulations in the banking industry, new global capital adequacy guidelines must be matched by careful internal reforms.

Publicly quoted companies must not only adopt reliable financial reporting practices, but also show greater market discipline in the economic environment(s) in which they operate. This is written in the full understanding that globalization and technology change the credit dimension, making markets more dynamic but also forcing companies to take more risk. Within this dual perspective of:

- Greater business opportunity, and
- Increasing amount of exposure

should be studied the need for companies and investors to gaining insight into forward financial conditions. This is essentially a preview of things to come and, like any prognostication, it has to be done within a certain level of confidence. Reading tomorrow's newspaper today has a cost. The question is 'How reasonable might that cost be?'

A great deal can be learned from what serious companies are doing. For instance, to overcome certain shortcomings of conventional accounting, Berkshire has established, and is regularly reporting, *look-through earnings*. These 'look-through' numbers include Berkshire's own accounting adjustments, plus Berkshire's share of the undistributed earnings of its major investees. Notice that such amounts are not included in Berkshire figures under conventional accounting.

- Look-through earnings exclude capital gains, purchase accounting adjustments and extraordinary charges or credits from investee numbers, and
- From the undistributed earnings of its investees, Berkshire subtracts the tax the company would have owed had the earnings been paid to it as dividends.

These are not pro forma reportings. These are Berkshire's version of forward-looking statements, and they are clearly outlined as such. As a consequence, investors are on the right track when interpreting the numbers. Proper identification of what a financial statement is and is not sets the right framework in computing, reporting and interpreting figures largely based on projections, hypotheses and a fair amount of luck.

A way of rephrasing what the previous paragraphs have explained is that the role of forecaster of business opportunity *and* of likely exposure is played by *forward-looking statements*. In addition to their release of regulatory accounting numbers which must be accurate and precise, companies may release information that constitutes an *educated guess* on coming events.

There is a significant difference between creative accounting and forward-looking statements. Creative accounting fiddles the financial numbers related to past performance. Forward-looking statements are projections which might or might not come true – and they should be appreciated as such. As an example, forward-looking statements may include issues relating to:

- Plans, objectives or goals,
- Future economic performance, or prospects,

- A certain number of contingencies, and
- Reasons affecting future performance.

Most critical to the reliability of a forward-looking statement is the outlining of assumptions which underlie it. Typically, words such as we 'believe', 'anticipate', 'expect', 'intend' and 'plan', and similar expressions, are intended to identify forward-looking pronouncements, but these are not necessarily the exclusive purpose of such statements. Moreover, companies do not intend to update forward-looking statements, except as may be required by applicable laws – or by major events.

The reader should appreciate that, by their nature, forward-looking statements involve inherent risks and uncertainties, both general and specific. The principle is that as long as investors understand the nature and intend of forward-looking statements, there is nothing wrong in publishing predictions and forecasts.

Of course, there is always the risk that predictions, forecasts, projections and other forward-looking pronouncements – whether described or implied – will *not* be achieved. This is precisely the cost of reading tomorrow's newspaper today, as the reader is already aware. A number of factors could cause end results to differ materially from plans, objectives, expectations, estimates and intentions expressed in a forward-looking statement. Reasons include:

- Changes in market psychology and trend,
- Significant volatility in interest rates,
- Volatility in exchange rates,
- Ability and willingness of counterparties to meet their obligations to *our* firm,
- Strengths or weaknesses of the economies of the countries in which our firm conducts its operations and in the global economy, and
- Effects of, and changes in, fiscal, monetary, trade and tax policies, as well as political and social developments, which upset established plans.

The good news about these and other reasons, which may affect the accuracy of a forward-looking statement, is that not all of them would move in a positive or negative way at the same time. This is known as the *Fermi principle*, named after Enrico Fermi, the physicist, who postulated that the art of making predictions benefits from the fact that each variable in a system has its own distribution – and, in an aggregate sense, the variance of one factor tends to cancel the variance of another.

The Fermi principle applies to all estimates, the more so as events described in forward-looking releases are not statements of historical facts. They address future activities, and their possible development that the company expects or anticipates; in short, something that will or may occur in the future. This, however, is no excuse for making such statements lightly, or misjudging 'potential', 'opportunity', 'risk factors' and 'uncertainties', which may cause actual results to differ materially from expectations.

In the majority of cases, the way they are practiced today, forward-looking statements typically relate to the implementation of strategic initiatives, including new business models, future business developments and expected economic performance. Therefore, the reader should be cautioned not to place undue reliance on forward-looking statements, which relate only to the day they are made.

A loophole with forward-looking statements is that companies are under no obligation to update or alter them as a result of new information, change in evaluation of future events or otherwise. This makes it easier to claim developments which, for one reason or another, do not materialize, and is a matter which should attract close scrutiny by regulatory authorities. As a remedy, the regular update of forward-looking statements – for instance, on a quarterly basis – will increase their:

■ Dependability, and
■ Appreciation by the market.

As an example, behind quarterly differences may lie problems with products in the pipeline, reputational risk events, a deterioration in credit risk, governmental and regulatory changes, volatility in local and global securities markets, swings in currency exchange rates and interest rates, competitive pressures, technological failures or changes in the financial position or creditworthiness of customers, obligors and other counterparties.

All these, and other major factors, can adversely affect business and financial performance contained in future filings and reports. Another reason of less than optimal dependability may be the negative effect of outsourcing expert opinion. Take option pricing as an example. Using brokers as consultants presents problems of conflicts of interest. Brokers have incentives to lean towards volatility estimates which assist in sales – as happened in 1997 in connection with option pricing.

Internal failures, too, might alter the contents of a forward-looking statement. For instance, management's inability to control for changes in laws and regulations; facing competition in geographic and business areas in which the company loses its market; retaining and recruiting qualified personnel; or timely development of new products and services.

Still other management failures which may upset forward-looking statements relate to mergers and acquisitions, which have turned sour because of overpaying for the acquisition, or an inability to integrate the acquired businesses, or mismanaging the risk involved in transactions and being unable to maintain state-of-the-art technology.

The foregoing list of important factors is not exclusive. Therefore, when evaluating forward-looking statements, one should carefully consider the different factors, other uncertainties and events, as well as the risks identified in any forward-looking statement which have been appropriately included to inform its reader. Forward-looking statements are necessary, but they also have to be reliable and explicitly state the level of confidence they address.

8.6 Virtual balance sheets and risk management

Not only public information of investors, and by extension market discipline, but also a rigorous risk management policy require forward-looking statements, able to project on business opportunities as well as on risks and uncertainties. This is written in the full understanding that actual results shown in regulatory balance sheet reporting could differ materially from those projected in a forward-looking statement.

For instance, as a global concern, a multinational company faces exposure to adverse movements in foreign currency exchange rates. Its exposures may change over time, as its business practices evolve, and could have a material adverse impact on the financial outcome. Therefore, management must be prepared to hedge against currency exposures associated with assets and liabilities, as well as against anticipated foreign currency cash flows. Hedging and speculation are two totally different things. Hedging:

- Addresses a commercial transaction which must be protected in the background,
- Is characterized by limits, such as no forward contract having a maturity greater than one year in length, and
- Contains no contract targeting gains to be realized beyond strictly defensive reasons regarding assets, liabilities and cash flows.

In a similar manner, a company may be exposed to interest rate risk associated with investments, loans, payments and so on. The interest rate of many contracts is tied to the London Interbank Offered Rate (LIBOR), and prudent treasurers evaluate the hypothetical change in obligations due to changes in LIBOR rate.

A valid modeling technique used for analysis of hypothetical changes in loan obligations, arising from selected possible changes in LIBOR, involves experimentation or exposure based on market changes: for instance, shifts in the LIBOR curve of plus or minus 100 basis points (bps), 200 bps, 300 bps and 400 bps over a twelve-month period.

Because, in general, a company also maintains investment portfolio holdings of various issues, types, and maturities, these securities must be recorded on the balance sheet at fair value with unrealized gains or losses reported as a separate component of shareholders' equity, net of tax. Table 8.1 presents an analysis of hypothetical change in fair values of public equity investments held by an industrial company,[8] which are sensitive to changes in the stock market.

The modeling technique measures the hypothetical change in fair values arising from selected changes in each position's price. Stock price fluctuations of plus or minus 10 percent, plus or minus 30 percent and plus or minus 50 percent were selected based on the probability of their occurrence.

Issuer	Valuation of securities given an increase in each stock's price of			Current fair value	Valuation of securities given a decrease in each stock's price of		
	10%	30%	50%		10%	30%	50%
Corporate equities	$197	$231	$257	$171	$146	$111	$86

Table 8.1 Estimated fair value of publicly traded corporate equities (in $ millions) at a twelve-month time horizon

Hedging currency risk, interest rate risk and equity risk is important for practically every company. The problem is that if need data becomes available only a month later, it is worse than useless because it can be outright misleading. To be of value, all tests which are part of an executive information system (EIS),[9] must be available *now*, the moment they are required for decision purposes – allowing time for calculating and compiling financial results.

This is the sense, and objective, of a *virtual balance sheet*, which (through high technology) can be produced very rapidly with ±3 percent to ±4 percent accuracy. The virtual balance sheet is not a regulatory reporting instrument and, therefore, it does not need to be precise. It is part of the EIS as well as an integral part of risk management at corporate level.

An admissible level of accuracy at ±3 percent to ±4 percent level is needed to permit a very fast response. Since the late 1990s, Boston's State Street Bank has been able to produce a virtual balance sheet covering its worldwide operations in less than thirty minutes. Other companies take one to two hours. Any firm which cannot now close its books in a matter of a few hours, at stated level of accuracy, is one characterized by:

- Poor technology, and
- A low level of management control.

In fact, the best organized companies are able to produce a virtual balance sheet in less than fifteen minutes. Using prognosticator models they are also able to know a month ahead what their earnings will most likely be based on their projected sales, expenses and gross margins. This is an area where forward-looking statements and virtual balance sheets meet.

High technology helps, but the most basic prerequisite is organizational, the need for change in corporate culture. Cisco provides an example. Because it structures its information system along the lines of an integrated supply chain, but in a way which promotes flexibility and personal accountability, every one of its employees can make decisions that might have had to go all the way to the president.

Cisco's CEO and CFO are credited with developing this virtual close. This is one of the first companies to generate hourly updates on revenues, product margins, discounts and bookings. It takes other companies five hours to do so, and some companies need a whole month. A virtual balance sheet and income statement permits an individual product line manager to see exactly what the gross margin is on his or her products, and whether it is above or below expectations. This is crucial in determining immediately if below expectation conditions were caused by:

- Delays,
- Costs escaping control, or
- Discounting by competitors.

Ultimately, the virtual close will become commonplace, but by then the leaders will have reduced the time required to a matter of minutes. Given the competitive advantages provided by a virtual balance sheet, there will come a day when even one day's delay in closing the company's books will be a throwback to the 'dark ages'.

Even if virtual balance sheets are for only the company's own senior management, and they not disclosed to the public, they help a great deal in transparency because managers who are in charge of the firm feel much more at ease in releasing financial information. On the contrary, people and companies misinformed or altogether ignorant of their exposure:

- Have every reason to be defensive, and
- Try to conceal, or even distort, the little bits of information they may have.

To be able to close the books on a virtual basis companies must follow very closely all their exposures, not just one or two. Since the mid-1990s, Perkin-Elmer, the instrument manufacturer, monitors foreign exchange contracts put out by finance officials in each country where the company does business. This has allowed the firm to centralize foreign exchange hedging, starting with six countries that represented half its foreign currency exposure.

By offsetting positions in different currencies against each other, companies try to optimize their finances regarding currency exchange risks, interest rate risk and other exposures. 'You take risks in whatever you do', Dennis Weatherstone, former chairman and CEO of JP Morgan, once suggested. 'But if you understand, measure, and account for them, that should keep you out of trouble.'

After he became the CEO of the Morgan Bank, Weatherstone saw to it that every day the bank's risk management unit compiled a one-page *4:15 report*: This became so known because it got handed to Morgan's top six executives by that time of day – with the goal of presenting a snapshot of the bank's entire foreign exchange, interest-rate, commodity trade, equity positions and all other exposures. Value at risk is based on the model underpinning this '4:15 report'.

Using heuristics and algorithms in connection with the trade book, banking book, investments in the portfolio, liquidity and volatility data, it is possible to calculate daily earnings at risk, providing senior management with intraday risk information which is factual and documented, albeit with an admissible ± 3 percent or ± 4 percent error rate. This should not be confused with VAR, which leaves extreme events out of the equation.[10]

Not only risk management reporting should be ad hoc actuated online by the senior executives themselves – rather than being given to them in a dull format on a piece of paper – but also it should be possible to take a fully interactive *market shock* approach. Every senior executive must be able to experiment through his or her workstation, by accessing distributed databases, with how the bank would fare in the event of a *worst-case scenario* like a sharp and protracted rise in interest rates accompanied by a significant movement in foreign exchange rates, a stockmarket crash and/or other sustained movements in key commodities. (More on risk management in Chapter 10.)

8.7   Compliance with the Sarbanes-Oxley Act

In July 2002, in the aftermath of Enron, WorldCom and other scandals, the Sarbanes-Oxley Act was passed by US Congress, establishing rigorous corporate governance rules. The Act set specific expectations for the reliability of financial statements of firms whose shares are traded on US stock exchanges. Section 302 of the Act requires CEOs and CFOs to certify the dependability of such statements, as well as that their companies have:

- An effective system of internal control, which includes issues related to external financial disclosures, and
- Procedures able to notify both external auditors and the firm's audit committee when significant control deficiencies are detected in their system.

The US's chief financial regulator, the SEC, is charged by the Sarbanes-Oxley Act with writing the rules that implement its requirements. In this connection, the SEC has already passed a requirement that senior executives of all listed companies swear to the accuracy of their financial statements, and it has given an indication that it will not grant exemptions.

Section 404 of Sarbanes-Oxley requires a firm's external auditor to report on the reliability of management's assessment of internal controls. Both sections 302 and 404 raise important questions in terms of corporate governance; for instance: how many and what type of control deficiencies may the CEO and CFO not report to external auditors and audit committee, without violating the Act? Which is the threshold over which the SEC and civil courts will have to take action?

Only jurisprudence, which takes years to develop, will establish tolerance levels for violations and answer questions regarding senior management assertions about control effectiveness. Till then, lawyers will use other, relatively similar cases, that have been decided by the SEC and the courts, as well as their knowledge of the general legal standards of duty of care. No doubt, there will also be complex technical issues involved, and these must be understood to provide a defensible legal court case. In all likelihood, the most important violations leading to court action, will involve primarily several issues identified in the following paragraphs.

- Creative accounting and other financial scams.

As we have already seen on several occasions in this text, to boost profits, companies have been causing their earnings statements to balloon through different gimmicks. These approaches range from changing critical assumptions to omitting or redefining traditional expenses, issuing highly biased pro forma statements, and using different forms of creative accounting.

The nemesis of creative accounting may well be an activist investor population which is increasingly referring such cases to the State Attorney's office, as well as the fact that the implementor of Sarbanes-Oxley is the SEC. This duality will, in all likelihood, add to prosecution cases' reasons described below.

- Circular dealing.

This involves the conflict created when securities analysts use their research to carry favor with companies, in the hope of landing investment banking business for their firm. Corrective measure call for better disclosure, changes in analysts' compensation to play down incentives to be involved in circular dealing and stronger patrols of the division between a bank's analysts and deal-makers, and its effectiveness.

■ Regulation FD.

A legacy from the Arthur Levitt SEC, this Regulation FD bars companies from selectively and pre-emptively sharing information before its public release. This regulation seems to be detested by the securities industry, but it is instrumental in safeguarding inventors' interests – hence it is a good reputation, whose violators should be brought to justice.

■ Outright fraud.

In this are included not only clear-cut scams but also cases where members of an entity's senior management mislead unwary investors about the real financial state of their company. Many of the fading dot-coms and plenty of other firms have hyped their earnings. They have tortured accounting to produce income statements that would be applauded by Wall Street, helping to sell the company's equity and bonds just prior to its collapse. In late 2003 this happened with Parmalat (see Chapter 15).

Significant help in shaping the jurisprudence for assertions by CEOs and CFOs, under section 302 of the Act, will be provided by post-mortems. For instance, in 2003 executives at HealthSouth, a recent massive US corporate governance disaster, asserted that they had an effective system of internal control, despite accounting disclosures being since proven wrong by billions of dollars.[11]

One of the aftermaths of Sarbanes-Oxley is that certified public accountants, too, must be very careful in deciding about the need to qualify statements – not only in their quantitative aspects, but also in regard to internal controls. Essentially, this will be tantamount to agreeing or disagreeing with the opinion reached by the CEO and CFO when forming their opinion on control effectiveness.

Similarly, the SEC and the courts will have to decide on thresholds for penalties regarding undocumented or fake CEO and CFO assertion, as well as for the related opinion(s) expressed by the external auditor. To a significant extent, every party's written opinion will make references to the more detailed guidelines to be established by the new Public Company Accounting Oversight Board (PCAOB) and its policies on the auditing standards to be used in forming section 404 external audit reports.

For evident reasons, Sarbanes-Oxley is not the most popular Act. Like some of its European counterparts, the Japanese Business Federation has been lobbying on behalf of the country's largest companies to exempt them from the new law passed in response to the wave of corporate scandals. The Japanese Federation said its members should be able to retain a more 'Japanese-style' corporate governance regime – whatever this might mean.

Some of Japan's most influential executives are concerned that the requirement to set up an audit committee of the board comprising independent directors is unsuitable for the Japanese corporate environment. A number of German companies have expressed similar worries – which not only do not make sense but also are signs of poor corporate governance, because only people unsure of themselves and their abilities try to protect their flanks by changing the law.

8.8   Appendix: the European Union's version of the Sarbanes-Oxley Act

In a way similar to America's Sarbanes-Oxley Act, which came on the heels of the 2003 corporate governance and auditing scandals, the EC came up with proposals intended to go well beyond the auditors' self-regulation prevailing so far in the EU. These proposals call for individual countries to set up regulators which will emulate the new US PCAOB – albeit within a less rigorous framework.

The Commission also wants to oblige public companies to establish independent audit committees, as in the USA, with the authority to hire and fire auditors. The rules, under discussion at the time of writing this book, would require non-EU auditors to register with local authorities, which is similar to a provision in the Sarbanes-Oxley Act.

It is good news that the mood in the EU has finally turned toward tougher sanctions for misbehaving accountants and companies' CEOs and other executives who fail to follow ethical standards. Another piece of good news is the increased co-operation among various EU supervisors. To strengthen the supervisors' role, the Commission would give individual countries the option of making compulsory the regular rotation of auditors or, at least, of the senior partner dealing with a company account.

On the whole, the Commission's rules do not seem to be draconian – standing below the level of those imposed by Sarbanes-Oxley. Moreover, the US rules are much more prescriptive. To make its own rules prescriptive, the EU can learn a great deal from the Parmalat experience, and its players, their dirty tricks and the aftermath, including the participation by Italian shareholders in American class actions against Parmalat.

Class actions are not yet common in Europe, but what happens anywhere in the Western Hemisphere has an impact on financial litigation in the EU. European countries definitely need more far-reaching legislation similar to Sarbanes-Oxley, or even beyond it. An Act focusing on sound corporate governance helps in producing *performers* – that is, people who know enough and care enough to manage themselves and their companies.

Notes

1 D.N. Chorafas (2004). *Corporate Accountability, with Case Studies in Finance.* Macmillan/Palgrave.
2 *The Economist*, 24 January 2004.
3 D.N. Chorafas (2001). *Implementing and Auditing the Internal Control System.* Macmillan.
4 D.N. Chorafas (2003). *Stress Testing: Risk Management Strategies for Extreme Events.* Euromoney.
5 *Business Week*, 21 January 2002.
6 D.N. Chorafas (2003). *Stress Testing: Risk Management Strategies for Extreme Events.* Euromoney.
7 D.N. Chorafas (2004). *Economic Capital Allocation with Basel II: Cost and Benefit Analysis.* Butterworth-Heinemann.

8 As shown in the company's annual report.
9 D.N. Chorafas (2005). *The Real-time Enterprise*. Auerbach.
10 D.N. Chorafas (2002). *Modelling the Survival of Financial and Industrial Enterprises: Advantages, Challenges, and Problems with the Internal Rating-Based (IRB) Method*. Palgrave/Macmillan.
11 *Global Risk Regulator*, **1** (7), July–August 2003.

9 A private investor's self-protection

9.1 Introduction

The goal of the Sarbanes-Oxley Act in the USA, and of its European equivalent, is to provide legal grounds for investor protection. Regulators should always be on the alert for malfeasance in the capital markets; that is what they are paid for. But regulators cannot be a substitute for the investors' own defenses, which must be:

- Properly engineered,
- Frequently revised, and
- Used all the time.

The best protection a private investor can have is to be in charge of his or her own account. To do so, he or she must first learn the nuts and bolts of investing, which has been the objective of Part 1. After appreciating what investing is and is not, the private investor must acquaint him or herself with risk management (see Chapter 10), which is every investor's business, and has to be done in a fully objective manner.

This does not mean that emotions can be taken out of investment decisions. Julius Baer, the Swiss private bank, puts its thoughts in this way: 'If you think money has nothing to do with emotion, then try tearing up a 100 euro note, sometime.' It is no less true, however, that emotions are the enemy of investment decisions – and most particularly of what it takes effectively to control risk.

One of the emotions which should definitely be avoided is that of lost opportunity which 'has to be recovered at all costs'. The *tenth golden rule* in investment is 'never chase the return of shares you did not buy'. There is an old proverb that crying over spilt milk is more than a waste of time, because it negatively conditions the individual doing so. What the tenth golden rule says is that:

- Running after an elusive goal often colors people's perceptions of the future, and
- Chasing the return of shares you did not buy can be risky because it often leads the investor to buy at the peaks.

Eugen Buck agrees with this rule, and would add that investors will be well advised to do post-mortem simulations on their equity choices, because they can teach valuable lessons. For instance, what if I had bought that equity? What kind of effect would it have in my profit and loss of the year? What can I learn from this walkthrough? In the opinion of Bob Keen, what this rule says is very true. No one, not just investors, should worry about something that did not happen to them.

As a principle, the rationale for resisting a last-minute rush and for not regretting what one had not done at that time, is not widely appreciated. One of the flaws in managing equity investments is that people often try to catch up with a lost opportunity, and/or tend to trade far too frequently because they are trying to emulate returns on shares they had bought earlier. This is one of the ways in which investors get burned. By contrast, mature investors never pursue:

- What they do not have, and
- What they do not need.

In the 1950s, when I was a graduate student at UCLA, my professors taught their students what it takes to make a sound investment, and then they advised: 'stick to it' (the investment). Today, this is half-true, because the market is much more dynamic than it was fifty years ago. Still, as already emphasized, too frequent movements in and out of the market are unwise for investors, though they do provide a stream of fees for brokers and investment advisers.

This and other unwise investment moves should be contrasted to the sound policy of directly owning a diversified group of equities that benefit from growth in the economy, and consistently earn above-average returns on capital. Our choices, however, should always be conditioned by our ability to assess the quality of the company's management. First-class management shows itself in bad times, not in good times which lift all company's.

Moreover, management's quality should be checked periodically against results. This does not only mean EPS (see Chapter 7) but also policies like retaining earnings by assessing whether retention, over time, delivers shareholders at least $1 of market value for each $1 retained; as well as, whether management giving itself stock options and other handouts, at shareholder expense.

'Good investment ideas', advises Warren Buffett, 'are rare, valuable and subject to competitive appropriation just as good product or business acquisition ideas are. Therefore we normally will not talk about our investment ideas.' But though Buffett may be unwilling to explain in detail risk and reward connected with specific equities, he freely discusses his business and investment philosophy. One of its elements is that as far as the allocation of capital is concerned,

- One does not need good hand-eye co-ordination or well-toned muscles to push money around.
- As long as one's mind continues to function effectively, he or she is well positioned to do a good investment job.

And this job can be done at low overhead, contrary to what some asset management entities practice. As an investment manager, Berkshire presents an excellent example of cost-effectiveness. Though the companies the group controls have about 33 000 employees, only twelve of these are at headquarters, occupying themselves with investment decisions. This speaks volumes for the fact that sound investment management needs brains, not numbers.

9.2   Investing in large caps versus small caps

As it will be recalled, the fifth golden rule of investments, particularly important for retail investors, is to invest only in stocks quoted in big boards. This has an evident impact on a distinction traditionally made by investment advisers, that one should be breaking down the range of equities offered on stock markets into three categories:

- Small caps, typically less than $1 billion of capitalization per company,
- Mid-caps, $1 billion to $5 billion, and sometimes up to $10 billion, and
- Large caps, over $10 billion of capitalization per company, and usually much more.

Big boards tend to have large cap stocks and the upper range of mid-caps. There was a time when these were offering better investor protection, if for no other reason than information about these quoted companies was more generally available – and it also tends to be more reliable, though there are exceptions. While there may be good value with small cap entities,

- Not much is known about them,
- Analytical information is scanty, and
- They can have hidden liabilities which, one day, will haunt the investor.

Besides the better visibility in regard to entities behind large cap stocks, several research projects indicate that large caps correlate better with the growth in the economy, and at the same time they are the driving forces behind the growing capitalization of domestic shares as a percentage of GDP. Reference to this issue has been made in Chapter 4. Figure 9.1 presents statistics from the USA and Europe based on the European Central Bank's, Monthly Bulletin of February 2002.

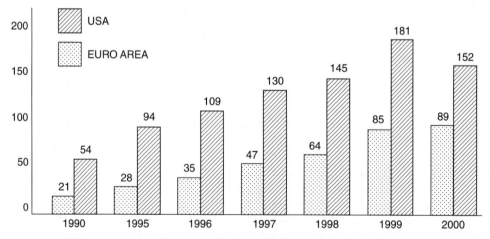

Figure 9.1 Market capitalization of domestic shares as a percentage of GDP (*Source: The Monetary Policy of the ECB*, 2nd edn, Frankfurt, 2004, table 2.8 on page 34. Reproduced with permission)

Market capitalization is being increasingly taken as an indicator of a well-performing company; investors should, however, understand that it is volatile. On 15 April 1999, on its way to its high water mark, Microsoft's market capitalization of $448.5 billion was a higher multiple than that of venerable General Motors, which stood at $56.5 billion. Microsoft and GM are both large caps. Investors flocked to Microsoft because of its market dominance.

- Its Windows operating systems run on 90 percent of the world's personal computers, and
- Its Office Suite commanded just slightly less than half the market for office productivity applications.

As should have been expected, however, when the technology bubble burst (in late March 2000), Microsoft's capitalization went down much faster than that of GM, and even more so than that of companies like Johnson & Johnson. On the other hand, the capitalization of Internet companies collapsed, and people investing in them lost a huge amount of money, while those who stuck with Microsoft faired much better.

The question about investing in large caps versus small and medium caps has no single answer. A great deal depends on investor risk appetite – and greed. In fact, closely associated with this is that of investing in one's own national capital markets versus following a policy of international diversification both for:

- Greater business opportunity, and
- Better possibilities for damage control, in a downturn.

For all practical purposes, a factual and documented answer to these two queries is what *asset allocation* is all about. Table 9.1 presents suggestions for asset allocation connected to five alternative portfolio strategies which range from super-aggressive to conservative. True enough, as Bob Keen points out, one can use different labels for these classes. For instance:

- Aggressive growth, instead of super-aggressive,
- Growth rather than aggressive,
- Income and growth, instead of moderately aggressive,
- Income, rather than moderately conservative, and
- Capital Preservation rather than conservative.

In fact, the labels in the above five bullet points are more common than those in Table 9.1. The choice of rather dramatic headers, however, has been intentional, aimed at avoidance of ambiguity on the investors' side. For instance, as a label, 'growth' does not convey, by itself, that there is a significant amount of risk associated with this investment strategy.

- Practically everybody would like to see his or her capital grow,
- But not everybody has the risk appetite which is inseparable from an aggressive growth policy.

	Domestic		International equities[1]	Alternative investments	Bonds	Cash	Total
	Large company equity	Small caps					
Super-aggressive	35	15	35[1]	10	–	5	100
Aggressive	40	20	30[1]	5	–	5	100
Moderately aggressive	35	15	25[1]	–	20	5	100
Moderately conservative	20	5	10[2]	–	50	15	100
Conservative	20	–	5[2]	–	60	15	100

Notes:
1 Including 'emerging countries'.
2 No 'emerging countries'.

Table 9.1 Suggested asset allocation in aggressive and conservative portfolios

Another suggestion made by the experts who contributed their know-how to this research, is that ranges might be better than expected values. For instance, Bob Keen said that an investor could have a super-aggressive strategy with large company equities ranging from 30 percent to 60 percent, and small caps ranging from 5 percent to 25 percent. Also, international equities in the portfolio may range from 30 percent to 60 percent, alternative investments from 0 percent to 15 percent, and cash from 0 percent to 10 percent.

While it is true that this type of presentation would help cover market variance, it would also make the target matrix fairly complex. Furthermore, if the aim is to address market variance and trend, then instead of ranges it would be better to have standard deviations from the mean value (expected value), at different levels of significance.

Keen is right. Using both expected value and variance will improve the asset allocation matrix, and professional investors should do so for the funds under their wing. Alternatively, retail investors should keep the matrix simple and understandable because most likely they will not have the technology, skills or time to develop and sustain sophisticated solutions for planning and controlling their investments.

Moreover, as cannot be stated too often, only the conservative and moderately conservative options should be considered by individual investor – particularly those keen to protect their interests rather than being taken for a ride by the market. As an old proverb has it, small ships should keep close to the coast. If they imitate the big ships and venture on to the high seas, they will sink.

Perhaps I should have written it as a golden rule that capital markets work by the *law of the greater fool*: 'No matter how stupid are the investments one makes, there might be (but not always) a greater fool ready to pay what it takes to own them.' Historical evidence suggests that this started in the mid-seventeenth century when some players passed their tulip investments on to others, who thought they were the chosen ones to benefit from ever rising tulip prices.

There is a parallel between the tulip bubble and the stock market's geared environment of the late 1990s. At about 1635, regular markets had been established for selling and buying tulips through the exchanges of Amsterdam, Rotterdam and other cities. Because these trades had become quite profitable, many people thought it near-sighted to restrict their activity to winter months. In 1636, a *futures market* developed for tulips.

- Traders would issue contracts at any time during the year, with delivery specified in the following winter.
- Futures contracts could be sold and bought several times, before the tulips actually arrived.

There is some evidence that this futures market for tulips was followed by an options market with calls and puts on the favored tulip – and with investors (not only specu-lators) betting that tulip prices would keep going up. This scenario, which became popular, became known as *Windhandel*, or trading air – a label which fits perfectly the Internet companies' craze of the late 1990s.

A good rule of thumb to keep in mind, in connection with equity investments, is that if EPS, P/E and other critical ratios (see Chapter 4) cannot get better, then they can only get worse. This turns out to be the case when relatively grim news follows a period looking like a support level for the next lift-off. Such events repeat themselves from time to time, with early 2004 their most recent appearance.

When the market is sensitive to bad news for equities, the more a portfolio is loaded in growth stocks, in comparison with other investments like bonds, the risk of landing in a tulip-type debacle increases. This has been accounted for in the classification of strategies for asset allocation in Table 9.1.

Note that the five strategies for asset allocation shown in Table 9.1 are not necessarily what investment banks are advising their clients. Based on statistics published in *The Economist* on 17 January 2004, Table 9.2 presents the investment advice given by other parties active in brokerage and asset management.

Other things being equal, the higher the equities share in the portfolio, the more homework the investor must do in following up the fortunes of his or her holdings.

	Equities[1]	Bonds	Cash	Alternative investments
Crédit Suisse	35	35	10	20
Henderson	65	30	5	N/A
ISIS	60	35	5	N/A
Julius Baer	45	42	8	5
Lehman Brothers	70	30	0	N/A
Robeco Group	50	50	0	N/A
Standard Life	55	45	0	N/A
Average	54	38	4	N/A

Note:
1 Including large caps and small caps, domestic and international.

Source: *The Economist*, 17 January 2004

Table 9.2 Asset allocations advised by different firms
(percentage)

Note: Share price index, start of June 1999=100

Figure 9.2 Upside and downside: price movements in the equity market (Reproduced with the permission of Deutsche Bundesbank)

This is particularly true of stocks characterized by high volatility. A very important issue regarding asset allocation, which is not shown in Table 9.2, is the industry in which one chooses to invest.

The impact that whole industry sectors have on wealth management is revealed by two trend lines in Figure 9.2, for TMT and non-TMT equities respectively. (This figure is published with the permission of the Deutsche Bundesbank):

- The first quarter of 2000 TMT equities rose fast, then came the deep downtrend.
- By way of contrast, non-TMT equities held a relatively small slope line, both in the upside and in the downside.

An investor has to take risks if he or she wants to get ahead of the game in return on investment, but because the investor puts personal savings on the line, he or she should also fully understand the risks being taken – as well as whether or not he or she can afford them. This is a basic principle which contributes a great deal to self-protection and damage control. The principle behind this statement can be expressed as:

- Markets are markets. They are difficult things to read, no matter what 'expert' one claims to be, and

- In the last analysis, the only person on whom the investor can depend for protection is him or herself.

Pity the investor who depends on 'others' to read the market signals and interpret market trends for him or her. That is why it is a 'must' to understand what investments are all about, that is, their risks and when and how these risks can be kept within reasonable limits. Moreover, it is more important to finish in good order, in asset management, than to finish 'first'. As Warren Buffett aptly says: 'To finish first, you must first finish.'

9.3   A prudent policy for investors: equities versus bonds

Though based on different frames of investment advice, the statistics in both Tables 9.1 and 9.2 are simple to understand and the advice behind them is visible. As a rule, the investor's self-protection runs against the sales person's talk that he or she has nothing to worry about the proposed purchase of equities, because 'I know my client's investment style'. Nothing should be taken for granted, including assurances that equities offered as a 'buy' have been subject to due diligence at the broker's headquarters. For instance, that they have been subjected to:

- *sector and group analysis*, identifying what sectors and groups are signaling the strongest quantitative insider buying,
- *technical stage ratings*, incorporating insider consensus on stocks in technical stages – along with the (meaningless) argument that 'technical stage analysis is superior to technical analysis',
- *highest dividend yields*, which are 'sure' to provide gratifying investment results, since the sales person's offer lists those 'insider stocks' that have yields of 3 percent or greater, and
- an oral assertion about *largest number of insiders buying* as the listing includes all stocks with a significant number of operational insiders that have been buying these equities on the open market over the past months.

This, and similar types of double-talk should be of absolutely no interest to the serious investor. 'Technical stage analysis', the number of 'operational insiders' and other hollow statements are thrown in to confuse the buyer. At the least, they make the investment process – starting with investment choice – more complex and less easy to understand than it might have been. The moment he or she goes for catchwords, the investor lets down all his or her defenses and becomes pray to small talk.

Equities is not the only type of investment which is subject to double-talk. Annuities from companies which look like being beyond any doubt or reproach, is another. Equitable Life, the venerable life insurer, provides an example of how its sales people took their clients for a ride.

In March 2004, a report published by the British government blamed the downfall of the world's oldest life insurer on mismanagement. For years, its executives and its sales people promised policyholders more in bonus payments than the company's assets could justify. In the aftermath, losses are estimated at £3 billion ($5.4 billion), and who pays for them is the insured public.

Other investors have chosen as partners to their retirement, mutual funds rather than life insurance companies and their annuities. But this strategy, too, has its risks. In March 2004, Bank of America and FleetBoston Financial agreed to pay $675 million to resolve separate charges that they were involved in the improper trading of mutual funds.[1] (At that time, Bank of America, aimed to complete a $47 billion acquisition of FleetBoston, scheduled for April 2004.)

Neither is real estate a risk-free position. Take the case of Australia as an example. In the early years of the twenty-first century, a booming business of new construction has produced a glut of homes, with the result that net rental yields, after maintenance and other cost, have gone down to 2 percent, way under the 7 percent mortgage rate most investors were counting on. Some people have kept on buying in the hope of capital gains, which contributed to causing a bubble, but only in Ponzi scams do capital gains seem as if they 'increase forever'.

Note that with the real estate bubble, the Australian economy, too, got leveraged. In the aftermath of this housing boom and bust, household debt, including mortgage financing, grew from 85 percent of disposable income in 1996 to about 140 percent at the end of 2003. Moreover, as in America,

- Consumers have borrowed more money against the rising value of their homes.
- They extracted some of their capital gains and spent more than their income.

This proved to be a very poor strategy because it caused the Australian consumers to be most exposed to higher interest rates or recession. In fact, the housing example we have just seen, should bring to the reader's attention the second golden rule of investing particularly important at retail level: 'Do not borrow, do not buy on margin and do not leverage yourself' (see Chapter 1). This advice is valid not only for equities, but for all investments.

Moreover, the third golden rule of investment has prodded the reader to 'decide whether he or she invests for income or for growth, and to diversify'. Real estate is a good option if you buy your own home, but speculating on real estate is not for everybody. Debt instruments are better fitted for this role. This is not a book on bond investments, but the issue of choice between equities and fixed-income instruments is crucial. In the past few years, capital markets have been characterized by a diverging trend in total returns – comprising price movements, interest and dividends – between the:

- Equity market, and
- Bond market.

With some exceptions, between March 2000 and March 2003 the share index of major capital markets lost around three-quarters of its value. In the same period the yields on ten-year euro-denominated government bonds fell from approximately 5.5 percent to below 3.5 percent by the middle of 2003. In the aftermath, the prices of bonds rose significantly and their investors reaped significant profits. This, however, does not mean that bonds are investments free of any risk. As we will see in section 9.8, bond investments have both interest rate risk – which is market risk – and credit risk.

A balanced way of investing in bonds and stocks helps not only in building up the investors defenses through diversification, but also in capitalizing on market trends. This is written in full appreciation of the fact that, by historical standards, a negative correlation of the magnitude between the equity market and the bond market tends to be an exception.

- If the relation between these two markets is observed over a long period of time,
- Then, on average, one finds that there exists a positive correlation between the weekly yields, but the coefficient is less than 0.3.

This 0.3 is a relatively weak correlation. Had it been a stronger one, such as 0.5 or higher, then falling equity prices would generally be accompanied by falling bond prices, hence higher yields. If we make the hypothesis that equity prices reflect their future discounted dividends, and bond prices reflect their future interest payments, a positive correlation could be explained up to a point by the fact that the two markets depend on a common discounting factor which tends to come into play in the absence of change in inflationary expectations.

Furthermore, several studies suggest that periods of negative correlation between equity markets and bond markets are often accompanied by significant volatility in stocks, and a great degree of price uncertainty measured by implied volatility of options on the equity market. Other things being equal,

- In times of crises investors shift their assets away from equities and purchase bonds, perceived to be safer, and
- The negative correlation is driven by equity market volatility which leads to a flight toward fixed income instruments.

To recap, a positive correlation between stock markets and bond markets sees to it that rising equity prices are accompanied by rising prices in the bond market and falling yields. By contrast, if a negative correlation prevails between the two markets, then the rising equity prices are accompanied by falling bond prices, and therefore rising yield.

9.4 Data analysis is at the core of the investor's homework

To a fairly substantial extent, statistics underpin investment decisions, and statistics are supposed to be reliable. But sometimes even official statistics are massaged. Inflation figures are an example; references based on accounting data is another. As we saw in Chapter 8, the standards of accounting have been established to promote disclosure, but in many cases financial reporting is twisted in a way that hides the true risks.

This applies equally to equities and bonds. In cases such as Enron, WorldCom, Parmalat and many others, both shareholders and bondholders were cheated not only because they did not receive full information about the real level of debt, profits and losses of the company, but also because they received manipulated financial data. There is a long list of tricks used in manipulating statistical and accounting evidence, making it possible to lie with statistics.

It may not be easy to believe, but looking at data and comprehending the message they convey is no simple and linear matter. Today we practically have an unlimited computing power, but our data sources are not well organized, and the information elements in our databases are often incomplete or obsolete. This means they are not dependable, even when they are not manipulated.

Because of this, investors should appreciate that the first step of a statistical analysis is looking at data and presenting it in a form which is simple and comprehensible. A graphical presentation is a good step prior to proceeding with rigorous analysis. Examples are histograms, box plots, regression lines, and normal distribution like the one in the upper part of Figure 9.3. Other examples are correlograms, statistical quality control charts, and Pareto diagrams, as the in the lower part of Figure 9.3.

The quality of financial information used by investors can vary tremendously between good and bad; or it may be simply unknown. Rarely is there assurance of its standard and of its dependability. Yet, in terms of end results, much depends on the integrity of the information being provided – not only on the analyst's skills. Every investor should appreciate these facts.

Some banks and brokers have found out that if the financial information which reaches them is of an average quality, then they should be using two heads (two analysts), rather than one. Subsequently, they analyze the results each analyst reaches, to find out differences in their perception of facts and trends. This permits a system of checks and balances, which can be built into every procedure.

Note that part of this work of testing different interpretations of the same information elements can be automated, with knowledge artifacts (agents) providing invaluable service in flushing out inconsistencies in data streams and in database contents. Then, when database contents and incoming data streams have been tested and proved to be reliable, there must be available a dependent methodology and *common framework* regarding:

■ Findings, and
■ Conclusions.

Filtering statistical evidence to flush out inconsistencies and intentional twists, is not easy but it is possible. My experience with statistical analysis suggests that three of the most frequent reasons a trained eye can see that figures and statistics stand out as being wrong are that:

■ They are surprisingly precise,
■ They are improbably pertinent, and
■ They are given wholesale.

Either of these reasons ensures that statistics-based statements may collapse under a second careful look. Figure 9.4 gives an example of how to lie with statistics. The data comes from a referendum which took place in a democratic country on 24 September 2000, amid the greatest ever voter apathy and abstention. The 18 percent of voters carried the day, even if though it was a small minority.

Also present in a statistical survey are two tendencies. To boast, and to understate, which do not cancel each other out. Another factor often at fault is the sampling

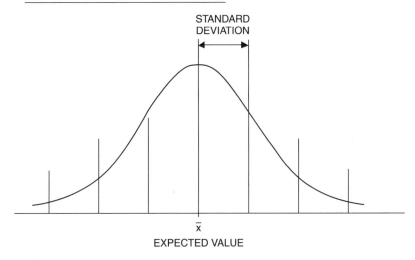

NORMAL DISTRIBUTION OF VARIABLE "x"

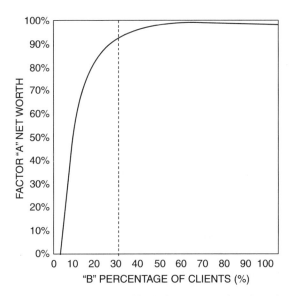

PARETO DISTRIBUTION OF FACTORS "A" AND "B"

Figure 9.3 Distributions, where applicable, help in comprehending the message conveyed by data

method. Weak (that is statistically invalid) and/or loaded samples are found at the heart of many false statistics. Even in scientific analysis the samples being used may be:

- Too small,
- Biased, or
- Plainly irrelevant.

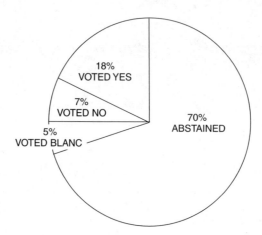

Figure 9.4 How to lie with statistics: The 24 September 2000 referendum where the
18 percent won

It goes without saying that the results of every statistical study are no better than the sample on which it is based. A valid sample has a minimum of twenty-five elements taken out of the population under study and subjected to measurement; fifty is better. Both the absolute number of elements in the sample and the percentage of the population this sample contains, have an impact on the operating characteristics (OC) curve and therefore on the level of confidence.[2]

In finance the accuracy associated with sample size and with measurements themselves has a good deal to do with materiality – a concept whose origin is found in accounting. Regulators and standards committees have often tried to clarify which events and data are important enough to be considered *material*.

Materiality relates to the size of the company business, but criteria and standards associated with judging materiality are often loose. In some cases, anything less than *x* percent of earnings or assets is considered 'immaterial' to overall performance, and thus could be left out of the statements. Sometimes this *x* is equal to 5 or 10 percent, which of course is absurd. That is why, when discussing virtual balance sheets in Chapter 8 I stated that a 3 percent to 4 percent error is admissible, I immediately added that this is a virtual statement only for the company's own executives.

Recently, the SEC made it clear that the materiality issue must be addressed both qualitatively *and* quantitatively, but new firm rules are still not available. Therefore, companies have an interest in establishing their own rigorous standards on materiality, as well as on the level of statistical error acceptable in connection with financial information. It needs no explaining that this level must be very small.

What I just stated about materiality and an acceptable level of error (or approximation) can be best appreciated if we return to the fundamentals. The reason why we use statistics, as well as statistical tests, is to see more clearly and be able to appreciate a certain situation. This is nearly synonymous with saying that statistics must help to create value. No innovation, no technology and no new product is worth anything if it does not create value.

Statistical tools such as, for instance, correlation coefficients, make it possible to think about relationships between different factors. The example we saw in section 9.3

was price correlations between equities and bonds – which are pertinent to asset allocation. Investors have today at their disposal plenty of statistical tools that help to understand what drives market dynamics within a market, and between markets.

Statistics are also making possible peer-to-peer comparisons. Peer analysis by a given firm's shareholders is valuable when it is based on reliable information. Prior to investing in a given equity, it is wise to compare one company with another in the domain of one's choice. But while peer analysis can be rewarding, it is not easy because:

- There is no industry standard on how to do it,
- The notion of economic risk capital is not a universal metric,
- Modeling assumptions are often vague or unreliable,
- Underlying data may be biased or incomplete, and
- Implementation specifics vary widely from one analytical process to the next.

These issues can leave investors with a dilemma. Shareholders often lack appropriate documentation to serve their peer analysis objectives. They generally are swayed by high profits which are unsustainable; are impressed by entities that carry high risks, which are not under full control; and are unaware of whether or not an institution is poorly capitalized. Only after the facts are revealed, frequently through bankruptcy proceedings, does it become known that a given entity failed because of major acts of mismanagement, systemic problems, poor asset quality, or for all three reasons.

9.5   Investors should always consider the contrarian's advice

Harry Truman is rumored to have said: 'I am looking for a one-armed economist.' When asked by other members of his cabinet 'why', he reportedly answered: 'So that he would not give me an advice, and right after that add "On the other hand …".' For every critical issue there is always at least an opposing view, and this is not likely to be complementary but contrarian.

- If, as so often happens, numbers and statistics are not reliable (as section 9.4 has demonstrated),
- Then a critical view which is contrarian, and goes beyond the confines of analysis, becomes very important.

The *eleventh golden rule* of investing is to 'always listen to contrarian opinion'. It is likely that a contrarian opinion will contradict the results and findings of a fundamental analysis, of a technical analysis, or of both (see Chapter 6). When this happens, so much the better for the investor – because it gives him or her food for thought.

In the opinion of Bob Keen, it would be forcing open doors to argue about the need to listen to contrarian opinion. The big question, Keen suggested, is how fast an investor acts when that opinion becomes available. Here is a practical example: Goldman Sachs makes a market report and sends it to its customers who are both:

- Private clients, and
- Institutional investors.

The better managed institutional investors debate the contents of this Goldman report immediately upon receipt, and they decide quite rapidly on whether they should or should not move. That is what good professionals do. By contrast, individual investors who receive from a major broker a market report, typically read it and sit on it for a week or two, before making up their mind on whether they should move. By then,

- What the report has stated may well be obsolete, and
- The window of opportunity has closed, and only the fast-moving investors took advantage of it.

'It should be evident that listening to contrarian opinion in no way relieves the investor of the need to decide what to do', said Eugen Buck, who summed up beautifully this issue by stating: 'Listen to contrarians but make your own investment decisions.'

The reader should also note that the seventh and eleventh golden rules correlate. Listening to contrarian opinion is an integral part of an investor's homework – just as important as learning how to do fundamental, technical and quantitative analysis. These approaches are necessary to exploit business opportunity as well as being able to keep risk under lock and key.

Going back to the fundamentals, there is an important difference between a theoretical contrarian and one dealing in pragmatic terms. In practice, to win as a contrarian one has to have not only a clear enough vision as to why things are *not* as they are generally accepted to be – but also the proper strategy and the right timing. In a way, the true contrarian is not going against 'any' trend, because he or she appreciates there is no general pattern of successful investment activity that holds good all the time.

Listening to contrarian opinion and weighing it on an equal basis with one's own is something rarely taught in schools, yet it is cornerstone to good management. Traditionally, organizations weed out the non-conformist elements, with the result that they respond slowly to change. Eliminating dissent creates the illusion of a homogeneous group aligned behind one approach. However, this makes it difficult to predict a valid path – let alone the best one.

Basically, the contrarian spirit says: 'Never follow conventional wisdom in the market.' To go counter to this means that an investor has to learn how to think for him or herself. Most people do not want to increase the effort to do it, or they simply do not know how to do it. For this reason, they prefer being the followers of a trend, but do not appreciate that:

- Even riding the wave requires thinking,
- Thinking is indispensable in facing the different twists and potholes in the investments road,
- Sometimes one does exceptionally well on the strength of a few chosen stocks while others are, at least temporarily, left by the wayside, and
- In other years, one makes (or loses) a fortune because as a contrarian he or she is the first (last) to be on the right side of the market, which reduces as others come on board.

Neither are contrarians limiting their options to market trends and timing, in coming in and out of positions. In fact, one of the interesting characteristics of several contrarians is their disdain for diversification. They believe that diversification is a hedge for ignorance, and that one can be much better off owning only a few stocks but knowing a great deal about them. This is a thesis this book supports.

Some contrarians are among the most respected names in asset management. They have made a lot of money for many of their clients, which is not forgotten. This, however, does not mean that contrarians are always right. If a contrarian opinion can prove to be quite valuable, it is just as true that in other cases the contrarian's judgment on the timing of a stock market rise or crash is indeed premature. But which is more honorable?

- To keep out of equities when one thinks they are overvalued?
- Or, to keep on buying and remain fully invested since, well, this is only the clients' money?

Because of the strength that comes from dissent, contrarian opinions are important and they should always be considered. Contrarian opinions often have associated with them a breadth of vision. Their implementation, however, requires strength of character to break with the past – or with the ongoing trend – which could no longer serve as a reliable guide to the future. In that respect, a great deal can be learned, from the leaders of industry. An example is provided by Alfred P. Sloan Jr, GM's former chairman and CEO.

As CEO, Alfred Sloan appreciated that an industrial company, credit institution or any other organization that tolerates dissent is able to respond to market shifts in a flexible way. It is more successful, because it can easily change the allocation of its resources if the market moves in a different direction than originally expected. Business life teaches that:

- Perfectly aligned organizations tend to reduce creativity,
- While dissent forces a company to face constraints more effectively and produce better rounded solutions.

Rubber-stamping and its associated intolerance of dissent, causes the board and senior management to consider few alternatives, leads to miscalculating the chances associated with today's decisions, and helps in exaggerating one's prospects of success and/or underestimating exposure. In short, there are major risks embedded in too much alignment, the greatest peril being that of moving blindfolded to a hidden crevasse.

Clear-thinking CEOs appreciate these issues and, by so doing, they are ahead of the game. Alfred P. Sloan Jr once said at a GM board meeting: 'Gentlemen, I take it we are all in complete agreement on the decision here.' When the assembled executives all nodded their assent, Sloan stated: 'I propose further discussion on this matter is postponed until our next meeting to give yourself time to develop disagreement, and perhaps gain some understanding of what the decision is all about.'

Following Sloan's leadership, CEOs will be well advised to provide, for themselves and their immediate assistants, a mechanism that brings constantly across their desk the query, 'What are *my* alternatives?', along with a reminder to every manager that some crucial questions are associated with each alternative:

- What is the upside and its chances?
- What is the downside and its likelihood?
- Where is the evidence that our last policy has been working?
- Are we ready to implement our chosen alternatives?

Investors should ask themselves very similar questions to those just outlined, and they should answer them in a factual and documented manner. This cannot be effectively done without paying attention to contrarian opinions, for the simple reason that such answers will totally miss the downside.

Any answer worth its salt must incorporate Truman's 'on the other hand . . .' remark. The upwards movement of the equity market may seem to be unstoppable; on the other hand . . . Not only contrarian opinion is crucial but it has also to be comprehensively phrased. To be able to drive his or her company in an effective manner, the chief executive has to convey only a few simple ideas, and be accountable for his or her decisions,[3] which must be:

- Clearly stated,
- Unambiguous, and
- Able to give direction.

If a decision can be misunderstood, it will be. If a decision is misunderstood, then the CEO will get the most of what he or she wants least, his or her people will be overcome by trivialities and the company will lack direction. But making a clear decision requires skill, practice and daring to provide *future vision*. With only minor rephrasing, these same statements are valid for investors, conditioning the nature of tools they use.

Here is an example of how lack of dissent leads to situations which can become ridiculous, and can lead to major exposures. The 1996 Market Risk Amendment by the Basel Committee on Banking Supervision advanced a measurement known as value at risk. As we saw previously, this was designed originally by the Morgan Bank for *market risk*, and even though subsequent practice has shown that it is mathematically unsound, its usage has expanded.

Then, in 2003, following somebody's one-track mind, several credit institutions transplanted VAR into *credit risk*, as $CVAR_{99.97}$. In this case, 99.97 means the level of confidence – which is evidently high, except for the fact that the whole VAR algorithm is weak and inappropriate for credit risk.

Models have locality. It is an aberration to use a model written for market risk for credit risk control purposes, and vice versa. Basically, credit risk and market risk are totally different exposures from one another, even if the one may lead to the other. Mixing them up practically means illiteracy both:

- In banking, and
- In the use of models.

It is not just a matter of dissent for the use of $CVAR_{99.97}$ and similar half-baked metrics.[4] All models are more or less wrong, but some can be valuable as eye-openers – but *not* $CVAR_{99.97}$.

While all human-made mathematical tools are imprecise, some are more accurate while others can be outright misleading. When this happens, the result is that senior management decisions based on them turn sour. Vigorous dissent in connection with model development and usage is vital in an environment of risk control.

(Note that in January 2004 the Gordian knot was cut by the Basel Committee on Banking Supervision with its publication of *Modifications to the Capital Treatment for Expected and Unexpected Credit Losses in the New Basel Accord*. This outlines the algorithm which should be used by credit institutions for their estimate of unexpected losses, leaving $CVAR_{99.97}$ in the dust.)

9.6 Value stocks, growth stocks and intrinsic value

Torrents of ink have run in arguments about the better choice of equities: Is investing in value stocks better than in growth stocks, or vice versa? Behind this query lies the fact that most stocks can be identified as either *value* or *growth*. As we saw in section 9.2, they can also be segregated into large caps, mid-caps and small caps, according to the total market value, or capitalization, of the company's shares outstanding. In principle,

- *Value stocks* are those perceived as priced below their true worth, and
- *Growth stocks* are those expected to grow faster than average.

Quantitatively, this classification of equities as *value* or *growth* depends on their price to book value ratio; or the P/BV's inverted presentation as book to market ratio. This is done in reflection of the fact that book value does not really mean much in terms of the equity's worth in a free capital market.

Yet, in terms of market sentiment book value still counts. Typically, value-oriented shares are those issued by companies whose market capitalization is considered relatively low to book value. The opposite is true of growth-oriented shares. In other words, at equity level:

- A low P/BV tends to indicate 'value', and
- A high P/BV is taken as indicator of 'growth'.

This relatively simple approach is at the basis of the S&P Growth/Value Index, based on an algorithm by Dr Barro, which is frequently used as a benchmark. Another hypothesis, supported by Dr Sharpe, is that there is a positive correlation between companies with a low P/BV, high dividend yield, relatively low P/E ratio, moderate earnings growth and modest ROE (see Chapter 7).

The S&P/Barro Index was launched in the 1970s. Over that period, neither the growth nor the value track outperformed one another in the long term. The only tangible result, which I know of, is that returns for each investment style tend to display longer-term cycles that are usually divergent. The S&P 500/Barro Growth

Index did better than the Value Index from 1994 to spring 2000. But after the Internet bubble burst, investor interest swung back toward value equities, which tended to hold the upper ground – or so investors thought.

While generalizations are dangerous, and often enough they are not rewarding, there is evidence that growth stocks tend to outperform value stocks over intermediate time periods ranging from three to eight years. By contrast, over long periods, of a decade or more, the difference in the performance of these two asset classes tends to diminish.

Generally speaking, growth investors look for companies with strong revenue and a trend in earnings making it possible to predict profits and cash flows in the future. This is not the criterion in cherry-picking by value investors, who seek out bargains, trying to buy stock for less than it worth. Approaches vary within this perspective:

- From buying stocks that have just had bad news, or are out of favor because of the market's overreaction,
- To the use of quantitative analysis, looking for critical ratios which help to predict future value performance.

A key component in a search for equity investments is the concept of *high-quality* stocks. The S&P definition is that high-quality stocks are those that have maintained a stable or superior growth rate for the latest ten years. High-quality stocks also tend to have larger market capitalization. Growth stocks may be high quality if they:

- Exhibit superior growth characteristics,
- Capture investor attention, and
- Have higher valuations than the average high-quality value stocks.

In contrasted to high-quality stocks, lower-quality stocks are those that have weak and unstable growth characteristics, tending to outperform only when the profits cycle accelerates. These are the basic notions but they are not always applied in that way. For instance investors, generally, tend to equate:

- Growth with *high-quality stocks*, and
- *Value* with *lower-quality stocks*.

These are associations which are rarely, if ever, correct. Therefore, they do not serve the investors. While value stocks tend to have more conservative valuations than most other stocks, they may well be high-quality equities. Only an entity-by-entity test can tell what lies behind the market's numbers, and the quality it represents. This in practice means homework.

A distinction between growth stocks and value stocks can be more meaningful if the investor uses a dynamic approach to valuation. Static approaches to the value versus growth argument are too simplistic. Investors need dynamic investment models based on intrinsic value such as *discounted cash flow* (DCF), to complement their quantitative and qualitative analysis. Moreover, the model we use must provide a framework to evaluate future prospects.

Intrinsic value analysis through DCF is a sound method, because it is a matter of good management that a company generates real, rising cash flows that match and exceed investment requirements. Therefore, analysts and investors should consider the future prospects under intrinsic value benchmarks, before making buy/hold/sell decisions. To begin with, *intrinsic value* is the discounted value of cash that can be taken out of a business during its remaining life. Theoretically, its calculation looks like being straightforward; practically, it is not that simple because intrinsic value:

- Is an estimate rather than a precise figure, and
- It must be changed if interest rates move or forecasts of future cash flows are revised.

This makes it possible that two analysts or investors looking at the same facts may come up with different intrinsic value figures because of differences in the assumptions they make. By contrast, another metric, the *per-share book value*, is easy to calculate, but it is of limited use owing to the fact that, as already stated, book value is historical evidence which may be far different from market value.

A paradigm Warren Buffett uses to explain the differences between book value and intrinsic value is that of looking at college education as a form of investment – which it is. One can think of education's cost as its book value. If this cost is to be accurate, it should include:

(a) The earnings that were forgone by the student because he or she chose to study in college rather than taking a job, and
(b) The earnings the graduate would receive over his or her lifetime, after graduation, subtracting those he or she would have got without college education.

In this case, the investment horizon is one's lifetime. The resulting excess earnings figure of b minus a must be discounted at an appropriate interest rate back to graduation day, to give the intrinsic value of education. One of the key points of interest in analyzing any acquisition for intrinsic value, is the relationship between this intrinsic value and the market price of that asset and their interdependence. In Buffett's example, for instance, the intrinsic value of college education is direct function of market value of skills reflecting an attained college degree.

9.7   Importance of the investment horizon

Siegmund Warburg used to evaluate his fellow bankers, treasurers of corporations, major investors, as well as heads of state, on the basis of whether or not they knew the difference between *Kairos*, or short-term time, and *Chronos*, long-term time. He did the same with his associates and his assistants, teaching them that important events happen in the longer term, and benefits come to those who can wait.

The *time horizon* one adopts is most critical to practically every investment he or she makes. More often than not, it would be a key factor in deciding whether this investment has been fruitful or turned sour. Moreover, the time horizon helps to differentiate between investors and speculators:

- Investors have a long time horizon, but
- Speculators are characterized by a very short one.

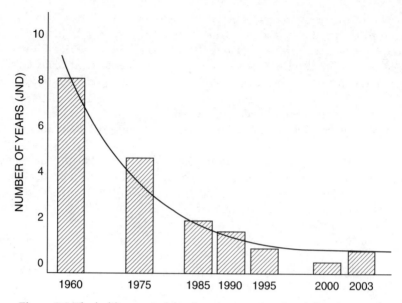

Figure 9.5 The holding period for American equities has fallen drastically

This being said, it is no less true that the holding period of US equities has been shrinking over the last four decades. This is particularly valid in regard to publicly traded companies on the NYSE, as shown in Figure 9.5. The trend curve identifies a significant change in attitude, which adds to the volatility of markets.

More traditional economists are of the opinion that shortening the time horizon is a negative for investors. They believe that global diversification and oft-neglected long-term thinking are crucial factors for the successful management of equity investments. I made reference to this when I stated what my professors at UCLA taught this to their students in the 1950s. Beyond this, according to some fairly recent calculations,

- There is approximately a 20 percent probability that an equity safekeeping account's value will diminish after one year,
- But when the investment horizon is stretched to ten years, the likelihood of a negative performance drops to 3.4 percent, and this figure sinks to a mere 0.5 percent for a twenty-year investment.

In finance, short term typically means less than one year; though, in some jurisdictions, for credit institutions under its authority the central bank defines short term as less than six months (France and Italy are examples). What is meant by short, medium and long term for an investor?

- If an investor has a three- to five-year time frame, then he or she thinks for the short to medium term.
- Five to ten years is medium term, and
- A long-term horizon is ten years or more.

The question to ask yourself about the long term, suggests Warren Buffett, is how you would feel about putting your family's entire net worth into a chosen investment and owing it forever. And he adds: if you invest for the short term you are leaning towards the greater fool theory, that is, there will be somebody else more silly than you, to buy what you are selling.

One of the ironies with investments is that overall, long-term shareholders benefit from a sinking stock market, like a family benefits from declining food prices. There-fore, when the market plummets, as it does from time to time, equity-holders should neither panic nor mourn; it may be good news.

Warren Buffett suggests that success in investment often depends on picking the right stocks and then doing nothing. As he stated in a report to Berkshire shareholders in the mid-1990s: 'We continue in our Rip Van Winkle mode: five of our top six positions at year end 1994 were left untouched during 1995.' But Buffett prudently puts a personal factor in this model.

- He gets to know management at companies he invests in, and
- Gains an insight into the entity's longer-term stock price, based on management quality.

An investor who cares to hold his or her place for the long term, and improve it, does not need to predict all the currents that will move in the stock market. Rather he or she concentrates on how his or her assets will change in value whatever the currents may be (see Chapter 10 on risk management). That is where scenario analysis and stress testing can provide significant hindsight.

From qualitative scenario analysis to quantitative stress tests, investors must keep in mind that the time horizon they choose has much to do with their personality and their risk profile – and with the time and attention they are devoting to managing their assets. One of the problems of *Kairos* is that nobody seems to have enough of it, yet everyone has all the time that is available. People make uneven use of their time. Many lack the concept of time management, while time moves faster for those who work faster. This is the concept of *intrinsic time*.

- Time moves fast in the New York market. The American trader takes a sandwich for lunch and eats it at his or her desk while working.
- Time moves slower in Tokyo. The Japanese trader will go to a sushi bar and wait to be served, while business opportunities come and go.
- Time moves very slow in the Middle East and in countries where people have the habit of leaving important work for tomorrow.

Because time moves faster for those who work faster, people who work under a tight schedule accomplish more in the same amount of clock time than people who work at normal pace or slower. The different economic theories typically fail to account for the arrow of time, just as they do not pay enough attention to the repetition of certain events.

Kyrtosis is the fourth momentum of a distribution (the mean $\bar{x}$ is the first momentum, standard deviation s the second, and skewness the third). It is only during the last ten years that financial analysts started using Hurst's exponent, also known as fat tails.[5]

Hurst was a British engineer studying the floods of the Nile river when he observed events were not normally distributed as if nature had a memory.

- A flood tended to be followed by another flood, and
- A draught tended to be followed by another draught.

In other words, more recent events have greater impact than distant events; there is residual influence. A system that exhibits Hurst coefficient, is the result of a long stream of interconnected events which mathematicians, engineers and financial analysts do not quite understand. The basic concept is that 'where we are now is a result of where we have been in the past', particularly in the more recent past.

This is a different way of saying that time matters. Both *Chronos* and *Kairos* are present. In this case, events ripple forward in time but the size of the ripple diminishes until, so to speak, the ripple disappears. This concept of a time arrow runs afoot of traditional econometrics, which assumes that time series are invariant. Yet, there is a difference, made by dynamics.

Hurst's findings refute the static econometric theories, and the notions underpinning them. Not only distributions of events may be leptokyrtotic or platokyrtotic – as contrasted to normal or bell-shaped – but also the time series may be antipersistent or ergodic. The output of the underlying system can be *mean reverting*.

- If that system has been up in the previous period, it is more likely to be down in the next period.
- If it was down before, it is likely to be up in the next period – which is the trend shown as a sinusoidal curve.

Markets follow quite closely this antipersistent behavior which switches positive and negative correlation of key factors. Time series of this kind would be typically choppy, reflecting the fact the market is volatile and there are mean reversals. Moreover, there may be a widening or shrinking standard deviation, if the time series produce a normal distribution in the first place. There may also be non-linearities in the capital market behavior, which tend to leave the long-term investor unaffected.

9.8   Factors affecting return on investment

It needs no explaining that private investors, institutional investors and any others like to get a return for their money. The questions are: what kind of return? At what risk? On the basis of which investment horizon?

Section 9.7 advised that serious investors concentrate on the longer term. However, while an investment policy may (indeed, should) have a longer-term horizon, the results of such a policy will come to the investor's attention both in the short and in the long term. This is an important distinction which should be kept in mind when we talk of return on investment.

Let us start with certain fallacies. Investors often tend to expect that short-term results, when positive, will hold true in the long term. This is false. Other investors believed that the great returns of the late 1990s signaled that big gains in the stock market would continue indefinitely. Then, 2000 proved this is not so. More to the point, by 2002 many investors were just as sure that stocks will not rise again. A year later, the tune has changed.

What these examples should teach us is that outperformance and underperformance are both natural parts of complete market cycles. For example, between 1945 and 2000 the S&P 500 slid into ten bear markets, defined as declines of 20 percent or more. Reaching the bottom took from three months (in 1990) to thirty-seven months (1946–48 and 2000–03). Both were well within historical precedent. After bottoming, the stock market has typically recovered in less than twenty months.[6]

These historical references not only signal the ups and downs which exist in equity markets, but they also show that the results of a return on investment analysis are highly dependent on the investors' time horizon. The evaluation of an investment made, for instance, in mid-1997 will be different in terms of results if the investment horizon is five years or six years – because 2002 was a low in the market while 2003 saw a reasonable recovery.

By March 2003, just before the market turned around, the negative performance by the DJIA was not historically unusual. The turnaround which took place thereafter tends to suggest that the longer the investor held his or her stocks, the better the chances of being rewarded. Stock portfolios are subject to *market risk* because of volatility in the prices of securities reflecting changing conditions in financial markets and/or general market sentiment.

The reader should always bear in mind that even a generally positive market sentiment does not lift all stocks. A portfolio invested in equities is also subject to *company risk*, that is, the possibility that current earnings will fall or that the company's overall financial soundness will decline, reducing the security's value even if the stock market is in positive territory.

Take Royal Dutch/Shell as an example. Following its announcement that it found it necessary to restate its oil and gas estimated reserves, the market punished its stock. Then pressure on the company mounted even more as law firms began preparing class-action lawsuits alleging deception by the oil company's management. Company memos suggested that top managers knew from the start that there were potential problems with its system for classifying oil and gas reserves,[7] and the evidence seems to reveal that management was more interested in its own survival than in shareholder value.

In spite of these ups and downs, there is a saying on Wall Street that, in the longer run, ROE investments outperform returns on bonds. This is not necessarily true in the short term, or even in the medium term. Statistics show that during any five-year holding period, there is a 26.7 percent chance that stocks will not outperform US Treasury bills. This is what 1997 research by Professor Jeremy Siegel of the Wharton School of the University of Pennsylvania has shown.

- To be at least 90 percent sure of beating Treasury bills returns, investors historically have had to hold stocks for twenty years or more.[8]
- Siegel, however, speaks of market risk and of Treasury bills not of any bond instrument.
- There is plenty of credit risk with corporate bonds which must be factored into the investment.

All bonds have credit risk, but the so-called junk bonds have much higher credit risk than the others. *Credit risk* reflects the possibility that the issuer of a fixed income security will not be able to pay principal and interest when due. Bonds also have interest rate risk, which is market risk. Therefore, investing in fixed income securities is subject to *interest rate risk* (see also the discussion in section 9.3 on bonds and equities).

The debt instrument's value may decline if interest rates change. A rise in interest rates causes the market value of bonds to go down. On the other hand, a rate decline results in an increase in the market value of fixed interest rate securities. Waiting to see which way interest rates go by parking the money in a money market account is a solution which has *current income risk*.

- Other things being equal, falling interest rates will cause the investor's income to decline, and
- Money in bank savings accounts, or time deposits, usually pays less interest than bonds and has credit risk (other than with deposit insurance).

Based on empirical results, another concept on Wall Street suggests that expected returns on bonds and shares are higher when the economic conditions are bad, and lower when economic conditions take a turn for the better. Behind this, experts say, may be some linkages in the pricing of financial markets, with business activity and interest rate tending to co-vary with one another.

What all this suggests is that in terms of return on investment, nothing is 'sure' for the investor. Risks are present whether he or she chooses fixed income, equities, real estate, mutual funds or any other instrument. Moreover, risk has the nasty habit of increasing more than the increase in yield, as the instrument in which one is investing becomes more complex.

- Complexity means that the unknowns grow fast and this impacts on volatility.
- In the longer run stocks may be more rewarding than bonds, but they are also more volatile.

Beyond the issues treated in the preceding paragraphs come the gimmicks. Every time the term 'enhanced' is used by investment advisers, it is likely that the risk goes up. For instance, an enhanced fixed income portfolio may have junk bonds in it, typically called high interest bonds to attract unaware investors. It is enhanced in the sense its average interest rate is higher, but it also represents *more exposure* of which the investor is not always aware.

Other risks are inherent to funds invested in foreign securities traded on foreign exchanges. These go beyond exposures taken in domestic investing, including changes in currency exchange rates; lower foreign accounting standards; questionable liquidity and higher volatility in some foreign markets; the impact of political, social, or diplomatic events; possible imposition of market controls or currency exchange controls; withholding taxes on dividends and interest; likely seizure, expropriation or nationalization of assets; and so on.

All the risks I have just mentioned must be analyzed in regard to their likelihood and the effects they have, and will have, on the investor's portfolio. It is not easy monitoring both risks and portfolio performance for needed restructuring, but it is possible. This is the subject of Chapter 10, which concentrates on risk management, and of the other chapters of Part 3.

Notes

1 *The Economist*, 20 March 2004.
2 D.N. Chorafas (1995). *How to Understand and Use Mathematics for Derivatives, Volume 2: Advanced Modelling Methods.* Euromoney Books.
3 D.N. Chorafas (2004). *Rating Management's Effectiveness with Case Studies in Telecommunications.* Macmillan/Palgrave.
4 D.N. Chorafas (2004). *Economic Capital Allocation with Basel II: Cost and Benefit Analysis.* Butterworth-Heinemann.
5 D.N. Chorafas (1995). *How to Understand and Use Mathematics for Derivatives, Volume 2: Advanced Modelling Methods.* Euromoney Books.
6 *Wall Street Journal*, 6 March 2001.
7 *The Economist*, 13 March 2004.
8 *New York Times*, 4 August 2002.

Four

Execution risk and damage control

10 Investors' responsibility in risk management

10.1 Introduction

The fairly affluent society in which we live, as well as the fact that pension schemes and social security programs no longer provide the assurance they once did,[1] have seen to it that, suddenly, plenty of people are eager to learn more about investments. How do they work? What are the fundamentals that drive the business? How does one sort of investment compare to other types in the modern economy? Where are the similarities between private and public investment solutions? The contradictions?

These are legitimate queries for every investor who wishes to be ahead of the game. But an equally important, perhaps even more so, requirement is to learn the theoretical and practical foundations on which rests the management of risk associated with investments, and its principles. The investment world does not yet seem to have discovered the strategic importance of managing risk. Yet, without control of exposure wealth embedded in investments can turn to ashes.

Risk management has two sides. One is quantitative, based on data and models. We will talk more about this in section 10.7. The other, to which the present and subsequent chapters are dedicated, is qualitative. Mastery of the qualitative part requires a fruitful dialogue with different stakeholders in and constituents of the investment arena, to help develop a better understanding of the holistic aspects of risk management:

- It's goals,
- Its tools, and
- Its shortcomings.

These two sides, qualitative and quantitative, are linked together through a methodology, which integrates them and drives the risk manager's hand. An important part of this methodology is a questioning attitude which challenges the 'obvious'. For instance, Chapter 9 has demonstrated that statistics and other information cannot always be trusted. There is an *information risk* confronting investors, and a *model risk*.

Information risk frequently is accentuated because of hidden *leverage risk* whose magnitude becomes known only at the time of bankruptcy. This was the case with Parmalat, WorldCom, Global Crossing, Enron, and many others. The case study of Parmalat can be found in Chapter 15.

Investments also have *legal risk*, some of which is predictable while another, often the larger part, is unexpected.[2] For instance, in January 2004 a French court ruled that Morgan Stanley, the investment bank, had issued investment research that was biased against LVMH, a French luxury goods company, causing it 'financial and reputational harm', while praising the performance of Gucci, a rival luxury goods firm and a client of the American investment bank. Morgan Stanley was ordered to pay LVMH 30 million euros ($38 million) to compensate for damaged 'morale' while a further payment for material damages is still to be assessed.

Another example of legal risk is the EU's 24 March 2004, 475 million euro fine of Microsoft, and its decision to oblige the software maker to share proprietary information and unbundle its media software from its Windows operating system. Even the mid-March threat that Microsoft was expected to face fines running to millions of dollars when a final decision was issued had a devastating effect on the company's shares.

In other cases it is market volatility which turns the tables, and brings companies and investment plans to the edge of the abyss. There is also a *volatility risk* which is not always appropriately appreciated, as we will see in Chapter 12. The same chapter will explain why *liquidity risk* can be deadly. Under tense market conditions, it is sometimes difficult to distinguish between liquidity and solvency risk.

What the previous paragraphs have stated in terms of investment risk is true equally for companies and for private investors. Far from being a one-off affair, risk management is a polyvalent enterprise which must steadily face not only adverse market conditions, but also new inventions siphoning the investor's wealth out of his or her pocket. For instance, those who promote and those who buy alternative investments have thought about the means but not about the consequences. As an old Indian proverb has it: 'A fish eats its victims in the water, a dog on earth, and a bird in the air, but somebody's fortune is eaten up in all places.'[3]

10.2   Risk management requires a lot of homework

Since Chapter 1, it has been emphasized that doing one's own homework in a diligent and methodological way is tantamount to never believing that one 'knows the market'. The market is bigger than anybody, and it goes where it wants to go. It does not ask the permission of a banker, of a broker, of an analyst, of an investor or of the prime minister to make a sudden move, which may be fatal to a lot of its players.

Starting with the most basic of all notions, the risk an investor is taking can be best expressed as *future cost*. At the bottom line, this risk creates claims on income, and it does so in a manner which might be seen as similar to interest expense and overhead. But because *risk claims* are prospective and contingent, cash-equivalent costs do not initially appear on the books; later on, they may do so, as for instance when a bank purchases third-party insurance.

The good news connected to this kind of exposure is that, up to a point, the qualification and quantification of risk, as a cost, is possible if we have refined information going beyond transaction pricing and capital allocation. This information should be treating risk as a dynamic entity which changes over time, using market prices to steadily calibrate exposure to:

- Credit factors,
- Market factors, and
- Operational or execution risks.

Traders and investors who are serious about risk management, and therefore about the job they are doing, are concentrating on finding strengths and weaknesses in the instruments in which they deal and in the market at large. They not only want to understand the facts affecting market behavior, but also to appreciate future costs due to risks being currently assumed. This is critical in computing in an accurate manner risk and return – and that is where technology can be of help.

But way ahead of technology come decisions concerning investments, and the homework associated with them. Shortcuts do not lead anywhere. People who do not work hard enough to be ahead of the game find themselves among the losers. Yet, surprisingly, many investors and traders are walking in and out of the market betting on a 50/50 chance. As Warren Buffett aptly asks: 'Would you jump out of an airplane with a parachute that has a 50 percent chance to open?'

The worst possible investment mistake is the 'going bust' trade, which often results from a spur of the moment decision. There is probably no class of trades and investments with a higher failure rate than those of an impulsive type, which sometimes are presented as 'intuitive'. For instance, putting on an unplanned trade because somebody just recommended it, or liquidating a position before a predetermined limit is reached because some adverse price movement might have suggested doing so. In contrast to such hit and run approaches, doing one's homework in the control of exposure means following clear enough guidelines:

■ Assessing and reassessing one's risk tolerance.

While the market is rising, it is easy to think one can handle larger and riskier investments. But little by little the assumed level of exposure may be more than the investor wants, or actually needs, to take. The assessment or risk tolerance must be accurate, not precise. It is not possible to kill the two birds of accuracy and precision with one well-placed stone. Figure 10.1 shows the difference between the two.

■ Lowering short-term expectations to meet market reality.

During the 1990s, and similar periods in the past, many investors have become accustomed to annual returns of 15 percent to 20 percent, or more. Not only is this well above the S&P 500's historical average of 11 percent, from 1926 through 2000, but it also translates into huge risk – hence future cost.

■ Focus on the longer term and have confidence in your projections.

As we have seen in Chapter 9 in connection with investment horizon, it is always wise to establish an investment period. Within this time horizon, market uncertainty should always be kept in perspective. Volatility may sometimes be unpleasant, but it is not unnatural. Investors who have the time, patience, and discipline to do their homework regarding their investment program, are rewarded in the longer run.

By contrast, investors who think they do not need homework because their superior knowledge of the market made them then enough money to put nineteenth-century robber barons to shame, eventually suffer from self-inflicted wounds. At the time of the French resistance against German occupations, 95 percent of *resistants* and agents

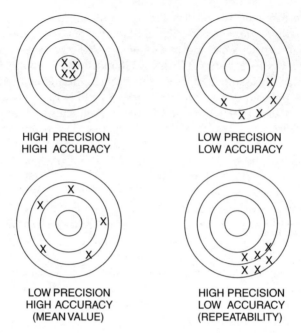

HIGH PRECISION
HIGH ACCURACY

LOW PRECISION
LOW ACCURACY

LOW PRECISION
HIGH ACCURACY
(MEAN VALUE)

HIGH PRECISION
LOW ACCURACY
(REPEATABILITY)

Figure 10.1 Accuracy and precision are not the same: for risk control, accuracy is more important

caught owed their arrest to their own carelessness or indiscretion, says Douglas Porch.[4] The counterpart of this in investments is the misjudgment of:

■ One's own risk tolerance,
■ The exposure being assumed, and
■ The amount of research necessary to keep risks under control.

Exposure to adverse market conditions may come from everywhere. Under the title 'Risks related to our business', the 2003 annual report of a telecommunications equipment manufacturer had this to say on assumed risks.

If we fail to keep pace with technological advances in our industry or if we pursue technologies that do not become commercially accepted, customers may not buy our products and our revenue may decline. The demand for our products can change quickly and in ways we may not anticipate, because our industry is generally characterized by:

■ Rapid, and sometimes disruptive, technological developments,
■ Evolving industry standards and changes in customer requirements,
■ Limited ability to accurately forecast future customer orders,
■ Frequent new product introductions and enhancements, and
■ Short product life cycles with declining prices over the life cycle of the product.

As this short list documents, risks are not only financial. They may be managerial, technical connected to product obsolescence, representing marketing failures or owing to other reasons. When they are left unattended, many of these 'other reasons' turn into financial risks and may bring the entity to its knees.

The annual report went on to say that because many current and planned products are highly complex, they may contain defects or errors that are detected only after deployment in commercial applications and, if this occurs, it could harm their reputation and result in reduced revenues or increased expenses, cancellation of orders, product returns, repairs or replacements, and diversion of resources. Also, legal actions by customers or the customers' end users can have financial consequences such as penalties, increased insurance costs, and other losses.

Moreover, the same annual report informed the company's investors of the lack of diversification characterizing the telecoms' suppliers industry, and its aftermath. Because sales are concentrated on a limited number of key customers, the company's revenue may materially decline, if one or more of these key customers do not continue to purchase the firm's existing and new products in significant quantities. The message is that this company's customer base is highly concentrated. Its top ten end customers accounted for approximately 60 percent of its revenue in fiscal year 2003. If any one of these key customers decides to purchase significantly less from that firm, or to terminate long-term relationships:

■ Revenues would cave-in, and
■ Profits may turn into losses.

The analysis of each of these risks, and many more the same annual report described, is an integral part of an investor's homework, including the likelihood of adverse events and the impact on the bottom line if they happen. Competition in the computers and communications industry, and in fact in any industry, is based on a long list of factors whose interrelationship is fairly complex. Examples are:

■ Performance,
■ Reliability,
■ Price,
■ Time to market,
■ Product footprint,
■ Compatibility with other products and protocols, and
■ Ability to offer integrated solutions.

There are more factors whose impact may turn the tables on the investor; for instance, breadth of product line, the supply chain and its automation, logistics and planning, cost of production, quality of manufacturing, sales costs, and high standard of after-sales service.

A company may believe it is competitive on the basis of all these factors, but it cannot afford not to be aware of the fact its competitors may compete more favorably on the basis of price, quality, performance, or on delivering products to market more quickly. Each of the aforementioned issues, and in cases many more, is a potential market advantage – and at the same time a potential market risk.

Neither, in the longer run, should investors feel comfortable because the company, or companies, in which they are shareholders has an established good record. Take

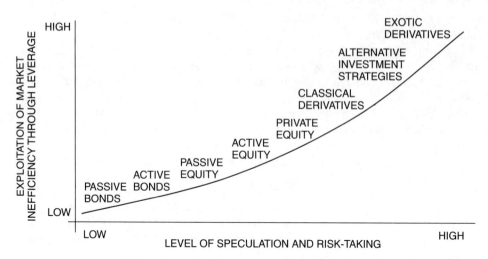

Figure 10.2 The exploitation of the market's inefficiency is not the same for all investment vehicles

Liberty Media, whose boss John Malone is known as a capable entrepreneur, as an example. Liberty reported a $931 million loss in the fourth quarter of 2003 despite surging revenues.[5]

All these examples are evidence of the polyvalence of exposure which can be found in an investor's portfolio, particularly if the instruments which it contains have been designed to exploit market inefficiencies through leveraging. Risk increases significantly with exploitation of market inefficiencies, and the pattern is shown in Figure 10.2. Eventually exposure escapes control, and what happens after is what took place at Long Term Capital Management in spite of its Nobel prize winners, or may be because of them.[6]

10.3   The importance of rigorous risk management standards

Because exposure is inseparable from every market activity, and from every instrument one holds in a portfolio, the *twelfth golden rule* of investments focuses on the need for rigorous risk management – rigorous in the sense that it must be seen as a discipline which reflects both ability and willingness to:

- Put up a considerable amount of effort for damage prevention and control,
- Employ the best available technology, to be ahead of the game in damage detection, and
- Accept with good grace the aftermath of one's hypotheses about market evolution and investment moves.

Risk management should be seen from two different viewpoints by the individual investor and the professional fund manager, suggested Gordon Midgley. In his opinion, for the individual investor, the primary exposure is that of risk associated with his or her savings objectives. Because this is the principal concern of a saver, he or she should avoid:

- Being a forced seller, or
- Being obliged, because of leverage, to crystalize the paper loss.

Other experts suggested that practically the same principle is basically valid for professional fund managers, though specifically the latter must be concerned about being in charge of their exposure to particular entities, specific risk factors, and overall results of a diversification policy.

To cope with these requirements, some entities have a separate department, sometimes known as the Performance Monitoring Unit, which also monitors and evaluates not only risk positions but also profits and losses by activity managed by the firm. 'They have to do so', Midgley said, 'because their major clients employ independent companies to do the monitoring of performance.' Eventually, over the years, this builds into a mandate.

The reader should appreciate that in the most basic sense the essence of risk management is not that of avoiding mistakes but of foreseeing the aftermath of both 'right' and 'wrong' moves, and of being prepared for it in time. This is written in direct reflection of the fact that risk-taking and the control of risk are the two most significant traits of every winning trader and investor – and that successful professionals are proactive in the market, while understanding that this is a necessary but not sufficient condition to win.

The alter ego of market activity is the ability to analyze the after-effect of entering into a given transaction. Challenging the 'obvious' permits the investors to determine whether a transaction is suitable for him or her. For instance, derivatives which are based on leverage and speculation are of particular concern, and therefore require much more by way of exposure control than cash transactions.

As previously mentioned, challenging the obvious is so important because investors must reach their own decisions and take responsibility for them. Amadeo P. Giannini provides an excellent example of how he trained his people in the art of assuming their own responsibilities – tossing out unconventional ideas, and being suspicious of people who seemed overly eager to agree with him. 'Are you yessing me?' he would shout.

Giannini surrounded himself with the best talent he could find and drove his professionals and his executives to the limit, but also gave them a free hand in running their departments. 'Come to me for advice, if that's what you want, but don't come to me for a decision', he would instruct them. 'If a decision is involved, bring it with you.' He had no patience with committees, and organizational flow charts, but he could tolerate mistakes, provided they were not of a lazy or careless type. And he did not easily forgive those whom he judged guilty of incompetence.[7]

Amadeo Giannini appreciated that to survive in banking, trading, and investing, he had to be able to reach his own decisions rather than depending on others to make them for him. He also had great respect for the fact that credit risk and market risk may have disastrous consequences, and used every manager's and executive's personal accountability as the method for an effective risk control.

If we do not care for credit risk and market risk, each on its own merits as well as in synergy, sooner or later the market will get us and teach us a bitter lesson. This will be a pity, because everybody has the option to control risk preventively by applying basic principles from stops and limits for damage control (see section 10.5), to the analysis of different types of exposure embedded in the portfolio of assets and liabilities. Analysis enables one to gain insight on exposure.

It is beyond any doubt that, in trading and investments, rigorous risk control is a most important discipline, both to the asset management firm and to the individual investor. Some people find it difficult to understand the reasons for steady and focused control of exposure, yet people with experience advise 'undertrade, undertrade, undertrade' – and correspondingly, 'underinvest rather than lose your fortune'.

- The way to recognize novice traders and novice investors of all ages, is that whatever they do they do it four or five times too big.
- Therefore, whatever one thinks his or her position ought to be, he or she should cut it at least in half, and even this may leave too much exposure.

A lesson can be learned from mature traders who follow the rule of taking more than 1 percent risk per transaction, compared to the worth of their assets (see Chapter 2). The advice never to risk more than 1 percent of total equity on any trade is an integral part of risk control. Keeping the risk relatively small and constant is the sign of a serious market player, who is in charge of his or her investments and/or trades.

From board members and the CEO to traders and investment managers, everybody must have a strong *respect for risk*. And there should also be on hand the risk manager who tells how much one can speculate and if everybody is within his or her limits. Respect for risk is nearly synonymous to traders' and investors' acceptance of responsibility for their own decision – which is the *thirteenth golden rule* of sound investing.

- This responsibility is continuous because investment decisions are made day by day, while they may have short-, medium-, or long-term effects.
- In the medium to longer term, no investment decision is, or has ever been, a 'wonderful idea from an imaginative brain'; all investment decisions can turn sour.

In the exchanges, with futures and with stocks, policing is done with margin requirements. But in OTC deals margin requirements are practically non-existent. For instance, depending on maturity, traders of Treasuries can finance up to 98 percent of their purchases through leveraging. This gives a gearing of 50-to-1; and more than that if one accounts for the fact that some of the money being used is itself borrowed. Because of leveraging:

- In many markets, and transactions, there are no constraints worth talking about.
- Only a rigorous internal risk control system and real-time reporting to senior management, can put the brakes on traders' speculation.[8]

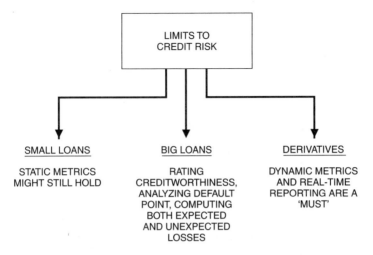

Figure 10.3 The concept of static limits is totally inadequate in connection with new financial vehicles

Precisely because overtrading is both a trend and a habit, risk management is the key to successful trading and investing. Moreover, part and parcel of a sound risk control policy is the ability to decide on an exit point (and associated conditions), before putting on a trade. In evaluating portfolio-wide risk and exit strategies, risk managers should appreciate that the overall portfolio exposure is likely to be much greater than the arithmetic sum of its parts because of synergy between different positions.

This then leads to the question of limits, which is not served through generalizations. Limits must be specific and commensurate with the exposure being taken and with the investor entity's risk appetite – now and in the future. Figure 10.3 makes this point with credit risk limits at three levels: small loans, big loans, and counterparty to derivatives deals.

An integral part of this concept is the fact that respect for risk is not just a matter of trading and of investing. It is a concept and a policy which applies to all types of business decisions, because there is no risk-free business activity, just as there is no 'free lunch'. Disrespect for risk is akin to a person who finds him or herself in the middle of an investment minefield, and who closes his or her eyes and walks through it as if there was no danger.

Computers and models can help in a significant way with risk control by flushing out alarm signals, and by calculating correlations in the portfolio as well as in trades about to be made (see section 10.7). However, both computers and models act as instruments assisting in decisions; they are not a substitute for the decision-maker. A risk management system that forgets about the human role in the control of exposure is very poor indeed. A sound approach to providing assistance for risk control would:

■ Pay great attention to correlations of different positions,
■ Measure total risk intraday as positions are added or sold,

- Update exposure figures as market prices change, and
- Bring to trader(s), investment executive(s), and senior management attention the aftermath of market moves – current, likely, and resulting from spikes.

Fulfilling what it takes to deliver the message in these four bullets requires real-time data-mining and a computer analysis able to establish the synergy of one's positions.[9] Bitter experience teaches that a mistake in correlation of position is the root of some of the most serious problems to be found in exposure. It is likely, in risk control terms, that:

- If we have ten correlated positions,
- Then it is as if we are really trading one large position.

Section 10.7 will explain why one of the basic contributions of technology in fund management is to identify and document not only item-by-item exposure, but also synergies which may not be apparent at first sight. The hidden synergy of exposures often sees to it that no matter what information the investor or trader has, and no matter how well he or she does what he or she is doing, he or she can be proved wrong. But,

- If he or she knows what the worst possible outcome is, then almost everything else will be a better result, and
- If he or she never bets his or her lifestyle, from a trading viewpoint, nothing terribly bad is likely to happen to him or her in the longer run.

Basically, this is the very essence of prudential risk management. Behind this lies the fact that, while we cannot quantify reward, we can quantify risk. This gives relative freedom of action. Beyond that, wise traders and commensurate investors do not just look at the risk, they control it. They know that run-away exposures are highly contagious, they appreciate that every minute counts, and they act fast in an informed and sensible way to avert a crisis.

10.4   Investors should never hesitate to cut losses

Able investors and good traders learn the most through adversity, because adversity teaches them that *the first loss is the best loss*, and that they should not do any trade or commit themselves to any investment till they are sure they have got it right. Based on these premises, the *fourteenth golden rule* is never hesitate to cut losses. Cutting losses quickly is one of the pillars in risk management. Selling at limits, when the limits are properly studied, helps in implementing a damage control strategy. That is why successful professionals love them.

Cutting losses is part of a rigorous risk management policy and practice, suggested Eugene Buck, adding that the twelfth rule and the fourteenth rule work in synergy. Up to a point, this has also been the opinion of Bob Keen who advises that individual clients should decide where the bottom line is, with the dual objective of:

- Limiting losses, and
- Bringing home profits.

Another advice given by winning practitioners in the capital markets is that if one sees a surprise move against his or her position(s), and does not understand its reason(s) or implication(s), then one should get out of this (these) position(s) and look for the reasons later. This can be written as the fourteenth golden rule. Quite similarly, when in doubt one should move out of his or her position(s) and get a good night's sleep. It is likely that next day, after a good night's sleep, the investor would be better positioned to solve the puzzle.

The chances are that part of the solution to the market's puzzle would be the re-evaluation of stops (see section 10.5), in a way to allow the trader or investor to hold on to his or her winners and cut the losers. One of the investment principles is that if the trader or investor does not stay with the winners he or she will not be able to pay for his or her losers and have a profit. Sometimes the losers multiply and, when he or she sees that in the portfolio is a 'can of worms', he or she has to play the executioner.

From real-time computers systems to knowledge-enriched models, technology provides traders and investors with significant support in identifying winners and losers. This, however, is no substitute for guts. Many investors and traders are good holders of winners, provided they properly identify them. By contrast, they tend to hold their losers too long – which makes damage control difficult and goes against the best practices on record. The task of cutting losses is so much more challenging because financial theory has not developed a precise quantitative guidepost. Past experience, however, suggests that:

- The maximum loss good traders allow is 7 percent, and
- Usually they manage to get out of a loser much quicker.

The strategy is to make money on the few stocks that during the year might double in price. Some traders hold their winners for six to twelve months, limit the time of holding stocks that are not that strong to three months, and keep their losers for two weeks or less. That is aggressive trading in equities, as contrasted to investing, and it is not a strategy advisable for the typical investor. As I have already mentioned, investors have a longer time horizon.

A question often posed is how to deal if one buys a stock at what proves to be a new high and then it pulls back into a lower range. Should he/she decide that this was a false breakout? The answer given by some of the successful traders is to cut 50 percent of the position if the stock keeps at the upper end of the range; and more than that if it gravitates towards lower values. Also, to watch out carefully for signs of a bear market.

This brings up the question of how to recognize a bear market. One way is to watch how individual stocks in one's portfolio are doing. If during the bull phase, the leaders start losing, this indicates that a bear market is developing. Another signal for a bear market is divergence between the Dow Jones index and the daily *advance/decline line*, which shows the cumulative net difference between the number of NYSE stocks advancing each day versus the number declining.

In principle, advance/decline tends to top out a few months before the Dow does. A similar watch is necessary regarding close follow-up of each individual equity in which one has invested. Frequently, when a stock drops to its mid-range it goes all the way down to its lower range. When this happens, mature traders consider it to be *capital at risk* and their decision usually is to cut their losses quickly. Traders, whose experience taught them over the years to do so, have learned:

- How to take losses, and
- How not to fall in love with commodities.

Many investors say, 'I cannot sell that asset because it has been for years the jewel of my portfolio' or 'If I sell, will be taking a loss.' These arguments miss the point that if the asset is below the price one has paid for it, selling it is not really the reason for the loss; the loss has already been incurred and it should be recognized in the virtual profit and loss statement an investor should provide *for him or herself* – preferably on a daily basis. Here, again, technology can help.

Letting losses run is one of the most serious mistakes repeatedly made both by investors and some traders. Not everybody understands the wisdom of cutting losses quickly. Yet, this is the best strategy for repositioning oneself against market forces and their swings.

- We should steadily watch out for the day the winners in our portfolio lose their appeal, and
- We must always cut back not only the losers, but also the least attractive good positions to make room for new winner(s).

Still another subject requiring steady vigilance is our ability to deceive ourselves, as well as to be deceived by our opponents. The best method for detecting repeated self-deceptions is *post-mortems*. Post-mortems are plan versus actual evaluations which can be instrumental in evaluating deliverables against expectations:

- From budgetary allocations and investments,
- To investment results, projects, other operations and their aftermath.

Not every project goes according to plan, whether a civilian or military operation. Take the French Indochina War of the 1950s as an example. According to Douglas Porch, in retrospect, it was not Henri Navarre, the French commander in Indochina, but Vo Nguyen Giap and Ho Chi Minh who could more plausibly claim to have been stabbed in the back. Though the Chinese greatly supported the Vietminh, in the Geneva peace negotiations Vietminh and Chinese interests were shown to diverge.[10]

In 1949, Porch suggests, communist China had come to the support of the Vietminh largely because it had wanted to eliminate Tonkin as a possible base for a Nationalist Chinese resurgence. But after Dien Bien Phu had achieved that goal, China needed time to put its domestic house in order and end its diplomatic isolation with openings to the Western powers. As an asset, Ho Chi Minh came way down the line of Chinese priorities.

Therefore, Zhou Enlai, the Chinese premier, agreed to the partition of Vietnam, undercutting the Vietminh desire for unity under their rule. When Soviet Russia backed the Chinese view, Ho had no choice but to accept a cease-fire based on the temporary partition of Vietnam. Thus, Dien Bien Phu was at the same time a victory and a trap for the Vietminh, as much as it had been a defeat and a trap for Navarre and the French forces. This is a political and military example but similar traps exist everywhere in business, and many of them have their origin in:

- Conflicting goals,
- A variety of complexities,
- Conflicts of interest, and
- Being afraid to cut losses.

Complexities can lead to catastrophes because, as many people fail to appreciate, they usually involve inefficiencies of scale. For instance, as size increases, planning and control mechanisms are overwhelmed and, beyond a certain point, efficiencies of scale turn into inefficiencies.

Other things being equal, increasing beyond a certain level the number of positions in a portfolio diminishes the freedom to move in and out of these positions in a dynamic way. This affects the returns in a negative way. Notice that the level of diminishing returns is no single, magic point. Rather it is a regression line with confidence intervals, but there is always a point beyond which the returns curve bends.

10.5 Damage control through limits and profit targets

Whether to buy or sell – an investor has the choice between giving his or her broker an order to do so at *market price*, which is the best price available when the order reaches the trading floor, or he or she can place a *stop order* to buy (or sell) only at some lower (or higher) price than the current one, in which case it becomes a market order. This is a *contingent order* which, usually, cannot be filled immediately. Generally, stop orders are of two types:

- A *buy order* is usually placed below current market value, and
- A *sell order* is typically put above the current market price.

Both become market orders, executed when the market goes the investor's way. It needs no explaining that buy orders are used to open new positions, while sell orders are put in place to limit losses. Therefore the latter are frequently known as stop-loss orders.

The rule for stop losses is fairly simple. Whenever we enter a position, we must have a predetermined *stop*, which means we should know where we are getting out, and we should decide on this before getting in. Evidently, this is part of the homework the investor should be doing. Expert traders advise that:

- The stop must be calculated on a technical basis, and
- The position size on a trade should be determined by the stop.

For example, if the market is in the middle of a trading range, it makes no sense to put the stop within that range, since it is most likely that the position will be taken out. The stop should be placed beyond some technical barrier, which can be identified in either of two ways:

- Through an absolute number, such as a percent below the buy price, or
- One (or two) standard deviations of the distribution of prices, which accounts for the trading range.

The latter is my preferred method, provided it is possible to easily data-mine the distribution of prices in a particular commodity, when the order is placed and along with it the stop loss. If the goal is to lock-in a gain, then the target gain, too, should be properly computed (more on this later).

A variety of the contingent order described in the preceding paragraph, usually known as *stop order*, is the so-called *limit order*. The latter tells the broker to buy or sell at market price or better. Stops and limits orders given by the investor to the broker by the customer have execution restrictions:

- The specified price, and
- The fact they can be executed only if the market reaches or betters the set price.

Another variety is the *market-on-close order* which instructs the floor broker to buy or sell for the customer at the market, during the official closing period – provided the market price falls within the range of prices traded during the official close of the contract month on the exchange that day. Still another species is the *discretionary order*, which gives a specific amount of discretion to the broker. For instance, he or she may be given discretion to buy when prices exceed the limit price, and to sell when prices go below the limit price.

These examples lead us to the *fifteenth golden rule* of investing: do damage control through limits and profit targets. This should be accomplished in a methodological way through both the market's ups and its downs. Stops commit the trader and the investor to get out of a position at a certain point without having to follow a fire-brigade approach. Behind this advice lies the fact that:

- There is no doubt commodity prices will fluctuate, but
- Nobody can really say all of the time 'when' and by 'how much'.

While there has been surprising little dissent on the wisdom of using stops and limits, opinions have been divided on whether, on the sell side, it is better to place them in absolute values, at a given percentage above or below the purchase price or other target(s) connected to an equity, or to take a normal distribution of the stock's values and put the limit at 'x' standard deviations from the mean.

Some of the experts said that they prefer the percentage basis, because it helps to mind how much the stock is costing the investor. Others were of the opinion that basing the limits on standard deviation is a more sophisticated approach. Bob Keen combined the two:

- Institutional investors should set limits at 2 or 3 standard deviations, and a maximum of 5.

■ By contrast, individual investors can better understand and manage limits based on percentages of a target value.

Whichever method is adopted, traders, investors, and professional asset managers should appreciate that without defenses which enable damage control, a sudden major drop in market prices may be devastating. 'You can predict nothing with zero tolerance', said Dr Heisenberg on *physics* and physicists, and his dictum is just as valid for investors.

From physical laws to engineering specifications and financial investments, whether these are equities or debt instruments, there is always a confidence limit and a broader or narrower band of tolerance. 'Because nothing walks on a straight line', we have to conceive an investment management process characterized by:

■ Mean tendency, and
■ Upper and lower tolerance limits.

Alert investors appreciate that within tolerance limits, which relate to their risk and return goals, there should be control limits that establish when a process tends to get out of control and the sort of corrective action needed in that case. The concept and process behind it are shown in Figure 10.4. 'The difference between genius and stupidity', Winston Churchill once said, 'is that genius has limits.'

A limits process depends on business decisions and analytics. The latter requires accurate measurements, a methodology, and technology providing support for risk evaluations. When analysis replaces subjective judgment, then the old saying that there are four kinds of trades – good, bad, winners, and losers – takes on a new meaning.

Most people think that a losing trade, or investment, is only the result of a bad bet. That is not accurate. One can lose money even on a good bet, or win money on a bad one, because of chance. But chance will favor one investor or another. It will *not* provide an edge. In the longer run, results are brought in by the winners who have a better methodology.

Part and parcel of this 'better methodology' is the investor's willingness and ability to bring home profits. A brief reference to this has been made in an earlier part of this

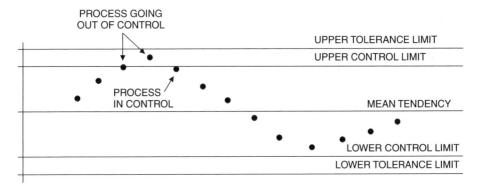

Figure 10.4 Nothing works in a straight line, therefore it is important to define quality control limits and tolerances

section, in connection with the fact that stops and limits help both in damage control and in locking-in target gains.

The principle which could well be written as the fifteenth golden rule is that, *unless one is a long-term investor, he or she should put a target on expected profits*. Like any other commodity, equities have ups and downs. The advice 'Cut your losses and let your profits ride', meaning hold on to winning stocks for a long time, can be full of risks. A sound principle is to set an objective of, say, a return of 50 percent on the investment. The difficulty associated with this advice is to find another equity investment that meets the initial requirements, so that one can make the switch.

A similar concept applies to stop losses. Where should be the limit to stop bleeding depends on risk appetite and risk aversion – markets can turn around and/or have a step down well below the buy limit one has placed. Because of this, contrarians say that use of limits may be harmful to the investor. Up to a point this may be true, but without limits it is not easy to undertake damage control.

To provide the reader with a better perspective on both sides of the limits argument, it is appropriate to recall that, for any practical purpose, the stop is a technical limit. Precisely because the use of limits may work in both a positive and a negative way, it is very important to analytically determine the technical barrier. In principle, if the computation is right,

- The market should not easily reach that barrier.
- The stop will come alive if the price move comes as a surprise, or nearly so, bringing the trader or investor out of that deal.

Having explained the procedure, it should be added that the overall strategy with limits varies among professionals. Several experienced traders choose to allocate a predetermined maximum dollar risk in a trade for a smaller number of contracts, while using a wider stop. They prefer this to the alternative of having to watch for more contracts, each with a smaller risk margin.

This method has its merits, but the reader should be aware that it is contrary to that used by the typical trader who tries to limit the loss per contract while trading in as many contracts as possible. There are upsides and downsides with every approach. Among the downsides of limits setting are the facts that:

- Nearby stop-loss limits often result in many good trades being stopped out, before the market moves in the anticipated direction.
- Wider limits on fewer contracts tend to maximize the chances that positions will not be stopped out of a trade that proves correct, but they also increase the amount of red ink in adversity.

Ideally, the concept behind stop-losses is to place limits at a point that, if reached, will reasonably indicate that the trade is wrong. That is why I advised the use of a statistical distribution which helps in conjunction with quality control charts based on tolerances, like the one shown in Figure 10.4.

The message to be retained from all this is that, for orderly control reasons, traders and investors must have available a system that not only permits the placement of stops, but also makes it possible to identify thresholds and keep them updated. If, for instance, in the trader's judgment, at a given price there will tend to be a lot of stops by other market players, then this is not the right price to put a stop because of the likelihood of a skid. (A *skid* is the difference between a theoretical execution price on a trade, such as the midpoint on the opening range, and the actual fill price.)

In conclusion, stops and limits should not be used in a haphazard way. It is always wise to watch out for convergence and divergence of market opinions – including that of contrarians – and to regularly review the stops. Traders and investors must appreciate that stops essentially mean time stops. Few people truly understand the importance of time as a critical business factor. If a trader thinks the market should break and it does not, then this may be a good point in business time to get out. (See also the discussion in section 10.6 on flexibility.)

10.6 Flexibility is one of the investor's best friends

The *sixteenth golden rule* in trading and investing states that flexibility is one of the investor's best friends. Neither a good trader nor a sound investor can afford to be rigid. Being open to see anything that moves and anything that does not move, as well as the ability to turn on a dime, is a raw ingredient of successful business – yet many people do not appreciate the benefits they can derive from adaptation to changing circumstances.

'I agree that flexibility is very important', said one of the experts. 'The question is how people are going to make use of it.' In his opinion, as far as flexibility is concerned, much depends on the type of investor one is. For instance,

- The speculator would listen to any new idea, and if he buys he will reposition his portfolio.
- But the long-term investor should not do too frequent portfolio repositionings, even if the new idea sounds great.

Another expert suggested that the investor's age also plays a role because flexibility tends to diminish with age. Many people become less flexible as they become older, while the young listen more eagerly to ideas. Flexibility is not always the best friend of the retail investor, said a third expert, because it leads to removal of constraints, limiting the ability to use damage control.

All told, the sense of the meetings has been that flexibility in trading and investing becomes easier when people have confidence in themselves, but without the heavy baggage of a big ego. 'No big ego' means they do not allow prestige, glory, or posterity to get in the way of a trade, because they understand that this is counterproductive. Successful investors often swallow their pride, eat their words, and get out of cherished positions before they are covered by red ink.

Konrad Adenauer, the German chancellor in the post-World War II years, answered remarks that from time to time he changed his mind, with the argument: 'What can I do. God makes me wiser and wiser every day.' There are many cases where sticking to one's past position proves to be wrong, because it reflects yesterday's realities rather than those of today or tomorrow. The necessary complement of flexibility is adaptation:

- Decreasing one's commitment when the market goes poorly, and
- Increasing the money invested in positions when fundamental and technical analysis suggest the market will improve.

Successful investors have been taught by experience, often the hard way, that no deals should be made in situations one does not fully understand, let alone cases whose outcome may be uncertain. For instance, one should not put at risk a significant amount of money before Fed decisions which, according the prevailing market opinion, may represent a switch, or the release of key indicators and other statistics which can upset a jittery market. This is tantamount to saying:

- Do not be a market hero,
- Always question yourself, and
- Challenge your ability to interpret market news and views.

Each of these bullets is a cornerstone to risk management. The market's reaction to the news is a popular game full of misconceptions. Too many people expect the market to react to certain news – but they do not know in which way the market initially will go; it may break out sharply, or it may quickly return to the previous trading range. At the same time, if a market does not respond to important news in the manner that it should, it is telling something very important:

- It is either not ready for any move, or
- It may be breaking out exactly in the opposite direction to that which the news suggests.

For instance, when the Iran–Iraq war started, gold was only able to move up a couple of dollars. Alert traders interpreted this as advance notice of a great sale, and so it was. The market broke down sharply after that. Furthermore, when a market makes a historic high, it is also giving a message. The fact that the price hits a new high mark indicates something has changed: most likely, the market has got ahead of itself and it gets ready for a turnaround.

Market reversals baffle many investors who sell on the news, then watch the market change course. Several people blame different institutions for using news as a means for pushing the market higher (or lower), but what this argument fails to realize is that a market that is fundamentally and technically poised to move higher (or lower) is not going to reverse because of a news item – even if it were a dramatic one.

- Being flexible is not at all a matter of being jumpy.
- Flexibility is the ability to adjust to changing circumstances, in a factual and documented way.

Part and parcel of flexibility by traders and investors is the policy never to wait for the ultimate 'high' or 'low' – or try to do one last 'kill'. A wiser, but not fail-safe, course is that of testing several combinations and variations of factors involved in a system of past market behavior, evaluating outcomes, and their likelihood, prior to making a move. The problem with this approach, which some people consider to be fine-tuning, is that:

- The link between past and future performance is quite often questionable, and
- Even at best, this link between past, present and future is a rough one.

Therefore, experienced traders and investors do not attempt to be perfect; they do not look for the 'optimum', whatever this may mean. Anyone can devise a 'perfect system' for the past. What is important, and at the same time very difficult, is to handle future uncertainty. This requires rigorous self-discipline and some time-tested rules. For instance:

- If the market looks its very best and going up,
- Then this can nicely be the best time to sell.

This suggests that some of the most successful traders and investors are contrarians. They do not like to follow the herd, but base their decisions on their own research, and on the way the outcome of this research shapes their mind. I have a friend who is contrarian and he says he and his like play *great defense*, not great offense. Playing great defense means he never forgets that with every move he takes his number one priority is risk control.

Being flexible and being contrarian correlate. The latter in practice requires looking at the other side of the coin, the one that is hidden. If a company talks about its comprehensive income, one should examine with great care its *comprehensive loss*, and the factors which affect its P&L performance without any creative accounting attached to it.

Basic and diluted profit (or loss) per share should be calculated by dividing net profit (loss) by the weighted average number of outstanding common shares. Total comprehensive profit (loss) includes, in addition to net profit (loss) changes in equity that are excluded from the consolidated and combined statements of operations, and are recorded directly into a separate section of stockholders' equity/invested equity on the consolidated balance sheet. Adjustments may include,

- Foreign currency translation adjustments, and
- Unrealized gains and losses on cash flow hedges and investment holdings.

It is always important to be prudent with foreign currency translations, because exchange rates provide opportunities for manipulating P&L statements. Gains and losses resulting from foreign currency transactions, which are transactions denominated in a currency other than the entity's functional currency, must be included in the consolidated and combined statements of operations. Another subject often massaged to enhance financial statements is inventories.

One more issue underpinning flexibility in trading and investing is to do nothing, absolutely nothing, unless there is something worthwhile to do. There is no point to always playing the market in order to be busy, and losing your money in the process. In an uncertain market, it is better to miss the opportunity that develops because you cannot give to it your undivided attention from the start, than misinterpret market facts and lower your defenses.

10.7   Using mathematical tools and appreciating they are not fail-safe

Chapter 9 presented to the reader some aspects of the use of technology in trading and investing. For instance, it has been said that models are at the core of interactive computational finance, they have locality, and they are of many sorts. Some are deterministic, others are stochastic, still others are enriched with knowledge engineering; many models are simple, but a growing number are becoming quite complex.

Results expected from models are often unrealistic. The downside of models is that the hypotheses behind them may not be sound and/or the mathematical formulas being used may fall under algorithmic insufficiency. Therefore, results can range from fairly accurate to totally inaccurate. One short sentence, from Tim Thompson of Barclays Bank, encapsulates everything that can be said about mathematical artifacts: 'All models are wrong, but some are useful.'

The most useful models are based on analogical thinking. They aim to represent in mathematical terms a real-life situation. This means a great deal of simplification based on abstraction and on hypotheses, which are essentially tentative statements. The process of simplification is cornerstone to modeling. It is also the Achilles heel in the use of models – whether in finance or anywhere else.[11]

A second weakness of models is that the data being collected and used may be inaccurate (see section 10.2), obsolete, or both. Accuracy and timeliness of data, as well as success or failure in abstraction and simplification, are at the roots of strengths and weaknesses of models. Figure 10.5 shows *where* data, abstraction, and algorithms come into the modeling process. Typically, in technical terms:

- 80 percent of the challenge is having reliable data, and
- 20 percent roughly corresponds to algorithmic developments and tests.

That is the *quantitative part*. Hypotheses, abstractions, and simplifications constitute the *qualitative part* of modeling. In essence these hypotheses are no different from the assumptions and tentative statements characterizing the judgmental process a trader uses in his or her daily decisions. As such, they have locality. That is why Chapter 9 said that:

- Models developed and used for one specific situation are not general purpose.
- Companies which use models indiscriminately are definitely looking for trouble.

One way to classify models is to distinguish between proprietary (or eigenmodels), and those which are generally available as a commodity. Proprietary models belong to their developer; commodity models are sold for a price, and regulators are promoting some standard models like VAR[12] – introduced in Chapter 9 under the very negative aspect of CVAR as an example of model misuse.

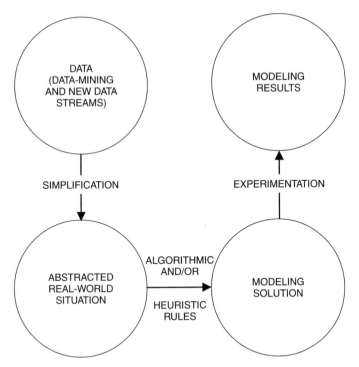

Figure 10.5 The strengths and weaknesses of models are simplification and accuracy of data

Value at risk is a good case study on the role of hypotheses, abstractions, and simplifications. It is a tool developed to help in making market exposure more transparent and comprehensive to senior management. As the reader will recall, VAR was designed and implemented in the early 1990s, when the then CEO of JP Morgan asked for a 4.15 p.m. report to bring his attention, and to that of his immediate assistants, market risk embedded in the bank's portfolio at that particular time.

At the time, the JP Morgan rocket scientists did a number of abstractions and simplifications in computing value at risk at the bank's portfolio. They had to do so in order to answer the CEO's request for a daily bird's-eye view of exposure. But the fact that the use of this model expanded tremendously in the financial industry, and became a sort of regulators' reporting standard, made several of the simplifications questionable.

Value at risk is also an example of a model which is not mathematically complete, as the Swiss Federal Institute of Technology, in Zurich, has demonstrated. It is also one which has been highly misused because of being transferred from market risk into credit risk, specifically for calculating (in a highly unreliable and misleading way) unexpected credit losses. We spoke of this in Chapter 9. Banks which did so, violated the principle that a model must be:

- Mathematically solid,
- Operationally comprehensive, and
- Have an output appreciated both by supervisors and by implementers.

With this background, the *seventeenth golden rule* in trading and investments is that models should definitely be used in asset management and other activities, but with great care, and with full understanding of their weaknesses including the fact that they are not fail-safe. Moreover, whenever and wherever they are used, models should, in principle:

■ Work in real-time,
■ Mine online rich databases,
■ Interactively visualize results for their user, and
■ Explain how these results were reached.

Whoever uses mathematical models should understand that there is model risk, said one of the experts. Another cautioned that, typically, the majority of models currently available will not tell their user something unless it has happened. Still another expert's viewpoint has been that, when models fail, the mistake is with the user(s) of models, not with the models themselves. For instance,

■ Few people currently work on the distribution of tail events,
■ Yet, in any distribution the understanding of outliers, and of their meaning, is most fundamental.

Moreover, because they are based on assumptions about specific environments or instruments, and situations within those environments, models have locality. Therefore, they should be used specifically on *one* job, and they should never be employed outside the domain for which they have been developed.

By contrast models, particularly those that are knowledge enriched, can help different masters. For instance, models which exploit patterns may be portable from one trader to another within a given domain. This is practical when the patterns they exploit tend to be similar and the background factors are practically the same.

The reader should also be aware that there is plenty of hype with models. When this happens, it takes away the models' domains of opportunity. Patterning is an example of opportunity for model usage. Pattern analysis is very important both in trading and in investments because, as experienced people appreciate, it is unwise to be misled by day-to-day price fluctuations. Rather, investors should focus on whether:

■ A pattern is shorter term or longer term,
■ It is deterministic or heuristic, and so on.

As Chapter 6 on charting has demonstrated, pattern analysis is one of the best examples of what can be achieved with properly designed models. We examine the characteristics of different patterns because we want to be better focused than everybody else or to perceive things other people cannot see. These are the hallmarks of successful traders and good investors, since they:

■ Help in being ahead of the game, and
■ Position them against the hysteria which sometimes dominates the ups and downs of the market.

As with any other instrument, there exist also some technical problems with algorithmic solutions beyond those of incompetence, or irrelevance, we already examined. For instance, models can be good at analyzing market patterns when there are precedents leading to clear hierarchies of information. The latter enable the development of crisp rules. This is not always the case in finance because:

■ Investment rules keep changing and, at the same time, trading decisions encompass many types of knowledge which may have been left out in the abstraction.
■ Models suffer from the lack of dependable, long, historical time series, while people expect them to deliver well beyond what they can reasonably do.

In conclusion, the reader should keep in mind that while the usage of models – and of the process of modeling – is recommended, their presence in no way guarantees success. Basically, many models are too inaccurate to be of any help. Curiously enough, as a general trend, the profitability of model-based trading systems seems to be moving in cycles in emulation of Malthousian logic.

■ There are periods in which trend-following models are successful, leading to their increasing popularity.
■ But as their number and that of their users increase, the market shifts from trend-tracking to a sort of directionless action.

An aftermath of overkill through computer-based models is that trend-tracking solutions become unprofitable. When this happens the deliverables leave much to be desired, the use of quantitative approaches bends, and the algorithms or heuristics behind them are criticized by investors and traders as inaccurate. Then, new improved versions appear giving model-based traders an edge.

Speaking from personal experience with models, I would strongly suggest that, as a policy, the learning features associated with modeling should be highly developed. This is not so easy because the culture of using computer-based models for training is still in its early stages. Therefore, many people and companies fail to take advantage of models as a learning tool. Yet, paraphrasing what Dwight Eisenhower once said about planning: 'The model is nothing. Modeling is everything.'

Notes

1 D.N. Chorafas (2004). *Corporate Accountability, with Case Studies in Finance*. Macmillan/Palgrave.
2 D.N. Chorafas (2004). *Operational Risk Control with Basel II: Basic Principles and Capital Requirements*. Butterworth-Heinemann.
3 Panacatantra (2001). *Les Cinq Livres de la Sagesse*. Editions Philippe Picquier.
4 Douglas Porch (1996). *The French Secret Services*. Macmillan.
5 *The Economist*, 20 March 2004.
6 D.N. Chorafas (2001). *Managing Risk in the New Economy*. New York Institute of Finance.
7 Felice A. Bonadio (1994). *A.P. Giannini*. University of California Press.

8 D.N. Chorafas (2001). *Implementing and Auditing the Internal Control System.* Macmillan.
9 D.N. Chorafas (2005). *The Real-time Enterprise.* Auerbach.
10 Douglas Porch (1996). *The French Secret Services.* Macmillan.
11 D.N. Chorafas (2002). *Modelling the Survival of Financial and Industrial Enterprises: Advantages, Challenges, and Problems with the Internal Rating-Based (IRB) Method.* Palgrave/Macmillan.
12 D.N. Chorafas (1998). *The 1996 Market Risk Amendment: Understanding the Marking-to-Model and Value-at-Risk.* McGraw-Hill.

11 Independent equity research and management risk

11.1 Introduction

The central theme of this chapter, which follows on from the rules applicable to risk management, is *equity research* and whether or not it contributes to control the exposure taken with investments. Is equity research really independent, or is it for some reason biased? Is it effective in foreseeing equity values (see also, on this issue, Chapters 12 and 13), or ineffective and therefore of little use. Furthermore, is there anything that could be done to improve equity research results?

Closely associated to these queries is the method, if any, which would help in better interpretation of results obtained through financial analysis. Many of the participants in the research project leading to this book pointed to the problem of 'tailoring' equity research: results are either interpreted or massaged in ways to fit with predisposition of higher-up echelons in institutions for which the analysts are working (see sections 11.2 and 11.3).

At the beginning of the twenty-first century, an article published in the *Financial Times* indicated that some 86 percent of fund managers think that sell-side recommendations by analysts dilute the value of their holdings, and the appeal of their services to institutional investors. Sell-side recommendations are also anathema to the corporate financial division of investment banks.[1] In a survey, commissioned by Reuters, of eighty-four fund management groups responsible for investing $65 billion in European smaller equities, Tempest Consultants found that:

- Brokers' analysts were widely perceived by fund managers to spend one-third of their time on corporate finance work,
- While they spend just one-quarter of their time carrying out fundamental research, and less than a fifth of their time on company visits.

It does not take two heads to appreciate that, as far as research results are concerned, this allocation of human resources is counterproductive. Indeed, fund managers participating to the Tempest study indicated they would prefer brokers to spend less than 10 percent of their time on corporate finance work, some 29 percent on company visits, and about 45 percent on fundamental research – as quoted by the *Financial Times*.

Other studies made along similar lines have raised the problem of special favors. As a matter of professional principle, no broker, fund manager, or member of a stock exchange should be allowed to provide one investor with a 'service' that makes it possible for him or her to take advantage of another investor who has not the leverage or influence to get such special service. The payment for and receipt of special services or favors should be prohibited.

Special favors are not what equity research is all about. Instead, its goal should be to provide strategic and tactical reasons for investments and disinvestments in equities, bonds, or other instruments. To gain its readers' confidence, financial analysis should make explicit how it collects information, as well as which factors and distortions influence the search that is made. It should also focus on:

- End-user expectations,
- Trade-off attributes, and
- The understanding of the analyzed company's product and market strategy.

For instance, is the company's management targeting markets in which potential profits are high? Avoiding markets in which competition is intense? Recognizing the importance of competition from the viewpoint of its suppliers and distributors? Identifying how to improve the company's bargaining position? Behind these queries lies the all-important issue of quality of management.

A similar critical list of queries applies to new product development including potential markets and trade-offs between risk and reward. To appreciate the importance of this subject, the reader should keep in mind that only around 5 percent of new product development projects are successful. Reasons for failure have to do with:

- Product design and cost factors,
- Dynamics of diffusion, and
- Technical change in a given industry.

Also, with the sources of technical change, how fast it is going and what are the technical parameters in the market to which the company undergoing analysis addresses itself? Is the company ahead of its competitors in realizing market changes and taking advantage of them, or is it sticking to obsolete strategies which have failed?

These are issues most crucial to equity analysis, as well as to research intended to unearth elements which sustain an opinion about an equity's value and creditworthiness. Yet, as the Tempest research indicated, they are not necessarily taken into account – since equity analysts spend less than 10 percent of their time on company visits. Product and market factors are necessary supplements to the analysis of accounts books – which, let us never forget, mainly deal with yesterday's facts and figures.

11.2   The bottleneck is at the top of the bottle

An integrated equity research program should be closely supervised by the board of directors, CEOs, and their immediate assistants. It should include both quantitative and qualitative criteria – such as product and market strategy, discussed in section 11.1 – and rely on open communications between all levels of the organization. Effective forward-oriented communication of an entity's strengths and weaknesses requires a company-wide view based on personal appreciation by the analysts of:

- Board members,
- CEO, chief operating officer (COO), CFO, chief information officer (CIO) and other executive vice presidents,

- All other senior bank personnel, including research and development (R&D) and marketing,
- The stand taken by supervisory authorities, and
- The market's appreciation of an entity's future.

The breadth of involvement identified by these five bullets reveals that beyond the common vocabulary, methodology, and the system on which it will be based, integrated capital management requires a significant commitment to research and analysis. Notice that both activities are also vital to the capital allocation process.[2] This, in turn, calls for a theory able to help in finding fundamental value-creating characteristics.

Senior investment advisers suggested that at the top of the list of subjects to be particularly well researched, is dividend policy, stock buybacks, executive options and their costing. Also the reasons why a growing number of companies use their cash for stock buybacks must be analyzed. By reducing shares outstanding, buybacks can conceal the true cost of lavish stock options.

In fact, this policy of generous handouts to corporate executives, which increased at the end of the 1990s, is one of the reasons why investors start questioning the options programs. Both the amount of cash paid in buybacks and the likelihood that companies cannot buy back enough stock to offset the dilution, have come under the magnifying glass.

Moreover, dividend policy is a theme which has returned for several reasons. One of these is that some firms have given away billions in excess profits to poor investments such as Microsoft's $5 billion stake in AT&T. Another reason is that companies are hoarding cash; Microsoft had in its treasury some $50 billion, in early 2004. 'Their returns are actually being dragged down by how much cash they have, because it's causing them to make poor investments', argues Robert Schwartz, an analyst at Thomas Weisel Partners, on this and other company cash hoards.[3]

Another reason is that investors have grown much more skeptical about declared accounting profits, in the wake of Enron, WorldCom, Parmalat and so many other fake accounts. They now wonder if evidence of profitability in the form of a dividend check might help them to sleep more easily. Even George W. Bush is trying to boost the popularity of dividends, by proposing to scrap income taxes on them.

As will be recalled, in the mid to late 1990s, companies, particularly those considering themselves part of a growth industry, established the policy of paying no dividends in spite of all their talk about 'shareholder value'. Investors were supposed to profit from the rise in capitalization of the firm, since management was reinvesting the money rather than taking loans. The 2000 to early 2003 severe market downturn shattered this argument.

Indeed, research projects undertaken in the aftermath of the bubble's bursting have found that paying no dividends works *against* shareholder value, and this not only because they are deprived of a regular income. When the company's management has little cash to spare it will spend it on few good projects. But when it has lots of money available:

- It will fund more and more ill-screened projects and different abstract ideas,
- It will pay only lip service to project management, thereby delivering disappointing returns.

Not only investors, but also, increasingly, analysts start criticizing the no-dividends policy saying that too much cash burns a hole in the managers' pockets, and it is leading them to ill-conceived corporate strategies; for instance, the usual practice of making disastrous acquisitions in unrelated areas – as happened so often in the 1990s.

In contrast to these facts of industrial life, the benefits of earnings retention theory are by no means supported by historical evidence. Researchers who are respected and who look carefully at the history of the payout ratio for US companies in the S&P 500 index from 1950 to 2001, have found that future earnings growth positively correlated with the payout ratio, and

- When the payout ratio is low, future earnings growth also tends to be low,
- While in the opposite case, when the payout ratio is high, so is earnings growth.

This new-found respectability of dividends runs contrary to one of the unfounded and ultra-light Nobel prize winners' theories which suggested that whether or not a firm paid a dividend should make no difference to the value of a firm to investors. According to this hypothesis, which proves to be increasingly irrelevant,

- Every share's value is based on the future cash flows from a company (which is true).
- 'Therefore', it does not matter whether those cash flows are paid out in dividends or kept as cash on hand by the firm (which is false).

Influenced by this and other theories of economic behavior, during the 1990s many boards concluded that if they did not have to pay a dividend, why do so? This is evidently a false conclusion based on fake premises and, as such, speaks volumes for the quality of boards and CEOs who reach such ultra-light decisions. As an old saying has it: the bottleneck is at the top of every bottle.

Dividends matter. Up to a point – that is, as long as they are not based on disposal of assets and other one-off income – they are an evidence that senior management runs the company for profits, and does not make silly investments just because other people's money burns holes in the company's pockets.

Telecommunications companies provide an example of capital mismanagement. During the last decade they have spent heavily on projects such as laying miles of fiberoptic cables, and investing in third generation (3G) mobile phones. Much of that now looks to have been wasted capital. Also because of what seemed to be an unlimited amount of cash, mergers and acquisitions (M&A) exploded in spite of all the evidence that most takeovers fail to add value to shareholders.[4] (More on M&A in sections 11.3 and 11.4.)

11.3   Legal risk in equity research and analysis

Investor misinformation because of conflicts of interest and other reasons involved in equity research and analysis, has raised the issue of the existence of a new type of legal risk. In mid-March 2004 it has been reported that, according to documents filed in a federal court in New York in February 2001, analysts at JP Morgan,

Deutsche Bank, and Bank of America downgraded their verdicts on the creditworthiness of WorldCom – but senior management did not pass the warning to the bank's
client base.

Indeed, always according to press reports, a Deutsche Bank analyst even recommended to his institution to limit its loan exposure to WorldCom, and not lend the telecom
more money. Management ineffectiveness is proved by the fact that not only the banks
did not share these worries with their clients, but also all three aforementioned institutions helped WorldCom sell $12 billion in debt – in what became the third-biggest
debt offering ever.[5]

I had a professor of management at UCLA who taught me that even human stupidity has its limits – and where stupidity ends, the conflict of interest starts. The
aforementioned case is conflict of interest at its best, most likely influenced by the fact
that all three institutions were active in mergers and acquisitions, and WorldCom was
a sought-out client, since it had an insatiable merger appetite.

Precisely because past actions and their bias weight heavily both on reputational risk
and on legal risk, after 2003 several investment banks and brokers have become more
careful. For instance, some major institutions now oblige their investment bankers
and financial analysts to be chaperoned by a lawyer whenever they talk to each other.
There are some institutions where analysts' security passes do not work on bankers'
floors, and vice versa. The building of computer firewalls to block emails between
the two groups is another example of attempted separation of functions. Moreover,
in certain cases analysts can now turn to an internal ombudsman if they feel under
pressure from:

- Investment-banking colleagues, or
- Clients who want them to say nice things about the companies they cover.

The better managed institutions add a sort of *analyst certification* to the opinion the
person gives. Here is as a real-life example from the 18 March 2004, 'Introducing
bond notes', by Merrill Lynch:

I, . . . , hereby certify that the views expressed in this research report accurately reflect my personal
views about the subject securities and issuers. I also certify that no part of my compensation was,
is, or will be, directly or indirectly, related to the specific recommendations or view expressed
in this research report.

This leads to two observations. First, it is *good practice* that not only CEOs and
CFOs sign financial statements, as dictated by the Sarbanes-Oxley Act (see Chapter 8),
but also equity analysts and bond researchers are responsible for their opinion – and
they countersign it. Every professional should be accountable for and countersign
whichever opinion he or she gives to investors.

The second interesting observation is that investment banks have already taken steps
to reorganize the importance of debt research, thereby complementing the advice given
to investors through equity research. Apart from the aforementioned Merrill Lynch
example, Morgan Stanley, which also provides fixed income analysis, announced on
12 March 2004 that it had installed new firewalls at its offices in New York, London,
and Tokyo. These separate fixed income research from traders and sales staff.

Morgan Stanley is reported as having said that traders would always be tempted to look at unpublished credit research, and analysts to peek at non-public trading positions, if they continued to sit together. But there is also a contrarian opinion. 'Debt analysts, traders and sales staff should still talk, because otherwise analysts would not be relevant', suggested Justin Simpson, head of interest-rate strategy at Morgan Stanley.[6]

This is a new-found conscience about the need for carefully policing the division between 'this' and 'that' line of business which might mix and lead the bank into a conflict of interest. Similarly, in March 2004 the Association of Investment Management and Research and the National Investor Relations Institute, released an ethics code for equity analysts. This is good news as far as *quality of management* is concerned.

In fact what has been written in section 11.2 is by no means a wholesale critique of management. A good deal of the wrongdoings were the exception. On the other hand, as an old adage has it, sometimes the exception proves the rule.

Another indication that quality of management may be improving is that during the last few years boards of directors have become smaller, more hard-working and more independent. In the mid-twentieth century, corporate boards in America generally had sixteen to eighteen members; today, less than twelve is more common. Experts suggest that being of smaller size has probably made boards more effective. It is, however, also true that smaller size is not the only ingredient improving the quality of management.

A crucial variable in the board's effectiveness is the directors' skills and experience, as well as the time they devote to this job.[7] Some studies indicate that the time individual directors spend on board issues has risen significantly over the last few years – from thirteen hours a month in 2001, to almost nineteen hours a month in 2003. It is not easy to verify these statistics, therefore what the reader should rememeber is that this is the trend.

One of the knowledgeable people participating in this research suggested it is not unlikely that more effort is devoted to the company's business because boards are becoming better paid. Average cash compensation has gone up from $41 000 in 2001 to $64 000 in 2003, reflecting the growing difficulty of finding the right people to sit on a board. Compensation also accounts for the greater amount of time board members must spend on company matters, including board level committees. The pattern in Table 11.1 comes from the 2003 annual report of a well-known American high-tech company.

Another trend to remember is the tendency for boards to meet in *executive sessions* of their own, which exclude the CEO and all of the company's other operating executives. Among the entities that belong to the Business Roundtable, 97 percent of boards now meet at least once a year without the chief executive, and 55 percent do so up to five times per year.[8]

In the USA, the UK, and continental Europe, there is plenty to be done in terms of upgrading corporate governance. A 1997 study by the Bank of England found that the main reason for bank failure is indeed mismanagement, as Table 11.2 demonstrates. Also there is a need for a clean bill of health regarding the CEO's behavior as a person, which goes beyond good corporate governance.

The reader should never forget that a CEO's legal risk could be detrimental to the company. Not only have investors lost money in a big way as each company's capitalization sinks in the aftermath of a CEO's lack of ethical standards, but also

Director	Investment/Finance Committee	Audit Committee	Acquisition Committee	Compensation and Management Development Committee	Nomination and Governance Committee
Mr A			X	Chair	
Mrs B	X				Chair
Mr C			Chair		
Ms D					X
Dr E				X	X
Dr F					
Mr G		X			
Mr H	Chair			X	
Mr I	X		X		
Mr J	X		X		
Mr K	X	Chair			
Mr L		X			

Table 11.1 Board of directors of a high-tech company and its five committees

Identifier of institution	Mismanagement	Poor assets	Liquidity problems	Secrecy and fraud	Faulty structure	Dealing losses
I	X			X		X
II	X				X	
III	X	X		X	X	
IV	X	X		X		
V	X			X		X
VI	X	X				
VII	X	X	X	X		
VIII			X		X	
IX	X	X	X			
X	X	X	X			
XI	X	X	X	X		
XII			X			
XIII	X	X	X			
XIV	X	X	X			
XV	X	X				
XVI	X	X				
XVII	X	X				
XVIII		X	X			
XIX	X	X				
XX	X	X				
XXI				X	X	
XXII	X	X				

Table 11.2 Why banks fail – findings of a research project by the Bank of England

plaintiffs' lawyers may seek redress for money lost when the company's equity price fell. No wonder that, as reported in the press, a company's directors were still debating what to do about their chief executive and the situation in which the company found itself.

In conclusion, from the quality of corporate governance to legal risk, there is plenty of issues which have not entered the domain of equity analysis. Yet there is a growing amount of evidence suggesting that legal risk and equity exposure associated with management quality and ethics correlate. Financial analysts will have to factor into equity research what Maynard Keynes called the 'animal spirits'.

11.4   Quality of corporate governance affects investors and the companies themselves

In the second trimester of 2003, critics of equity research pointed to the Settlement which has been reached on 28 April of that year between the SEC and a number of New York investment banks, including foreign financial institutions operating in the USA. What this Settlement meant and the reasons behind it have been discussed in Chapter 5, while the penalties applied were presented in Table 5.1 of that same chapter.

As will be recalled, at the root of the findings of unfair practices which led to the Settlement was meticulous work by state prosecutors who unearthed plenty of evidence of misbehavior and in misinformation of investors. The prosecutors were led by Eliot Spitzer, the New York attorney general. As this evidence documented, biased equity research:

- Promoted certain stocks in a way which has been unfair to the investors, and
- In the late 1990s also led to an overbought situation, followed by more than three years of depressed markets.

While biased equity research has helped the few at the expense of the many, another issue which has been recently under critique is that of inefficiencies embedded in mergers and acquisitions generally – and who profits from these inefficiencies. This is an argument which goes beyond the collusion existing between financial analysis and investment banking.

For instance, as a news item in the *Financial Times* has it, Bruce Wasserstein who succeeded Michel David-Weill at the helm of Lazard Brothers, the international banking house, built up Lazard's investment banking franchise, 'but he has done so on the traditional Wall Street model, with all the rewards going to the bankers rather than the shareholders.'[9]

Revenues at Lazard Brothers have doubled, however, and even members of the founding Lazard families, as well as the Eurazeo investment company, have seen their income slashed. Eurazeo's Lazard holdings, equivalent to 15.8 percent of the bank's capital, provided 32.8 million euros in the first half of 2002. That plunged to 6.2 million euros in the first half of 2003, in spite of a prosperous investment banking activity.

The flaw with this policy of 'management takes all' is that the risk stays with the shareholders, who are in no way rewarded for the exposure they assume. Section 11.2 has already made the point that, for shareholders, dividends represent a tangible reward for their investment which not only provides income but also 'proves' the earning power of the company through profits.

As if disrespect for shareholder value has not been enough, there is also a great number of scandals connected with equity research, which started in the 1990s and came to the public eye, in a big way, in the first years of the twenty-first century. 'The problems revealed by the scandals were systemic, not the result of a few bad apples', said the 30 December 2002 editorial in *Business Week*. While only a few CEOs may go to jail for breaking the law, the breakdown was endemic in both the corporate and financial systems. The same editorial pointed out the conflicts of interest of Wall Street analysts who:

- Sit in on board meetings,
- Go on a company's road shows,
- Mislead the majority of investors, and
- Feign objectivity by getting paid for generating investment banking business.

Such behavior, *Business Week* aptly suggests, is not synergistic; it is corrupt and counterproductive to capital-raising and investment in the economy. The lack of virtue in the late 1990s and the first years of the new century is also reflected in the failure of boards to do their job as shareholders' representatives and advocates. Many boards rubber-stamped CEO demands for:

- Millions of options,
- Personal loans,
- Repricing of underwater options,
- Creative accounting, and
- A loose code of ethics.

Corrupt companies may be only a fraction of the approximately 16 000 publicly owned enterprises in the USA, but the fact that by and large the virtual theft of company property has gone for so long unpublished, sets a very bad example for the majority of entities which have abided by the accepted rules of:

- Corporate governance,
- General accounting, and
- Financial reporting.

Chief executive officers who respect themselves, their employees, shareholders, and the general public look with dismay at opinion polls which say that Americans regard chief executives of big companies with contempt. In the aftermath of major scandals people who run big companies are now mistrusted and reviled. Yet, they were until recently feted and admired.

Shaped by creative accounting, lavish but unjustified options, and other huge take-aways, by 2002 investor opinion of professional managers reached an all-time low. That is why sections 11.2 and 11.3 so much pressed the point that equity analysts should look very carefully at management quality. It has been always difficult to pick a first-class leader of a big public company, because the job requires many different, and difficult to find, skills. A chief executive must:

- Know a lot about the business he or she runs,
- Face successfully key day-to-day issues, and
- Be able to take substantial strategic decisions, which may mortally wound the firm if he or she gets them wrong.

At the same time, however, the chief executive's decisions and actions must be characterized by high moral values. He or she is under no condition expected to plunder the company he or she leads, or to show little regard to the interests of shareholders and employees. And even when no wrongdoing is alleged, huge pay awards are provoking growing outrage, as Richard Grasso, the former chairman of the NYSE, found out when he became a symbol of excess almost overnight, after it was revealed that he was due to receive $188 million in 'accumulated benefits'.

Not only are the different forms of golden parachutes for the top executives causing public indignation, but also there is little to justify the fact the average pay of executives skyrockets – especially in America, though it also has started taking place in Europe. In 1980, the average pay for America's CEOs at the big companies, was about forty times that of the average production worker.

- In 1990, it was about eighty-five times, and
- In 2004, this has reached about 400 times.

While, curiously enough, such lavish salaries have gone uncontested, profits of big firms fall and shares are still well down on their record high. No wonder market research results indicate that 80 percent of people believe that many CEOs and other senior executives are overpaid.[10]

Another noticeable trend in corporate governance, of which to take account, is that the tenure of CEOs has been significantly shortened. The average tenure of a chief executive of a big American company declined from nearly nine years in 1980 to just over seven in 2001, says Rakesh Khurana of the Harvard Business School. The reason is not just that bosses leave sooner, but that a growing proportion is fired for poor performance. A study by Booz Allen Hamilton of 2500 major publicly traded companies around the world, found that 39 percent of cases where a corporate leader was replaced in 2002 were sackings for underachievement.[11]

Have these issues had an impact on equity values? You bet they have. Are they taken appropriately into account in equity analysis? On this, the evidence is negative. Yet, financial analysts should pay due attention to them. Golden parachutes and lavish payouts are not only costly in themselves, but they can damage the company's image and franchise because:

- Pay packages which are excessive or unfair destroy morale among the rest of a company's workforce, and
- Bosses who manipulate corporate results to fill their own pockets give a message of poor ethical standards.

Because the different excuses found for overpay increase in frequency and magnitude, investors generally must pay attention to them, and institutional investors should make better use of the powers they already possess. In 2003, in the UK, shareholders received the right to vote on top executives' remuneration. All stakeholders need to be far more diligent, demanding full transparency about executives' pay as well as a better focused control on the quality of corporate governance.[12]

11.5   Can independent research be an effective solution?

The concept of independent equity research, and most particularly its efficiency, finds no unanimous opinion at Wall Street. According to Benn Steil, a senior fellow at the Council on Foreign Relations in New York: 'The settlement (Wall Street firms reached with SEC) is more bull than the market whose collapse precipitated it.' Steil adds: 'Mass distribution independent research financed by banks as part of their parole agreement can only serve to further discredit and devalue research', and he outlines the reasons for his statement in three bullet points:

- The very definition of 'independence' has been crafted solely to dissociate it from investment banking.
- Empirically, there is no evidence that what the settlement defines as independent research is actually better than non-independent.
- Many prominent independent research houses also manage money or broker trades – both of which give them a clear incentive to urge investors to buy stocks.[13]

What Steil is essentially talking about is management risk associated with independent financial analysis. Should equity research be the exclusive domain of investment banks and brokers – or of 'independent' outfits spun off from, or financed by, investment banks? Or should other entities enter this domain, for instance independent rating agencies which look after creditworthiness, and therefore address management issues discussed in sections 11.2, 11.3 and 11.4?[14]

An answer to this query must go beyond fundamental and technical analysis (see Chapter 6) to include credit rating and the capital market (see Chapter 3). The evolution of the capital market and that of the credit rating industry correlate. As the reader will recall, it was the British and other European investors' interest in the American railroad and canal companies, in the middle of the nineteenth century, that gave early impetus to both of them – and helped in developing the capital markets mechanism.

Today, credit rating agencies employ armies of analysts and rating experts. There are about 1250 at S&P alone. But unlike the equities markets, where analysts from many different organizations provide opinions and forecasts on the prospects for companies and industry sectors, the fixed income markets are dominated by the big four ratings agencies: S&P, Moody's, Fitch and A.M. Best. To these could be added a smaller agency, Dominion Bond Rating Service, to make up the list of those recognized by the SEC.

It should not escape the reader's attention that research on equities and research on debt (loans and bonds) correlate, though this does not mean that the viewpoints of shareholders and bondholders are the same. In fact, they are not.[15] These two types of analysis work in synergy because, first and foremost, they must both examine very carefully management quality. Beyond that,

- What a shareholder is after is a company able to survive, increase its capitalization, and pay a good dividend.
- What a bank giving a loan and an investor buying a bond want to see is a company able to survive, pay the interest, and repay the principal.

These two bullets are contrarian to the opinion prevailing in the market that financial analysts working for investment banks specialize in equities, and financial analysts working for credit rating agencies address the debt industry, therefore the interests of bondholders. But is this distinction correct?

Basically, ratings of creditworthiness, criteria used by commercial banks for giving loans, *and* equity research look after the entity's ability to stay in business, overcome market competition, and prosper – in short, its *future* prospects.

It follows that if equity research outfits become really independent from investment banks, then one way to survive is to cover the whole domain identified by the preceding two bullets, expanding into the arena of independent rating agencies which will most likely enter into equity research. But will equity analysis outfits really become independent? How will this happen?

Different scenarios have been suggested to answer such query. One of them talks of a forced separation not only of research, but of all trading in equities, bonds and derivatives from their corporate-advisory work. Some experts are suggesting that this will change the nature of financial markets, and it could make even the biggest markets – including those of foreign exchange, government bonds, interest rate swaps – less liquid.

According to the opinion of these experts, should this happen bid/offer spreads would widen, and there might be less dealing volume. At worst, these same people suggest, the banks' customers might also suffer as companies and investment firms could find it more expensive to hedge their risks or to react to changes in market conditions. This is too pessimistic and it is unlikely, but it is not altogether impossible.

Another interesting question is whether equity research constitutes the only issue to be taken care of in a separation of duties and responsibilities. It does not seem so. The way an article in *The Economist* had it, an amendment to the directive on market abuse by the EU, approved by the European Parliament, could significantly change the way that firms use privileged knowledge about their customers' intentions.

Inside information, this amendment says, also means information related to the client's *pending orders* which, if it were made public, might have a significant effect on prices. As the reader will recall, this is the issue discussed in Chapter 5 in connection with the *specialists* at NYSE. A strict interpretation of this EU amendment would prevent an investment bank from:

- Advising a client on a complex securities transaction, and
- Giving him or her a firm price for the transaction.[16]

The Economist takes this argument further by suggesting that the work of market-makers will also change, given the fact that the distinction between market-making for customers and proprietary trading is often blurred. This is particularly true when the market-maker and proprietary trader sit together, or even are the same person. Such duality of function ensures that:

- The market-maker positions him or herself so as to get a good price for a client.
- At the same time, he or she is dealing ahead of the client to make a profit for him or herself essentially at the client's expense – a practice known as *front-running*.

An alternative scenario of financing independent equity research would be that of developing ways and means of funding it. Being 'independent' in doing equity research means that financial analysts will not be paid by the investment bank – in order not to be influenced in their opinion by investment bankers. As it will be recalled, this has happened in a big way recently with recommendations to investors regarding Enron, WorldCom, and so many other firms which went bankrupt.

Given such misbehavior, confirmed by the 28 April 2003 SEC Settlement, there is no argument that the concept of independent equity research is sound. The question is, who pays? The leading idea after the Settlement had been a $100 million, five-year commitment by brokerage firms to fund independent research arms, free of conflicts of interest. It is not difficult to appreciate that such financing is substandard; $100 million is peanuts – and with peanuts you get only monkeys.

Even *if* the question of financing was not present, there is another salient problem which has to do with lack of consensus on the definition of 'independence', plus the questions of: how much should each brokerage pay up? To whom should be sent the research results? And whether investors should pay for it?

For a few months following the bad publicity because of biased equity research, brokers were bound to do something. Many of them were embarrassed by their relationship with now defunct formerly high market performers and by the investors' outcry about conflicts of interest over financial research. This is a subject, however, which now relegated to the closet.

After the April 2003 Settlement, for example, Citigroup responded to investigations of conflicts of interest at its investment-banking arm by splitting the unit in two. The former Salomon Brothers continued with investment banking, but Smith Barney returned to its role as a stockbroker. Part of Smith Barney has been the research unit accused of skewing its findings to win investment banking business.

Two conclusions can be reached from the discussion in this section. One is that the question of an effective separation between equity research and investment banking is still looking for an answer – moreover this is by no means the only conflict of interest with investments in stocks. The other conclusion is that there exists much more common ground than meets the eye behind the substance of titles like 'equity research' and 'rating of creditworthiness'. Eventually this may have considerable impact in reshaping independent investment research.

11.6 Very often, analysts' pickings are mediocre

Chapter 10 explained why, to effectively manage their exposure, investors need timely and accurate information. 'Buy' and 'sell' signals by equity analysts were supposed to be a significant input to this process, but they are not. As we will see in this section and in section 11.7, generally, equity research findings have been characterized by asymmetries loaded on the *buy* side (see section 11.7). Asymmetries work both ways:

- The buy side is promoted in many words and figures when the market goes up.
- The sell side is king when the market falls, but this is done (often massively) through short-selling by hedge funds and traders, rather than being publicly promoted through analysts reports.[17]

In making up their mind on which investment strategy to follow, investors find themselves in the middle of a conflict because of these asymmetries, and because of the 'free advice' traders and fund managers often give: to be *market neutral*. Experience teaches it is unwise to believe in market-neutral trades. I know of several cases with *delta neutral spreads* in options which turned sour.

In theory, a market-neutral strategy means balanced positions. Their value is supposed to change very little for small price moves in either direction. In practice, they are 'neutral' only in a dream world; what surrounds the market-neutral argument is highly misleading. Not only is the concept questionable, but the timing and execution are often wrong.

- Instead of just getting right out, traders and investors decide to move out of the position one leg at a time.
- By the time they finish liquidating that position, they may well go through all of their portfolio's capital.

Neither is the use of options the financial markets' penicillin, as some brokers advise. A study done in the 1980s for the SEC, when options had attracted a great deal of market attention, found that 90 percent of all options expired at losses to the holder. Long option positions cost dearly, and they are not a winning strategy, no matter what the brokers say.

If new methods of dealing with market uncertainty provide very little by way of protection, it is no less true that in the more traditional areas of investing, those connected with the choice of equities, very often analysts pickings are mediocre. Here are some examples.

In late November 2002, at the *Institutional Investor* magazine's All-American Research Team Awards dinner, Eliot Spitzer, New York State attorney general, said his office commissioned independent research firms to analyze recommendations made by more than 400 analysts, covering fifty-one industries ranked at or near the top by *Institutional Investor*.

Based on their actual stock picks over the 1999 to 2002 time frame, analysts who were ranked number one in their fields actually had mediocre performances. Spitzer went on to say that average investors would not know the truth because Wall Street promoted the rankings of their analysts but withheld data on their efficiency in stock-picking.[18] This statement followed on the heels of another action, this time by the SEC, which also had to do with stock picks.

On 26 June 2002, the SEC said that would require Wall Street analysts to certify that their stock picks are not influenced by pay packages, or investment-banking relationships. The rule discussed in the US Congress is a 'start on the road to improving investor confidence', said the then SEC chairman Harvey Pitt. This commentary concerned investment suggestions given by analysts in interviews, public appearances, and reports.

The SEC wanted comments made in public by equity analysts to include statements pledging the ratings are not influenced by compensation or any other relationships with companies concerned in such comments. Also, in a rare move, the National Association of Securities Dealers (NASD) notified Jack Grubman that it was weighing possible punishment for making recommendations to investors without a 'reasonable basis'.

In mid-2002, the NASD investigation concerned Grubman's coverage of Winstar, which he continued to recommend to investors even as it unraveled. Winstar, a client of Citigroup's Salomon Smith Barney investment-banking unit, sought bankruptcy protection in April 2001. A similar experience, to the detriment of investors, has characterized Grubman's upbeat recommendations on WorldCom.

Another example of how biased stock pickings can be is that concerning Citigroup, Sandy Weill, Grubman and AT&T. In an email, dated 13 January 2001, Grubman wrote to Carol Cutler, an analyst at a money-management firm: 'I used Sandy to get my kids in the 92nd Street Y preschool (which is harder than Harvard) and Sandy needed Amstrong's vote on our board to nuke (John) Reed in showdown. Once the coast was clear for both of us (ie Sandy clear victor and my kids confirmed) I went back to my normal self (on AT&T).'[19]

The message behind this message was that Jack Grubman, a long-time bear on AT&T, upgraded the stock in late November 1999 to the equivalent of a 'strong buy' from a 'hold'. Grubman's children were admitted into the school around the time that Citigroup pledged a $1 million donation, which came after Citigroup's chief executive, Sanford I. Weill, urged Grubman to 'take a fresh look' at upgrading the stock of a major corporate client, AT&T.

The *fresh look* on AT&T that Grubman took helped sell shares particularly in AT&T's wireless division (which in February 2004, years later, was bought by Cingular). But by the time Grubman downgraded AT&T again, in October 2000, the company *and its investors* had lost 50 percent of capitalization.

- The stock traded at $28.82, down from $57.43, and
- Losses mounted to $80 billion, a huge amount of red ink for investors.[20]

This incident aside, it should also be noted that Jack Grubman's reputation as a Wall Street analyst suffered when WorldCom, Global Crossing and other telecommunications companies he promoted as strong buys crashed into bankruptcy. Even so, the disclosure of the emails suggesting that Grubman might have altered his stock picks to help his twin daughters get into an elite New York nursery school marks one of the most bizarre incidents in a year full of Wall Street scandals.

In another incident, Jack Grubman threatened to 'put the proper rating' on a stock whose executives were complaining about the tone of one of his reports. In yet another, ex-Merrill Lynch analyst Henry Blodget derided as 'this piece of junk' a stock Merrill was recommending to private investors. And there is the case of allegations by regulators, citing emails from brokers, that Credit Suisse First Boston improperly obtained outsized commissions in exchange for hot allocations of initial public offerings.

That is the so-called *spinning* which consists of awarding customers shares in popular public offerings in exchange for future investment banking business. Spinning is one of the issues at which Eliot Spitzer and his assistants have been looking very carefully for possible criminal charges, including bribery. Investigators from Spitzer's office have been instrumental in unearthing cases unworthy of Wall Street, with emails at the center of many of high-profile probes of alleged wrongdoing during the stock market bubble.

Investment bankers should take very seriously allegations on conflict-of-interest stock picks, spinning and other scams, not only because the authorities seem determined to come down hard on them, but also because improprieties tarnish their image and their reputational risk. 'The only way you're going to end this kind of practice (spinning), is to persuade people that they're doing it at the peril of criminal conviction', says William Galving, the Massachusetts Secretary of State.[21]

11.7 Buy-side asymmetries in the experts advice

In a way, the equity analysts' picks are a prognostication, and prognostications can go wrong. Eurostar provides a telling example of how deadly wrong earnings projections can be, because of mixing of real facts with wishful thinking. Ten million Eurostar passengers were expected to use the link each year. In 2003 only 6.3 million did. Moreover, instead of 5 million tons of freight, only 1.7 million tons were transported. Behind this shortfall lies the story of Eurostar's huge losses, compound by the fact that tickets and freight were based on an expectation of much higher usage than the tunnel has been able to attain.

Therefore, rather than concentrating only on picks, it is wise to take a wider view by looking for asymmetries in the experts' advice, of which there is plenty. For starters, *asymmetries* are part of life, and as a matter of course they exist everywhere; for instance, in management directives, market responses, data streams coming from the market, hedge coverage, insurance coverage, inflation effects, deflation effects, changes in supervisory rules, and hidden correlations.

One of the greater risks associated with asymmetries is that people think: 'They do not matter.' That is the wrong approach to real-life events. Apart from the fact that in equity research asymmetries are human-made, and they can be very damaging to investors, market-based asymmetries are imbalances which should serve as warning signs because they can:

■ Create a perfect storm, and
■ Lead to a serious rise in delinquencies and losses.

This is precisely the reason why asymmetries in buy and sell advice are not at all welcome. When and where they exist, they lead to overbought (or oversold) situations, blurring the judgment of investors in regard to what they need to do to keep their exposure under lock and key, along the lines discussed in Chapter 10.

This policy of favoring 'buy' over 'sell' recommendations, with neutral a small number in between, has had its peak in the mid to late 1990s. But it has also

	Count
By 'A', a banking company	
Buy	49
Neutral	3
Sell	8
Companies followed	60
By 'B', a brokerage	
Buy	420
Neutral	21
Sell	45
Companies followed	486
By 'C', a brokerage	
Buy	250
Neutral	20
Sell	37
Companies followed	307

Table 11.3 Coverage universe of buy versus sell opinions by equity analysts at the end of 2002

continued in the early years of the twenty-first century, albeit in a less pronounced mode. Table 11.3 presents as an example a small sample.

The distribution of 'buy' and 'sell' recommendations was even more asymmetric in the 1990s. The distribution changed a little only after the debacles of 'buy' signals for Enron, WorldCom, Internet outfits, and so many other companies. These were entities highly rated as 'buy' till a relatively short time prior to their bankruptcy.

Only by the end of 2002, about twenty months after the bubble years were over, the number of stock 'sell' recommendations by Wall Street analysts jumped up to a little over 10 percent of total advice. This was four times higher than two years earlier.

In a way, this rise in 'sell' recommendations reflected the efforts by brokers to respond to criticism about biased stock research. It also followed regulations that came into force in September 2002 obliging investment banks to include information on their total proportions of 'buy', 'sell' and 'hold' recommendations to investors – as well as pressure from securities regulators to make Wall Street research more reliable and independent.

In the aftermath, some investment banks, such as Morgan Stanley, revamped their ratings system to make it easier for investors to understand. The reader should notice that buy, neutral, sell is not the only terminology in use. There exists as well other graduations like strong buy (which in the late 1990s popped up even more frequently than buy), outperform, underperform, and so on.

It would be a mistake to believe that the severe market downturn from early 2000 to early 2003 has radically changed the attention paid to equity research – and to what may go wrong with a company. Sometimes opinions are divided. A short time before Adecco lost 35 percent of its value in one day (see Chapter 14), its equity was rated in

Firm name	Recommendation	Last update
Bank Leu	Hold	15 January 2004
Smith Barney	Hold	14 January 2004
Julius Baer Brokerage	Hold	13 January 2004
Crédit Suisse First Boston	Outperform	13 January 2004
Goldman, Sachs	Suspended coverage	13 January 2004
Deutsche Bank	Hold	13 January 2004
Dresdner Kleinwort Wasserstein	Buy	13 January 2004
Petercam Nederland	Sell	12 January 2004
Zuercher Kantonalbank	Underperform	12 January 2004
Effectenbank Stroeve	Sell	12 January 2004
Pictet & Cie	Buy	12 January 2004
Bank Sarasin & Cie	Reduce	12 January 2004
Fortis	Sell	12 January 2004

Table 11.4 The equity rating of Adecco mid-January 2004 at about the time its equity crashed

a very contradictory way by different investment houses as shown in Table 11.4. Out of thirteen institutions:

- one rated it outperform,
- two rated it buy,
- four rated it hold,
- two rated it underperform or reduce,
- three rated it sell,
- one suspended coverage.

'Suspended coverage' is an expression often used to mean that the analyst following this stock has left and no replacement is available yet. With this exception, as the reader will observe, there is no pattern in this rating. Though the higher frequency, by a notch, is 'hold', 'outperform/buy' and 'sell' show up with exactly the same frequency.

Such wide and incoherent spread of investment opinions is rather surprising because, after all, all aforementioned institutions base their advice on largely quantitative information to form a learned judgment. Examples of the type of information include:

- *Financial statement analysis*, what can be learned from a company's income statement and balance sheet, and how it applies to running the organization.
- *Financial evaluations*, using current information to project future funding requirements, including need for external financing.
- *Sustainable growth*, understanding the link between operating strategy, product strategy, market strategy, financial strategy, and likelihood of further expansion.
- *Optimal mix* of debt and equity financing, costs of financing, industry and company traits, as well as how taxes affect the firm's capital structure.

■ And (hopefully) an analysis of the *quality of management*, including the company's competition, and business standing.

The first four bullets are quantitative valuations, though there is some subjective judgment in market and product development, also in financial considerations in making recommendations. The job of the financial analyst essentially boils down to communicating such value propositions to investors. This is a reality check on projections before the market does it for him or her.

In conclusion, as the examples we have seen in this and the preceding chapters show, the way it is currently undertaken, equity research is not providing able assistance to investors in terms of risk management. While no one can predict the future performance of the equity markets, and past performance cannot guarantee future results, the information investors obtain should be timely, accurate and unbiased, so that the risks they take are transparent and well documented.

Notes

1 *Financial Times*, 16 May 2001.
2 D.N. Chorafas (2004). *Corporate Accountability, with Case Studies in Finance*. Macmillan/Palgrave.
3 *Business Week*, 20 January 2003.
4 D.N. Chorafas (2004). *Rating Management's Effectiveness with Case Studies in Telecommunications*. Macmillan/Palgrave.
5 *The Economist*, 20 March 2004.
6 *The Economist*, 20 March 2004.
7 D.N. Chorafas (2004). *Rating Management's Effectiveness with Case Studies in Telecommunications*. Macmillan/Palgrave.
8 *The Economist*, 25 October 2003.
9 *Financial Times*, 29–30 November 2003.
10 *The Economist*, 11 October 2003.
11 *The Economist*, 25 October 2003.
12 D.N. Chorafas (2004). *Corporate Accountability, with Case Studies in Finance*. Macmillan/Palgrave.
13 *Financial News*, 1–7 September 2003.
14 D.N. Chorafas (2000). *Managing Credit Risk, Volume 1: 'Analyzing, Rating and Pricing the Probability of Default*. Euromoney.
15 D.N. Chorafas (2004). *Corporate Accountability, with Case Studies in Finance*. Macmillan/Palgrave.
16 *The Economist*, 16 November 2002.
17 D.N. Chorafas (2003). *Alternative Investments and the Mismanagement of Risk*. Macmillan/Palgrave.
18 *BusinessWeek*, 2 December 2002.
19 *Wall Street Journal*, 18 November 2002.
20 *International Herald Tribune*, 18 November 2002.
21 *BusinessWeek*, 7 October 2002.

12 Volatility, liquidity, leverage, and their impact on investments

12.1 Introduction

Economic and market conditions that cause volatility in the value of commodities cause the worth of an investor's portfolio to fluctuate. There is no assurance that one's equities, bonds or other investments will appreciate. In regard to equities, not only might dividends not be paid because of adverse conditions, but also the investor's net worth might shrink as stock market prices fall. Therefore, three principles characterizing a sound investment strategy are:

- The investor with financial staying power finally wins,
- Time in the market is more important than timing the market, and
- The good stocks to buy are the ones that everybody is selling.

Liquidity is behind the first bullet, while what the second says is that a longer time horizon may counterbalance the effects of volatility. Behind the message of the third bullet is the advice of mature investors not to panic when confronted by market volatility, but instead to look at it as an opportunity to increase one's positions in sound equities.

Taken together, all three bullets constitute the alter ego of sound risk management, leading to the *eighteenth golden rule* that changes in volatility and liquidity must be studied in unison, as well as in connection with the investor's financial staying power and his or her gearing.[1] Figure 12.1 gives a snapshot of this three-dimensional frame of reference.

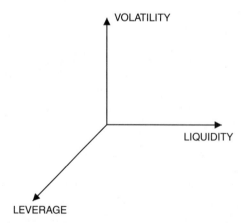

Figure 12.1 A frame of reference which helps to reposition our portfolio against market forces

Volatility is a measure of the variability of the price of an asset. It is usually defined as the annualized standard deviation of the natural logarithm of asset prices, but other metrics are used also. The distribution of prices of a given commodity over a longer period of time is usually taken as being normal (bell-shaped), even if everybody knows the normal distribution is an approximation of real-life events – whether of market prices or of any other variable.

Because volatility is so important and its effects so devastating, one of the missions critical to any system put in place to manage risk is to track the fluctuation in market prices. If the volatility of a market becomes so great that it adversely skews expected risk and return, then wise people would stop trading in that market. They may liquidate existing positions, and will not take any new ones on till they can see clearer and be able to interpret the market's moves. Attention to volatility is vital because it is likely that volatility swings:

- Transgress well-defined limits, and
- Upset carefully calculated risk/reward ratios.

For investors and traders, volatility changes on the upside must act as alarms. Moreover, they should always keep in mind that volatility occurs at different levels, and tracking changes in volatility is as important as understanding the impact on one's holdings of the current level of volatility.

Experienced traders have a rule to get out of the market when the volatility and momentum become absurd. This happens from time to time and therefore, for risk management reasons, volatility must be steadily followed and interpreted in terms of its effects:

- For each commodity being traded, and
- In every market in which one is active.

Like volatility, liquidity is a salient problem to investors in equities, bonds, derivative financial instruments, and other commodities. It is also a leading trading and investment yardstick. Well-managed banks develop measures of both global and local liquidity in order to help themselves and their clients, because they appreciate that efficient money management requires the ability to confront both lack of liquidity and excesses of it:

- Excess liquidity, is that which is surplus to the needs of the real economy.
- When it is invested in financial assets, it influences market behavior on the upside, creating a sort of inflation in financial instruments.

Even hedging is an empty concept without methods and means for measuring current volatility and liquidity, as well as projecting future volatility and liquidity. The opposite to excess liquidity is a liquidity squeeze. Leveraging and liquidity correlate. High leveraging (see section 12.6), has an impact on market psychology and, along with other reasons, leads to a liquidity squeeze. Another aftermath is growing credit risk – one of the main determinants of a downturn.

Liquidity, like volatility, is a crucial factor in asset allocation, as well as in investment and trading decisions. One of the lessons of real business life, which is not properly taught in schools, is that people and companies who are leveraged and pay scant attention to their liquidity, dig themselves into a deep hole. When volatility increases and they finally realize how deep in a hole they are, they panic and rarely find the means to get out of it as a wholesome entity. Look at LTCM[2] as an example.

12.2 Volatility, volume of transactions, and volatility index

Market illiquidity and market volatility tend to correlate among themselves, and with the fact of highly leveraged trading. Their synergy increases when trading involves instruments which are inherently geared, because market prices of these instruments are highly volatile and materially affected by unpredictable factors or events. As a result, even relatively small price movements may produce a large profit or loss.

In addition, some of the trading entities, such as hedge funds, enter into borrowing arrangements for purposes of leveraging their proprietary dealing chores. This increases the vulnerability of banks lending to hedge funds, and makes risk management, even by entities and investors who do not enter into leveraged deals, so much more complex.

A different way of making the foregoing statement is that while on the upside volatility and gearing increase the potential for profits, they also directly affect the risks associated with trading and investing. The combination of leverage and volatility can subject the value of portfolio positions to sharp fluctuations, either positive or negative. Investors must appreciate that not only volatility, liquidity and leverage must be studied in unison, but also their cumulative effect should be projected in conjunction with prevailing market conditions.

This polyvalence in approach must be considered both from the narrow perspective of a given asset, and from the overall viewpoint of a portfolio's diversification in relation to:

- The market direction, and
- The investor's goals in terms of risk and return.

To get a clear idea of the market's direction and its sustainability, investors should be looking at price trends and the volume of transactions. The volume of trade in a stock is a measure of supply and demand. When an equity starts to move to a new high ground, volume tends to increase by at least 50 percent over the averaged daily volume in most recent months. As far as an individual equity is concerned, in principle,

- A pickup in volume is an early indicator that a stock starts to move, and
- A collapse in volume gives the message the stock is tapering off.

Within the framework suggested by these two bullets, the trading price of a common stock may fluctuate significantly in response to a number of events and factors. Examples of macroeconomic factors are general economic conditions, changes in interest rates, trends in a given industry, such as telecommunications, wider stock market volatility; there are also microeconomic factors. For instance, for a specific company, stock price volatility may be due to quarterly variations in operating results; innovation or absence of it in products and services; favorable or unfavorable strategic developments; new business combinations, or the unraveling of business partnerships; actions by competitors; changes in financial and other estimates by securities analysts, and their recommendations; and significant changes in capital structure. The issuance of additional debt or equity to the public is an example. Other company-specific factors are the departure of key personnel, corporate restructurings, changes in valuation methodology, new regulations, or pure speculation.

The metric *beta* (β) measures volatility of a security relative to a benchmark. Any equity with a β higher than, for instance, that of the S&P 500, is considered to be more volatile than the market. The volatility of any security with a lower β than the benchmark is rising or falling more slowly than that of the market. The S&P 500 has a volatility of 1.

The β of individual equities is frequently given in financial analysis but, as instruments become more complex, sources which provide volatility estimates decrease, and such estimates are not very frequently updated. Therefore, financial analysts tend to develop their own algorithms, or adapt to their needs some of those already existing. An example from the stock market is the use of measures of volatility such as:

- Standard deviation of S&P composite daily price changes,
- Average spread between daily high and low prices for the S&P composite, and
- Volatility index (VIX) by the Chicago Board Options Exchange.

VIX is an index of implied volatility of options on America's S&P 500 stockmarket index. It is specifically designed to measure the cost of buying options. In January 2004, VIX fell to 14 – its lowest since 1996. This is a long way from its 1998, 2001 and 2002 peaks. On 23 July 2002, for instance, it had soared to 52.

Investors follow VIX quite carefully because as volatility falls, they can make profits on risky assets. This is particularly true of those investors who have been selling options and by so doing they have been selling volatility too.

- Indeed, mid-2004 saw lots of people and companies being short on volatility.
- However, markets are renowned for turning around without warning, and therefore *shorting volatility* is a very dangerous game.

By being short on volatility speculators, and those investors emulating them, expose themselves to complex financial deals that they do not really understand. Shorting volatility involves mountains of uncertainty, and a change in market sentiment can be lethal. Both for speculation and for risk control reason, VIX acts as indicator of *implicit volatility* and, as such, it starts being closely watched.

The attention investors pay to VIX is particularly intense in connection to financial lows. For instance, significant has been the fact that in July 2002 VIX closed above 50 for the first time since October 1987, when the Dow fell 22 percent on Black Monday. Two days later, came yet another sharp decline in the technology-heavy NASDAQ Composite index. Notice that on 23 July 2002, implicit volatility at 52 was not too far from the high water marks of VIX:

- 57 at the height of the panic selling after 11 September 2001, and
- 60 during the Russian financial crisis in August 1998.

Volatility started falling in late 2002, and by the end of 2003 it had reached roughly half its previous peak. The more conservative market players took heart when the VIX fell from over 50 percent in July 2002 to a low of 14 percent in January 2004, its lowest level since 1996, though it rose again to over 18 percent in February 2004.

The market's mood, however, never stays still over a long period of time. From the middle of January 2004 investors started to dump risky assets with high P/E ratios. Two months later, this pace picked up and stock markets fell. By 15 March:

- The S&P 500 stood at 5 percent off its mid-January high, and
- The capitalization of technology stock of NASDAQ dropped some 10 percent.

Worst hit by the equities retreat has been the auto sector, down 17 percent January to March 2004 – one of the worst performing in the S&P 500. With this change in market mood, the VIX has been climbing sharply, and so have bond spreads for investment-grade corporates. Even non-investment grade bonds benefited from narrowing spreads when compared with Treasuries.

As a commonly used measure of implied volatility, the VIX says roughly by how much shares are likely to move, which is market risk, but it also has a message on credit risk. Because of the fall in both leverage and volatility, in February 2004 Moody's KMV predicted that the likelihood of an average company defaulting over the next year had fallen to just over 1 percent – a significant reduction from the early years of the twenty-first century. In January 2004, an investors' report by Merrill Lynch had this to say on investor sentiment and VIX behavior in 2003:

We saw violent swings in investor sentiment which is why low-quality stocks did so well. We went from extreme 'risk aversion' at the start of the Iraqi war to significant appetite for risk. We saw the VIX measure of equity volatility practically halve over the year. We saw US high yield spreads practically halve too. We saw investors go from 'above normal' cash levels to 'normal' cash levels, as equities went from 'undervalued' back to 'fair value'.[3]

Based on data from January 1998 to January 2002, Figure 12.2 plots the behavior of the S&P Composite Index and the CBOE VIX. The reader will notice the two most pronounced peaks in this chart:

- The first with two nodes corresponding to the August 1998 Russian crisis and September 1998 LTCM meltdown, and
- The second, a spike created by the 11 September 2001 terrorist attack in New York and Washington.

These peaks have been followed by a return from the VIX of nearly 50 to one just above 20. In both cases the sharp reduction of the volatility index has been a sign that the market fever has calmed down.

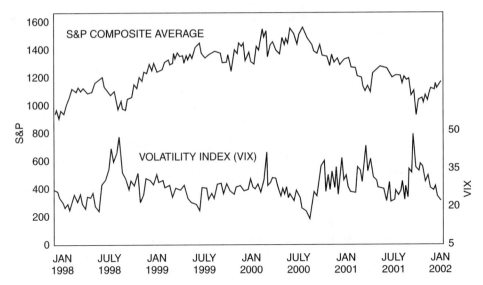

Figure 12.2 Volatility index (VIX) and S&P composite average (*Source:* Merrill Lynch. Reproduced with permission)

Of course, while important, volatility is not the only variable affecting the market. Globalization has introduced equity correlations. For instance, many stock analysts base their research and prognostication on the impact of the S&P equity index. A 10 percent rise in this index tends to boost European equities by 9 percent.

Currency exchange and interest rates are other crucial variables affecting prices. A 10 percent appreciation of the euro against the dollar tends to hurt European equities by around 7 percent. While a 10 percent rise in US bond yields, for instance from 4 percent to 4.4 percent, tends to boost European stocks by 2 percent. This latter factor serves two purposes.

■ It captures global trends in credit spreads, and
■ Provides some guidance about the cyclical environment.

As a rule of thumb, the US government bond yields tends to be inversely correlated with high-yield spreads, which in turn is indicative of the health of corporate balance sheets. Better documented is the statement that volatility in the equity markets increases during times of uncertainty over economic growth; as well as that equity markets have a propensity to fluctuate wildly when the overall economy approaches a peak.

12.3   The concept of implied volatility and its use

Measures of implied volatility can provide valuable information on the uncertainty prevailing in the market with regard to future developments. This is as true of equities as it is of short-term interest rates. Estimates of implied volatility which increases day to day, week to week, or month to month, create a certain level of anxiety in the market and investors got to pay attention to them.

Implied volatility is normally calculated on the basis of option pricing models to obtain an estimate of expected dispersion of future percentage changes. Take short-term interest rates as an example. A value of implied volatility equal to 20 percent would indicate that on an annual basis the best estimate of the market's expected dispersion of implied interest rate, over the remaining life of the futures contract, is 20 percent of the current level of this interest rate.

In Euroland, stock market uncertainty is measured by the implied volatility extracted from options on the Dow Jones EURO STOXX 50 index (see Chapter 4). For example, in the period after mid-March 2003, the ten-day moving average of implied volatility dropped and, in tandem with this, stock prices, as measured by the broad Dow Jones EURO STOXX index.

On the other hand, while the implied stock market volatility extracted from options prices is an important measure for gauging the degree of uncertainty prevailing among market participants, it is not always clear whether changes in implied volatility are created by the aggregation of uncertainties relating to specific firms of sectors of the economy, or whether they are caused by general uncertainties relating to:

- Specific firms,
- Sectors of the economy, or
- The market as a whole.

Many analysts believe that by examining the implied volatility of individual stocks as a complement to the analysis of implied volatility of market indices, it is feasible to make inferences which are fairly well documented. This requires special care, such as the ability to ascertain that the implied volatility of a given stock market index indeed measures the expected volatility of a well-diversified portfolio of stocks – where, to a large extent, the ups and downs of individual equity price counterbalance one another.

To appreciate the sense of the foregoing statement, it is appropriate to keep in mind that the risk embedded in a portfolio of stocks is determined by a number of components, such as the variance of the price of each of the individual stocks in the inventory, and the extent to which individual stock prices move in unison, hence they correlate. Also, bear in mind the ability of implied volatility extracted from options prices on a stock market index to reflect expectations about:

- The future correlation between these stock prices, and
- The future volatility of the individual stocks within the index.

Price correlations have an impact on decisions by investors and asset managers who seek the benefit of diversification. On several occasions, however, the benefits of port-folio diversification have been minimal, as revealed by episodes where measures of volatility converge. Convergence of volatility metrics can occur when the correlation between stocks rises because of:

- General market concerns,
- Contagion effects, and/or
- Heightened uncertainties about stability of financial instruments or entities.

An example of the third bullet point is the discovery of accounting irregularities at Enron, WorldCom, Tyco, Parmalat and other firms, when the confidence of market participants in the information disclosed by corporations was severely impaired. Another reason for volatility convergence is systemic uncertainties taking hold in stock markets against a background of concerns about the possibility of war, or of a widespread financial crisis.

In principle, the higher the correlation among equities in a portfolio, the higher the volatility of the inventoried positions. Also, the closer the composition of the portfolio, the higher the volatility of the inventoried positions. On the other hand, the closer the composition of the portfolio resembles the stock market index used as proxy, the better the prognostication of its volatility.

To determine the extent to which implied volatility of a stock market index is driven by expectations of volatility in the individual stocks that make up the index, the implied volatility of each of the individual stocks has to be examined. One way to do so is by taking an appropriately weighted average of the implied volatility of each of these stocks. This helps to reveal the extent to which the implied volatility of say the EURO STOXX 50 index is due to be expected volatility in the individual stocks. By comparing this average with the implied volatility of the stated index, inferences could be made about the extent to which volatility in the stock market reflects expectations about correlations between these stocks.

A similar statement is valid about any other established index. Figure 12.3 presents 2000–01 data on implied volatility in the USA and Euroland. The time series reflects the expected standard deviation of percentage stock price changes of options on stock price indices. (Dow Jones EURO STOXX 50 for the Euroland and the S&P 500 for the USA). Notice that the 11 September 2001 spike has been more pronounced in Europe than in the USA.

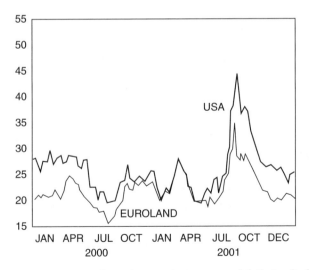

Figure 12.3 Percentages per year and ten-day moving average of daily implied equity volatility in the USA and Euroland

Implied volatility proved to be a useful tool, and has led to greater sophistication in its study. Several studies now distinguish between total volatility, equity market volatility, and specific volatility. Take volatility in the German equity market as an example. It rose considerably in conjunction with the stock market boom in the late 1990s, but also in the subsequent severe price corrections.

An interesting observation is that, quite often, days on which the DAX (the German share price index) is highly volatile are followed by days with great fluctuations, characterizing a fat tails distribution. (The DAX volatility seems to follow a leptokyrtotic distribution Hurst coefficient.) The measure of incidence of major price swings is characterized by kyrtosis.[4]

A study of the equity yield fluctuations of the DAX index by the Deutsche Bundesbank has shown a significant increase in volatility over the 1997 to 2003 time frame, with mid-1997 identified as the turning point. In fact, the DAX itself became more volatile and there has been a sharp increase in the volatility of individual stocks on which the index is based.

A GARCH model developed by the Bundesbank, focusing on data before and after the 1997 turning point, shows an unconditional variance more than 2.5 times higher than normal – as well as an increase in the persistence parameters after 1997. By comparison, a Markov model with high and low volatility based on historical data from 1965 demonstrated that, although temporary phases of high volatility occurred prior to 1997, they all lasted less than a semester. Decomposing the monthly realized volatility of a typical DAX-listed enterprise into

- A company-specific component, and
- A general market component

the Bundesbank researchers found that, although market volatility has increased over time, the change in specific volatility has been more pronounced. The divergent trend in the volatility of individual stocks and that of the DAX is probably explained by a declining correlation between the yields on individual DAX stocks.[5]

The Bundesbank study points out that, on one hand, this improves the opportunity for risk diversification. But, on the other hand, the significant rise in and this in spite of the effect of declining correlations.

A similar development has taken place in the American stock markets during the late 1990s. In that case, investments were characterized by a rush out of old economy shares and into new economy equities. Johnson & Johnson, for example, dropped from $103 to the mid-1970s signaling the existence of two different equity markets prior to the year 2000 crash:

- For most technology stocks share prices kept on rising.
- For all other shares, there has been the nearest thing to a bear market.

In fact, this event was global and has accelerated ever since the summer of 1998, becoming particularly pronounced in January–February 2000. As will be recalled, at that time the Dow Jones Industrial Average slipped by 15 percent from the record level of 11 723, while at the same time, the NASDAQ rose by 12 percent.

At the time experts said that the extent of the market's split personality was not captured by broad indices because a mere handful of shares had been driving the market up. The valuation of Terra, a mobile communications spin-off from Spain's Telefonica, implied that each of its customers was worth almost eight times as much as a customer at America On-line (AOL), while shares of Carrefour, the French food retailer, were down 30 percent from their peak in autumn 1999, and those of Volkswagen, the German car manufacturer, were off by 25 percent. As will be recalled, both Terra and AOL Time Warner crashed after the late 1990s came to an end.

12.4   Solvency and liquidity feed upon one-another

There are different definitions of *liquidity* ranging from quantitative to qualitative. The quantitative targets the amount of money in the market and is expressed through the algorithm

$$MS = MB \bullet v \tag{12.1}$$

where MS is the money supply, MB the monetary base, and v the velocity of circulation of money. Notice that there are different metrics of MS: M0 which is practically the amount of money issued by the central bank in notes and coins (roughly corresponding to MB); M1, M2, and M3 which measure the amount of money in circulation expanded by the banking system (explained in Table 12.1).[6] MB and v are established by monetary policy targets.

'There is no limit to the amount of money that can be created by the banking system,' Marriner Eccles, a former chairman of the Fed, had warned, 'but there are limits to our productive facilities and our labor supply.'[7] In conjunction with the interplay of supply and demand for liquidity, these limits lead to liquidity's qualitative definition by Dr Henry Kaufman as the 'feel of the market' which connects to market psychology.

The earliest known manipulation of liquidity on a grand scale by the state goes back to Augustus, the Roman emperor, and Tiberius who succeeded at the helm of the Roman empire. The seeds for the panic of year AD 33 were sown BC in the time of Augustus, who had established a government policy based on the triple principle of:

■ Deficit financing,
■ Low interest rates, and
■ Steady increase of monetary base.

The aftermath has been plenty of liquidity and growth, but a financial system without limits could not last for ever. When he became emperor, Tiberius tried to right the balances by following precisely the opposite strategy. He greatly reduced state expenditures, limited the monetary base, and let the interest rates follow a course upwards. This led to massive bank failures – the first global banking crisis on record.

Moreover, Roman money was drained by the Middle East and Asian countries, which furnished the Romans with plenty of goods. The similarity to the huge current account deficits of the USA is inescapable. With the Roman globalization, prices were falling, interest rates zoomed, and creditors ran after debtors. Trying to get

	Liquidity providing	Liquidity absorbing	Net contribution
1 Monetary policy operations of the Eurosystem	195.3	0.8	+194.5
Main refinancing operations	122.5	–	+122.5
Longer-term refinancing operations	60.0	–	+60.0
Standing facilities	0.5	0.8	−0.3
Other operations	12.4	–	+12.4
2 Other factors affecting the banking system's liquidity	383.7	450.8	−67.2
Bank notes in circulation	–	298.0	−298.0
Government deposits with the Eurosystem	–	43.5	−43.5
Net foreign assets (including gold)	383.7	–	+383.7
Other factors (net)	–	109.4	−109.3
3 Credit institutions' holding on current accounts with the Eurosystem (1) + (2)			127.4
4 Required reserves			126.4

Notes:

1 European Central Bank (2002). *Monthly Bulletin*, January.

2 Daily average during the reserve maintenance period from 24 November to 23 December 2001; totals may not add up to rounding.

Table 12.1 European Central Bank: contributions to the banking system's liquidity (in billion euros)[1,2]

hold of the situation, the Roman Senate issued a decree which made matters worse. Finally, Tiberius ended the crisis by recapitalizing the banks through taxpayers' money throughout the empire.

The Roman banking crisis should serve as a warning to all Western governments. In the 1990s, the Japanese probably did not learn the lesson from nearly twenty centuries ago, and they had to reinvent ways and means from getting out of the abyss of *their own* banking crisis. Commenting on how Japan was handling its economic and financial lows for nearly thirteen years, a 2004 report by Merrill Lynch pointed to the mobilization of extraordinary high liquid balances:

■ In 2004, Japan's currency in circulation has been 15 percent of GDP, up from the historically stable 7 percent,

■ But Japanese banks have not yet been adequately recapitalized, and liquidity alone will not close the deflation gap characterizing demand and supply.

One of the points made by the aforementioned Merrill Lynch study is that once expectations turn from deflation to inflation, the power of *cold money* turning *hot* could quickly drive up inflation.[8] This is the other side of the liquidity equation, $MS = MB \bullet v$. Once the velocity of circulation of money escapes control, it carries along with it a price spiral.

As these examples demonstrate, it is quite understandable that central banks watch most carefully for signs of a balance between provision and absorption of liquidity in the economy, with particular emphasis on contributions by the bank system to liquidity. An example of metrics used to track liquidity, and of associated statistics, is provided by Table 12.1. The statistics come from the European Central Bank's *Monthly Bulletin*.

The preceding paragraphs made reference to interest rates. Liquidity is significantly influenced by the cost of money expressed through interest rates, which essentially are a pricing mechanism. Money may become available at a high price while it is unavailable at a lower one.

Another way of looking at liquidity, this time from the more narrow perspective of a company, is as money in the bank, cash flow and liquid instruments versus the timing of the firm's assumed obligations. This narrower definition overlaps with the concept of *solvency* (more on this later on). At corporate level:

- Liquid assets include cash, balances due from banks and short-term investments.
- Typically, these are assets that mature within the next three months and should be presented in the balance sheet at fair value.

Significant risk is associated with lack of liquidity, which impacts on solvency. The FSA defines *liquidity risk* as the risk 'that a firm, though solvent, either does not have sufficient financial resources available to it to enable it to meet its obligations as they fall due, or can secure them only at excessive cost'. This, FSA says, is a basic business risk faced to some degree by most financial services firms.[9]

Theoretically, liquidity and solvency are two different concepts. Practically, however, this is not always the case. In the stock market crash of October 1987, a key question for the Federal Reserve was the likelihood of systemic risk. Was a big bank in trouble? Was it insolvent? Could its failure tear apart the financial fabric?

'In the short run, (Gerald) Corrigan (the president of the New York Fed) argued, there was no way to tell the difference between just short term liquidity problems and outright insolvency.'[10] Tail events in credit risk and market risk may damage the bank's liquidity, solvency or both. Therefore, a financial institution must watch carefully:

- Its own and the market's liquidity as a whole, and
- Its own solvency, including the possibility of fast realization of assets under conditions other than a fire sale.

A good way to measure a firm's solvency, indeed one which is often used, is to divide its current assets by its current liabilities. This is known as current ratio or acid test:

$$\text{Acid test} = \frac{\text{Current assets}}{\text{Current liabilities}} \qquad (12.2)$$

The acid test provides a rough measure of the safety afforded the firm's short-term creditors. Though its minimal acceptable value varies from one sector of the economy to the next, classical economic theory considers a current ratio of 2 as the floor for solvency reasons.

Behind the statement just been made lies the fact that in the event of technical liquidation, current assets are less likely to yield their expected value, while current liabilities will haunt the firm. At the same time, current assets will probably yield a higher percentage of their real value than fixed assets.

■ Short-term lenders regard current assets as the ultimate source for the repayment of their loans.
■ Consequently, the higher the current ratio the greater is their feeling of security.

The reader should, however, notice that this working capital ratio might be misleading as a tool for financial management. To calculate it, the acid test figures are taken from the balance sheet, reflecting past activities of the firm. Though it may comfort a manager to know that his or her current ratio was in satisfactory form two months ago, he or she knows nothing about its present state. Balance sheets:

■ Always represent the past, and they are also summary statements of accounts.
■ They do not include information on timing, with reference to the periods within which current liabilities become due.

For instance, a company could have a current ratio of 3 to 1 at the time of its audit, but if its current assets are primarily made up of goods in process and most of its current liabilities are due at the end of the current month, it might face a severe cash shortage. On the other hand, a firm that acts as an agent buying and selling finished goods could have a low current ratio and still be in good liquidity position.

One way of coping with inadequacies embedded in the current ratio is to consider not current assets but liquid assets. These include cash, investments and securities which can be realized without difficulty (known as near cash), cash value of debtors (accounts receivable), and a conservative assessment of cash value of raw materials, goods in process and finished goods held in stock. Dividing liquid assets by current liabilities gives the so-called quick ratio, or liquid ratio:

$$\text{Quick ratio} = \frac{\text{Liquid assets}}{\text{Current liabilities}} \tag{12.3}$$

This ratio's significance is that it takes accounts of timing between receipts generated by liquid assets and payments falling due, providing a suitable balance. If timings are balanced, liquid assets and current liabilities should be managed so that the quick ratio is better than 1. If it is less than 1, liquid assets no longer cover the payments due, while if the value is much greater than one, scarce resources are being wasted by being kept in idle liquidity.

Notice that, up to a point, diversification and liquidity correlate with one another. As Figure 12.4 suggests, diversification helps in times of tight liquidity, because not all sources connected to the company's liquid assets are expected to be under stress at the same time. Senior management should keep in mind that the quick ratio is a dynamic measurement which can change significantly over time.

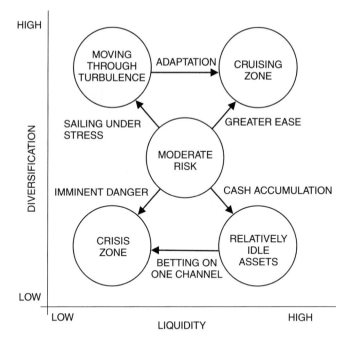

Figure 12.4 Diversification helps in terms of tight liquidity

12.5 Liquidity management and risk control

There exist core principles for liquidity management, one of these being the existence of an appropriate contingency plan. This liquidity management principle aims at damage control in the aftermath of exposure and it concentrates on the probability of a liquidity crisis. Another principle relates to the establishment of *liquidity risk limits*, such as a net overnight funding limit. This, too, is a risk management tool.

As these principles demonstrate, the proper handling of liquidity requires establishing a comprehensive framework of policies and risk limits. It also demands tight control on both the global cash position and the stock of highly liquid and discountable securities. The goal is to ensure that the entity will always have sufficient liquidity to meet its liabilities when due (see section 12.4), without compromising its ability to respond quickly to strategic market opportunities.

Companies with experience in this domain appreciate that sound liquidity management must be based on an integrated framework that incorporates assessment of all known cash inflows and outflows, as well as the availability of high-grade collateral. This could be used to secure additional funding if required. Well-run organizations see to it that at all times,

- Their liquidity position is prudently managed under a variety of potential scenarios, and
- Stress factors are taken into due considerations, including the administration of stress tests.[11]

The liquidity scenarios to be covered should incorporate both normal market conditions and extraordinary factors, reflected under stressed conditions. These may be specific to both our company, or related to different types of market crises. An example of the former are unexpected losses at 99.97 percent level of confidence – which corresponds to AA credit rating.[12]

In line with the acid test and the liquidity ratio we examined in section 12.4, for each scenario the short-term liquidity position arising out of non-trading activities must be determined by matching liabilities running off against maturing assets. Quite often there is a gap, which is augmented by that of the trading book. The trading book gap is ascertained by comparing the value of assets which could be liquidated with the liabilities which would have to be repaid. If there is no gap in the banking book, then the stress test should concentrate on the trading book.

To handle their liquidity exposure in an able manner, tier-1 banks and other institutions watch their liquidity position intraday, because they appreciate that liquidity issues are dynamic, changing with transactions and with market pricing. Figure 12.5 provides an example. Well-managed banks also establish *liquidity limits* based on two levels:

■ *Liquidity risk* – by risk type, risk factor, currency, and market.
■ *Liquidity volume* – by open position, individual security, and type of transaction.

Independent rating agencies are following quite closely liquidity risk and its underlying factors among the entities they cover. Following the liquidity crisis which in 2000–02 savaged Internet companies and telecoms, even the biggest carriers and their suppliers, credit rating agencies give more frequent commentary on *liquidity risk factors*.

Simple statistics on transactions can tell a story, for instance, that a company may be doing a lot of telecom trades, but they would not necessarily indicate the worth of such:

■ Bandwidth trades, and
■ Network swaps.

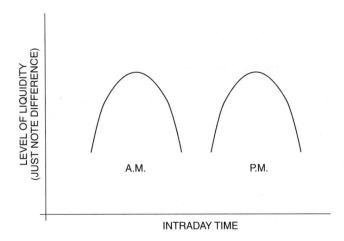

Figure 12.5 A bank's liquidity position changes intraday with the volume of transactions

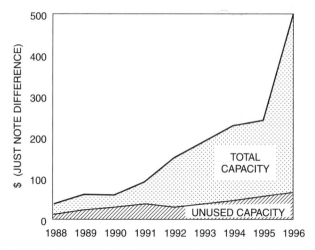

Figure 12.6 Submarine fiber-optic cables and their utilization

Therefore, statistics must be supplemented by information on used capacity versus unused but available telecommunications capacity. As the scams of capacity swaps and subsequent bankruptcy of Global Crossing, WorldCom and other companies demonstrate, such information is vital to investors, in appreciating a company's and an industry's business – as well as its ability to survive in a highly competitive market.

Taking submarine underwater cables as an example, Figure 12.6 demonstrates that since 1996 it has been clear that unused capacity had become a high multiple of used capacity, and this was most likely to lead to a financial earthquake. The rapid build-up of capacity has absorbed the telecoms companies' liquidity like a sponge, but with such capacity remaining idle:

- The cash flow has been pitiful, and
- The quick ratio equation has turned on its head (see section 12.4).

Such happening should have been a powerful warning signal for telephone companies. Yet, in spite of such evidence, at the beginning of 2000 leading international banks formed a mobile commerce power-play known as the Mobey Forum, to get a piece of the action in future telecoms capacity. The prevailing hypothesis, at that time, was that telecoms were surely inheriting the Earth – in spite of the fact all available evidence indicated that:

- The communications industry was losing the battle to manage its own networks, and
- As new technologies were introduced, changing the rules of the game, good money was thrown after bad by following obsolete principles.

One of the most flagrant examples of miscalculation has been the 3G mobile network spectrum auctions in Europe, which brought disaster to the telecoms industry and its suppliers.[13] It led big and small carriers into a bear trap of billions of dollars from which there is no easy or even visible way out. The fortunes telecom companies paid to European governments for 3G bandwidth:

■ Drained their liquidity, and
■ Increased their leverage beyond any reasonable proportion.

Misfortunes rarely comes singly; in 2002 telecoms companies came under scrutiny for their accounting practices. The cases brought to public attention include not just Enron Broadband Services and Global Crossing, two of the most spectacular failures, but also KPN of the Netherlands, a former postal, telegraph and telephone company, which according to a shareholder group had an inflated balance sheet with at least 10 billion euros ($12.5 billion) in doubt. Another example is Optus of Australia, whose parent company (Singapore Telecom) wanted some costs previously hidden on the balance sheet moved onto the trading account.[14]

Liquidity woes saw to it that in the 2001–04 time frame business prospects were not bright even for those telecoms which had not been fiddling the books. The hopes of telecommunications companies and their suppliers for double-digit *revenue growth* were far from being met. By 2002 it became evident that revenue growth stood at zero to 5 percent per year, a long way from the expected 25 percent to 35 percent annual growth.

Liquidity crisis is an inescapable aftermath of leverage (see section 12.6). When it started in the telecoms industry, analysts said that carriers and the telecom equipment industry needed 50 percent to 70 percent annual *traffic growth* just to produce *flat* revenues, and more than that to restructure their balance sheet. By contrast, with an appreciable 30 percent to 35 percent traffic growth, revenues were falling because the *average selling price* declined very fast. For example, if a unit of bandwidth in 1990 cost $100, in 2002 the cost of the same unit of bandwidth was $1.

The semiconductor industry has also been subject to a liquidity squeeze. In February 2001 plunging computer-chip prices battered South Korea's Hyundai Electronics Industries, the world's second-largest maker of memory chips, leading the company into financial difficulties. As a result, its American subsidiary, Hyundai Semiconductor America, was unable to meet a $57 million repayment on a project finance loan in early March of that same year.

In Seoul, Hyundai Electronics informed creditors, led by JP Morgan Chase, that it will soon repay the loan on behalf of the US unit. The parent company was expected to capitalize on a decision by state-run Korea Development Bank to roll over $2.3 billion in Hyundai Electronics bonds due in 2001. However, the Korean government-arranged relief program covered only about half of the $4.5 billion in interest-bearing debt owed by the company and due.

To make up the difference, hyundai Electronics slashed 25 percent of its workforce and raised $1.6 billion through asset sales. It also undertook fresh borrowing and made a plan to generate at least $600 million in additional cash. But with so many ifs in that company's strategy to get out of stress conditions, analysts said Hyundai Electronics was unlikely to avoid a liquidity crunch unless semiconductor prices turned around quickly. The analysts were proved right. Hyundai Electronics had failed in its risk management, though it continued limping on as Hynix Semiconductor.

All sorts of companies succumb to a liquidity squeeze because they do not use foresight in their financial planning. The building boom in Las Vegas, Nevada, too, inevitably resulted in overcapacity, with each new 'palace' taking business from its predecessors. By the end of 1998, the building of the Bellagio had nearly doubled Mirage Resorts' debt load, and the revenue was falling short of what was needed to service the loans. Moreover:

- The Bellagio took business from Mirage, and
- The Venetian and Paris took business from Bellagio, leaving Mirage Resorts ripe for takeover.

In 2000, Kirk Kerkorian's MGM Grand appeared like an invading army on the horizon and made a $6.7 billion hostile offer for Mirage. Within twelve days, Mirage belonged to Kerkorian, and Steve Wynn – who engineered the Mirage Group's ascent – was pushed out. Wynn subsequently announced he would build an even more lavish casino than Bellagio, to be named La Rève.

Ground was broken on the $1.85 billion project in November 2002, and the opening is scheduled for 2005. La Rève will include a human-made mountain, in addition to its mountain of debt. To pay for it all, Wynn Resorts planned a $408 million initial public offering and $1 billion in bank loans from a consortium led by Deutsche Bank, Bear Stearns, and Bank of America.[15] All this means leverage and more leverage, with a liquidity squeeze at its heels and debtors queuing up to recover part of the money they foolishly spend.

12.6 Risks associated with multiply-connect leverage

Leverage means living beyond one's means through borrowing. A leveraged company is loaded with loans. A leveraged buyout is a takeover of another company whose purchase is financed by a large amount of borrowed money. The BIS defines leverage as *a low ratio of capital to total assets*.[16] All banks are leveraged, but some are much more leveraged than others and these are the most exposed to a collapse of their balance sheet, leading to counterparty risk.

During the last couple of decades, leverage has taken on a broader meaning: the use of a small amount of funds to gain control over an entity or an instrument whose worth is many times the own funds the acquiring entity is putting up. This practice, which has become widespread, is sometimes referred to as a gearing leverage, or simply *gearing*.

Notice that the two terms: gearing and leverage are often used interchangeably. However, no matter which word is employed, there is a significant degree of danger with leverage, particularly so when it involves *multiple layers*. For instance, three kinds of leverage may support and feed upon one another:

- Borrowing from bank(s),
- Buying stocks on margin, and
- Using collateral with inflated stock prices, because the companies issuing the equity are highly leveraged.

The risk associated with this practice is known as multiply-connected leverage. Exposure to multiply-connect gearing is unstable, because failure of any one of them will both amplify and speed up the destabilization of the others. Subsequently, this will spread very fast across the stock market, punching the *bubble* and leading to panic selling.

Any model made to study the instability due to, and aftermath of, multiply-connect leverage, should account for the fact that, in general, six factors characterize a financial bubble:

- High liquidity,
- Increased use of leverage,
- Significant volatility,
- Accelerated turnover,
- A growing number of investors join in, and
- New issuance of instruments or real assets.

The growing number of investors plays a key role because many newcomers are inexperienced and easily carried away by a profits mirage. As for new issuance metrics, an example in the housing market is the case of house 'starts'. Investors should appreciate that exponential price increase is not among the factors mentioned in this list, because it is the aftermath rather than a primary reason for financial bubbles.

Bubbles burst for several reasons. One of these is that investors and other market players run out of money – even borrowed money. This starts a process of *de-leveraging* which at the bottom line is characterized by default. For instance, there may be an increased density of debt problems, concluding in bankruptcies, or going up to the limit of default.

Default does not need to come only from the leveraged investor's side, neither is it always true that some entities are 'too big too fail'. In the area of business debt, companies that go bankrupt range in size from big entities to a swarm of smaller firms. Nobody is immune to the risk of failure.

A similar principle applies in regard to consumer debt, as households may have difficulties paying off their credit card payments, medical bills, mortgage payments, and other financial obligations they are assuming without thinking that bills come due. Some ways of personal leveraging are relatively new. Credit card debt was virtually unknown before the late 1970s.

Another principal sector where debt has accumulated is government, at all levels, from municipal, to state and federal. In the economy as a whole, the multiply-connect effect is biting because it is these same consumer households that are investors, and these same businesses at bankruptcy's edge are the object of investment. Eventually growth of whatever,

- From earnings
- To the level of gearing,

might not be sustainable because, to a significant extent, there is a zero-sum relationship between the household and the corporate sectors. When productivity and/or profitability start to decelerate, the servicing of debt faces discontinuities which bring up the rate of defaults, lead to further profits recession, and result in market downturns with everybody getting poorer.

No doubt, in a healthy economy, there will always be an element of debt, which in itself is not a problem. The problem comes when such debt grows at unsustainable levels, most specifically as a substitute for what should be income streams of households; industrial, agricultural and service firms, and government entities coupled with:

- Failure to match cash inflows and outflows,
- Inability or unwillingness to control expenses, and
- Rapid growth in the speculative side of the economy.

Taken together, these three bullets make up the start of *leverage risk*. A leveraged economy wounded by a burst bubble takes long, painful years to a growth path. As an example, let us return to ask the Japanese about their 1990 to 2004 experience, from the time the equities and real estate bubble burst till the start of a recovery based on a significant amount of deleveraging and increased ROE:

- In 1998, about halfway through the Japanese economy's depression, leveraging was nearly 70 percent and ROE 6.5 percent.
- In 2004 the Japanese economy's leveraging stands at 32 percent, while ROE seems to have zoomed.[17]

In this specific case, as well as in many others, leverage is expressed as the ratio of *net debt over equity* (ND/E, expressed in percent). Wise investors will also carefully watch the *debt per share* (DPS) of companies they are following. Although only one number, DPS tells a long story about the entity's quality of management, and its inclination to safeguard shareholders' interests.

Another important leverage ratio is that of *debt service coverage*. It is computed as earnings before interest and taxes over interest due (EBIT/interest) and is considered to be highly predictive. This is a vital tool in discriminating between lower and higher gearing exposure, with all this means in terms of credit risk.

The reader should appreciate that the thesis supported in this text is not against all levels of leverage but, rather, its excesses. It is a statement of fact that leverage exists everywhere in the economy, whether the investor buys bonds, purchases stocks, or does some other transaction. Every company runs on borrowed capital, and credit institutions do so more than most. But, as Figure 12.7 suggests, institutions which overleverage themselves with geared instruments, like derivatives, are heading for a very uneasy future.

One more example helps in appreciating this reference on leverage. The reader will remember that banks generally operate with an equity cushion of only 8 percent. This has been established through the 1988 Capital Accord, and it also characterizes the standard method with the New Capital Framework (Basel II) by the Basel Committee on Banking Supervision.[18]

- Eight percent capital requirements equates to a leverage factor of 12.5, or 1250 percent.

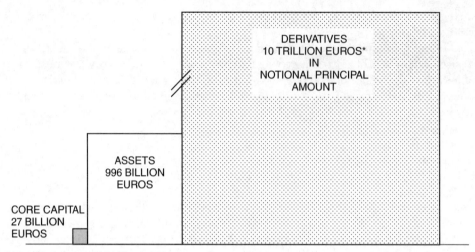

Note: Statistics as of 31 March 2001

Figure 12.7 Deutsche Bank joins the club of superleveraged financial institutions (*Source*: BIS)

When John Law issued paper money through his Banque Générale, he kept gold coin reserves of 25 percent of printed money which corresponds to 'only' 400 percent leverage. Eventually, as business expanded, this ratio was geared up. There was a run on the bank, and Law's Banque Générale was saved through royal handouts, till it got further overleveraged and it finally crashed.

■ With derivative financial instruments leverage has reached for the stars. When LTCM crashed, in September 1998, it had a leverage factor of 350 or 35 000 percent.

Some experts think that commercial and investment banks today move in the same LTCM direction, not only because they themselves are very active with derivatives but also because they loan money to, and invest big money with, hedge funds. Such highly risky investments exploit a loophole in the capital requirements guidelines, because the banks doing the exploiting do not need to report them as part of their trading book exposure.

Superleverage is done against all good sense. As the Basel Committee wisely advises when banks operate with very high leverage, they increase their vulnerability to adverse economic events, and boost the risk of failure. Even if they do not go bankrupt, they put at risk their future, their earnings, and what they call 'shareholder value'.

Notes

1 D.N. Chorafas (1998). *Understanding Volatility and Liquidity in Financial Markets*. Euromoney Books.
2 D.N. Chorafas (2001). *Managing Risk in the New Economy*. New York Institute of Finance.
3 Merrill Lynch (2004). *2004: The Year Ahead*. January.

4 D.N. Chorafas (1995). *How to Understand and Use Mathematics for Derivatives, Volume 1: Understanding the Behaviour of Markets*. Euromoney Books.
5 Deutsche Bundesbank (2003). *Monthly Report*. December.
6 D.N. Chorafas (1996). *The Money Magnet*. Euromoney.
7 William Greider (1987). *Secrets of the Temple*. Simon and Schuster/Touchstone.
8 Merrill Lynch (2004). *2004: The Year Ahead*. January.
9 Financial Services Authority (2003). *Improving Liquidity Handling to Head Off Financial Failures*. FSA/PN/115/2003.
10 Bob Woodward (2000). *Maestro: Greenspan's Fed and the American Boom*. Simon and Schuster.
11 D.N. Chorafas (2003). *Stress Testing: Risk Management Strategies for Extreme Events*. Euromoney.
12 D.N. Chorafas (2004). *Economic Capital Allocation with Basel II: Cost and Benefit Analysis*. Butterworth-Heinemann.
13 D.N. Chorafas (2004). *Rating Management's Effectiveness with Case Studies in Telecommunications*. Macmillan/Palgrave.
14 *CommunicationsWeek International*, 18 February 2002.
15 *Executive Intelligence Review*, 19 December 2003.
16 Basel Committee on Banking Supervision (2002). *The Relationship between Banking Supervisors and Banks' External Auditors*. BIS, January.
17 Statistics and forecasts from Merrill Lynch (2004). *2004: The Year Ahead*. January.
18 D.N. Chorafas (2004). *Economic Capital Allocation with Basel II: Cost and Benefit Analysis*. Butterworth-Heinemann.

13 Methods for judging quoted equities

13.1 Introduction

Comprehensive, accurate and up-to-date information is a key requirement for corporate management, the regulators' oversight activities, and decisions made by traders and investors. To safeguard their interests, investors must attentively follow and analyze developments in the market(s) in which they are active, and in the companies they entrust with their money.

As the preceding twelve chapters have documented, the scope of investment analysis goes beyond embracing publicly accessible information or specifically requested material. What is generally available must be enriched by means of simulations, extrapolations and interpolations based on data streams by the companies themselves and by information providers. The aim of information enrichment is to provide the investor with insight, which is particularly important in estimating a future course of action and its risks.

For instance, with hindsight, it is clear that Swissair's strategy of rapid expansion by taking stakes in smaller airlines was misguided. But was it possible to foresee that Switzerland's prestigious airline would go off the cliff? And could a forecast be made about the prospects of Swiss, formed from the remnants of Swissair plus Crossair, a regional carrier? Here is the answer to these queries, in a nutshell.

Swiss was launched straight into the huge slump in the world's aviation industry caused by the 11 September 2001 terrorist attacks on America. Therefore, the travel environment was as a whole negative, and Swiss's prospects were further diminished by the fact that the new company tried to attack at the same time two totally different markets: short-haul and long-haul.

Astute analysts were not surprised by the fact that in its first year of operation the newcomer lost nearly 1 billion Swiss francs ($770 million). Belatedly, in June 2003, to improve its balance sheet, Swiss embarked on a round of major cost-cutting. A few months later, in September of the same year, it joined the OneWorld alliance, a consortium led by British Airways and American Airlines. But this does not mean its future is secure.

To answer queries of the type outlined in the preceding paragraphs in a factual manner, an investor must have not only qualitative and quantitative information, but also dependable metrics, including gauges of performance and of expected risk(s). As far as management performance is concerned, the old yardstick is *return on equity* (see section 13.2), but this only mirrors financial data while, as we have seen in a number of examples, a qualitative evaluation of management performance is just as important.

Hence the wisdom of using measurements like corporate performance management (CPM), enriched with variables able to map enterprise risk, and lead to a realistic evaluation of business risk (see section 13.3). Business risk has many aspects. One of these is that the company loses its license or its brand name; or, in the case of a financial institution, that investors and depositors withdraw their funds.

For instance, in July 2002, in the middle of the severe rollback of the US stock market, individual investors withdraw $52.4 billion from equity funds. This was the second-biggest cash-out as a percentage of assets, and the largest ever in sheer dollar volume. Many market watchers interpreted such capital flight as evidence that individual investors had given up on the market and the economy – because of spreading pessimistic views of equity performance.

Optimists said at the time that if history is any judge, such a retreat of individual investors may be the signal that things are just about to turn around. They pointed out that, as suggested by historical data, big redemption sprees are generally followed by rising markets a little later.

Pessimists answered that these are not waves in business opportunity lifting all boats. This thesis brings us back to the fact that to identify companies in which it is worth investing we must have criteria helping to judge intrinsic equity performance. For instance, a new operating benchmark is employed by mobile operators in the USA – cash cost per user (CCPU), per month.

JP Morgan Chase calculates this CCPU ratio by dividing network costs plus general and administration expenses and retention costs, by the number of subscribers. In early 2004, costs for US mobile operators come in the range of $21–$31 with:

- The lowest ratio by Verizon Wireless, and
- The highest ratio by AT&T Wireless.

A CCPU of $21 is not an easy target, but experts think that operating at that level of efficiency would add 5 percent to EBITDA margins. On the other hand, it is hard to make up for the corrosive effect of declining voice revenues hitting fixed network operators, and Verizon's business is heavily weighted in fixed lines traffic.

As these examples demonstrate, the traditional operating and financial company reports do not tell the investor everything about either capital or operating results. Astute investment analysts have plenty of questions about an equity's deliverables to its shareholders. This is the issue that this chapter addresses. Of course, there is no guarantee that analysts and investors will be always right with new metrics. Rather, the way to view this is that without better focused metrics they will most likely be wrong.

13.2   Rethinking the metrics which we use

Since Chapter 1 the reader is aware that the doors of risk and return are adjacent and identical. Therefore, a good policy of self-protection is to scoff at the claim that investors can get high returns at low risk using a 'magic' stock market formula – no matter from where such an argument or suggestion might come.

The moment one believes in miracles, that is, in things he or she does not understand, anything can happen. For instance, in the mid to late 1990s investors were sold the idea of the 'Magic Dow 10'. First there was the formula of the Dow 10 which suggested that taking the thirty blue-chip companies that make up the Dow Jones industrial average as a point of departure:

- One should invest at the start of each year equal amounts of money in the ten stocks with the highest dividend yields among these thirty.
- Then, at the end of twelve-month period, one should sell the stocks, and repeat this process with the new top-yielding companies.

The hypothesis behind this magic formula for 'winning' in the stock market was that when a year started well, it could not be otherwise that it ends even better. Only the rating of the top ten Dow companies might have changed. Some believers questioned, 'Why the Dow 10? Why not merely buy the top three or five high-yielding stocks, but bet bigger amounts on each?' Others said: 'Why only Dow? Why not the top-yielding three, five or ten international stocks, at least from Group of Ten stockmarkets.'

Still other self-proclaimed investment experts thought of a different way of how to make fast bucks in equities markets. These were of the opinion that rather than looking at big companies which make up the Dow 30, an astute investor should concentrate on small, growing companies. In theory, these are easier to evaluate than blue-chip stocks, as:

- They are usually involved in just one line of business, and
- Their fundamentals may be simpler to understand.

In practice, however, the standard criteria for assessing the quality of a small-capitalization stock, like P/E ratio, ROE, and even book value, are almost impossible to apply in the case of growing companies with short histories. As a result, investors in these stocks tend to fall back on:

- Tips from their broker,
- Misinformation from their friends,
- Different market whispers, or
- Simple guts and instinct.

On repeated occasions this book has brought readers' attention to the fact that a systematic approach to investing requires a great deal of homework. It has also emphasized the importance of reliable information. This comes not only from analyzing the balance sheet and income statement, but also from getting to know the management of the firm.

Of course, most private investors cannot contact senior management on a whim. What they can do is to follow market volatility and size up the risk it represents to their investments. The concept underpinning market volatility has been discussed in Chapter 12. What has not yet been brought to the reader's attention is the fact that the metrics and criteria one is using in judging the market price of equities are themselves volatile.

The very popular P/E ratio provides an example. Figure 13.1 shows P/Es of forty-five large market cap companies. These have ranged from a one-digit number to nearly 200 at the high-water mark of the Internet and TMT bubble. With only one exception,

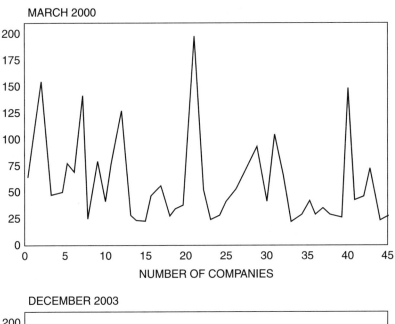

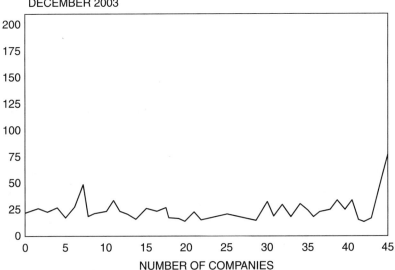

Figure 13.1 The striking pattern of P/E ratios in the middle of the bubble and over three years later (Copyright FactSet Research Systems Inc., reproduced with permission)

in December 2003 the P/E ratios of these entities were severely re-dimensioned below 50x. This is a striking pattern. (See also in section 13.7, Figure 13.4, the trend line of EPS over nearly two decades)

Both the impact of volatility on metrics used in investment decisions, and correlations targeting assumed exposure are most crucial in risk management. A relatively recent concept is that both investment criteria and metrics should look at the volatility of an entity's assets and prevailing correlations between them. This enables an assessment of how much one can lose if the bet goes sour. In principle:

- The lower the volatility,
- The smaller the correlation coefficient between exposures inventoried in the portfolio.

Small correlations improve the prospects of keeping assumed risk in control. This is, of course, a conditional statement because volatility can change almost overnight while assumed positions often have a long life cycle. And, as far as a financial institution, or any entity active in the market, is concerned, correlations change as new transactions are steadily completed and old ones die out.

With these references on models and correlations in mind, investors should appreciate that part and parcel of sound equity research is paying close attention to changes affecting the standards we use. Challenging the standards means questioning the 'obvious'. When the criteria revert themselves, the company's books contain errors and its forecasts contain caveats; in which case the investor should retreat to the sidelines. A sound piece of advice is:

- To be wary of a company that shows a sudden hike in profits just before flotation, and
- Keep away from companies which are poorly capitalized and depend on leveraging to survive.

An integral part of the P/E ratio pattern is the yield the investor obtains from the equities in his or her portfolio. Companies with high P/E ratios tend to pay minor or no dividends, on the hypothesis that their shareholders would have plenty of satisfaction from price appreciation, which means an even higher gearing of the P/E. However, as we have seen in the preceding paragraphs, P/E ratios have the nasty habit of significantly deflating, thereby deeply hurting investors.

Hence the query: equities or bonds? A factual and evidence-based answer is critical to every investor, and the response has to be specific, not general. Investors must keep in mind that in any particular year bonds may widely outperform stocks.

Statistics from Geneva-based Banque Pictet, a leader in private banking, indicate that in year 2001 bonds gave a return of 3.8 percent. Stocks had a negative performance of 22.0 percent – leading to an eye-popping 25.8 percent better performance of bonds over equities. Even by taking the three-year 1999–2001 average, the answer is that bond performance is better than that of equities, though at a much lower degree of 3.1 percent. In the 1999–2001 time frame:

- Stocks had a negative performance of 0.8 percent, and
- Bonds a positive performance of 2.3 percent.

However, the laurels of better investment performance change heads if longer time frames are considered. In a five-year period, 1997–2001, stocks gave an average annual return of 11.8 percent and bonds of 3.6 percent – providing equities with an advantage of 8.2 percent. Even if the 1929–32 depression is included, equities seem to perform better. Over a seventy-five year period, 1926–2001, stocks provided an average return of 8.32 percent and bonds of 4.8 percent, giving equities an advantage of 3.8 percent, according to Pictet statistics.[1]

On the other hand, while there are unquestionable advantages in taking the longer look, analyzing rate of return over three, five, or ten years, the most recent hecatombs of years 2000, 2001 and 2002 suggest that analyzing the rate of return over the annual period, even quarterly results, is a most worthwhile exercise. It is just as important to ensure within this three-, six- and twelve-month time frame that management is not enriching itself at shareholders' expense through lavish equity options, personal loans, extravagant expenses, and other tricks – which brings our discussion back to the issue of management's quality and ethics.

13.3   New measures for judging equity performance

From management quality to financial deliverables, performance metrics have a dual objective. One is to inform the investor about an equity's potential value; the other to avoid turning the organization into a parking lot for non-performing managers, engineers, and marketing people. When this happens, the end result is poor.

Appropriate metrics can help to understand the impact on performance of what are sometimes called *technical gatekeepers*, which keep efficiency out but let in a horde of inefficiencies. This negative contribution is due to bottlenecks which may be organizational, technological, or cultural. To do away with bottlenecks, senior management must reward business units in a way that:

■ Gives them ammunition for their efforts, and
■ Creates a common language to help eliminate resistance to change.

Appropriate measurements of performance can lead to better intrinsic motivation, by contributing to an incentive system which rewards results but also singles out failures, and brings them to general attention. In the last analysis, this is the longer-term objective of:

■ Measurements, and
■ Criteria used in evaluating the output of these measurements.

The reader is already aware of the importance of using both quantitative and qualitative criteria. The challenge in judging equity performance on the qualitative metrics side is that of integrating quality of management with ROE and other performance measurements such as economic return. Economic return is the ultimate driver of shareholder value. At least two levels should be considered:

■ Economic return by business unit, and
■ Total economic return for the institution as a whole.

This two-level approach is important inasmuch as *economic capital* (EC)[2] is allocated by BU. Hence, both the institution as a whole and each of its BUs should be taken as the basis of comparison in terms of return. With this in mind, critical algorithms for investment analysis are:

$$\text{ROE} = \frac{\text{Enterprise net profit}}{\text{Capitalization}} \qquad (13.1)$$

where in the ROE algorithm equity is taken not at book value but at market capitalization.

$$\text{ROEC}_i = \frac{\text{Net BU}_i \text{ profit}}{\text{EC allocated to BU}_i} \qquad (13.2)$$

where ROEC_i, the return on economic capital, focuses on EC allocated to each business unit i. Notice that:

$$\text{ROE} \leqslant \sum_{i=1}^{n} \text{ROEC}_i \qquad (13.3)$$

but in any case it should be that:

$$\text{Return} > \text{Hurdle rate} \qquad (13.4)$$

where the *hurdle rate* is the lowest rate of return at which an investor is willing to commit his or her money. Investors should also be aware that in practically every case:

$$\text{Shareholder equity} = \text{Risk capital} \qquad (13.5)$$

Up to a point EC and risk capital are synonymous, though they might vary because of industry sector differences as well as the way EC is computed and handled. A more fundamental algorithm would be:

$$\text{Risk capital}_{\text{Diversified}} = \\ \sqrt{\sum_i \sum_j \text{Risk capital}_{\text{standalone},i} \bullet \rho_{ij} \bullet \text{Risk capital}_{\text{standalone},j}} \qquad (13.6)$$

In this case, and in subsequent equations, EC includes regulatory capital. To a significant extent:

$$\text{Total EC} = \sum_{i=1}^{n} \text{Capital allocated to BU}_i \qquad (13.7)$$

Notice that, for sound management purposes, ROEC must be computed at different levels of confidence. This helps in prognosticating income in a way that conveys the likelihood of attaining the projection being made. For instance: ROEC_{50}, will give the expected value (mean value) of return on economic capital.

Another valuable equation for measuring economic performance is the return on risk-adjusted capital (RORAC).

$$RORAC = \frac{\text{Income} - \text{Costs} - \text{Expected losses} \pm \text{Capital benefit}^3 - \text{Taxes}}{\text{Risk capital}} \quad (13.8)$$

Moreover, economic return on equity should capture fair value changes not reflected in accounting *profit and loss* (P&L income statement) due to the use of accrual accounting or other reasons. In the insurance business, for instance, the difference between traditional accounting and economic return is particularly large.

Economic return on equity should integrate key performance indicators. However, to prevent creation of sub-optimal incentives, performance assessment in complex environments should not be done using just one type of measure. In every financial evaluation, profit is evidently a critical indicator and:

$$\text{Enterprise net profit} = \sum_{i=1}^{n} \text{Net BU}_i \text{ profit} \quad (13.9)$$

Or, more precisely:

$$\text{Enterprise net profit} = \sum_{i=1}^{n} \text{Net BU}_i \text{ profit} - \text{Holding costs} \quad (13.10)$$

Moreover, a critical indicator is that of economic value added (EVA):

$$EVA = \text{Return} - \text{Cost of capital (COC)}$$
$$= (RORAC \text{ (in \%)} - COC \text{ (in \%)}). \text{Risk capital} \quad (13.11)$$

Finally, because companies, like people, die, it is important to look at shareholder equity as being always at risk. Therefore, for every equity in the portfolio should be computed the corresponding default point (DP):

$$DP = \frac{\text{Equity capitalization}}{\text{Book liabilities}} \quad (13.12)$$

The DP defines the asset value at which a company will default in its obligation. The DP is a highly dynamic measurement, which must be constantly recomputed as both an entity's market value and its liabilities steadily change. Default points and default correlations are very important because they impact in a significant way on a firm's life cycle – from ratings and credit decisions to its survivability and wealth production, which essentially means on business risk.

13.4   Business risk and brand name

The original Capital Accord of 1988 (Basel I), by the Basel Committee on Banking Supervision, addressed credit risk. As its name implies, the 1996 Market Risk

Amendment has focused on market risk. Introduced in 1999 and generally applicable in 2006, the new Capital Adequacy Framework (Basel II) focuses on operational risk, and on restructured capital adequacy rules for credit risk including unexpected losses. No supervisory guidelines have a yet addressed business risk. Jos Wieleman, of ABN-AMRO, defines business risk as being:

- Caused by uncertainty in profits,
- Due to internal factors such as inefficiencies, shortfalls, price changes, and
- Influenced by external factors, like changes in the competitive environment.

Another important external factor is *rating risk*, because of market valuation, and therefore market discipline, through the proxy of independent rating agencies.[4] The lack of clear regulatory guidelines create a strategic gap which affects business risk. To overcome it, Wieleman advises:

- Taking the proverbial long, hard look in business strategy, and
- Going beyond the traditional, short one-year planning period.

According to ABN-AMRO, business losses can be directly traced to unexpected changes in the aftermath of failed strategic decisions; events that damage the bank's franchise; mismatch in pricing of products and services; adverse conditions affecting revenue, owing to changes in banking environment; as well as internal shortfalls in human resources, sales effort, outsourcing, and other factors.

My research has revealed that the large majority of investors do not pay as much attention to business risk, and its causes, as they deserve. Neither do they see that business risk can act as multiplier of other risks, by magnifying their impact. Hence, the *nineteenth golden rule* of investments: both individuals and companies should appreciate the impact of business risk.

'For the retail investor,' said Eugen Buck, 'business risk is the loss of his job. For the institutional investor and the fund manager, business risk is the loss of his clients.' Another knowledgeable banker suggested that, when it comes to business risk, he would be tempted to combining the viewpoints of institutional and retail investors' exposure: the failure of big companies in the early years of the twenty-first century, for example, hit both the retail investors' jobs and the funds which had invested in these entities. When this happens, the business plans of:

- Retail investors,
- Pension funds,
- Asset managers,
- Insurance companies, and
- Other firms 'too big to fail'

are turned on their head. After stating that business risk is a tough issue on which to give good advice in connection with investments, one of the experts suggested that Enron, Global Crossing, Adelphia, WorldCom, Eurotunnel, and Parmalat, can be seen as blips in the economy's radar screen. 'The majority of managements are honest,' this expert said, 'but investors must always watch out. Too many aspects come into business risk, and not all of them are well understood.'

In my experience, no two entities follow the same procedure in evaluating business risk and in taking measures to right the balances. Among the different approaches it uses for accounting for business risk and its after-effect, the top management of a money center bank takes a commissions and fees forecast, and it examines the shortfall, if certain business risk type events happen. Such shortfall varies by business unit and channel in terms of:

- Its impact on a BU's P&L, and
- Its snowball effects within the institution.

For instance, the shortfall from mergers and acquisitions activities has significant after-math, because of high fixed cost characterizing M&As. On the contrary, in private banking (see Chapter 2), the aftermath of a shortfall is much lower, since the fixed cost is not as high as with M&As.

Different institutions use different approaches to compensate for business risk. Some banks deduct 60 percent or more of goodwill from shareholder equity. The sense of such sharp reduction in goodwill rests on the fact that business risk often involves a significant amount of damage to the company's brand name.

Brand name risk is reputational risk and it can come from several sources; for instance, somebody knowingly, or by mistake, is abusing the regulations. As a real-life example, the executive responsible for the operations in India of a major financial institution, sold short securities. In America and most of Europe there is nothing illegal in selling short. But it is punishable in India.

As this case documents, globalization brings to the fore huge differences in cultures and in regulations, making compliance so much more complex (see also section 13.7). Business risk is not a healthy situation, but it is a fact of life. Here are a couple of other examples.

- The products of a company as a whole, or of some of its BUs, drift in quality.

Many small companies have become big by betting on innovation and on produc-ing first-class goods, or providing unmatchable services. As they become bigger and bigger, however, several companies lose interest in high quality and associated control procedures. As a result, there are slippages which damage their brand name. The case of quality problems with Mitsubishi autos is an example.[5] Other examples are:

- Billing mistakes which become a kind of poison to a company's brand name.

Consumers in America are complaining that telecom billing is no longer honest. In 2003, billing complaints by households against US phone companies increased sig-nificantly. For instance, complaints against MCI rose 310 percent in the first half of 2003 compared with the previous half-year. That was the biggest jump connected to any major carrier, as shown by data secured via the Freedom of Information Act from the Federal Communications Commission.

James Thomas, of Hartford, Connecticut, was quoted by *USA Today* as having said
he was billed more than $1300 in July for MCI long-distance calls that should have
cost $20.[6] Qwest Communications also saw billing complaints rise. AT&T Wireless
has been facing a class action lawsuit from 600 000 subscribers over claims of billing
contract violations. Subscribers say that the operator is delaying billing for roaming on
other networks and then charging users for exceeding their monthly limits in the month
billed.[7] This AT&T Wireless case follows similar actions against Sprint and Nextel.

■ Accounting snafus, let alone creative accounting scandals, can also greatly damage
the brand name.

The cases of creative accounting at Enron,[8] Adelphia Communications, WorldCom,
and many others are too well known to be retold. That of Parmalat is discussed in
Chapter 15. But the more common accounting restatements can also damage the brand
name of a firm. For instance, in late 2003 AT&T said 2001 and 2002 expenses had
been understated by $125 million because two workers had circumvented internal
accounting controls.[9]

In the opinion of the majority of senior executives, the fact that a brand name is
of great value to the firm is beyond question. Notice, however, that its impact tends
to be much more important in connection with technology and media companies, as
demonstrated through the statistics in Table 13.1.

On the other hand, not all brand names seem to be equally valuable to their owners.
To be ahead of the game, some companies decide to establish their own brand name,
even if the firms they acquire have a first-class brand name record. This is a policy
increasingly followed by global financial institutions.

Siegmund Warburg had been a banker who left Nazi Germany in 1934, established
the New Trading Company (NTC) in London, and right after the end of World War II

Brands	Estimated brand value in billions[1]
Coca-Cola	$73
Microsoft Windows	$70
IBM	$53
Intel	$39
Nokia	$39
General Electric	$38
Ford	$36
Disney	$34
McDonald's	$28
AT&T	$26

Note:
1 Forbes 2 October 2000. The dollar figures have been
rounded to two significant digits

Table 13.1 Six of the most valuable brand
names are technology and media companies

(in 1946) restructured NTC to create the SG Warburg firm. Many years after the death of Siegmund Warburg, in 1995, Swiss Bank Corporation (SBC) acquired SG Warburg renaming the investment banking unit SBC Warburg. The same year, SBC acquired Dillon Reed renaming the unit SBC Warburg Dillon Reed.

A few years later, in 1998, SBC acquired UBS and assumed UBS as its brand name. In 1999, the company's investment banking operations have been renamed Warburg Dillon Reed. Then, in 2000, UBS acquired PaineWebber and, in 2002, UBS management decided to drop both the 'Warburg' and 'PaineWebber' brands.

It has taken UBS seven years to take out of its label the Warburg brand name, but little more than two years to abandon the name of PaineWebber, a Wall Street brand which dated back to 1880 when William Paine and Wallace Webber set up their Boston brokerage. Note that the financial cost to UBS from the change in name-plating is not insignificant.

The Swiss bank took a CHF1 billion ($660 million) non-cash write down in its fourth quarter of 2002 relating to the PaineWebber brand name, but its management believes it is worth it to have a shorter flagship brand. With this, PaineWebber and Warburg joined the roll of other illustrious brand names such as Morgan Grenfell, Bankers Trust, Manufacturers Hanover and Kleinwort Benson, which have been scrapped by their new owners.

13.5   A new method for measuring business risk

Business risk is as important to a portfolio of equities, as credit risk and market risk. All three, and their impact, are key elements in the portfolio's worth, but while the latter two are subject to marking-to-market for fair value reasons, this is not true of business risk (except the case of deduction from goodwill we saw in section 13.3).

This raises the matter of the wisdom of marking-to-model the business risk which has been, and continues to be assumed, in order to be in charge of it, and of its aftermath. For this purpose, Jos Wieleman suggests the *corporate performance management* (CPM) method,[10] an umbrella term describing:

- Methodology,
- Metrics,
- Processes, and
- Technology.

Wieleman is one of the experts who stress the need to monitor and manage business performance and its after-effects. In his opinion, business risk is a concept still in a stage of development and, in all likelihood, it is an underestimated risk type. Hence, a focused effort is necessary to help bridge the strategic gap created by the failure to account for associated business risk.

As shown in Figure 13.2, ABN-AMRO's CPM method divides overall business risk into two major classes: core and non-core. Each of these classes consists of two major component parts, with the concept of strategic performance omnipotent in all of them. Strategic performance and business risk correlate.

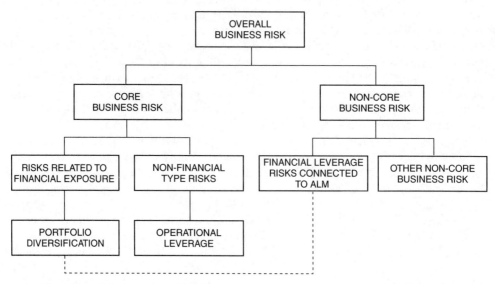

Figure 13.2 The corporate performance management method used by ABN-AMRO

It is possible to proceed with further subdivision within this general framework, as well as to combine certain elements. *Revenue risk*, for example, connects to *operational leverage* which is the degree in which a given change in sales affects EBIT.[11] In principle,

- The higher the degree of operational leverage, the higher the portion of fixed costs, and
- The higher the entity's fixed costs, the more EBIT will fluctuate in response to changes in sales – thereby increasing business risk.

Wieleman suggests that, based on this notion of operational leverage, managers can modify a firm's business risk through their choice of crucial industrial factors, such as product line(s), production technology, overheads, assumed fixed costs and chosen variable costs. According to this definition, business risk can and should be managed at strategic level by setting the entity's:

- Business mix,
- Operational leverage, and
- Fixed and variable cost structure.

Note that in a thoroughly studied corporate finance approach, the parameters of targeted or expected EBIT are supposed to be dynamic. They are driven by the long-term cost structure, including investments in real and contingent assets as well as goodwill.

This concept integrates into current industrial and financial policies. Well-run institutions appreciate that the cost structure is influenced by choices made about critical resources, such as labor costs, capital expenditures, depreciation, and amortization. Another crucial variable which relates to business risk, within an entity's cost structure, is long-term financing of investments. Still others are:

- Expected cost of debt,
- Implied cost of equity,
- After-effect of financial leverage,
- Weighted cost of capital,
- Equity surplus, and
- Liquidity needed to cover the variability of the business.

Both in computation and in evaluation of the aforementioned list of factors entering into business risk, there may be conflicts of interest which distract senior management's attention in identifying the causes and in doing damage control. This leads to the *twentieth golden rule* of investments: look at conflicts of interest as part of daily life – and factor them into your decision-making process.

'The nineteenth and twentieth rules correlate', said one of the experts. 'Investors must always be careful about who the counterparty is, and examine its past history of conflicts.' Indeed, there may be many conflicts of interest between a new party in a transaction and an old acquaintance. It is likely, however, that of the two the new relationship would have more unknowns – things we do not know about, which a superficial examination will always fail to reveal.

Database mining can help in finding information on past conflicts of interest to use them as guidelines. Can models be of help? On this issue opinions were divided. Some experts said opinion that business risk could be followed through models and some types of conflicts of interest could be simulated, but everybody agreed that it is very difficult for individual investors to do so since they do not have the models and they lack the appropriate information. What is in abundance is rumors which may help in certain cases, but they are in no way a risk management support.

In contrast to private individuals, institutional investors can do scenario analysis, Monte Carlo simulation and stress testing based on the identified business risk variables. Through experimentation, a planning process will be instrumental in producing a probability distribution for business risk taking. The latter should include adjusted earnings, taking into account path dependencies based on reasonable assumptions.

Among other benefits, simulation and experimentation made around a kernel of business risks assists management in avoiding a tunnel vision – which may result because of the strong focus on economic capital and regulatory capital, as well as the way the financial risks are usually being managed. Tunnel vision, for instance, would cause certain financial principles to fund investments in real assets are often overlooked.

Wieleman suggests the usage of two internal operational performance indicators: ROIC and return on funding capital (ROFC), which provide useful metrics, and should be added to the list of twelve return measurements (equations 13.1–13.12) in section 13.3. Both ROIC and ROFC help in thinking by analogy and in comparing

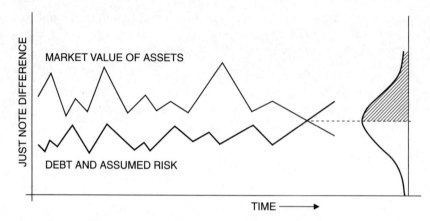

Figure 13.3 The need for follow-up on credit risk, market risk and business risk is steady

obtained results with those attained by peers. The algorithms are:

$$ROIC = \frac{Earnings}{Used\ assets + Additional\ risk\ capital} \qquad (13.13)$$

$$ROIC = \frac{Earnings}{Funding\ capital} \qquad (13.14)$$

where Funding capital = Equity + Debt.

Other useful metrics are estimates of the probability distributions of business losses; operating profit(s); main risk drivers, such as sales; as well as probability distributions of transaction numbers, transaction volumes, margins, and adjusted expenses. Estimates of volatility of underlying risk drivers, sensitivity of earnings, and a horde of correlations have an important impact on business risk.

Experts participating in this research project suggested that a good deal of the attention paid to business risk by credit institutions stems from the fact that advances made to date in curbing costs and in risk provisioning, need to be complemented by progress on metrics focused on the income side. Both convincing business strategies and a clear orientation towards profitable business segments and customer groups, are necessary to generate new sources of income.

The objective of new income-side metrics should be to assist management in steering the company to a sustained earnings path, as well as to provide early indicators when such earnings path may be abruptly interrupted because of reasons associated with business risk. The after-effect of cross-border M&A provides an example.

At a time when M&A activity is gaining momentum again, alert management should pay attention to costs associated to the subsequent financial integration. Research by the European Central Bank (ECB) suggests that change to a pan-European market entails costs associated with switching from one set of organization, practices, conventions, rules and infrastructure, to another.[12] Currently in the EU, each national market has:

- Its own co-ordinated arrangements, and
- Its own internal network externalities.

These constitute a major cost chapter for cross-border M&A. Lack of political will and switching costs are slowing down the transformation from a juxtaposition of national systems into a genuinely integrated financial and industrial landscape. It does not take two heads to understand that effective integration requires co-ordinated arrangements, with the aim of lowering switching costs while maximizing benefits provided by the broader market to be created. But the political will in the different EU countries is not standing squarely behind such effort.

13.6   Fair value accounting and its impact on equities

The regulation of the IASB adopted by the European Commission on 19 July 2002 requires, from 2005, that all listed companies in the EU draw up their accounts, or at least their consolidated financial statements, according to the IAS. Beyond this, is the EC regulation of 29 September 2003 adopting certain international accounting standards.

The objective of these decisions, which become the law of the land in European countries, is to harmonize accounting practices to ensure that European capital markets function efficiently and that accounting information is homogeneous and generally understood. Beyond this comes the projected convergence between IAS and the US GAAP, aiming to achieve an acceptance of European companies' annual financial statements in the USA.

With the exception of IAS 32, and IAS 39, which are currently being revised and are subject to fierce stonewalling, all IAS standards were translated into European law in a bloc endorsement. Indeed, this IAS translation into European law has followed the path of a fairly complex procedure aiming to enable the aforementioned accounting standards to be further developed by IASB.

What the reader needs to appreciate in connection to the impact of IAS on equities is that, as an international accounting standard, IAS has (correctly) upset and replaced the elder rules of accruals accounting, by introducing fair value accounting into business practice. Although proposals for full fair value accounting in the IAS have failed in the past, owing to massive and broad-based opposition, the IASB's proposal to revise IAS 39 includes the option of valuing all financial instruments at their fair value.

A successful implementation of this *policy decision* requires consistent valuation methodologies across jurisdictions and across equities, particularly those equities of similar types and styles. This is absolutely necessary if performance, and most particularly *risk-adjusted performance*, is to be comparable between jurisdictions – which is not the case today. For instance, research by the Alternative Investment Management Association (AIMA) has found that:

- 22.2 percent of convertible bond funds make adjustments to net asset value (NAV) of varying sizes, and

- By contrast, the other 77.8 percent, hence the majority, do not make any adjustments.

As another example of the potential magnitude of valuation differences created by different pricing approaches, the AIMA reviewed the dealer prices provided for a mortgage hedge fund as at 31 December 2000 and found differences between the prices provided by five dealers of CMOs, which ranged from 6 percent to 44 percent.[13]

Such findings are typical of both accounting-type difference and of policies followed by companies in the companies' financial reporting throughout business and industry in different jurisdictions. Correctly, therefore, the intention of a revised IAS 39 by IASB is to:

- Avoid problems which arise from presenting risk-compensating hedging relationships between different business transactions – which is practically hedge accounting.
- Come up with standards which allow hedges to be accounted for at portfolio level.
- Eventually, this is a macrohedge approach to be part of revised IAS 39.

In the experts' opinion, the aims IASB has made for itself correspond to state-of-the-art risk management and they are on a par with approaches applied by the best managed companies in the banking industry. Still unresolved, however, are the issues of properly accounting for premature repayments in the context of requirements for:

- Measuring effectiveness of hedging relationships, and
- Including core deposits, such as sight deposits and savings deposits in the hedged net portfolio position.

Even so, the fair value option in which both the underlying transaction and the hedging transaction can be shown at fair value is of significant importance. It is quite likely that on this basis accounting practices will gradually move towards full fair value accounting, essentially overtaking the traditional book value-based solutions – that is, the value of assets at the time they enter the balance sheet.

Experts favorable to NAV accounting point out that book value accounting has been discredited in terms of its ability to represent what a company is really worth, because the current method of accruals gives very little insight. When IBM bought Lotus, the software firm, the latter had a book value of around $500 million. But IBM actually paid $3.5 billion. The additional $3 billion, representing Lotus's intellectual assets and goodwill, swamped the company's book value.

Precisely because of book value's shortcomings in representing what an equity might be worth, a good metric of whether or nor a financial institution is being overvalued by the market is to measure the ratio of its *book value* to its *market value*. Several studies have targeted this ratio and they have found that, on average, companies that have high book-to-market ratios tend to earn excess returns over long periods.

Closely connected to this issue of an entity's valuation is whether investors are rational or irrational. Jeremy Stein, an economist at the Massachusetts Institute of Technology (MIT), offers an answer to this query. If investors are rational, he says, then the volatility measurement β cannot be the only measure of risk (see Chapter 12).

Conversely, if investors are irrational, then β is still the right measure in many cases.[14] Stein argues that:

- If an equity's volatility captures an asset's fundamental market risk,
- Then it often makes sense for managers to pay attention to it, even if many investors are failing to do so.

There is, or at least should be, little argument that the market value of assets is a rather accurate way of measuring what an equity is worth at a given point in time. It cannot be otherwise, because it represents the market's opinion. As a dynamic fair value measure, market value is never steady. It typically rises when assets are in demand, and drops, sometimes sharply, when equities get in a tailspin and/or the company needs to dispose of part of its property at a fire-sale price because of liquidity pressures (see Chapter 12).

The problem with using the market value of assets is that many instruments, portfolio positions, and entities have no easily defined market value. They are priced only twice: when they are bought and when they are sold. Over-the-counter derivatives are the traditional example of what I am saying, but they are not the only ones. Non-quoted equities is another, and the same is true of a myriad of assets which are not commonly traded.

Moreover, knowledge of future market value of assets is always sketchy, yet investments, the assumption of debt, and risk-taking are essentially akin to betting on the future. This is precisely the reason why book value accounting is unreliable.

The downside of estimates based on marking-to-model is that, quite often, expectations turn out to be erroneous, and economic consequences of unfavorable sales or cost developments are rarely accounted for. One day the company may reap the benefits of unexpectedly favorable market developments, and the next it may be faced with negative factors of which it had only incomplete knowledge. This is the essence of business risk, discussed in section 13.5:

- Risk-taking is a very serious matter requiring steady vigilance, measurement and control.
- At the same time, without the willingness to incur risk by betting on the future, all long-term economic activity would cease.

Rigorous risk control and market value of assets correlate. The challenge of improving upon fair value is increased by the fact that uncertainty involves entrepreneurial opportunity. Greater business opportunity, however, does not mean an unlimited freedom of action. One of the limits is prudential safeguards; another is the fact there is always a probability that the firm's assets will fall below market value, as shown in Figure 13.3.

Some of the experts suggested that marking-to-market should pose no problems. Practically, however, there is a number of challenges associated with dealers' practices in valuation of securities, lack of uniform policy on time horizons, wide variety of methods used by exchanges in closing transactions, and the fact that model risk is omnipresent.

Moreover, the wide range of methods for pricing complex instruments ends in incompatible results. For instance, OTC options are valued at in-the-money amount. Other methods are interpolation, matrix pricing, parity calculations, general partner valuations, and third party valuations. A study by AIMA found that there is no consistency in market practices on how dealer quotes are incorporated into valuations.[15] Of the participants who use dealer quotes:

- 44 percent use an average,
- 18 percent use the median, and
- 27 percent make a subjective judgment.

The same AIMA study documented that among participants indicating source of valuations, nearly 30 percent use dealer quotes, 24 percent follow Bloomberg, 14 percent Reuters, while the balance of securities are valued on the basis of other sources, including brokers. A slight majority of respondents said that they marked their long positions to the midpoint, others use the more conservative approach of bid side, mark to last trade, or last bid offer.

13.7   Globalization increases the complexity of evaluating equity performance

In a book which he published in the 1970s, Burton G. Malkiel, of Princeton University, made the case that stock prices are as unpredictable as a random walk.[16] The reader would remember that the random walk of a drunk underpins the method developed in the late nineteenth century by Lord Raleigh, and by consequence Monte Carlo simulation, which is based on it. However, other economists disagree, suggesting that shrewd investors can beat the market.

What the random walk hypothesis essentially says, is that investors cannot beat the stock market because news travels too rapidly. When a new data-stream or even some bits of information emerge, investors react almost instantly, bidding a stock's price up or down until it reaches a new equilibrium. According to this theory, the only things that the market has not taken into account are things that have not happened yet, which are by definition random – making brokers' advice essentially worthless.

Though Malkiel does not seem to explicitly say so, this random walk hypothesis implicitly espouses, at least to a significant extent, the so-called efficient market theory. The latter says that the market is efficient as far as the pricing of assets is concerned. In other words, the market immediately integrates and accounts for publicly available news. Not all economists agree with this argument.

For instance, two other economists, Andrew W. Lo, of MIT's Sloan School of Management, and A. Craig MacKinlay, of Wharton School, University of Pennsylvania, reject Malkiel's concept.[17] Their opinion is that the best professionals can still beat the market by analyzing financial and other data, and exploiting the subtle regularities or irregularities they discover. Random walkers answer that this process occurs so quickly that extra profits are a mirage. Not so, say Lo and MacKinlay: 'As different trading strategies emerge, new anomalies can appear, or past anomalies can reappear.'[18]

In the opinion of Lo and MacKinlay, computers processing newly available, tick-by-tick feeds of market transactions can detect regularities and irregularities in equity prices that would have been invisible a few years ago. For example, one of the reasons behind market irregularities is *clientele bias*, making certain stocks popular with investors who have specific trading styles.

Even if the efficient market theory was able to hold within a country's own exchange(s), which is not necessarily the case, it would be nigh on impossible to do so in a globalized economy, where many exchanges impact upon each other's performance within and across time zones. For better or worse, globalization generally – and more specifically globalization of equity markets – has changed the rules of the game in this and in other domains.

A most interesting input, along this line of thought, comes from Germany. In its *Monthly Report* of March 1998, the Deutsche Bundesbank noted that, over the past few years, the globalization of securities business has had an interesting aftermath: It adversely affected the recording of the securities component in the balance of payments statistics.

As a result of this bias, the Bundesbank study advises, it is not possible to make a precise allocation of holding gains to credit institutions, enterprises and individuals since no specific information is available on the valuations used in the balance sheets. Owing to the existing reporting system and its limitations:

■ Transactions by private investors cannot always be determined with the desired degree of accuracy, and
■ Business transacted by residents abroad is not fully reported; hence accounting for foreign assets held by residents is probably too low.

On the other hand, according to the Bundesbank study, the holdings of German securities ascribed to non-residents (liabilities) has possibly been set too high, since foreign purchases also include orders placed by residents abroad. Because estimates for closing these gaps are still subject to appreciable margins of uncertainty, financial information is not fully reliable and the market cannot be efficient even if the mechanism of doing so was on hand – which is not the case.

With globalization bringing these and many other issues to the fore, comparing today's market valuations with historical reference to the value of equities, can be an error-prone job. Indeed, an argument often made about bias associated with historical comparisons is that they are citing too-high or too-low valuations, as well as some which are largely subjective.

The changing composition of market measures, such as S&P Composite or Dow Jones, make historical comparisons tricky. Moreover, for equities, a key question is one of rate of increase of the P/E multiplier. The reader will remember that Figure 13.1, in section 13.3, has shown how the P/E readjusts itself downwards when market psychology is negative; indeed, the resulting pattern is most significant.

The highs and lows of the P/E ratio tend to follow a trend line. The same is true of earnings per share. As shown in Figure 13.4, over time the trendline of EPS is rising. Because this happens for no evident reason, it is another nail in the coffin of the efficient market theory. If the market was efficient, how can the growth in EPS

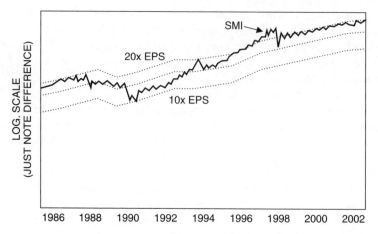

Figure 13.4 The 1986 to 2002 trend line in EPS ratios for the Swiss equities market
(*Source*: Statistics by global investor, Credit Suisse Private Banking)

and P/E be justified, particularly in light of unconvincing profit figures and negative market psychology?

Some experts say that historical comparisons may be further biased by structural factors, globalization being only one of them. Others are of the opinion that change in the mix of businesses characterizing an index has an aftermath. For instance, the S&P Composite is currently skewed toward services as opposed to manufacturing industries, which was the case in the past. This has probably raised the underlying earnings-growth rate in the USA.

The bottom line is that if it becomes impossible to draw in retrospect truly analytical comparisons using historical market valuations, then it is even more difficult to do so on a nearly real-time basis as the efficient market theory requires. At the same time, it is absurd to integrate market news into valuations based on book value and similar benchmarks without fair value adjustments, which are impossible to make precisely.

In conclusion, profits and cash flows are cornerstones to a company's survival, and information about them is not absorbed instantly by the market. Profits feed the dividends' stream and also permit self-financing of the firm's expansion and modernization. Substandard management is the main reason why companies fail in profitability goals, as well as in longer-term survival. Other reasons are poor products, poor marketing skills, the use of low technology, and the high cost of production and distribution. Insight into these factors, particularly in a global equities landscape, can be gained through painstaking analysis – not by means of 'theories', no matter how popular these may be.

Notes

1 Statistics published in *Cash*, the Zurich-based financial daily newspaper.
2 D.N. Chorafas (2004). *Economic Capital Allocation with Basel II: Cost and Benefit Analysis*. Butterworth-Heinemann.

3 Affected by unexpected losses.
4 D.N. Chorafas (2000). *Managing Credit Risk, Volume 1: Analyzing, Rating and Pricing the Probability of Default*. Euromoney.
5 D.N. Chorafas (2004). *Rating Management's Effectiveness with Case Studies in Telecommunications*. Macmillan/Palgrave.
6 *USA Today*, 2 September 2003.
7 *Total Telecom*, October 2003.
8 D.N. Chorafas (2004). *Management Risk: The Bottleneck is at the Top of the Bottle*. Macmillan/Palgrave.
9 *Total Telecom*, November 2003.
10 Not to be confused with the Critical Path Method (CPM) – also a management tool – dating to the early 1960s.
11 D.N. Chorafas (2004). *Operational Risk Control with Basel II: Basic Principles and Capital Requirements*. Butterworth-Heinemann.
12 ECB (2003). *Monthly Bulletin*, October.
13 *AIMA Newsletter*, no. 48, September 2001.
14 Jeremy Stein (1996). Rational capital budgeting in an irrational world. *Journal of Business*, October.
15 *AIMA Newsletter*, no. 48, September 2001.
16 Burton C. Malkiel (2004). *A Random Walk Down Wall Street*. W.W. Norton.
17 A.W. Lo and A.C. MacKinley (2002). *A Non-Random Walk Down Wall Street*. University of California Press.
18 *Business Week*, 31 May 1999.

Five

Case studies in investments

14 Case studies on equity values

14.1 Introduction

The ups and downs characterizing different equities in this chapter's case studies document the wisdom behind the dictum, 'Do not invest any more money that you are prepared to lose', as well as of another sound piece of advice: 'Do not put all of your investments into one asset class or sector.' Every initiative the investor takes has an associated execution risk. Hence the need to be always ready to implement damage control (see section 14.2).

The reader is by now well aware that a prudent investor must diversify between securities (bonds, equities) and among stocks, selecting equities from a variety of economic sectors rather than just one or two. Diversification could help in reducing risk and in protecting potential returns in volatile markets, but it does not do away with the need for steady and focused exposure control. Investors should pay particular attention to companies which try to leverage themselves through hedging, as well as reinventing themselves (see section 14.3).

Investors must also appreciate that, while by large majority they look favorably at a rising equity market, not all stocks perform in a positive way. Near the high-water mark of the mid to late 1990s the price action of two well-known stocks – General Electric (GE) and Xerox exemplified the split nature of the market.

- General Electric's price suggested that not only was this stock a leader, but also that its strength was intact.
- This was not the case for Xerox, whose stock topped out in early 1999, and not only has it not been able to regain its lost momentum but has also experienced sharp decline.

As this GE/Xerox example demonstrates, what counts is not just the macroeconomic factors and general market trend, but also management quality behind the securities themselves. Every equity has risks embedded in it, but few investors are careful enough to flush them out. These risks see to it that while in a benign environment equities are supposed to do well, some fall upon rough times – and this has been as true of mature companies as of start-ups since the beginning of the capital markets.

In the 1900–25 time frame there were an estimated 3000 automobile start-ups. To appreciate the aftermath of a high mortality rate, just count how many auto companies are left today – and even more important, how many of them are profitable and creditworthy.

Equity analysts who made a name for themselves, like Benjamin Graham and David L. Dodd, believed that stocks with undervalued assets would appreciate to their true market value. Graham said he would not buy a stock unless it had the potential to gain at least 50 percent within two to three years. Another piece of advice has been that it is best to buy stocks in companies which are selling for less than their intrinsic value.

The time of Graham and Dodd was different to today, at least in the sense that growth stocks in technology, media, telecommunications, and life sciences were the order of the day. But the wisdom of looking for stocks with strong long-term earnings growth prospects, and a healthy cash flow, has not changed. Overall revenues, too, should be a focal points because, on the whole, revenues are harder to manipulate than earnings.

- True revenue growth comes from organic growth: customers buying more merchandise at regular prices, rather than acquisitions or price discounting.
- But also, true revenue growth is more easily identified in companies that prize transparency and offer the public untainted earnings numbers.

Because there could be a revenue growth leveraged through the assumption of much greater risks, sometimes at a level which is unwarranted, a meticulous examination of a company's risk appetite, as well as of the quality of its risk management system, is inseparable from the search for sound equity investments.

As I never tire of repeating, management quality and ethics is a crucial reference. An investor's steady lookout is prized because the law moves too slowly for investors' comfort. Mid-February 2004 American prosecutors finally moved against Jeffrey Skilling, Enron's former CEO. His date in court came with the guilty plea of Andrew Fastow, Enron's former CFO, in January 2004 – but Enron had failed in early December 2001. The timelag has been twenty-six months.

In March 2004, Bernie Ebbers, former CEO of WorldCom, was charged with fraud and other offences centering around a major accounting scandal at the American long-distance phone company. Ebbers pleaded not guilty, but Scott Sullivan, WorldCom's former finance chief, pleaded guilty to similar charges. Since WorldCom went bankrupt in July 2002, in this case the timelag was twenty months.

As for Richard Scrushy, the former CEO of HealthSouth, he has been awaiting trial on charges relating to a $2.7 billion accounting fraud at the firm. In these and so many other cases, it is most commendable that the law enforcement industry takes action. But finding out whether the person at the top and his or her friends are ethical people or crooks is a long-term process for justice; in the short term it is part of investors' responsibilities.

Moreover, today many companies deliver hype embellished through smokescreens rather than shareholder value, in spite of statements to the contrary. Even annual reports have become an extended public relations exercise, with too much self-congratulation, too much glossy print, and not enough content on the economic fundamentals of the business. Beyond that, as we saw on many occasions, there has been a torrent of creative accounting practices. All this leads to lack of trust, and leaves investors with no alternative than to face the economic reality of our time.

14.2   Risk management, damage control, and hedging

The large majority of companies, let alone private investors, still do not have much of an idea about what is required for effective risk control. McKinsey, the business consultancy, points to this when it states that 36 percent of the corporate directors polled in one of its studies actually admitted that they did not *fully understand* the risks faced by their company. A study I myself did on this same issue demonstrated that many companies do not exactly appreciate the return they get on money spent on risk control.

An example is that of investments made to take care of risks associated to the year 2000 (Y2K) problem. In the late 1990s, companies spent millions on updating their computer systems to guard against the Y2K bug that was expected to create havoc on 1 January 2000. When nothing dreadful happened on that day, executives from several companies commented that such expenditures were a waste of money, if not an outright loss because of a hoax.

Careful scrutiny, however, would prove that executives who said this are, at best, muddle-headed. A practical example helps to explain why. During World War II, the British and American military authorities equipped cargo ships in a convoy with anti-aircraft cannons able to shoot down attacking German planes. A year after this initiative took place, statistics demonstrated that very few German planes were shot down by such guns. As a result, the authorities dismantled the cannons from the ships and put them in service elsewhere.

Thereafter, however, the statistics radically changed as many British and American merchant ships were sunk by German planes. It was therefore found, the hard way, that the real mission of the guns mounted on ships was not necessarily to shoot down German aircraft, but to dissuade the enemy planes from attacking and sinking the ships.

One of the purposes of a first-class risk control system is no different than that of the guns in the foregoing paradigm. The part of risk management which works hand-in-hand with internal control,[1] has as its goal the discouragement from taking on exposure beyond pre-established limits – whether abuses regard credit, market, operational, or business risks.

In Britain, in 1999, the Turnbull Committee set out a policy for internal control and risk management for all companies with stock market listing. Rather than laying down hard-and-fast rules, the Turnbull Committee required all corporate boards to identify and manage the risks as their own circumstances dictated. This is a flexible approach to damage prevention and control.

For instance, at Diageo, the liquor company, implementing the Turnbull Committee guidelines involves reporting from the bottom up on all the risks the firm faces. At board level, this information is distilled into what is known in company jargon as a *risk map* that describes both:

- The likelihood of a risk occurring, and
- The cost suffered by the company if it does.

High on the list of Diageo's risks is that of a change in the public perception (a business risk, see Chapter 13), and in the regulation of alcoholic drinks. At Danone, the foods company, risk management is closely linked to day-to-day delivery of products to the market. Similarly, for each individual investor, risk control should focus on the day-to-day valuation of his or her portfolio, with a pattern which shows the *best* and *worst* performers among the portfolio positions – during the day, week, and month.

This information is necessary because the other part of risk management is damage control, which must be a polyvalent exercise. For an investor, for example, damage control can be applied through stops and limits (see Chapter 10) before investments lose 75 percent of their value as in the case of Zurich Financial, or 50 percent of their value as with the San Paolo IMI equity. Both dives are shown in Figure 14.1.

For a manufacturing company, damage control has aspects which relate to its products and to its processes. With the crash of telecom start-ups, Cisco (see section 14.3) found itself confronted with the problem that a many of its switches just installed in failed companies could filter into the secondary market. Because of this risk, Cisco saw as its first priority the task of collecting and putting under lock and key all these materials, because fire sales would damage its product line (see section 14.3).

Another aspect of damage control is that of investments made to assure *business continuity* if and when adversity hits.[2] Building backup computer centers and fail-safe procedures may seem, to some companies, a waste of money. But backup computer centers are important for business continuity reasons. One of the most resilient companies after the 11 September 2001 terrorist attacks was Lehman Brothers, which had offices just across the road from the World Trade Center – almost at the front line.

For all practical purposes, immediately after the attack Lehman avoided a business interruption. Its systems solution allowed many of its staff to work from home, while others personnel installed themselves in hotel rooms or rented other space overnight elsewhere in New York. As a result, the investment bank came through the very difficult period after 9/11 better than some of its competitors that suffered much less physical damage and disruption, but were thrown off-balance with their information technology.

Some of the experts who participated in the research which led to this book pointed out that, at investor's level, damage control is done through *hedging*. Technically, this

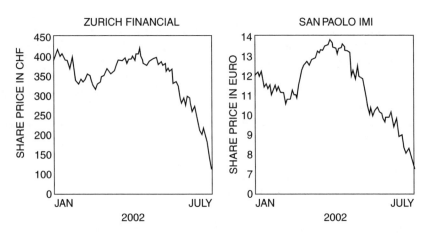

Figure 14.1 Equity dives in European financial institutions, end of July 2002

is true, one must be very careful, however, because hedging today means different things to different people. Also, hedging is quite often used as an excuse for assuming an inordinate amount of risk.

In its most genuine form, a hedge involves establishing a position, say, in the futures market that is equal and opposite to a position in the actual commodity. For example, a silver producer long 100 000 ounces of physical metal may hedge by going short in futures contracts by establishing an equal and opposite position.

- The concept of taking such equal and opposite positions in the cash and futures markets is that a loss in one should be offset by a gain in the other.
- In this manner, by using derivative instruments the hedger can fix a futures price for his or her commodity in today's market.

This process of hedging works because cash prices and futures prices tend to move in tandem, converging as each delivery month reaches expiration because of basis risk. Even if the difference between the cash and futures prices of a given commodity[3] widens or narrows as they fluctuate independently, the risk of an adverse change in this relationship is considered to be generally less than the risk of going unhedged.

Three decades or so ago, counterparties entered into hedging transactions in order to protect particular assets and cover their exposure to a given liability, or assure steady cash flow in spite of movements in a given market or markets. In that sense, transactions done for hedging purposes have generally been thought to be benign from the risk management officer's (RMO's) standpoint.

Traditionally, when an RMO analyzes a proposed transaction he or she mainly looks to see if the established hedge protects the company from price movement, or if there was some other reason for which the hedge was done. In the case of derivatives, for instance, if a hedge was properly constructed, loss on the underlier would be offset by gain on the derivative instrument, and vice-versa. In this way, no meaningful financial deterioration is likely to occur.

Along this orthodox concept of hedging, derivatives employed for hedging purposes assist in improving an entity's financial position. On the contrary, improperly structured derivative hedges or 'hedges' done for speculation rather than damage control can be financially disastrous. Hence the need to assure a hedge is both properly designed and operates as intended. This can be achieved through:

- Scenario analysis,
- Simulation, and
- Stress testing.

All this is written on the understanding that, as its name implies, a hedge is done for hedging reason, even if such approach is no longer the typical case. Increasingly, hedging has become synonymous with speculation – and it needs no explaining that speculation involves a most significant amount of risk.

If hedging is done for damage control, then it is proper to study the motivations behind it and, most specifically, whether it corresponds to a transaction which is calculated to provide financial cover. For instance, the treasurer may try to obtain a form of price insurance that:

■ Takes guesswork out of projections associated to future costs, or
■ Holds on a cash flow, without sustaining losses as a result of foreign exchange volatility.

In a way contrasting to the strategy of the hedger, who seeks to avoid risk, the speculator willingly assumes risk by trying to predict price movements before they occur and thereby profit from market volatility (see Chapter 12). Contrary to the hedger, who seeks merely to assure a certain stabilized economic result, the speculator makes his or her profits (and losses) from the uncertainty frequently associated with fluctuations in commodity price. Capitalizing on the highly leveraged nature of derivatives contracts, enables hedgers – when they get greedy – to turn to speculators.

14.3   Two technology companies: Cisco Systems and IBM

Cisco Systems is a new technology company which practically invented itself in the 1990s through a wave of mergers and acquisitions. At the height of his corporate power in the 1960s, Litton Industries' Thornton was asked by shareholders why he was so bent on buying other companies. To this he answered: 'I don't buy companies. I buy time.' This is essentially what Cisco's Chalmers repeated three decades later.

Cisco Systems is a global company specializing in telecommunications routers, local-area network (LAN) and ATM switches (its number one income earner), dial-up access devices, software products, as well as services. It operates in the USA, Canada, Mexico, Latin America, Europe, the Middle East, the Asia/Pacific region, and Japan.

Cisco's equity reached its high-water mark in mid-2000, as shown in Figure 14.2. Starting in 1996, by 1998 Cisco's rise in capitalization had left behind both the S&P 500 and the S&P Information Technology (IT) index. The gap increased in 1999, and

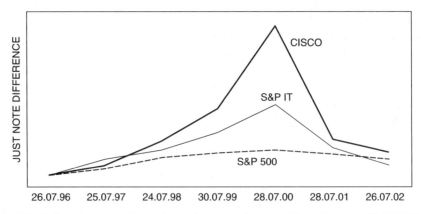

Figure 14.2 A six-year comparison of cumulative total return: Cisco Systems, S&P 500 index, and S&P Information Technology index

it became wider in 2000. By 2002, however, all three aforementioned metrics had met on the downside not far from where they had started five years earlier.

To face the challenges posed by the deep recession of 2001 in the telecommunications industry, in April 2001 Cisco surprised the investment community with an announcement that it would take a write-down of about $2.5 billion to cover excess inventory. The reason for the surprise was that in our epoch of just in time (JIT) manufacturing, material excess inventory write-downs have been rare.

- In its basic form, JIT is producing required items in exact quantities, precisely when they are needed.
- But a potential downside to JIT is running so lean that an unforeseen event can shut down the company; hence companies tend to keep buffers on the side.

On Wall Street, experts said that the rapid downturn in the outlook for communications equipment sales over the first quarter of 2001 qualified as an unforeseen event even among the better-managed firms. Therefore, most analysts considered Cisco's decision to write-down $2.5 billion in inventory to be appropriate and consistent with the company's prior practices of adjusting inventory levels to reflect changing demand.

The accounting for out-of-date or obsolete inventories is identical to the accounting for excess inventories. Inventory designated as 'excess' is segregated to ensure that it is not subsequently carried at more than its net realizable value. An excess inventory charge is taken when the inventory on hand, or the product into which it will be converted, exceeds foreseeable demand.

There are no clear rules as to how far into the future demand should be projected in this connection, but a period longer than one or two years is probably acceptable. Companies have an incentive to be conservative in measuring inventory write-downs, since this can be a way to use bookkeeping to produce higher future profits. In principle, after the inventory is identified,

- It should be written down to an amount not less than its net realizable value, and
- A write-down charge must be recorded in the operating income section of the income statement.

The principle is that such a charge should not be included as an element of cost of goods sold. It is levied against profits, and it is supposed to be objective. But the determination of the write-down amount involves a number of estimates, many of which are subjective.

If the write-down inventory's eventual selling price is higher than estimated, or its estimated completion and disposal costs are lower than estimated, profits will be higher than originally anticipated based on the written-down inventory costs. On the other hand, once the written-down inventory is exhausted, these extra profits may not be sustainable.

Post-mortem, as the telecoms market gave some signs of revival Cisco was proven right in its inventory write-down. It has a majority market share in enterprise data-networking, and it has been gaining share in carrier networking. By 2003 the company had a cash hoard of over $19 billion (mostly in bonds), and no debt. Another 'plus' is that Cisco is solidly cash flow positive. The way the Merrill Lynch analyst following the company phrased his thoughts, other pluses included:

- Market leadership,
- Unparalleled R&D spending, and
- Extended service capabilities.

The same analysis, however, featured some concerns like service provider capital spending and uncertainty regarding slowdowns in both service provider and corporate IT spending, owing to the state of the economy.[4] All companies have some reason for concern. Among the major equities in the technology domain, the most dramatic has been IBM's nose-diving in the late 1980s/early 1990s.

Contrary to Cisco, IBM is an old technology company which, by staying put on obsolete mainframe-based solutions, practically drove itself to extinction in the late 1980s. At the time, many investment analysts wrote off IBM as an entity because, as they put it, a battleship cannot make a sharp U-turn. But the board kicked out the old management, and new management saw to it that IBM reinvented itself.

In early 1993, IBM was skidding fast downhill, collapsing under the weight of its own bureaucracy and near-sightedness found all the way from product development to market sensitivity. As far as bureaucracy was concerned, some 26 percent, or 23 000 of its 90 000 employees in the Europe, Middle East and Africa area were riding desks rather than horses – operating in support as opposed to frontline functions.

To pull the company up by its bootstraps, in the late 1980s management had split the entity into dozens of independent fiefdoms, each with its own infrastructure – and a huge overhead. According to one estimate, within the IBM corporation there were 128 people who called themselves 'chief information officer'. Lou Gerstner changed all that when he became the CEO in 1993. He:

- Refocused the company on services, and
- Decided to keep most of the company together, even if the previous management had decreed that vertical integration was finished in the computer industry.

Having decided to steer away from strategies and practices followed by IBM's past mismanagers, Gerstner converted a failing manufacturer of mainframe computers into a thriving IT services outfit. He also offered the incentives that were needed to focus the stakeholders' minds on the rebirth of the company in which they owned equity.

Another of Gerstner's critical moves, based on the right hypothesis, has been that over time customers would become less interested in technological characteristics like chip speeds and proprietary operating systems. Instead, they would place much more value on solutions with the leaders in the computers industry becoming service led rather than technology led. With this in mind, IBM bought Lotus Development, and it went ahead with strategic alliances involving a myriad of smaller software firms.

Has this strategy reached its limits? Some analysts are suggesting that IBM went one acquisition too far with its purchase of Monday, the consulting arm of

PricewaterhouseCoopers (PwC). They are saying that the price IBM paid raised the questions: what is the value of assets? How much may be the difference between:

- Overpaying,
- A fire sale, and
- A fair price negotiated between a willing dealer and a willing seller?

This commentary should be seen within the perspective of the acquisition, when it happened. In the first days of August 2002, IBM announced that it was buying PwC Consulting, known as Monday, for $3.5 billion. The acquisition made Big Blue the biggest management consultancy by a margin. But was this a high price, right price, or low price?

To answer the foregoing query, one has to recall that a couple of years earlier Hewlett-Packard (HP) had negotiated with PwC to buy its consultancy arm. At the time, the certified public accountant had demanded an eye-opening $18 billion, and the deal fell through. There was no way for HP to profit from such a highly expensive acquisition.

At the time, analysts on Wall Street suggested that if PwC was less greedy and asked between $10 billion and $12 billion, HP would have gone along. But in the mean time the business climate changed, especially after the Arthur Andersen Certified Public Accountants (CPA) scandal, and the huge bankruptcies of 2002. Certified accountants came under scrutiny for conflict of interest, because of doing consultancy and auditing at the same time with the same clients.

- If $10 billion to $12 billion was the right price for Monday,
- Then at $3.5 billion, it was a fire sale, as the consultancy went for 30 percent of that amount.

But what if the originally asking price of $18 billion had nothing to do with reality, and even $3.5 billion was far too high for the asset? As this and many similar examples demonstrate, 'what is the value of assets' is a query which has no linear answers. The market price of a completed transaction may be too high or too low when compared with obtained results, so one has to look at the world and the transactions taking place, and try to learn from experience. That is why real-life case studies are so important.

14.4 Investors' appetite for Internet stocks

In May 1999, nine months before the crash of Internet stocks, the *Weekly Market Comment* by Donaldson, Lufkin and Jenrette, an investment bank, had this to say about Internet equities: 'Recent comments from Chairman Greenspan suggest that the drumbeat of a tightening bias by the Fed is highly likely in forthcoming meetings. Historically, this has been unkind to high-P/E growth stocks, and *it is likely to be particularly hard on Internet shares, which essentially are zero coupon bonds* ...'[5]

Donaldson, Lufkin and Jenrette's market report further explained that part of its optimism toward higher price levels was an expectation that the move toward money market funds that had begun in August 1998 would reverse course and shift into equity funds as market confidence was restored. There was a reason for such skepticism, but the fear that the equity bubble will be burst and Internet stock deflate was about two years ahead of its time.

By contrast, August 1998 saw the Russian meltdown, just as in mid to late 1997 had come the bankruptcies of some of the Asian Tigers. Together, the Asian and Russian events had created a genuine currency crisis in emerging countries. Currencies were in trouble and this did not make for a good market. It is not possible to sell financial products without a currency. And currencies which are too volatile are not stable products on which investors, traders, and speculators are willing to bet.

In the aftermath, investors felt more comfortable with dollar-valued products which they thought they knew how to analyze, or at least they understood better their volatility. As a result, 'Emerging products' and 'emerging industries' have been replacing emerging markets at focal points of investors' attention, making 1999 an exceptional period for technology stocks. However, at the same time, instantaneous communications magnified the volatility effect:

- Big changes took place in financial markets, particularly in intraday trades because of the Internet, and
- Emphasis was heightened on Internet stocks because they were perceived as growth engines – even if their P/E ratios were infinite as many of them had no earnings.

Prior to the Internet equities bubble, it used to be that professional investors and the institutions made the market. But in 1999 it was made seven days a week, twenty-four hours a day, by Internet fellows. Forgetting that there is always a learning experience with any type of stock, Wall Street analysts inflated the Internet equities bubble by suggesting that:

- Most of the Internet companies that would lead the technology wave were not yet conceived, and
- Because (in their judgment) there were relatively few companies in the Internet sector, these companies were not necessarily overvalued.

Durlacher is an example of an investment bank whose business was dominated by the dot-com boom, and which experienced a spike in its share price as shown in Figure 14.3. After the Internet stocks crash, it spent the time trying to start a new life as just another ordinary investment bank. However, when the bubble burst and its clients disappeared, Durlacher went into a tailspin. To become a player in the financial market again, it now focuses on offering services to small and medium-sized companies neglected by big investment banks.

While the Internet equities mania spread, the bravest analysts dared to say that even if the price of these stocks continued to increase, eventually they would cave in. In the late 1990s, however, negative sentiments were easily discarded though there were clouds on the horizon. The outcome of a vote taken at Comdex '98, involving some

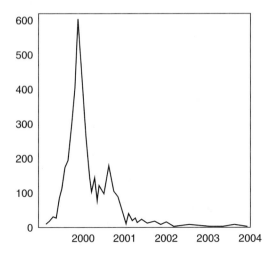

Figure 14.3 Durlacher's share price (in pence) has seen a blip

300 people with experience in Internet companies and their stocks, suggested of the Internet equities that:

- 69 percent were expensive,
- 24 percent were valued correctly, and
- 7 percent were still too cheap.

The irony is that for nearly two years this 7 percent carried the day. The sense of the meeting involving the majority of the participants at this same Comdex '98 event was that the company that wins in a new market becomes very big – but which company? Experts said that the best way to answer this question is to respond to another one: 'How is franchise value being created?'

On Wall Street, analysts expressed the opinion that telephone companies seem to answer this criterion of franchise because telephone penetration in the world is low, below 20 percent – and 'in the coming years' it may push up to 40 percent with cellular and broadband in the lead. The meltdown of telephone companies and their suppliers (see section 14.5) speaks volume for the value of that projection.

Another choice by some of the experts was companies active in electronic commerce. The majority of names chosen as proxy for e-commerce had something to do with the dislocation in the economy which pushed away legacy systems. Most of these names have disappeared – but e-Bay, Yahoo! and Amazon.com survived and they prosper.

At the time, analysts sticking their neck out on the prospects of Amazon.com had shown a certain amount of courage because, as will be recalled, there had been a substantial fall of Internet stocks from May to the end of August 1999. This had caused a sudden loss of value which hit numerous small and large investors. Indeed,

- The entire market value of the fifty leading Internet stocks in the USA reached its high-point on 12 April 1999, with a value of $613.4 billion.

- On 9 August of that same year these equities were worth 'only' $374.2 billion, which corresponded to a loss of about 40 percent in capitalization in a matter of a few months.

Moreover, on 30 July in the middle of this very sharp correction the IMF had warned of significant risks, especially the danger of a substantial and abrupt fall of US stock values. And there was another curious phenomenon to cope with, as Figure 14.4 demonstrates: The growth in market capitalization of Amazon.com correlated with the company's financial losses – not with its profits, which in fact were non-existent.

   Amazon.com was one of the companies absorbing capital like blotting paper while showing no profits. On the upside, the company had something to offer for the risks investors were taking. It capitalized on the fact that modern industry was reorganizing along horizontal layers. Along with other Internet players, Amazon.com was horizontalizing the old vertical structure.

   Neither was Amazon.com staying put in terms of products. The Seattle-based company did not rest on its laurels and it was the first to open a mega-bookstore online, offering 2.5 million titles – many more than any bricks-and-mortar counterpart. Since practically its first year, Amazon provided a:

- Huge selection,
- Easy-to-use site, and
- Hacker-free track record.

All this helped propel 1997 sales to $132 million, up from $16 million in 1996. True enough, Barnes and Noble was fighting back, investing in its own Internet site, and

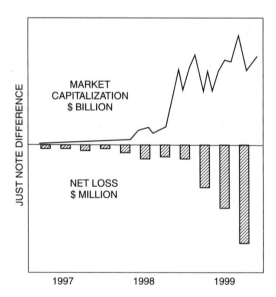

Figure 14.4 A curious phenomenon with Amazon.com: market capitalization and level of losses tend to correlate

Bookseller Borders also had a website. But neither could catch up with Amazon. Getting on the net early proved to be a huge advantage.

While big-name retailers could not afford to wait, those Internet start-ups who had both a product and a brand grew roots. Such firms, however, were a small minority when compared with the large and growing Internet company population. The large majority of online start-ups, which in the late 1990s attracted the attention of so many mature and novice investors, went with the wind. And money poured into them turned to dust.

14.5 Old-established companies, too, can be highly volatile

Lucent Technologies, the former Western Electric and owner of the famous Bell Telephone Laboratories, was spun off AT&T in the mid-1990s and for many years remained the favored entity of institutional investors. Nortel, the former Northern Telecom, has been the R&D arm of Bell Canada. As a self-standing entity, its equity represented an outsized portion of the Toronto stock market, leading many investors to overweight the stock, even when they thought they were diversifying by buying mutual funds.

At its peak in 2000, Nortel represented more than 36 percent of the Toronto TSE 300 index. Ironically, US rules that limit how much from retirement plans can be invested north of the border encouraged an overweighting in Canadian equities and most particularly in Nortel. It needs no explaining that investors suffered when Nortel stock fell from a peak of US$89 in mid-2000 to below US$8 in mid-2001 after the company stunned the financial world by posting a second-quarter loss of US$19.4 billion, one of the biggest ever.

The market punished Nortel's equity, and its investors, as illustrated in Figure 14.5. The reader will appreciate the similarity between Durlacher's chart in Figure 14.3 and Nortel's plight. In both cases, the rush to earn a quick buck ended badly. Quite

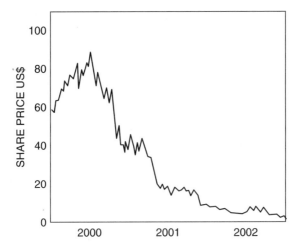

Figure 14.5 The rise and fall of Nortel equity as the former superstar came down to earth

evidently these were not healthy situations, but they have been one more reminder that markets are prone to mispricing.

The Canadian investors' exposure to Nortel was mostly through group pension plans and tax-sheltered registered retirement savings accounts. The Association of Canadian Pension Management estimated that group pension plans had total assets of 650 billion Canadian dollars (US$422 billion) at the end of 2000, with about 300 billion Canadian dollars (US$195 billion) more in individual plans.

Apart form their common origins in the Bell System, Lucent and Nortel share another characteristic. In spite of being former luminaries in telecommunications R&D, they have failed to capitalize on product innovation, leaving to newcomers like Cisco the routers, switches and access devices (see section 14.3), and to other newcomers, like Nokia, the leadership in mobile telephones.

This failure in product vision has become a classic in industry because top management does not conduct 'what if' analyses concerning major turns in the evolution of product lines. Examples abound. Automobiles were promoted by start-ups, not by established railroad companies; airplane manufacturers, too, were start-ups, not an outgrowth of the auto industry; mini and maxi computers were designed and marketed by new companies not by the mainframers; and the personal computers (PCs) made the fortune of start-ups while the mini, maxi and mainframe vendors resisted the PC.

Apparently none of the different pension funds, and other institutional investors who bled heavily with the telecom equipment vendors' fall from stock market grace, had done a stress analysis on losses in capitalization in case the telecom equipment manufacturing industry turned on its head. Yet, Nortel, Lucent, Alcatel, Ericsson, and others of the well-established telecom equipment vendors were open to two types of assaults:

- One by newcomers, particularly those specializing in optical switching like JDS Uniphase, and
- The other, by a downturn in overleveraged telecom carriers, who had totally miscalculated the market's potential and their own ability to withstand shocks.

Both in the USA and in Canada, with major losses suffered in official stock exchanges while investing in big name companies thought to be as solid as the rock of Gibraltar, many pension funds and individual investors tried to console themselves, and to assure their future, through highly illiquid alternative investments[6] – compounding one mistake with another.

What kind of lessons can investors learn from this more than 90 percent loss in capitalization by Lucent, Nortel, and the other big names in telecommunications equipment? I think the first is to shun companies unable to reinvent themselves and their products. This shows poor management (see also the case study on IBM in section 14.3). Although the plunge of its equity has been matched by that of many other communications and technology firms, the case of IBM is special because its stock had an unusually large place in rather conservative portfolios.

Spun off from AT&T in 1996, Lucent Technologies had damaged itself by bloated costs and management miscues. The excuse that economic slowdown in the telecommunications sector also hampered its recovery is not believed because Lucent was going downhill well before adversity hit in a big way. For the quarter that ended on 30 June 2001, Lucent's revenue was $5.82 billion, down 21 percent from a year earlier.

The next lesson is that half-baked measures do not bring commendable results. Lucent's management hoped that 20 000 job cuts and other measures announced by CEO Henry Schacht in late July 2001 would double the company's annual cost savings to $4 billion. However, by mid-2001 with the telecommunications industry in a depression, Lucent Technologies had little choice but to *both* cut costs most dramatically and reinvent itself in a bid to turn around its fortunes.

■ The market was moving away from its products, and
■ The company did not have in the pipeline enough *new* products and solutions, in spite of being the owner of Bell Labs.

Also, after adversity hit, Lucent's management tried to retain the investors' attention through spin-offs, rather than putting forward a plan enabling it to reposition itself and increase its market appeal. Little attention was paid to the fact that spin-offs often become a potential problem for entities that make a play on the unification of their business, priding themselves on holding every link in the chain to provide solutions to end-to-end connectivity. No wonder that, as shown in Figure 14.6, by mid-2002 Lucent's equity was further downgraded by the market both:

■ In absolute terms, and
■ Relative to two classical benchmarks.

There has been no fast recovery as the pressure levied by past mistakes on Lucent Technologies continued to weight, bringing to investors' mind the query: 'What is this equity's residual worth after the hardships it has gone through?' As if the product and market misfortunes were not enough, Lucent also faced a major shareholder class action, further draining its dwindling financial resources.

The company's 2002 annual report wanted to be reassuring about financial staying power, but only up to a point. Management stated that cash, cash equivalents, and

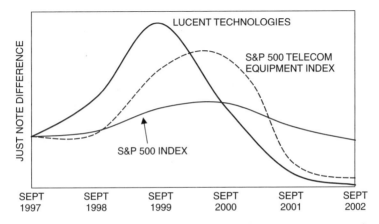

Figure 14.6 The rise and fall of Lucent's equity in the 1997 to 2002 time frame

short-term investments were sufficient to meet requirements in fiscal year 2003, but there was no evidence provided to assure shareholders that:

- More sources will be available if really needed, or
- Actual cash requirements will not be greater than those currently expected.

The annual report further said that if sources of liquidity were not available, or the firm could not generate sufficient cash flow from operations, it might be required to obtain additional sources of funds through more operating improvements (which should have been made in the first place), asset sales and financing from third parties, or a combination thereof. Management underlined that it cannot provide assurance that these additional sources of funds will be available or, if available, would have reasonable terms. All this was written in the 2002 annual report in a very negative climate in terms of Lucent's credit rating with:

- Long-term debt rate B– by S&P and Caa1 by Moody's – essentially junk and with a negative outlook,
- Convertible preferred stock was respectively rated CCC– and Ca, the nearest kind of default, and
- The rating of trust preferred securities had fallen to CCC– by S&P and Caa3 by Moody's.

In short, this meant that Lucent Technologies' credit ratings was well below par, a far cry from the investment grade it had enjoyed in the past. As a result of successive downgrades, the company no longer had the ability to participate in the commercial paper market and was unable to sell trade and notes receivables to the Trust. In addition credit downgrades:

- Significantly increased the company's cost of borrowing, and
- Affected its ability to enter into and maintain certain contracts on favorable terms.

Lucent did not benefit from a turnaround like IBM had done in 1993 (see section 14.3). Shareholder value fell as the company's equity dived to a level just above penny stock. This was a very sorry state of business for an entity which used to be one of the jewels of American industry, and a leader in R&D as owner of the famed Bell Telephone Laboratories.

Moreover, the fair values of Lucent's fixed-rate long-term debt, interest rate swaps, company-obligated 7.75 percent mandatorily redeemable convertible preferred securities, as well as subsidiary trust and short-term investments, were sensitive to changes in interest rates. Its portfolio of customer finance notes receivables predominantly comprised variable rate notes at LIBOR plus a stated percentage, and it has been subject to variability in cash flows and earnings due to the effect of changes in LIBOR.

Prior to May 2002, Lucent's debt obligations primarily consisted of fixed-rate debt instruments, while its interest-rate sensitive assets were primarily variable-rate instruments. In the latter half of fiscal year 2002, however, the company began to mitigate this interest rate sensitivity by adding short-term fixed-rate assets to the investment portfolio and simultaneously entering into interest rate swaps on a portion of its debt obligations, to make them variable-rate debt instruments.

The objective of maintaining the mix of fixed and floating-rate debt has been to mitigate the variability of cash inflows and outflows resulting from interest rate fluctuations. A further hope was that of reducing the overall cost of borrowing. According to its annual report, as of 30 September 2002, the company had in assets short-term investments of $1.5 billion, while in liabilities long-term debt obligations stood at nearly $1 billion. There were also company-obligated 7.75 percent mandatorily redeemable convertible preferred securities of subsidiary trust of $0.4 billion. All this did not add up to a sound financial basis.

14.6   Equity values of service firms also plunge

There is a widespread notion among investors that, other things being equal, equity values in the service industry are better protected than those in manufacturing companies. The rationale behind this notion is that the service market is dynamic, and it is the sector of the economy in ascendancy while manufacturing dwindles. Connected to this opinion is the notion that, at least in G-10 countries, services are the economy's true motor.

The hypothesis behind this is only partly right. In Western countries services are indeed the main motor of the economy, but this in no way means that equity value of service companies cannot dive. In mid-2001, the stock of Kuoni, the well-known Swiss travel-related network, went into a dive as can be seen in Figure 14.7. Service companies that go under, or whose stock takes a dive, are by no means one-off cases.

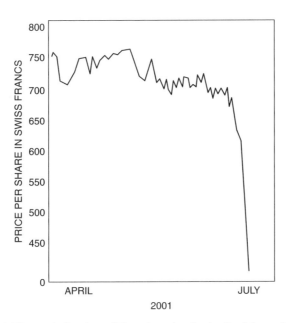

Figure 14.7 The capitalization of Kuoni crashes in the Zurich stock exchange

Adecco's shareholders learned this the hard way in 2004. Adecco is a Swiss-based but internationally operating personnel and temporary employment company. Not only does it supply personnel and temporary help, but also offers permanent placement services for professionals and specialists in a range of occupations on a global basis.

Mid-January 2004 Adecco's shares plunged by more than 48 percent, then recovered somewhat to close over a third down, after the agency admitted to 'material weaknesses in internal controls' at its North American operations. It also delayed publication of its accounts for 2003, till a month or so later.

Adecco assured investors that it did not face a Parmalat-style accounting scandal (see Chapter 15), but the precise nature of the problem remained unclear. Felix Weber, Adecco's Swiss CFO, and Julio Arrieta, the Spanish head of its US staffing side resigned. Both executives were ultimately responsible for group accounting and its larger activities – the areas believed to be at the center of the 2004 problems.

Investors had looked at Adecco as being much more than an employment agency. Not only it was global, but also itself employed 28 000 people, while nearly 640 000 people depend on it for finding temporary employment. Talking to the media after these events, John Bowmer, the firm's chairman, was unable to answer sixteen of the twenty-two questions which revolved around:

- Financial implications,
- Overall personnel policy, and
- Possible fraud accounting investigations.

According to the media, the reporters' queries were left unanswered 'on legal grounds'.[7] Independent rating agencies reacted without loss of time. Standard and Poor's downgraded Adecco's BBB+ to BBB−, just above junk bonds; and Moody's gave it a Baa3. In early January 2004, Adecco's total debt was estimated at 2 billion euros. Lacking information, which should have been provided by the company, on which to base their judgments, analysts made several hypotheses ranging:

- From a major accounting error,
- To outright accounting fraud.

Yet, according to some reports, Adecco's accounting errors seem to be worth about 50 million euros ($60 million), not as bad as the market thought after Adecco's first press release. This was stated by Rolf Kunz, an analyst at Zuercher Kantonalbank in Zurich, who advised clients to sell the shares. Adecco spokesman Simon Holberton declined to comment.[8]

Commenting on Adecco's future, some analysts said that its staffing operation is number one in the world. Overall, 90 percent of the firm's revenues are derived from this division. Markets such as France, the UK, Japan, Italy, and Spain did well. But business in countries like Switzerland, Germany, the Netherlands, and Belgium was weak. There were also margin pressures and negative currency effects in the USA.

Other analysts focused on the outlook for the world economy, and the way this had an impact on Adecco's services, noting that the future remains uncertain. However, in response to growth margin pressures, the company continued to reduce costs, while taking care not to damage its branch network and market position. Based on these references, some brokers gave a hold recommendation for the company's equities and bonds.

In fact, Adecco could also be seen as a positive case study compared with £145 million ($261 million) down the drain at the UK's SFI Group. This is no dot-com or high-tech outfit. It is a service company, more precisely a troubled pub operator that owns the Slug and Lettuce chains. SFI should have been a relatively stable little enterprise, but mismanagement saw to it that the investments of its shareholders were wiped out. In a letter addressed to them, Stuart Lawson, the executive chairman, admitted that SFI continued to trade only with the support of its banks, following the 2002 revelation of:

■ A £20 million ($36 million) accounting black hole, and
■ Its subsequent delisting from the exchange.

Lawson also stated that SFI has bank debts totaling £151.2 million ($272.16 million) while it owes £6.7 million ($12.06 million) in unpaid interest and fees. This is a case study not only on the mismanagement and bankruptcy of a service company, but also on the substandard policies on credit risk followed by commercial banks. Imagine banks giving loans of $272 million to a Slug and Lettuce outfit with a damaged balance sheet.

It therefore came as no surprise that Lawson added to his statement: 'Neither current nor projected trading is sufficient to support repayment of such a high level of debt, and the directors believe that the company's equity value is completely eroded.'[9] Add to this the fact that the Slug and Lettuce outfit also had 'further significant exposure arising from interest rate *hedges*' and you have two service industries:

■ One of them 'financial', and
■ The other one lettuce catering

whose management turned itself on its head. Till its crash, however, the Slug and Lettuce outfit obtained some hefty loans from the banks. That says much about foresight and insight on creditworthiness which credit institutions are sometimes proud of. Neither is this case of high finance an exception. Investors in other service companies, too, had their nightmares – because of misjudgments by people who are paid to know better.

On 4 April 2002, Ahold's shares fell as the released annual report by the Dutch food retailer brought the market's attention to items left undisclosed when full-year results for 2001 were presented. Ahold's 2001 annual report had shown an exceptional gain of 70 million euros ($84 million) the company had to disclose under US accounting standards. According to analysts, that gain came from a derivative trade made in currency hedging, and it implied the company's pre-tax profit was overstated by 4 percent.

In restating its figures to conform to US GAAP, Ahold's net earnings emerged 85 percent lower in 2001 compared with 2000, at 120 million euros (144 million). By contrast, under Dutch financial accounting principles they rose 36 percent to 1.5 billion euros ($1.8 billion) in 2001, hailed as something of a record.

That high figure was reached before write-offs on goodwill and exceptional charges. Financial analysts also pointed to another item in the reconciliation with US GAAP, under which Ahold had to comply with a new US standard governing how it treats derivative instruments and hedging activities. Compliance with accounting rules deducted a further 133 million euros ($159.6 million) from earnings, and further widening the financial reporting gap between American and Dutch accounting standards.

Not only financial restatements but also profit warnings lead to market downgrades, which can sometimes be severe. An example is the April 2002 profit warning by PeopleSoft, which led some analysts to argue that the company may be in violation of SEC disclosure rules. The software firm's management was also charged with barring analysts who issue a negative rating from access to senior executives – which is irrational and counterproductive, but also an expanding practice.

Under the SEC's rule known as Regulation Fair Disclosure, companies are free to talk to whichever analysts they like, and vice versa. However, a violation could be triggered if 'material' information that might potentially move the stock is released selectively to some analysts ahead of public disclosure. All sorts of companies have fallen into this trap. Under best conditions, this is part of *execution risk*, but it can also be willingly orchestrated, as WorldCom and so many other cases have demonstrated over the years. It is always rewarding to look at case studies on equity values.

Notes

1 D.N. Chorafas (2001). *Implementing and Auditing the Internal Control System*. Macmillan.
2 D.N. Chorafas (2005). *The Real-time Enterprise*. Auerbach.
3 Money, too, is a commodity.
4 Merrill Lynch (2003). *Cisco Systems Overview*. 10 April 2003.
5 Thomas M. Galving, in Donaldson, Lufkin and Jenrette (1999). *Weekly Market Comment*, 12 May (emphasis added).
6 D.N. Chorafas (2003). *Alternative Investments and the Mismanagement of Risk*. Macmillan/Palgrave.
7 FT.com, 16 January 2004.
8 *Bloomberg*, 19 January 2004.
9 *The Times*, 7 October 2003.

15 Parmalat: a case study on leveraging corporate assets

15.1 Introduction

An allegory by Sri Shantananda Saraswati, an old Indian sage, describes in a beautiful way Parmalat and all other business scams. Once four businessmen set out on a trip carrying firearms for protection. On their way they met a mahatma, who warned them not to go down a certain road as it was dangerous. They did not listen to him, answering that they were well equipped to face any danger.

As the four businessmen went farther, they found a bar of gold lying on the ground. Rejoicing at their luck they wrapped it up in a piece of cloth with the idea of dividing it among themselves in due time. Night fell, and two of the businessmen went to a neighboring village to buy food, while the other two stayed behind. After they had gone, those who stayed felt tempted to keep the bar of gold for themselves and conspired to shoot the other two when they returned with the food.

While the two businessmen who went to the village were returning with the food, they also succumbed to the temptation of keeping all the gold for themselves, and plotted to do away with their friends who had stayed behind. Therefore, they put poison in the food they were taking back to them. No sooner had the two travelers come back with the food, than the other two shot them dead. Thereafter, being hungry, they devoured the food brought to them by their murdered companions. With this, they fell asleep, never to wake again.

Next morning the same mahatma who had met the four businessmen the day before passed by on his way to the river for his daily bath. He found all four of them lying dead and the bar of gold wrapped in cloth. The mahatma threw the gold into the river so that it might not do further mischief.

Much too often, there is plenty of poison added to equities and to debt instruments, by unscrupulous individuals who are after the investor's gold. The question which transpires through this case study on Italy's Parmalat is, how could business people have been so blind to consequences of their own financial manipulations. The same query applies to companies such as Enron,[1] Adelphia Communications, Global Crossing, Tyco, Eurotunnel (see Chapter 1), WorldCom[2] and a score of others.

There is a growing opinion that our society has fostered an environment of corporate malfeasance. The current system of corporate governance has been exploited so much by certain interests that the existing system of checks and balances has become inadequate. Not only the moral code is left wanting but also supervision and regulation are in need of very significant reform.

One of the puzzling and most interesting questions concerning Parmalat and its sister companies in king-size fraud is whether this unprecedented poisoning of the equities market was due to ignorance – which is difficult even to imagine – or orchestrated on purpose to defraud people of their jobs, their savings, and their hope for a better future. The banking industry, CPAs, and the company's own management, all bent the rules – and WorldCom's precedence can be illuminating in answering the query posed in this paragraph.

'The corporate leader as a hero has been replaced . . . by a view of individuals that are immoral, incompetent and interested only in enriching themselves. Greed is addictive. Money replaced morality', said an article in *The Times*, on 8 June 2002 after the WorldCom scandal. And the *Evening Standard* wrote on 27 June 2002:

No one can recall a time in the past 30 years, when there was such scepticism about published accounts. It is inevitable that when the public discovers a bent policemen that it loses faith in law enforcement. That is why the world is finding it hard to live with the problem caused by the accountant's willingness to collude in the triumph of corporate greed.

There is not one but a torrent of questions springing out of big scandals in America and in Europe. Who have been the 'higher up' accomplices who permitted the Tanzis of Parmalat, Skillings of Enron, Ebbers of WorldCom, and scores of others, to prepare and eventually achieve masterpieces of public fraud, which from 2001 to 2003 went from $5 billion with Enron, to $12 billion with WorldCom, and $18 billion (14.8 billion euros) in Parmalat's case.

All governments should be keen to rush through rigorous laws for exemplary punishment of financial malfeasance, and for reforming regulation and supervisory rules in a way which enables the authorities to gain advance notice of the poisoning of equities and bonds that takes with it the savings and hopes of hundreds of thousands of investors. Governments, regulators, and the law enforcement industry should not be permitted to 'sleep on the job'.

15.2   Parmalat as a speculative hedge fund

There are reasons to believe that, and to be worried about, the collapse of the Parmalat bubble, which may not be just a WorldCom- or Enron-style debacle but, instead, a larger version of the financial crisis of the LTCM hedge fund type. As it will be remembered, in late September 1998 the failure of what was considered till then to be the Rolls-Royce of hedge funds with its Nobel Prize winners, shook the foundations of the world's monetary and financial system.[3]

The LTCM crisis put the New York Federal Reserve Bank into the front line in an attempt to solve it, and contain its aftermath, before it attained global proportions. With Parmalat, the main evidence has been that what happened was the same sort of crisis as LTCM, but probably more complex than its 1998 counterpart. At the center of the storm are the banks of the Italian hedge fund with a dairy products line on the side (see section 15.7).

There are also similarities between Parmalat and Enron, the hedge fund with a gas pipeline on the side, in terms of financial plotting and using dirty tricks which cost investors, employees and other stake holders dearly. These range from fiddling the books to:

- Playing in a big way the derivatives market,
- Engineering scams which deceive investors, and
- Penalizing the company's own personnel.

The Enron scandal came to the public's attention in December 2001, two full years before that of Parmalat. Since day one, the major financial press, including the *Wall Street Journal*, focused attention on a handful of Enron's thousands of subsidiaries, affiliates, ventures, and entities which were deeply involved in Ponzi games, as well as some of Enron's own executives and bankers. It took more than two years till, finally, in February 2004, Enron's CEO and CFO were indicted.

The bankruptcy of Parmalat warned Italian Finance Minister Giulio Tremonti, on 22 December 2003, of the risk of this leading to *general corporate insolvency* in Italy – if investor confidence is badly shaken and there is a run on corporate bonds. Indeed, after Parmalat, not only in Italy but throughout Europe, financial entities and industrial companies with loans contracted in the capital market became nervous about:

- The enormous sums of debt paper that went up in smoke, and
- The uncertainty about how far and where the trail of criminal investigation might lead.

In fooling investors and rating agencies, Parmalat had played its hand in a way that made the capital markets' deception bigger than it might otherwise have been. To give a false impression of financial staying power to banks, investors, credit rating agencies and regulators, the company had an American listing for some of its securities. The multiple frauds that took place in the 2001 to 2003 time frame exposed how vulnerable the financial system is when:

- Creative accounting calls the tune,
- A maze of offshore companies is ingeniously employed to hide the facts, and
- Safeguards are perverted, either deliberately or through huge incompetence.

'It fooled a lot of people that Parmalat was able to maintain a New York listing for its American Depository Receipts (ADRs)', said Christopher Seidenfaden of Unicredit Banca Mobiliare.[4] Investors were reassured that Parmalat was satisfying American regulatory requirements. In a letter to *The Economist*, François Veverka, Paris-based executive managing director of Standard & Poor's, stated that Parmalat and its advisers repeatedly provided the rating agency with detailed information about its:

- Liquidity position, and
- Size and type of its liabilities.

They did so in response to the rating agency's inquiries as recently as 5 December 2003 – just before the company's crash. This information essentially confirmed the audited accounts and it was enough to warrant a low investment-grade rating, such as BBB. But, as has subsequently been shown, just like the audited accounts themselves, the financial information the rating agency received was utterly misleading.

The point Veverka essentially made is that until it missed its bond repayment on 8 December 2003, there was no indication in Parmalat's accounts that the company faced an imminent liquidity crisis. This is a frequent occurrence when creative accounting holds the upper ground, and, therefore, what regulators, investors, and analysts receive is essentially financial misinformation.

Because human nature is what it is, all the talk about strengthening auditing standards is of no more than of theoretical interest. Neither are more onerous standards on the securities exchanges a magic solution – though, admittedly, they are necessary. The better answer is:

■ Prosecuting all wrongdoers more swiftly, and
■ Imposing very significant penalties for deep-seated financial fraud, which will make wrongdoers think more seriously before committing fraud.

Light sentences, including dubious prison terms, lead nowhere. They are regarded as a joke by the wrongdoer – while the stolen money is real and hidden away. As John Ashcroft, the US Attorney General, aptly said on 3 March 2004, when he announced the criminal prosecution of Bernie Ebbers, WorldCom's former CEO, the free enterprise system rests on:

■ Transparency, and
■ Reliable financial accounts.

The Italian government is aware of the systemic dimensions of the Parmalat crisis, at least in what concerns the country's bond market, shown by Tremonti's statement about 'general corporate insolvency'. 'Do you have any idea', Termonti asked his colleagues, 'of what would happen if the market demanded liquidation of money invested in corporate bonds? Therefore, we must quickly review current legislation protecting investors.'[5]

This preoccupation has been no different than the one in the USA in early to mid-2003 with the disaster at Freddie Mac, which threatened to set off a chain reaction leading to a collapse in the value of mortgages and blowing the real estate bubble.[6] Tremonti also referred to 100 000 Italian owners of Parmalat bonds, mostly families, who were advised by their bankers to buy the defunct company's paper when the scam was still under wraps. Parmalat's bonds are now worth nothing.

To put this investment scam into perspective, it is appropriate to notice that this is the third largest insolvency hitting Italian investors in a couple of years. The first, the Argentinean insolvency, wiped out 12 billion euros in bonds owned by 450 000 Italian citizens. Then came the bankruptcy of Cirio, another food company, which defaulted on 1.2 billion euros in bonds owned by 40 000 families. Critics say that:

■ Both Italian and international banks have lured unwary customers into high-risk investments, and
■ Pensioners, workers, and professionals did not know *where* their money was invested, because they were told it was '*safely placed*'.

As far as Italian and other investors are concerned, Argentina, Cirio and Parmalat acted as hit-and-run hedge funds – and the banks covered them. Worse still, they misrepresented their debt as being 'safe', and their different highly risky derivative financial instruments as 'best deals' (see in section 15.4 the reference to Bank 121). At times, the banks even unloaded the worst entities in their portfolio onto investors.

Moreover, Parmalat's collapse threw the spotlight on the colossal volume of non-transparent financial deals which capitalize on globalization. Several of them are being run both by doubtful operators and big international banks through offshore centers like Cayman Islands. Such transactions are often used to finance illegal and speculative high-risk deals, some of which are covered by political connections. The Parmalat scandal exposed this questionable substructure of the global financial system.

Acting as a hedge fund with a dairy products line at the front end and a giant financial speculation in the background, Parmalat was able to lure investors and siphon off their savings through a network of 260 international offshore speculative entities. These have been the black holes where the money disappeared. One of the entities at the receiver end of that scam, Cayman Islands-based offshore Bonlat, had allegedly invested $6.9 billion in interest rate swaps, which are high-risk derivative instruments – the sort of investments that lead to financial disaster.

In conclusion it can be said that Parmalat acted as a hedge fund with a long list of secretive deals and hundreds of empty shells as subsidiaries. But at the same time, it was the largest Italian food company and the fourth largest in Europe, controlling 50 percent of the Italian market in milk and milk-derivative products.

Parmalat's bankruptcy as a speculative hedge fund is not only the largest in European history, but also represents 1.5 percent of Italian gross national product (GNP). This is proportionally much larger than the combined ratio of the Enron and WorldCom bankruptcies in the USA compared with the American GNP – and, in GNP terms, is surpassed only by a banking scam which took place in Turkey.

15.3   A bird's-eye view of Parmalat's scam

Calisto Tanzi, whose family controlled 51 percent of Parmalat, was arrested on 27 December 2003, the day of his company's bankruptcy. Reasons for the arrest were suspicion of fraud, embezzlement, false accounting, and the misleading of investors. Prosecutors also alleged that Tanzi ordered the destruction of company documents, which makes the investigation into the scam so much more complex.

Prosecutors said they suspected Tanzi diverted 1 billion euros in company funds to his own use. The argument used by Tanzi's lawyer has been that no money disappeared. It was just a case of 'non existent assets . . .'. But Tanzi confessed to misappropriating 500 million euros. Prosecutors, however, believed the actual sum is much higher.[7]

In reality, nobody knows exactly how much money was stolen from Parmalat's coffers and how much was wasted in speculative deals. For instance, what proportion of the missing funds were used to plug operating losses, and how much cash was diverted to illegally enrich certain the company's management as well as other individuals who had a hand in the scam?

On 30 December 2003, Tanzi admitted to prosecutors that he knew the company's accounts were being falsified to hide losses of as much as $10 billion, mainly in Parmalat's Latin American subsidiaries. Allegedly the fake balance sheet figures enabled Parmalat to continue borrowing while it was virtually bankrupt (more on this later).

The Italian hedge fund with a dairy products line on the side had a hefty business in the Western hemisphere. Apart from its wheeling and dealing in South America, and its Central American hideout on the Cayman Islands, Parmalat had a $3.3 billion business in North America, where it sold its trademark milk-in-a-box and also owned Black Diamond Cheese, Archway Cookies, and Sunnydale Farms dairy. As stated in section 15.2, it also exploited the American capital market:

- Its shares traded in New York, and
- It had sold more than $1.5 billion in bonds to US investors.

The US SEC has sued Parmalat for misleading investors in a 'brazen fraud' but, as a regulator, SEC may have a much wider role to play in the investigation because surely Parmalat could not have acted alone in placing its American ADRs among US investors.

Moreover, supposedly, 38 percent of Parmalat's assets were held in a $4.9 billion Bank of America account belonging to a Parmalat subsidiary in the Cayman Islands. On 19 December 2003, however, Bank of America said that no such account existed. Subsequently, Italian prosecutors seem to have discovered that the hedge fund's/dairy firm's managers simply invented assets to offset up to $16.2 billion liabilities and falsified accounts over a fifteen-year period. This was facilitated by the fact that these accounts, and many others,

- Were characterized by total lack of transparency,
- Yet, there was no regulatory action even though this was a company of 36 000 employees operating in thirty countries.

Or, perhaps the regulators looked the other way. As reported on 29 March 2004, by the *Wall Street Journal*, a Deloitte Touche Tohmatsu auditor in Brazil raised concerns in 2001 and 2002 about a Cayman Islands unit of Parmalat, later found to be at the center of the dairy giant's accounting scandal. Citing Deloitte emails and memos, the *Wall Street Journal* said a message was sent from Brazil to Adolfo Mamoli, a partner at Deloitte Italy, in March 2001, with concerns about Bonlat Financing Corp's ability to repay debts of about $225 million owed to Parmalat in Brazil.

There is no evidence of corrective action being taken after this alarm bell rang. Instead, according to the ongoing investigation, auditors first inquired about the Cayman Islands account in December 2002, and in response they received a letter on Bank of America stationery in March 2003, confirming the existence of such an account. That letter is now said to have been a forgery, concocted by someone in Parmalat's Collecchio headquarters.

What surprised both the magistrates and investors is that when such a 'forgery' was produced nobody bothered to investigate. Yet, the billion-dollar size of the alleged account should have raised queries. As far as sound auditing practices are concerned, even a $1 million bank account must be cross-verified by the auditors. There is no evidence that this was done.

On CPAs' side, the Parmalat scandal has involved two major auditing firms. From 1990 to 1999 the company's auditor was the Italian branch of Grant Thornton, one of the larger American accounting firms. In 1999, under Italian law, Parmalat was forced to change its auditor, replacing Grant Thornton with Deloitte Touche Tohmatsu. Grant Thornton, however, continued to audit Parmalat's offshore entities, involving financial companies that were closed sown in the Dutch Antilles and re-established in the Cayman Islands.

According to press reports, Deloitte said that it first raised questions about Parmalat's accounts in October 2003.[8] This was just two months before the company's crash. Grant Thornton issued a statement calling itself a victim of the deceit. This is a thinly veiled excuse, and covert admission that their auditing responsibilities were not undertaken. The puzzle is how two major international auditors did not uncover over the years a blatant accounting fraud. After all,

- That is the largest part of their mission, and
- That is why they are paid by their clients, and trusted by the regulators, the markets and the public.

The crisis at Parmalat deepened on 21 January 2004 as people familiar with the group estimated that its gross debt could be more than 14 billion euros, while the company's operating units could be worth only between 1 and 2 billion euros. Another puzzle with this affair is that a month after the company was placed in bankruptcy protection, and investigative magistrates, bankers and outside accountants began combing its books around the world, not a trace of any cash seems to have been found.

'There's just nothing. Maybe we'll still find a Euro 500 million or Euro 1 billion hoard somewhere, but I doubt it. If there had been that cash, they would have used it to cover things up', one person familiar with the investigation said.[9] Experts suggested that the more than 14 billion euro gross debt estimate:

- Includes numerous off-balance sheet private placements, and
- Takes into account transactions where Parmalat created offshore trusts that claimed to be buying bonds, but in fact were used to cancel part of the issues.

All this is evidence not just of Parmalat's misdeeds, but also of the sophistication of operations which used the cracks in the regulatory armory to lead to a huge-scale deception of investors. Moreover, it is difficult to believe all this has been developed and put in action just by provincial headquarters of a milk company, located at a little sleepy town near Parma – a city known for its Parmesan cheese, not for its ingenuity in derivative financial instruments.

To shore up its balance sheet and for plain deception reasons, Parmalat used derivatives and other complex financial transactions for many years – something it could not have done without the active assistance of big money-center banks. Indeed, the now defunct company did these things through investment banks like Citigroup. In one 1999 deal with Citigroup, realized through a subsidiary of the bank, called Buconero (which means 'black hole' in Italian), the bank made a 117 million euro ($146 million) 'investment' in return for a chunk of the company's net profit.

By setting up this transaction as an investment and not a loan, which is ironically a legal maneuver, Parmalat made its borrowing costs appear smaller than they actually were. This is the dark side of financial engineering which, to be done in a masterfully covert way, requires an amount of skill nobody ever thought had existed around Parma.

While Parmalat had claimed to have bought back 2.9 billion euros of its own debt, to the prosecutors Calisto Tanzi admitted the entire amount was fictitious. Investigators have also found no trace of a 1.5 billion euro investment in grade bonds that Luciano Del Soldato, an imprisoned executive, claimed were on the books during a conference call with analysts in mid-November 2003, a month or so before the crash.

One person familiar with the company suggested that virtually none of the main subsidiaries, in particular the dairy operations in Italy, Brazil and the USA, was profitable. Parmalat's strongest operations appeared to be in Canada, Australia and South Africa, and some very small units in Eastern Europe. With red ink running all over the places where Parmalat was supposed to be profitable, financial engineering had turned the deep red figures into black.

15.4   Taxpayers, investors, and the control of malfeasance

In January 2004, Giulio Tremonti, Italy's finance minister, said the Parmalat affair would cost the state about 21 billion euros. That would offset almost exactly the sacrifices the government made in 2003, in public spending, to cut the budget deficit. Experts, however, suggested that the indirect effects may be even bigger – and both the direct and indirect effects were sure to land at the door of the Italian taxpayer.

One of the hilarious revelations from the Parmalat scandal has been that Italy's feared revenue police have been confronted by a claim from Fausto Tonna, Parmalat's former CFO, that his boss could fix the dates of supposedly random tax inspections. Bad news hitting the authorities never comes singly, and during the first week of February 2004 the prosecutors probing Parmalat came under a cloud when Giovanni Panebianco, the leader of one of the investigations, resigned after being charged with corruption.[10] This is the other side of the scam and shows that the old boys' network has also been at work,

■ With a business culture rooted in ties of blood and friendship,
■ Employing non-inquisitive public accountants and very co-operate bankers, and
■ Held together by a web of reciprocal political and other favors.

Immediately before the Parmalat malfeasance had been that of the Cirio Food company – involving Sergio Cragnotti, the CEO, his son Andrea, and son-in-law Filippo Fucile. Among the notable people interrogated by Italian magistrates were Cesare Geroni, president of Capitalia, the big Italian financial holding group which controls Banca di Roma, one of the top financiers of Parmalat (more on this in section 15.7).

Calisto Tanzi's family, too, his son Stefano and his daughter, were involved in the company's operations, right thorough to a subsidiary travel bureau which had been reportedly deep in the red. Parmalat Finanziaria said on 21 January 2004, that Stefano Tanzi resigned from its board and from eleven other units, relinquishing all operating functions at the hedge fund with the dairy products line. The founder's brother, Giovanni Tanzi, also stepped down from all positions he held at the company, and Paolo Tanzi, another family member, also quit his posts.

On 14 February 2004, Michele Ributti, the chief lawyer for Calisto Tanzi, resigned after he was placed under investigation for allegedly laundering his client's cash in Switzerland. Ributti was suspected by Swiss and Italian investigative magistrates of having laundered 1 million euros – peanuts compared to the size of the scandal.[11] Ributti's lawyer, Vittorio D'Aiello, rejected the allegation that his client laundered money, saying:

- The money was paid by Tanzi, for professional services, into a bank account belonging to Ributti, and
- The cash never left that account; therefore it cannot be considered money-laundering.

These allegations and counter-allegations are a sideshow to the global probe into the disappearance of more than 14 billion euros from Parmalat's accounts, and they highlight the complexity of Italian magistrates' efforts to tie together as many suspicious transactions as possible before pressing charges against Tanzi, many other former Parmalat executives and, possibly, bankers for the dairy group.

With Parmalat's scandal on the upswing, investigative magistrates hauled out of jail for interrogation two former executives, ex-CFO Fausto Tonna and accountant Gianfranco Bocchi, to help decipher accounts at the company's headquarters in Collecchio. According to people who know what went on at headquarters, Tonna had ordered the destruction of computers and their files before investigators arrived in late December 2003. According to published reports this destruction continued for several days, even after the magistrates arrived.

Italian investigators also sent requests for assistance to authorities in the USA, the Cayman Islands, Luxembourg, Malta and Monaco, said Silvia Cavallari, a magistrate in Parma. In Brazil, congressmen called company executives to testify about international money transfers involving the Italian company. Brazil's lower house set up a committee to investigate Parmalat's Brazilian unit after a jailed accountant in Italy said some of the missing funds may be in Brazil.

Also in South America, Parmalat Finanziaria's Chilean unit missed its self-imposed deadline to make a partial payment of debt it owed to milk suppliers. On 9 January 2004, Parmalat Chile had pledged to pay, on 19 January, some 20 percent of the $2.1 million it owed to 200 dairies for 10 million liters of milk purchased in December 2003. The rest was due by the end of January, but the company failed to make the payment by the deadline.

In fact, from France to Chile, individual milk producers who had sold their produce to Parmalat as well as milk producers' federations, were left high and dry as the hedge fund with the dairy products line stopped payments. This led to great distress for the large majority of little farms who had sold on credit to the Italian dairy company, and depended on its payments for their living.

Italian investors were in for more shocks as other companies, more accustomed to spending than controlling costs or living up to their responsibilities, felt the effects in their bottom line and in their treasury. A short while after the Parmalat scandal came that of Finmatica, an Italian software firm. This new scandal reinforced the feeling of a specific *Italy risk* attributable to:

- Opaque reporting,
- Poor governance,
- Weak regulation,
- Tolerance of corruption, and
- Lack of adequate supervision.

The next scam in the chain was revealed on 25 February 2004, with Italy's judicial system embroiled in a fresh controversy which involved a local bank as well as the Bank of Italy. This came to the public's attention after a public prosecutor placed Antonio Fazio, governor of the national central bank, under investigation in an inquiry into possible fraud at Bank 121, formerly known as Banca di Salento.

- The inquiry was into financial products sold by Bank 121 to ordinary Italian investors who did not know what they signed up to and what kind of risk they had assumed.
- The governor of the Bank of Italy has been one of thirty-eight people called up for the inquiry launched by the prosecutor's office in Trani, in the Puglia region.

This new scandal, the fourth in a matter of a few months, destabilized Italy's fragile banking industry and left more than a little dented the reputation of the country as a place in which to invest. The central bank has been criticized not only because it failed to spot the massive accounting fraud at Parmalat, but also – and most particularly – because it did not detect the huge risks embedded in the derivative financial instruments sold by Bank 121 to unwary investors. Some 100 000 savers, many of them of relatively low net worth, were caught in the net of that scam.

In Italy, experts suggested that the while 'investments' sold by Bank 121 were complex, this is only the tip of the iceberg of an affair which is much more complicated. Banca di Salento was a private bank which was for sale. Two of the institutions interested in acquiring it were San Paolo IMI, of Turin, and Monte dei Paschi di Sienna.

- By getting on board with derivative instruments from 100 000 customers, Bank 121 asked the bidders for a higher price.
- Besides that, allegedly, Monte dei Paschi (which finally got Bank 121) wanted to market to its own customers the derivatives product which behaved as a zero coupon bond.

No formal accusations were leveled at Antonio Fazio, with the inquiry seeking to establish whether he abetted suspected fraud in the sale of Bank 121's financial products. Much of the scam around the Bank 121 affair revolved around the sale (in 1999 and 2000) of financial products whose names sounded similar enough to Italian government bonds to lure savers and investors into thinking they were buying rock-solid securities – so solid that the value of some fell by as much as 70 percent!

The main concerns are for urgently needed more rigorous regulation, this need having become evident after the massive investor losses connected to Argentine government bonds sold on the Italian market. Because thousands of savers had been left with large losses – for some, a whole life's savings disappeared – the Berlusconi government sought to make reforms which could help toward restoring confidence in Italian capital markets, but critics say these did not go far enough.

According to a proposed law a new regulator, provisionally called the Authority for the Protection of Savings, will replace Consob, the current ineffective securities market watchdog. Dubbed Super Consob, this new regulator will likely be more powerful than its predecessor, taking over the supervision of debt issuance from the Bank of Italy, and also getting some of the central bank's staff and property.

But will it have teeth? The maximum prison sentence for market abuse will be twelve years, critics however say that most probably this will be greatly reduced with political patronage. Also scheduled is a new minimum fine of 500 000 euros ($600 000) for financial fraud. Still, these powers will fall far short of those, for instance, of the FSA in the UK, or Germany's BaFin, which put supervision of all markets under one roof.

15.5   Mr Fixit and the challenges of a turnaround

On 25 February 2004, Enrico Bondi, Parmalat's government-appointed administrator, secured that Banamex, a subsidiary of Citigroup, would unfreeze bank accounts held by Parmalat's Mexican subsidiary. This decision allows the subsidiary to resume payments to suppliers. It also shows how Bondi is trying to keep some control of Parmalat's sprawling but doubtful assets, in order to produce a viable rescue plan.

Bondi came into the picture a few weeks prior to Parmalat's bankruptcy. He was imposed on the firm on 8 December 2003, by Italian banks financing the hedge fund and its dairy line, after these creditor institutions had lost patience with the mismanagement by Tanzi and company, and got tired of always having their finger in the dike of bad loans to stop it from collapsing.

When Enrico Bondi's appointment took place, trading in Parmalat shares was suspended and the company's board was reluctantly convened the next day. Bondi was initially appointed as a consultant, because Calisto Tanzi would not relinquish his CEO job – though he seems to have accepted Bondi's presence as the price for the banks' continuing support. This saw to it that the executive powers of the turnaround specialist were rather limited – till a couple of weeks later when everything broke loose.

Enrico Bondi had made his name in previous rescue operations of Italian firms, where he had been fairly successful. Edisson, the energy company, is a case in point. Another Italian turnaround artist, not connected to Parmalat, has been Paolo Scaroni who in 2002 became chief executive of Italy's Enel, the publicly owned electricity authority. Overhauling Enel and grooming it for privatization had all the characteristics of an endurance feat – not unlikely that facing Bondi at Parmalat.

In 2002, Enel was a $25 billion ex-monopoly still 68 percent state owned, saddled with high costs and ill prepared for competition. A poorly timed diversification into telecoms by prior management was draining some $1.4 billion a year from Enel's cash reserves. Put together in the mid-1960s as the price for participation by the Socialist Party in the Italian government, Enel had greatly contributed to the ballooning of Italy's high public debt.

Some experts said that from one turnaround to the other, the specialist's job becomes increasingly more challenging. Bondi's responsibilities, for instance, were seen in order of magnitude as greater than those of Scaroni, because Parmalat represented war on a double front:

- On the one side, its bankrupt operations around the globe, and
- On the other, the banks with its own list of priorities which were largely in conflict with Bondi's intention to get back some of the money the banks received from their Parmalat deals.

Some experts suggested that one of the major hurdles to confront Bondi in his role as Parmalat's 'Mr Fixit', would be the hedge fund's curious relationship with the banks that have been both financing it and trading with it. Investigators believe that a long list of credit institutions and investment banks (see section 15.7), knew that Parmalat was bankrupt and its bonds were junk, but continued patronizing it and sold Parmalat bonds as 'sure value' to their clients.

Complicity in covering up the company's state of near-bankruptcy included the fact that Parmalat could write into its books a non-existent $4 billion account, to cover its losses and back up bond issues. Only in mid-December 2004, when the situation became unsustainable, did Bank of America drop the Parmalat connection by announcing that this big account was simply not in its books. The competition for Parmalat business was so high that, reportedly, Bank of America became Parmalat's main bond placer in 2001, displacing JP Morgan which, with 25 percent of the overall issues, estimated at 8 billion euros, is still the largest owner of Parmalat bonds.

The credit institutions' murky role in the corporate bond business has been exposed by one of Bank of America's former executives, Duncan Goldie-Morrison. On 13 November 2003, a short time before Parmalat's bankruptcy became public, Morrison submitted a complaint to the NASD, charging that the bank used creative accounting in regard to investments and junk bond portfolios.[12]

For regulators, the challenge posed by the Italian hedge fund and dairy products outfit may be even greater than that facing Mr Fixit because, as experts see it, countless Parmalats are out there still to be discovered. By all accounts, they contain a high multiple of the poison that so far has been uncovered in the rotten vaults of the Collecchio headquarters.

One of the rather curious challenges facing Parmalat's new management was that the company's financial accounts for 2002 had failed to disclose that 496 million euros ($600 million) of its cash had been invested in Epicurum, which supposedly was a mutual fund based in the Cayman Islands. Besides that 'investment', in a way reminiscent of how bankers play derivatives-and-loans games with other bankers, Parmalat had also entered into a huge currency swap with Epicurum.

The *Parmalat–Epicurum* connection is a classic example of the abyss into which a company can fall because of overleveraging and overgambling with derivative financial instruments. Yet, up to a certain time, the banks financing Parmalat considered it to be a rather well-managed entity with a relatively low credit risk. The curious relationship of the dairy products firm with Epicurum was disclosed only in November 2003, after Consob, Italy's stock market regulator, asked for information about it.

By then, the more naive bankers and some investors were getting wind that things were not as pristine as they were thought to be. Parmalat tried to quell market fears by saying, on 12 November 2003, that it would withdraw its money from Epicurum within fifteen days. This did not take place; what did happen, sometime later, was a disclosure that Epicurum was nothing more than a shell company.

Epicurum was one of the Italian hedge funds' smoke-and-mirror outfits which helped Parmalat's management to confuse and deceive everybody – including itself. This case is one more piece of evidence of the fact that when the quality of management is found wanting, if not outright treacherous, credit risk and market risk reinforce one another, and they see to it that events move way beyond anyone's control.

To appreciate the challenges Enrico Bondi faced in running Parmalat after it filed for protection against creditors, not only in January 2004 did Bank of America deny the existence of a 3.9 billion euro ($4.9 billion) bank account Parmalat claimed to control, but there was another case involving some $500 million of economic pain to Parmalat's investors. Bondi considered legal action in this case, since Italian law permits him to do so.

Indeed, at the core of the Parmalat scandal lies a letter, reportedly from Bank of America, in which the credit institution is said to have confirmed that Bonlat, a Parmalat subsidiary based in the Cayman Islands, had deposits of close to 4 billion euros ($4.8 billion) with the bank. Grant Thornton, the auditor of Bonlat, seems to have relied on this Bank of America letter for evidence of the Parmalat subsidiary's assets.

In mid-December 2003, however, Bank of America said that the document in question was a forgery; the asset simply did not exist. Without that money, Parmalat's empire came crashing down. Yet, while the party among Parmalat and its banks lasted, many investors were reassured by the repeated willingness of big international banks to underwrite new bond issues for the hedge fund with a dairy product line on the side: Citigroup, Bank of America, and Deutsche Bank are some of the institutions which underwrote Parmalat bonds.

Bondi has also been considering legal action against the Brazilian authorities to regain control over Parmalat's operations in that country. He effectively lost control over Parmalat Brasil, mid-February 2004, when a San Paolo court appointed a team of administrators headed by Keyler Carvalho Rocha, a former central bank director, to manage the subsidiary.

The bankrupt company's administrator is also fighting moves by some of Parmalat's creditor banks that could reduce his authority on other units outside Italy. For instance, in February 2004 he got a subsidiary placed under Italian jurisdiction, ahead of an attempt by UBS to put it under a Dutch court's authority. Also, Bank of America, a major Parmalat lender, has sought Eurofood's liquidation in Ireland. A court in Parma decided Eurofood should fall under Italian jurisdiction.

In another dispute, Bondi wanted a court in the Cayman Islands to remove Ernst and Young as an appointed liquidator for Parmalat units registered there. The appointment was made in December 2003 at the request of six US creditors, all of them life assurance companies. Among other reasons, losing judicial control over some financial units could make it harder for magistrates to access documents.

Indeed, letters sent by Italian investigators to US judicial authorities in New York ask them to check certain details about Bank of America, Citigroup, and Gian Paolo Zini, a former lawyer of Parmalat. Luxembourg authorities, who are investigating whether local Parmalat units were used to launder money, have confirmed that they received their first official request for help from Italian prosecutors. Italian prosecutors also found that both Parmalat and Cirio received help from the Camorra, Napoli's Mafia.

15.6   It is not easy to get out of bankruptcy unscathed

To cast some light into the dark corners of the crumbling Parmalat empire, in Milano, magistrate Carlo Nocerino and three officers of the Guardia di Finanza entered the offices of Nextra the fund unit management of big Italian bank Intesa, the country's largest lender. The Guardia di Finanza also searched the Milano office of Morgan Stanley and sought help from investigators abroad.

'Magistrates are obliged to look into everything now', said Andrea Fuccio, a fund manager at Banca Aletti, a unit of Banca Popolare di Verona e Novara.[13] In all these searches and confiscations of documents, prosecutors have been investigating the role of banks in helping to finance the wheelings and dealings of Parmalat, including its highly leveraged deals.

Lindsey Harrison, a Morgan Stanley spokeswoman in London, said Italian authorities had visited Morgan Stanley's office in Milano asking for documentation as part of the ongoing investigation into Parmalat. What was not stated is that the interests of Intesa and Morgan Stanley tended to correlate. In June 2003 Nextra had bought 300 million euros worth of Parmalat Finanziaria bonds from Morgan Stanley, and sold these bonds back to the US securities firm in September and October 2003 – about two months before Parmalat was declared insolvent. That is what Corrado Passera, Intesa's CEO said at a shareholder meeting in Milano on 13 January 2004.

In mid-January 2004, Italian magistrates raided the Milan offices of Deutsche Bank, seizing documents. Officials at Bank of America and Citigroup in Italy were also being questioned, as were the top executives of Italy's largest banks. Prosecutors suspected some outsiders from banks, law firms, and accounting companies were involved in the fraud, making it more difficult to detect. Two outside accountants for auditors Grant Thornton have been put under arrest, and twenty-five other outsiders were under investigation, including two Deloitte managers and a former Bank of America corporate banker in Italy.

In Milano prosecutors also searched the offices of UBS, looking for evidence in connection with a murky credit derivatives deal related to a Parmalat bond issue in the summer of 2003. In July of that year, some five months prior to its crash, Parmalat had issued 420 million euros in bonds in a deal organized by UBS. But the hedge fund with the dairy product line on the side got only 130 million euros, as it was forced to buy 290 million euros of bonds issued by Banca Totta, an institution controlled by Banco Santander.

The Totta bonds in Parmalat's portfolio were linked to a credit default swap, such that, in case of Parmalat's bankruptcy, those bonds were worth zero[14] – but UBS remains a creditor of Parmalat to the tune of 420 million euros and not of 130 million euros. This speaks volumes for why Parmalat resembles so much LTCM – the Rolls-Royce of hedge funds which, as we saw, crashed in September 1998.

Italian media also reported rumors that the 5 percent equity holding by Deutsche Bank in Parmalat was sold short in the stock market. The upshot of this has been that, allegedly, these securities came from securities lending by Deutsche's clients. If so, the clients were left with the almost worthless Parmalat shares returned to them after the crash, while the institution that shorted them reaped the profits – and very significant profits.

Also under close investigation by magistrates has been the fact that Parmalat's banks helped Italy's biggest food company sell more than 500 billion euros of bonds in the four years prior to the company's bankruptcy – at a time when its top executives allegedly were creating false assets. Those debt instruments found their way into the portfolio of institutional investors and private individuals – and with Parmalat's bankruptcy they became worthless.

For some credit institutions, rebuilding their reputation with clients and investors was their way of managing a turnaround from their involvement in the Parmalat scam. On 19 January 2004, Matteo Arpe, chief executive of Capitalia, Italy's fourth largest bank, announced a payback program for retail investors who, upon his bank's advice, bought bonds in Parmalat. Capitalia estimated the buyback of defaulted bonds will cost it some 60 million euros ($72 million) – small beer compared with the big scandal.

Capitalia is Italy's fourth largest banking group, embracing three banks: Banca di Roma, Banco di Sicilia and Bipip Carire. This group has been hugely exposed to Parmalat, as well as to Cirio, the other food outfit that controversially went bust in late 2002 and whose former chairman, Sergio Cragnotti, was accused of fraud and arrested in February 2004.

Sergio Cragnotti defended himself by saying that he had sold all the bonds of his defunct company to the banks not to savers. Back in 1991, Cragnotti was helped in his company's rise by Banco di Santo Spirito (Bank of the Holy Spirit) and Cassa di Risparmio di Roma (the Roman Savings bank, predecessor of Banco di Roma) – where the savers could be found.

Moreover, on the eve of the food company's insolvency, creditor banks rushed to dump their Cirio bonds, by selling them to their customers. Something similar happened with the dairy products company. Italian newspapers are now publishing letters by owners of Parmalat bonds, saying how they were still being sold such bonds by their banks on 11 December 2003,

- Two days after the first Parmalat default, and
- After Standard & Poor's had downgraded these bonds to junk status.

As usual, close personal relations, not an objective evaluation of credit risk, underpinned the banking loans and underwriting of bonds. As reported in the Roman daily La Repubblica, Cragnotti's letters to the bank started: 'Caro Cesare . . .' (Dear Cesar).[15] The Cesar in question was not the original but Geronzi – the general manager of Cassa di Risparmio di Roma, allegedly linked to the Sindona scandal of the 1970s, and now chairman of Capitalia.

From evidence which came to the public's attention post-mortem, it seems that, in Cirio's case, Cragnotti's longstanding relations with Cesare Geronzi, who hand-picked Matteo Arpe to run his banks, has been quite instrumental. By the time Cirio went bust, Cragnotti personally owed the bank around 500 million euros ($600 million) and his company owed much more.[16] A billion here, a billion there and pretty soon we talk about real money, as Everett Dicksen, the former Republican leader in the US Senate used to say.

A billion here, a billion there and Parmalat's accounts cannot be squared, as Enrico Bondi has found the hard way. This is not because of lack of trying because the turnaround specialist seems to have done a first-class job in the short period of three months, after being entrusted at the eleventh hour with the rescue operation.

When at the end of March 2004, he presented Parmalat's financial results, these amounted to liabilities of 14.8 billion euros ($18 billion) – of which 4.2 billion euros were bank loans. To square the circle, Bondi's proposal to the creditors has been that of reaching an accord through which, after a hefty write-down, creditors would convert their loans into equity in the company. Behind this is the hypothesis that after heavy cuts in operations:

- Reducing its debt by nearly 90 percent, to 500 million euros,
- Reducing geographic coverage from thirty countries to twenty, with commensurate personnel reductions,
- Cutting the number of its product labels from 120 to thirty,
- Downsizing its annual revenue from 5.8 billion euros to 3.8 billion euros, and
- Trying to double its operational margin from 3 percent to 6 percent, with 10 percent the longer-term goal,

the former hedge fund could convert into an operational dairy products outfit, coming out of bankruptcy in not too bad a shape. If it is approved, such a rescue plan will be implemented at great cost to Parmalat's bondholders and banks which extended its loans, most likely wiping out the equity of its shareholders as well as greatly downsizing its personnel.

Enrico Bondi's plan for saving the hedge fund and dairy company from the abyss, and from the financial scandal engulfing it, proposed swapping the 14.8 billion euros of debt for shares, and streamlining the firm by selling minor businesses. At the time of writing (end of April 2004) the die is not yet cast, particularly because the banks have not so far accepted Bondi's offer to lick their wounds and be happy with 12 percent to 14 percent of the face value of their loans, which would be converted into equity. The company which would come out of that deal, if it does, might make 7 billion euros per year – or at least that is what the turnaround specialist seems to hope.

15.7 The banks of Parmalat

Parmalat's scandal came only eight months after JP Morgan Chase, Citigroup, Merrill Lynch and other Wall Street firms coughed up $135 million, $101 million and $80 million, respectively, to settle charges over their role in Enron's fraud – albeit without admitting guilt. It is most interesting to notice how easily banks:

- Succumb to the temptation of fat fees taken out of transactions, and
- Leave the most important questions of exposure and reputational risk for later on (see section 15.8).

Senior management seem to forget that reputational risk can be devastating, a mighty negative business factor. That's what Italian banks have found out in connection with the Parmalat scam. In its aftermath, they are targeted by public opinion, the judiciary and, even, by Parliament – because they are considered responsible of what took place.

Legal experts were to comment that big and small banks which financed Parmalat and traded with it will not emerge from this company's wreckage unscathed financially, or with only minor reputational bruises. Indeed, popular resentment in Italy against the banks is real and, to a significant extent, well founded.

- There is a dramatic crisis of confidence in the banking system, and
- The population does not easily forget that hundreds of thousands of Italian families lost their savings.

Along with all the largest Italian banks, and many minor ones, prosecutors in Milano and Parma have been investigating Bank of America, JP Morgan Chase, Morgan Stanley, Citigroup, from the USA; ABN-AMRO, from Holland; Banco Santander, from Spain; Deutsche Bank, from Germany, and more. 'The banks put their gun at our', declared Parmalat founder Calisto Tanzi, after he has been under arrest.[17] One episode out of Tanzi's interrogation records, reported to the press, involves Morgan Stanley and it is taken by some experts as an example of how the banks might have blackmailed Parmalat into issuing bonds and, sometimes, into buying them back on short notice when the banks themselves needed liquidity.

Capitalia, Monte dei Paschi, Banca Intesa, BCI, San Paolo IMI, Unicredito (the former Credito Italiano), Banca Nazionale di Lavoro, Casa di Risparmio di Parma, and many more, have been Parmalat's main Italian financiers. As detailed in Table 15.1, Citigroup was one of the big American lenders to Parmalat, as well as adviser and partner in some deals. These and other credit institutions were the ones who:

- Lent to Parmalat,
- Underwrote its bonds, and
- Traded in derivatives.

The huge amount of exposure from derivatives trading led many experts to the suggestion that Parmalat's default cannot be compared with Enron, Global Crossing, Adelphia Communications or WorldCom, but to the LTCM debacle in

Italian institutions
  Banca di Roma/Capitalia
  Monte dei Paschi
  Banca Intesa BCI[1]
  San Paolo IMI
  Banca AntoVeneta
  Banca Popolare di Milano
  Banca Nazionale di Lavoro
  Cassa di Risparmio di Parma
  Unicredito/UBM[2]
  Banca Popolare di Lodi
  Banca Popolare di Emilia
  Credem
  Banca Lombarda (now Unicredito)
  Banca Etruria
  Banca Popolare Verona-Novara
  Banche Popolare Unite

Foreign institutions
  Citigroup (Epirucum, Bucco Nero)
  Deutsche Bank
  Bank of America
  JP Morgan Chase
  ABN Amro
  Morgan Stanley
  Banco Santander
  And to lesser extent Merrill Lynch, Bank of Boston, UBS, Nomura International and
  Barclays Bank

Notes:
1 An institution that integrated the Savings Bank of Milano (Cariplo), Comit and Ambrosiana Veneto, and whose investment banking arm is Nextra (see section 15.6).
2 Unicredito is the former Credito Italiano and UBM (Banca Mobiliare) its investment banking arm.

Table 15.1 The banks of Parmalat

September 1998. The similarity in systemic risk represented by the interconnection of a derivatives pyramid makes these two cases so much alike.

Moreover, the banks allegedly have been pushing Parmalat into issuing bonds, and the corporate bond sector has been used as a main vehicle for leveraging. One of the preferred instruments employed for this purpose are collateralized debt obligations (CDOs). As credit derivatives, CDOs are issued by banks and are based on a collection of corporate bonds. They are sold to:

■ Different investment funds,
■ Institutional investors, and
■ Private individuals.

Because the bond risk is spread out over the different corporate bonds contained in a CDO, banks can place them at a higher price. Some estimates put the overall value of CDOs at more than $500 million. This represents 10 percent to 11 percent of other estimates which put the banks' exposure to Parmalat at $4.5 billion to $5 billion, while some experts say that the figure is much more.

Parmalat's bankruptcy aside, what many investors who buy structured instruments do not appreciate is that a deep world recession can produce big casualties among corporate entities. This works counter to the bank's claim that CDOs offer minimal risk. In the case of defaults, losses would spread widely among investors. Fitch Ratings says that sixty-nine CDOs it rated had a total exposure of about 700 million euros to Parmalat; a figure which does not include those CDOs which Fitch does not rate.

In the period before its huge financial fraud came to light, Parmalat had become involved to the extent of over $1 billion in CDOs. This is one of the most rapidly expanding sectors of the global derivatives markets, and a highly risky one. Allegedly the CDOs strengthened Parmalat's relations with Bank of America.

Faced with a torrent of red ink, nearly thirty international banks have banded together under Citigroup's leadership to seek compensation from Enrico Bondi and Parmalat's remains. Among the worst hit seems to be Bank of America, with a $274 million exposure at the end of 2003 in loans and derivatives. The blow to Citigroup is even bigger, as it reported a $544 million after-tax exposure in 2003 due to Parmalat-related credit and trading losses – and there is rumored to be an up to $1 billion exposure by Banca di Roma, though officially it is only a fraction of this.

The love affair of Parmalat with Italian and international bankers did not develop overnight. Ironically, it came in the aftermath of the company's first near-bankruptcy. Parmalat was at the edge of an abyss in the late 1980s. It is said that Cirio DeMita, the then powerful secretary general of Christian Democracy, the mammoth Italian political party which ran the country for nearly fifty years after World War II, arranged a syndicated loan headed by Monte dei Paschi – and this let Parmalat off the hook.[18]

Some experts have suggested that this eleventh-hour salvage taught Calisto Tanzi, the company's founder, chairman and CEO, a lesson. This lesson is how easy it is to call the bankers as a fire brigade when you know somebody near the pinnacle of power. The experience has not been lost on Tanzi, and it said that this is behind the two strategic moves by Parmalat:

- Its international business expansion left, right and center, and
- Its conversion into a covert overleveraged hedge fund with no risk management whatsoever.

The evidence shows that Parmalat's American adventures started in 1997, when the company decided to intensify its campaign of international acquisitions, especially in North and South America. All this expansion was financed through debt, and in the process Parmalat became the third largest cookie-maker in the USA.

Management's ineffectiveness, however, seems to have matched the company's mountain of leveraging. A torrent of disconnected acquisitions brought no profits but red figures. Losing big money in what was supposed to be its productive activities, Parmalat shifted more and more to the risky world of derivatives and other speculations. Substandard management found itself confronted by two parallel adventures, both of them demanding.

On the one hand, huge sums were poured into different unrelated enterprises at home and abroad, like soccer-tour club Parma, which had been losing money from the very beginning. Parmatour, now closed, is said to have accumulated a loss of at least 2 billion euros, too high for a tourist outfit. The red ink's exact figures relating to the Parma soccer club are not fully known.

On the other hand, the derivatives gambles which resulted in fat commissions for the banks of Parmalat, do not seem to have produced profits for the company. Rather, the hedge fund side of the dairy products outfit has accumulating losses, and debt after debt to the banks.

From what has been revealed so far, one of the derivatives used by the milk company is the obscure 'self-referenced credit-linked notes' (CLNs). In these, Parmalat invested a rumored $30 million, and what it received essentially was an insurance policy written on itself. Such notes were issued by a vehicle set up by Merrill Lynch in 1999. The effect has been to paint, up to a certain time, a flattering picture of Parmalat's financial health.

The lesson the reader should retain from this debacle is that both Italian banks and global banks, including Citigroup, JP Morgan and Deutsche Bank, were too willing to earn lucrative fees by constructing derivatives deals by which Parmalat:

- Transferred funds offshore, and
- Speculated with them.[19]

One of the ironies of this silly pyramiding of derivatives exposures is the conflict of interest which developed on the bankers side. Even if they only suspected that a client like Parmalat had been using in a questionable way offshore vehicles propelled by derivative financial instruments, their duty was to severe relations with the wrongdoer.

One of the scams which have surfaced post-mortem relates to the New York-based Zini law firm. Allegedly through it, companies owned by Parmalat have been sold to certain American citizens with Italian surnames, to be purchased again later on by Parmalat.[20]

- The purpose of such fake transactions was to create liquidity in the books.
- In turn, this fictitious liquidity permitted Parmalat to continue issuing bonds.

In his interrogation by Italian magistrates, Calisto Tanzi allegedly declared that the fraudulent bonds system 'was fully the banks' idea'. Moreover, Fausto Tonna, Parmalat's former CFO, allegedly counterfeited Parmalat's balance sheets in order to provide security for the bonds. But 'it was the banks which proposed it to Tonna', Tanzi declared to prosecutors.

One of the troubles the banks are facing is that many of Tanzi's depositions have been confirmed by Luciano Spilingardi, head of Cassa di Risparmio di Parma and a member of the Parmalat board. Bond issues were ordered by the banks, Spilingardi said to prosecutors, according to leaks published in Rome's daily newspaper *La Repubblica*. 'I remember', Spilingardi stated, 'that one of the last issues, of Euro 150 million ($187 million), was presented to the board meeting to subscribe the entire bond. If I remember correctly, it was Deutsche Bank.'

Spilingardi added that he expressed 'perplexity' about the proposal, because a previous bond issue of 600 million euros in the spring of 2003 had failed, causing a 10 percent fall of Parmalat stocks in one day. But, finally, the bank's request was accepted and the last Parmalat bond was issued in the summer of 2003. The proceeds supposedly made their way to the Cayman Islands.

15.8   Conflicts of interest and reputational risk

In ways quite similar to those of Eurotunnel, Vivendi Universal, Enron, WorldCom, and other firms, Parmalat's financial problems have been ignored for too long by its managers, bankers, auditors, and supervisors. The reason may be because of inordinate laxity, or because bankers, auditors, and supervisors were taken in by the wrongdoers' constant self-promotion, and they did not have the sense to challenge the 'obvious'.

Credit rating agencies, too, have to do some explaining, though they may find refuge behind a statement that it is tricky for outsiders to monitor what had been going on behind closed doors. Like Vivendi, Parmalat failed to disclose lots of information to the rating agencies, but the agencies should not have issued investment-grade ratings on its bonds. Instead, they should have brought this lack of disclosure to the public's attention – alerting investors to the risks attached to the Parmalat name.

The banks found themselves in a conflict of interest because business with this 'dear client' was extremely lucrative for their own bottom line. Rather than refuse it, they have tended to take the fees while drawing up contracts designed to limit their own legal liability if, as expected, trouble hits. Yet, in doing so,

- The banks implicitly acknowledge that there may be something not quite right, and
- By selling unusual debt instruments to their clients, they left themselves wide open to a significant amount of reputational risk.

The way it has been reported post-mortem, Parmalat's largest bond placers have allegedly been Bank of America, Citicorp, JP Morgan, and Deutsche Bank. They were helped by Italian partners in the financial industry. The worse part of the story is that these worthless bonds were rated as sound financial paper, while the banks underwriting and selling them knew, or should have known, that they were worth nothing.

On Parmalat's part, in the meantime, fiddling the books has been matched by a maze of offshore mailbox companies. With the help of derivatives and other gimmicks, this network of shell firms has been increasingly used to massage financial results and conceal losses, by making the red ink appear as 'assets' or 'liquidity'.

Up to a point, concealment of financial black holes worked to perfection, and Parmalat started to issue bonds in a big way – with 'security' provided by the alleged liquidity represented by the offshore Ponzi games. The banks of Parmalat obliged.

When in mid to late December 2003 the Italian hedge fund with a dairy products line on the side announced the replacement of its CEO, it also made public the appointment of two banks to oversee its restructuring: Lazard Brothers and Mediobanca. The latter is a long-term lender Italian bank, allegedly closely allied with Trieste-based big insurance company Assicurazioni Generali.

It was not going to be easy for the company's new management or for the advisory investment banks to reconstruct the maze of financial and other operations to find out if Parmalat still had some assets. The underlying conflicts of interest masked the facts, and these seem to have gone on all the way from the company's rebirth in the late 1980s till its collapse.

After Parmalat went public, as a sharp operator, Calisto Tanzi lost no time tapping into the vast global capital markets. Between 1990 and 2003, the company's hedge fund side raised a total of about $8 billion in debt in the global market, according to unconfirmed reports.

Bank of America arranged $743 million in Parmalat debt sales between 1997 and 2002. Chase Manhattan, Bank of Boston, Deutsche Bank, Barclays, and Merrill Lynch sold billions of dollars of debt. These cash injections fueled fast growth, with seventeen acquisitions in 1993 alone. This boosted revenues from $800 million in 1990 to $9.7 billion, and

- It led to more and more loans by willing commercial banks,
- While, as we have seen, investment banks obliged by underwriting and selling Parmalat's bonds.

Along with details about conflicts of interest, it became known that Tanzi always found banks willing to do business with his hedge fund. In addition to underwriting Parmalat's last bond issue, of $350 million in September 2003, which paid interest of 6.125 percent at the time of offer, Deutsche Bank allegedly purchased over 5 percent of Parmalat's shares reportedly on the same date, but then managed to sell down the position to 1.6 percent on 19 December 2003. Investors who bought the equity based on the bank's analysts' positive comments cried foul.

The international bankers' collaboration enabled the Parmalat top executives to capture a respectable position in the corporate debt market. Even if some people seem to have raised questions about the company's policy of going for more and more debt, despite its seeming mountain of cash, this did not affect the banks' patronage. Yet, its strange asset allocation should have been an alarm signal.

After the event, some financial analysts pointed out that among the most strange issues in professional conflicts has been the fact that some banks came up with reassuring research reports. This type of investor misinformation continued until a month before Parmalat's collapse. An October 2003 equity report by Deutsche Bank:

- Rated Parmalat's shares a 'Buy', and
- Noted the strong cash flow, which warranted higher premium.

Citibank also issued an optimistic bulletin on the company in November 2003, shortly before Parmalat failed to meet a $184 million payment to bondholders, and admitted, after prodding from Deloitte, that it could not liquidate some $640 million it had said it held in a murky Cayman Islands mutual fund (Epicurum, see section 15.5).

To help untie some of the knots, Italian magistrates have been asked by Parmalat's government-appointed administrator to investigate whether some of the banks have charged excessive fees to Parmalat for loans of 1.85 billion euros ($2.3 billion) organized since July 2001. The investigators were expected to seek clarification from five institutions: Nomura International, UBS, Morgan Stanley, Deutsche Bank and UniCredito Italiano.

These inquiries are critical elements in the search for the 14.8 billion euros missing from the Italian dairy group. They are also one of the rounds between Enrico Bondi and banks that financed the bankrupt group. Under Italian bankruptcy law, Bondi can revoke deals Parmalat struck up to twenty-four months before it filed for bankruptcy on 24 December 2003, if those transactions can be seen as unfavorable to the bankrupt company.

Experts, however, suggest that, given the complexity of the deals and the abundance of derivative instruments proving that bank fees for complex and high-risk financial operations were excessive, this could be difficult. Parmalat's new administration bets on the fact that the law allows a bankrupt company to revoke agreements and puts the onus on the counterparty to justify the terms of the transaction(s) which took place.

To say the least, all this involvement of money-center banks with a mismanaged Italian hedge fund looks sloppy and controversial. For instance, beyond the aforementioned bond issue of September 2003 and voting rights to over 5 percent of Parmalat stock, Deutsche Bank also seems to have had other relationships with Parmalat.

Massimo Armanini, the German credit institution's top investment banker in Italy, worked for the dairy products company from 1998 to 2000. Moreover, as reported in the press, in late November 2003 Deutsche's ratings advisory team helped Parmalat draft a presentation to Standard & Poor's, the independent rating agency, to answer concerns about suspected liquidity problems. This took place about a month prior to Parmalat's bankruptcy.

Issues to which big banks seem to have been blind, were sensed by some private equity firms, which seem to have foreseen the impending disaster. In a last-minute maneuver, on 9 December 2003, Tanzi and his son Stefano met in Italy with executives of the Blackstone Group, to talk about a possible buyout. The meeting came a day after Parmalat admitted that it had not recovered a payment of $640 million from the Epicurum investment fund. Wisely enough, Blackstone did not become involved.

Not unexpectedly, with so many scams and conflicts of interest around, lawsuits have started to fly in America, where Parmalat sold more than $1.5 billion-worth of bonds to investors, including individuals and several big life insurance companies. While Italian magistrates are looking for Italian rules and laws that were broken by Parmalat and/or its auditors, the other jurisdictions are taking action because fraud went way beyond the country's borders. Financing by foreign investors enabled Parmalat to become an international business, and to exploit the differences between legislation and regulations which exist between jurisdictions.

Filed on 5 January 2004 on behalf of Parmalat investors, the US-based class action targeted Citigroup, Deloitte Touche Tohmatsu, and Grant Thornton international, in addition to Parmalat's management. The charges range from assisting in manipulative financial transactions to participating in the falsification of audit confirmation documents.

Deutsche Bank has not been named in the class action launched by one of the legal firms, Milberg Weiss Bershad Hynbes and Lerach, of New York, on behalf of Parmalat investors, But Darren Robbins, a spokesman for the law firm, said that this bank is 'in it up to the eyeballs'.[21]

For its part, on 29 December 2003 the US SEC sued Parmalat with fraud for filing misleading financial statements during 2002 and 2003. The suit in a New York court alleged that Parmalat 'engaged in one of the largest and most brazen corporate financial frauds in history'. An Italian judge said Grant Thornton, one of Parmalat's auditors, had advised the group to set up its now famed Cayman Islands subsidiary to 'modify the system used up until then to hide losses'. Arthur Andersen could not have done better.

15.9 Management accountability

In their way Calisto Tanzi and Fausto Tonna echoed the roles of Ken Ley, Jeff Skilling and Andrew Fastow at Enron; of Bernie Ebbers and Scott Sullivan at WorldCom; and of Dennis Kozlowksi and Mark Swartz at Tyco. (After a six-month long court procedure brought by Manhattan District Attorney General, Robert Morgenthau, the trial of the latter two ended in mistrial.) Everywhere, in all of these cases, there seem to have been employees who either knew or suspected what was going on, and bankers who:

- If they did not suspect the thinly veiled scams, were not worthy of their jobs, but
- If they did suspect them, and still continued dealing with the wrongdoers, have to be judged as accomplices.

While, at the time of writing, much remains unknown about the extent of the scam and those who profited most from it, what is known is that substantial assets have disappeared from Parmalat just as billions of dollars were siphoned off from Enron, WorldCom and the other former high-flying bankrupts or near bankrupts.

In Parmalat's case, Calisto Tanzi has admitted he diverted (read, misappropriated) funds from the group to the tune of 500 million euros, over seven or eight years. Tanzi told magistrates he moved that money from the company to tourism businesses owned by his family. The money was shifted into 'a series of companies that now we'll have to analyze one by one to verify the cash flows', Fabio Belloni – one of Tanzi's lawyers – told reporters outside Milan's San Vittore jail, where Parmalat's former boss has been held since his arrest in late December 2003.[22]

The founder, chairman and CEO admitted to top magistrates that he fiddled the books for more than a decade, skimming off at least half a billion euros from his publicly traded dairy company. For his part, Fausto Tonna the former CFO, provided hours of testimony to prosecutors detailing how he and Tanzi pulled off the biggest fraud in European financial history.

- Tonna told the Italian magistrates that he benefited personally from funds held by subsidiaries in Luxembourg, and
- He alleged that Parmalat took kickbacks from the Swedish packaging group Tetra-Pak, something the Swedish company has denied.

Milan judge, Guido Piffer, accused Tanzi of having 'perfect knowledge of the fraudulent mechanisms' that were used to inflate Parmalat's assets and conceal billions of euros in liabilities. This accusation, which does not amount to a formal criminal charge, was contained in a seven-page ruling drafted by Judge Piffer to justify the decision on 28 December 2003, to continue holding under lock and key Parmalat's former chief executive.

In his ruling, Judge Piffer alleged that Tanzi had 'instigated and endorsed' the financial schemes that led to the discovery of big black holes in Parmalat's accounts. 'It could not have been otherwise, taking into consideration the enormity of the financial breakdown that had to be concealed, and considering that Tanzi himself, and people in his family, were the beneficiaries', the ruling stated.[23]

To answer the question why Parmalat was boosting debt further and further when it had publicly stated that it had huge cash reserves, former CFO Tonna had a standard reply: the company was on an acquisition spree and needed cash, and the liquid funds were earning good returns, some 3.5 percent after taxes in 2003. This excuse is both thinly veiled and it rests on wrong premises.

As far as creative accounting and cash reporting by Parmalat is concerned, experts suggested that the group's parent company was offsetting high levels of debt on its balance sheet through presumably forged documents. These conveniently showed holdings at some of its subsidiaries, such as Bonlat, that matched the headquarters' liquidity requirements.

The Italian hedge fund's trickery was helped by the fact the company's auditors were not careful in their work. Deloitte seems to have accepted Grant Thornton's audits without any questioning. For their part, bankers and investors took the audited figures as reassurance that, although complex, Parmalat's finances were essentially sound.

'What is the one line in an audited balance sheet that no one questions?' asked a former auditor with Deloite and Touche. '(The) Answer (is) the cash and other short-term assets line. And that is precisely where this fraud was directed.'[24] Nobody seems to have asked the all-important question: had Parmalat engineered a sophisticated swindles scheme by inventing a cash cow?

- Basically, it was not sufficient for Bonlat, and other group entities, merely to claim fictitious cash balances.
- They also had to generate a paper trail of false sales to show to the auditors where the company's cash flow supposedly came from.

Only by mid to late 2003, after more than a dozen years of wheeling and dealing were equity analysts becoming increasingly skeptical about the company's prospects. A colorful aspect of this story is that some negative comments by analysts, as well as mounting criticism, led Tanzi to counterattack. On 20 March 2003 he sent a thirty-four page complaint to Consob, the Italian stock market regulator, charging Lehman Brothers and others with seeking to slander the company in order to make speculative gains on Parmalat's shares.

Tanzi had guts, but fraud was not the only of Parmalat's 'accomplishments'. Mismanagement was another. While Calisto Tanzi has been a star performer in manipulating bankers, investors, auditors, and regulators, some people suggest he was out of his depth as a manager. He had made acquisitions in Europe, the USA, and in Latin America that were largely unprofitable, but:

- He seemed to pay little attention to performance, and
- Instead, he focused all his attention on growth at any cost.

It is therefore not surprising that eventually the company's financial problems led to the crash. Indeed, in 1988, Tanzi had faced his first major debt crisis, after an acquisition spree. But as we have seen, the politicians helped him arrange a financial bailout. An estimated $80 million came from heaven, or more precisely from a seven-bank consortium led by Monte dei Paschi di Siena.

The reader will remember that after this salvage operation was successful, Tanzi learned his lesson and began creating a web of finance companies in the Dutch Antilles. These, magistrates believe, were used to hide liabilities from investors prior to listing Parmalat's shares on the Milan stock exchange. A big question is: did Tanzi act alone, or has there been a conspiracy?

'To last for the better part of 15 years, it must be that many gardens and pockets have been watered', said an Italian banker. 'This type of breaking news scandals don't happen accidentally. They are the result of nourishment by a lot of actors, whose cover-ups work till the bubble becomes way too big and finally gets punctured.' Others compared Tanzi to an acrobat, and those who supported him to the manipulators who held the safety net but one day pulled it away – so that when the acrobat fell, he crashed.

Business Week phrased its thoughts in the headline of a long article: 'Inside Parmalat. Many knew, no one talked. Why?'[25] The answer must be sought in doing secretive deals and in conflicts of interest.

The aftermath of Parmalat's patronage by big political figures and, through them, by both Italian and global banks, had serious implications. Did they, the safety net layers, know about the scams and deliberately ignore them? Were they capable or incapable of reading the warning signs? How high in the banks' chain of command had the huge Parmalat loans, bond underwritings, and derivatives trading gone?

- If the top brass at the banks did not know, then their senior executives were utterly incapable.
- If they did, then they are in a worse bind because they became accomplices.

In either case, the global influence of the Parmalat scam spread mayhem among investors, from Rome to Alaska. Some $1.5 billion in Parmalat bonds were sold to US investors alone, mainly through private placements. Whether incompetence or collusion, the aftermath has had a shocking impact.

'What's appalling is that the mistakes were made by many banks all over the world. Parmalat was a totally international affair', said Valter Lazzari, professor of banking and finance at Bocconi University, in Milan. Others add that it is absolutely ridiculous that bankers, accountants, legal advisers, politicians, even some members of Calisto Tanzi's family, all claim that they had no idea what was going on.

The huge losses aside, this is a case study which should be taught in all business management schools. As *Business Week* aptly commented, the Parmalat mega-scandal and Tanzi family saga, is a story of globalization gone wrong. Evidence is emerging that many investment bankers in Italy, Germany, the UK and the USA:

- Harbored doubts about the milk company's numbers for years,
- Were suspicious of its superheated growth, and
- Wondered why an Italian dairy company needed to raise so much debt if it had billions in cash.

Yet, in spite of their doubts, these institutions continued dealing with Parmalat, and evidence of continuing patronage indicated they liked what they saw. After all, Parmalat was a hedge fund with dairy products on the side, and they knew how to finance and trade with hedge funds. Parmalat was also a global fast-growing company with books audited by one of the Big Four – all good reasons to court it for its steady business in stock and bond offerings.

15.10   Parmalat bites back banks and auditors

By mid-2004, after seven months on the job, Parmalat's new management felt enough in charge of legal challenges facing the company, to bring to justice the banks and external auditors who allegedly contributed a great deal to its troubles. Two of the lawsuits are seeking $10 billion in damages against Deloitte & Touche and Grant Thornton, the certified public accountants (CPAs, Chartered Accountants) that for years oversaw the accounts of the bankrupt firm.

The legal action undertaken by Enrico Bondi, accuses both CPAs of improper auditing that allowed huge sums to be allegedly stolen, squandered or wasted by former managers. This legal action, which is bad news for the auditors, came only days after launching lawsuits against three banks:

- Citigroup,
- UBS, and
- Deutsche Bank.

As we saw in Table 15.1, all three, and others, were involved in financial dealings with Parmalat, before the massive fraud that caused the bankruptcy of the Italian hedge fund and food conglomerate.

Mid-August 2004, Bondi published a formal list of Parmalat's creditors, also explaining his reasons for rejecting numerous claims by several of Parmalat's lead banks, with Citigroup and Bank of America at the top of the list. If those rejections are upheld by the judge, the banks will not join the pool of creditors who stand to have their debt turned into shares. Therefore, they will have no say in future votes about Parmalat's restructuring.

The case of the two external auditors is different. The threat for Deloitte & Touche is that the Parmalat case may become what Enron was to Arthur Andersen; a huge reputational risk which led to the disappearance of the auditor. The federated structure of Grant Thornton, which is also a smaller and lesser known outfit than Deloitte, might help it to recover from business risk exposure, but this is by no means sure.

Some analysts expressed the opinion that Bondi's move was shrewd. He made all parties to lawsuits, filed by Parmalat in America, jointly liable for the $10 billion of damages the company asks as compensation. As a result, even if he only wins one case he still stands a chance to recover impressive compensation for Parmalat's legitimate creditors.

The climate created by these court actions brought some major queries to the foreground: How many hidden Parmalats exist in Italy and in the rest of the European Union at this moment? What may be the trigger that punches the bubble of highly leveraged financing? Are the existing bankruptcy laws able to handle 'hedge fund-and-something else' type of cases, or should the laws undergo radical restructuring procedures?

On September 20, 2004, in Milano, Fitch Ratings pulled the alarm bell when it released a special report on likely implications in the aftermath of the Parmalat affair. This report signaled out some other Italian companies at precarious financial conditions: Alitalia, Fantuzzi, FinPart-Cerruti, Finmatica, IT-Holdings, Italtractor, Stefanel, Tiscali, Versace.[26]

Fitch considers that the so-called Marzano Law, cut to the size of the Parmalat debacle, is not enough to protect investors in Italian business and industry. The rating agency also points out that contrary to the restructuring of French laws in connection to procedures relating to bankruptcy, Italian law does not guarantee the interests of lenders, because of the prevailing:

- Absence of a direct influence in bankruptcy procedures, and
- The long time taken by cases in the Court.

Both bullets lead to ineffective restructurings, which become more costly, more protracted and less well managed than they should be. While the Marzano Law has helped Enrico Bondi in elaborating a salvage plan for Parmalat, Fitch Ratings suggests that numerous other Italian enterprises, which are today at the edge of financial chaos, find it difficult to use the currently limited legal supports in order to redress themselves in good order.

15.11   Epilog

The best epilog to the Parmalat drama, as well as to the Argentinean debacle, and to all similar scams of garbage bond sales which took small investors for a ride, has been provided by a late July 2004 article by *The Economist*. This article stated that an estimated 400 000 Italians, the large part of retail clients of local banks, had been holding Euro 14.7 billion ($17.65 billion) of Argentina's bonds when that country defaulted in December 2001. These unlucky savers were sold the toxic waste in the vaults of their banks, through their banks' branches.

In Italy alone, another 100 000 small investors held Euro 1.9 billion ($2.28 billion) of Parmalat's bonds when the hedge fund, with a dairy product line on the side, failed in December 2003. The fraud did not end there. Still another 40 000 Italian savers were left holding Euro 1.1 billion ($1.3 billion) of Cirio paper when the food processor collapsed in 2003.

In short, in just these three incidents of inappropriate selling of highly risky debt instruments to small savers, $21.23 billion in individual savings went up in smoke. At San Paolo IMI, one-third of the 4000 customers who are Cirio bondholders and 10 percent of the 20 000 Parmalat bondholders have decided to seek compensation through legal means.

Quite evidently this did not please the bank's top brass. The way it has been reported, Alfonso Iozzo, San Paolo IMI's managing director, sees a risk of moral hazard if customers were given blanket reimbursement. 'People must learn to assess investments', he says, forgetting that:

■ These clients should not have been sold toxic waste in the first place, and
■ Small savers don't have the skill to recognize a rotten asset; therefore they are easy prey to malpractice.

But Capitalia, Italy's fourth biggest banking group, has chosen the opposite strategy. Almost all of its 3800 customers who bought bonds in Cirio, Parmalat and Giacomelli – another distressed and disgraced Italian company – have been reimbursed, either fully or at 50 percent, depending on whether or not the bank played a part in placing the bonds. 'Reputation is a bank's most important value. We wanted to settle quickly to keep our customers' trust', says Matteo Arpe, Capitalia's managing director.[27]

In the charged Roman climate of discontent among banking clients, Arpe's has been a wise move and, as such, it reminds us of how another genius has been able to move swiftly ahead of the curve. Caesar tripped when disembarking from a ship on the shores of Africa, and fell on his face. With his talent for improvisation, he spread out his arms and embraced the earth as a symbol of conquest.[28]

Capitalia's strategy was wise, and not only because of public relations reasons. It also protects the bank from legal risk and saves some bigger costs, as the cases of Citigroup in May 2004, and J.P. Morgan Chase in July 2004 demonstrate. Mid-July 2004, J.P. Morgan Chase, the second-biggest bank in the US, set aside $2.3 billion to cover the possible costs of litigation arising from the Enron and WorldCom affairs. A month earlier (in May), Citigroup paid $2.7 billion to settle a class-action lawsuit related to WorldCom's troubles, and put aside nearly $5 billion provisions for Enron-related and other court actions.

All this speaks volumes for corporate governance, as well as for some bankers and politicians. It also brings to mind a first-class dictum by Confucius every executive and every investor should keep in front of him or her: 'The man who knows the principles of right reason is less than the man who loves them, and less than the man who makes of them his delight and practices them.'

Notes

1 D.N. Chorafas (2004). *Management Risk: The Bottleneck is at the Top of the Bottle.* Macmillan/Palgrave.
2 D.N. Chorafas (2004). *Rating Management's Effectiveness, with Case Studies in Telecommunications.* Macmillan/Palgrave.

3 D.N. Chorafas (2001). *Managing Risk in the New Economy*. New York Institute of Finance.
4 *The Economist*, 17 January 2004.
5 *Executive Intelligence Review*, 16 January 2004.
6 D.N. Chorafas (2004). *Corporate Accountability, with Case Studies in Pension Funds and in the Banking Industry*. Macmillan/Palgrave.
7 In early March 2004 it was reported by the media that Calisto Tanzi had hidden in credit institutions in Montevideo, Uruguay, a hoard of $870 million – allegedly protected by banking secrecy laws in Uruguay.
8 Which contradicts the *Wall Street Journal* news item that Deloitte's first alarm bell rang in 2001.
9 FT.online, 22 January 2004.
10 *The Economist*, 7 February 2004.
11 *Financial Times*, 14–15 February 2004.
12 *Executive Intelligence Review*, 23 January 2004.
13 *Bloomberg*, 21 January 2004.
14 *Executive Intelligence Review*, 20 February 2004.
15 *La Repubblica*, 26 February 2004.
16 *The Economist*, 21 February 2004.
17 *Executive Intelligence Review*, 23 January 2004.
18 In Italy it is also said that in exchange De Mita got from Parmalat a factory in his native Nuscho, a town near Naples, and possibly other favors.
19 *The Economist*, 20 December 2003.
20 *Executive Intelligence Review*, 16 January 2004.
21 *The Economist*, 17 January 2004.
22 *Bloomberg*, 30 December 2003.
23 *Financial Times*, 30 December 2003.
24 *The Economist*, 17 January 2004.
25 *Business Week*, 26 January 2004.
26 Les Echos, September 21, 2004
27 *The Economist*, July 24, 2004.
28 Anthony Everitt, *Cicero. A Turbulent Life*. John Murray, London, 2001.

Acknowledgements

(Countries are listed in alphabetical order)

The following organizations, through their senior executives and system specialists, participated in the recent research projects that led to the contents of this book and its documentation.

Austria

National Bank of Austria
Dr Martin Ohms
Finance Market Analysis Department
3, Otto Wagner Platz
Postfach 61
A-1011 Vienna

Association of Austrian Banks and Bankers
Dr Fritz Diwok
Secretary General
11, Boersengasse
1013 Vienna

Bank Austria
Dr Peter Fischer
Senior General Manager, Treasury Division
Peter Gabriel
Deputy General Manager, Trading
2, Am Hof
1010 Vienna

Die Erste (First Austrian Bank)
Franz Reif
Head of Group Risk Control
Neutorgasse 8
A-1010 Vienna

Creditanstalt
Dr Wolfgang Lichtl
Market Risk Management

Julius Tandler Platz 3
A-1090 Vienna

Wiener Betriebs- and Baugesellschaft mbH
Dr Josef Fritz
General Manager
1, Anschützstrasse
1153 Vienna

France

Banque de France
Pierre Jaillet
Director, Monetary Studies and Statistics
Yvan Oronnal
Manager, Monetary Analyses and Statistics
G. Tournemire, Analyst, Monetary Studies
39, rue Croix des Petits Champs
75001 Paris

Secretariat Général de la Commission Bancaire – Banque de France
Didier Peny
Director, Control of Big Banks and International Banks
73, rue de Richelieu
75002 Paris
F. Visnowsky
Manager of International Affairs
Supervisory Policy and Research Division
Benjamin Sahel
Market Risk Control
115, Rue Réaumur
75049 Paris Cedex 01

Ministry of Finance and the Economy, Conseil National de la Comptabilité
Alain Le Bars
Director International Relations and Cooperation
6, rue Louise Weiss
75703 Paris Cedex 13

International Marine Insurance Consultants
Alain Bernard
7 Bd du Jardin Exotique
98000 Monte Carlo, Monaco

Germany

Deutsche Bundesbank
Hans-Dietrich Peters

Director
Hans Werner Voth
Director
Dr Frank Heid
Banking and Financial Supervision Department
Wilhelm-Epstein Strasse 14
60431 Frankfurt am Main

Federal Banking Supervisory Office
Hans-Joachim Dohr
Director Dept. I
Jochen Kayser
Risk Model Examination
Ludger Hanenberg
Internal Controls
71–101 Gardeschützenweg
12203 Berlin

European Central Bank
Mauro Grande
Director
29 Kaiserstrasse
29th Floor
60216 Frankfurt am Main

Deutsches Aktieninstitut
Dr Rüdiger Von Rosen
President
Biebergasse 6 bis 10
60313 Frankfurt-am-Main

Commerzbank
Peter Bürger
Senior Vice President, Strategy and Controlling
Markus Rumpel
Senior Vice President, Credit Risk Management
Kaiserplatz
60261 Frankfurt am Main

Deutsche Bank
Professor Manfred Timmermann
Head of Controlling
Rainer Rauleder
Global Head Capital Management
Hans Voit
Head of Process Management, Controlling Department

12, Taunusanlage
60325 Frankfurt

Dresdner Bank
Oliver Ewald
Head of strategic Risk & Treasury Control
Dr Marita Balks
Investment Bank, Risk Control
Dr Hermann Haaf
Mathematical Models for Risk Control
Claas Carsten Kohl
Financial Engineer
1, Jürgen Ponto Platz
60301 Frankfurt

Volkswagen Foundation
Katja Ebeling
Office of the General Secretary
35 Kastanienallee
30519 Hanover

Herbert Quandt Foundation
Dr Kai Schellhorn
Member of the Board
Hanauer Strasse 46
D-80788 Munich

GMD First – Research Institute for Computer Architecture, Software Technology and Graphics
Prof. Dr Ing. Wolfgang K. Giloi
General Manager
5, Rudower Chaussee
D-1199 Berlin

Sparkasse Lüneburg
Lothar Arnold
Organization & IT Department
Tibor Kuloge
Organization & IT Department
And der Münze 4–6
21339 Lüneburg

Hungary

Hungarian Banking and Capital Market Supervision
Dr Janos Kun
Head, Department of Regulation and Analyses

Dr Erika Vörös
Senior Economist, Department of Regulation and Analyses
Dr Géza Nyiry
Head, Section of Information Audit
Csalogany u. 9–11
H-1027 Budapest

Hungarian Academy of Sciences
Prof. Dr Tibor Vamos
Chairman, Computer and Automation Research Institute
Nador U. 7
1051 Budapest

Iceland
The National Bank of Iceland Ltd
Gunnar T. Andersen
Managing Director
International Banking & Treasury
Laugavegur 77
155 Reykjavik

India
i-flex
H. S. Rajashekar
Principal Consultant, Risk Management
i-flex Center
146 Infantry Road
Bangalore 560 001

Italy
Banca d'Italia
Eugene Gaiotti
Research Department, Monetary and Financial Division
Ing. Dario Focarelli
Research Department
91, via Nazionale
00184 Rome

Istituto Bancario San Paolo di Torino
Dr Paolo Chiulenti
Director of Budgeting
Roberto Costa
Director of Private Banking
Pino Ravelli
Director Bergamo Region

27, via G. Camozzi
24121 Bergamo

Luxembourg

Banque Générale de Luxembourg
Prof. Dr Yves Wagner
Director of Asset and Risk Management
Hans Jörg Paris, International Risk Manager
27, avenue Monterey
L-2951 Luxembourg

Clearstream
André Lussi
President and CEO
3–5 Place Winston Churchill
L-2964 Luxembourg

The Netherlands

ABN Amro
Jos Wieleman
Senior VP Group Risk Management
PO Box 283
HQ 2031
1000 EA Amsterdam

Poland

Securities and Exchange Commission
Beata Stelmach
Secretary of the Commission
1, Pl Powstancow Warszawy
00–950 Warsaw

Sweden

The Royal Swedish Academy of Sciences
Dr Solgerd Björn-Rasmussen
Head Information Department
Dr Olof Tanberg
Foreign Secretary
10405 Stockholm

Finansinspektionen
Anders Bredhe
Capital Adequacy Expert
Sveavägen 167
SE-113 85 Stockholm

Skandinaviska Enskilda Banken
Joar Langeland
SEB Group Basel II Project Manager
Bernt Gyllenswärd
Head of Group Audit
Box 16067
10322 Stockholm

Irdem AB
Gian Medri
Former Director of Research at Nordbanken
19, Flintlasvagen
S-19154 Sollentuna

Switzerland

Swiss National Bank
Dr Werner Hermann
Head of International Monetary Relations
Dr Bertrand Rime
Vice President, Representative to the Basle Committee
Prof. Urs Birchler
Director, Advisor on Systemic Stability
15 Börsenstrasse
8022 Zurich

Federal Banking Commission
Dr Susanne Brandenberger
Risk Management
Renate Lischer
Representative to Risk Management Subgroup, Basle Committee
Marktgasse 37
3001 Bern

Bank for International Settlements
Mr Claude Sivy
Head of Internal Audit
Stephen Senior
Member of the Secretariat, Basle Committee on Banking Supervision
Hirotaka Hideshima
Member of the Secretariat, Basle Committee on Banking Supervision
Herbie Poenisch
Senior Economist, Monetary and Economic Department
Ingo Fender
Committee on the Global Financial System
2, Centralplatz
4002 Basle

Crédit Suisse
Dr Harry Stordel
Director, Group Risk Management
Christian A. Walter
Vice President, Risk Management
Paradeplatz 8
8070 Zurich
Ahmad Abu El-Ata
Managing Director, Head of IT Office
Dr Burkhard P. Varnholt
Managing Director, Global Research
12/14 Bahnhofstrasse
CH-8070 Zurich

Bank Leu AG
Dr Urs Morgenthaler
Member of Management
Director of Risk Control
32, Bahnhofstrasse
Zurich

Bank J. Vontobel and Vontobel Holding
Heinz Frauchiger
Chief, Internal Audit Department
Tödistrasse 23
CH-8022 Zurich

United Bank of Switzerland
Dr Heinrich Steinmann
Member of the Executive Board (Retired)
Claridenstrasse
8021 Zurich

UBS Financial Services Group
Dr Per-Göran Persson
Executive Director, Group Strategic Analysis
George Pastrana
Executive, Economic Capital Allocation
Stockerstrasse 64
8098 Zurich

University of Fribourg
Prof. Dr Jürgen Kohlas
Prof. Dr Andreas Meier
Department of Informatics
2, rue Faucigny
CH-1700 Fribourg

Swiss Re
Dr Thomas Hess
Head of Economic Research & Consulting
Mythenquai 50/60
PO Box
CH-8022 Zürich

United Kingdom

Bank of England
Richard Britton
Director, Complex Groups Division, CGD Policy Department
Ian M. Michael
Senior Manager, Financial Industry and Regulation Division
Threadneedle Street
London EC2R 8AH

Financial Services Authority (FSA)
Lieselotte Burgdorf-Cook
International Relations
7th Floor
25 The North Colonnade
Canary Wharf
London E14 5HS

British Bankers Association
Paul Chisnall
Assistant Director
Pinners Hall
105–108 Old Broad Street
London EC2N 1EX

Investment Management Association
Dr Gordon Midgley
Director of Research
65 Kings Way
London WC2B 6TD

Accounting Standards Board
A. V. C. Cook
Technical Director
Sandra Thompson
Project Director
Holborn Hall
100 Gray's Inn Road
London WC1X 8AL

Barclays Bank Plc
Tim Thompson
Head of Economic Capital
Julian Knight
Manager, Group Risk Analysis and Policy
Alan Brown
Director, Group Risk
54 Lombard Street
London EC3P 3AH

Citigroup
Dr David Lawrence
European Head of Risk Methodologies and Analytics
33 Canada Square
Canary Wharf
London E14 5LB

Rabobank Nederland
Eugen Buck
Managing Director
Senior Project Manager Economic Capital
Thames Court
One Queenhithe
London EC4V 3RL

Abbey National Treasury Services plc
John Hasson
Director of Information Technology & Treasury Operations
Abbey National House
2 Triton Square
Regent's Place
London NW1 3AN

ABN-AMRO Investment Bank N.V.
David Woods
Chief Operations Officer, Global Equity Directorate
Annette C. Austin
Head of Operational Risk Management Wholesale Client
250 Bishopsgate
London EC2M 4AA

Bankgesellschaft Berlin
Stephen F. Myers
Head of Market Risk
1 Crown Court
Cheapside, London

Global Association of Risk Professionals (GARP)
Dr Brandon Davies
Member, Board of Trustees and Executive Committee
150–152 Fenchurch Street
London EC3M 6BB

Standard & Poor's
David T. Beers
Managing Director, Sovereign & International Public Finance Ratings
Barbara Ridpath
Managing Director, Chief Credit Officer, Europe
Walter Pompliano
Director, Financial Institutions Group, Financial Services Ratings
Broadgate West
9 Appold Street
London EC2A 2AP

Moody's Investor Services
Samuel S. Theodore
Managing Director, European Banks
David Frohriep
Communications Manager, Europe
2, Minster Court
Mincing Lange
London EC3R 7XB

Moody's K.M.V.
Alastair Graham
Senior Vice President, Director of Global Training
Lynn Valkenaar
Project Manager, KMV
Lars Hunsche
Manager
Well Court House
8–9 Well Court
London EC4M 9DN

Fitch Ratings
Charles Prescott
Group Managing Director
David Andrews
Managing Director, Financial Institutions
Trevor Pitman
Managing Director, Corporations
Richard Fox
Director, International Public Finance

Eldon House
2, Eldon Street
London EC2M 7UA
Andrew Fishman
Managing Director, FitchRisk Advisory
101 Finsbury Pavement
London, EC2A 1RS

A.M. Best Europe
Jose Sanchez-Crespo
General Manager
Michael Zboron
Managing Senior Financial Analyst
Mark Coleman
Financial Analyst
1 Minster Court
Mincing Lane
London EC3R 7AA

Merrill Lynch International
Bob Keen
Director of Global Private Bank Group
Bart Dowling
Director, Global Asset Allocation
Elena Dimova
Vice President, Equity Sales
Erik Banks
Managing Director of Risk Management
Merrill Lynch Financial Center
2 King Edward Street
London EC1A 1HQ

JP Morgan
David Marks
Managing Director
JP Morgan Securities Ltd
125 London Wall
London EC2Y 5AJ

Dresdner Kleinwort Wasserstein
Duncan H. Martin
Director, Head of Strategic Risk Management, Global Risk Management
PO Box 560
20 Fenchurch Street
London EC3P 3DB

AON Limited
Daniel Butler
Executive Director, Professional Risks
Geoff Perry
Director, Professional Risks
8 Devonshire Square
London EC2M 4PL

The Auditing Practices Board
Jonathan E. C. Grant
Technical Director
Steve Leonard
Internal Controls Project Manager
PO Box 433
Moorgate Place
London EC2P 2BJ

International Accounting Standards Committee
Ms Liesel Knorr
Technical Director
166 Fleet Street
London EC4A 2DY

MeesPierson ICS
Arjan P. Verkerk
Director, Market Risk
Camomile Court
23 Camomile Street
London EC3A 7PP

Charles Schwab
Dan Hattrup
International Investment Specialist
Crosby Court
38 Bishopsgate
London EC2N 4AJ

Charity Commission
Susan Polak
Mike McKillop
J. Chauhan
13–15 Bouverie Street
London ECAY 8DP

The Wellcome Trust
Clare Matterson
Member of the Eexecutive Board and Head of Policy

210 Euston Road
London NW1 2BE

Association of Charitable Foundations
Nigel Siederer
Chief Executive
2, Plough Yard
Shoreditch High Street
London EC2A 3LP

IBM United Kingdom
Derek Duerden
Technical Strategy, EMEA Banking Finance & Securities Business
76 Upper Ground
London SE1 9PZ

City University Business School
Professor Elias Dinenis
Head, Department of Investment
Risk Management & Insurance
Prof. Dr John Hagnioannides
Department of Finance
Frobisher Crescent
Barbican Centre
London EC2Y 8BH

TT International
Timothy A. Tacchi
Co-Chief Executive Officer
Henry Bedford
Co-Chief Executive Officer
Robin A. E. Hunt
Martin House
5 Martin Lane
London EC4R 0DP

Alternative Investment Management Association (AIMA)
Emma Mugridge
Director
10 Stanhope Gate
Mayfair
London W1K 1AL

Ernst & Young
Pierre-Yves Maurois
Senior Manager, Risk Management and Regulatory Services
Rolls House

7 Rolls Buildings
Fetter Lane
London E4A 1NH

Brit Syndicates Limited at Lloyd's
Peter Chrismas
Marine Hull Underwriter
Simon Stonehouse
Marine Hull Underwriter
Anthony Forsyth
Marine Underwriter
Marine, Aviation, Transport & Space Division
Box 035
Lloyd's
1 Lime street
London EC3M 7DQ

Trema UK Ltd
Dr Vincent Kilcoyne
Business Architecture
75 Cannon Street
London EC2N 5BN

STP Information Systems
Graeme Austin
Managing Director
16 Hewett Street
London, EC2A 3NN

United States

Federal Reserve System, Board of Governors
David L. Robinson
Deputy Director, Chief Federal Reserve Examiner
Alan H. Osterholm, CIA, CISA
Manager, Financial Examinations Section
Paul W. Bettge
Assistant Director, Division of Reserve Bank Operations
Gregory E. Eller
Supervisory Financial Analyst, Banking
Gregory L. Evans
Manager, Financial Accounting
Martha Stallard
Financial Accounting, Reserve Bank Operations
20th and Constitution, NW
Washington, DC 20551

Federal Reserve Bank of Boston
William McDonough
Executive Vice President
James T. Nolan
Assistant Vice President
PO Box 2076
600 Atlantic Avenue
Boston, MA

Federal Reserve Bank of San Francisco
Nigel R. Ogilvie, CFA
Supervising Financial Analyst
Emerging Issues
101 Market Street
San Francisco, CA

Seattle Branch, Federal Reserve Bank of San Francisco
Jimmy F. Kamada
Assistant Vice President
Gale P. Ansell
Assistant Vice President, Business Development
1015, 2nd Avenue
Seattle, WA 98122–3567

Office of the Comptroller of the Currency (OCC)
Bill Morris
National Bank Examiner/Policy Analyst
Core Policy Development Division
Gene Green
Deputy Chief Accountant
Office of the Chief Accountant
250 E Street, SW
7th Floor
Washington, D.C.

Federal Deposit Insurance Corporation (FDIC)
Curtis Wong
Capital Markets, Examination Support
Tanya Smith
Examination Specialist, International Branch
Doris L. Marsh
Examination Specialist, Policy Branch
550 17th Street, N.W.
Washington, D.C.

Office of Thrift Supervision (OTS)
Timothy J. Stier
Chief Accountant
1700 G Street Northwest
Washington, DC, 20552

Securities and Exchange Commission, Washington DC
Robert Uhl
Professional Accounting Fellow
Pascal Desroches
Professional Accounting Fellow
John W. Albert
Associate Chief Accountant
Scott Bayless
Associate Chief Accountant
Office of the Chief Accountant
Securities and Exchange Commission
450 Fifth Street, NW
Washington, DC, 20549

Securities and Exchange Commission, New York
Robert A. Sollazzo
Associate Regional Director
7 World Trade Center
12th Floor
New York, NY 10048

Securities and Exchange Commission, Boston
Edward A. Ryan, Jr
Assistant District Administrator (Regulations)
Boston District Office
73 Tremont Street, 6th Floor
Boston, MA 02108–3912

Microsoft
Dr Gordon Bell
Senior Researcher
Bay Area Research Center of Microsoft Research
455, Market Street
Suite 1690
San Francisco, CA 94105

American Bankers Association
Dr James Chessen
Chief Economist
Mr Douglas Johnson

Senior Policy Analyst
1120 Connecticut Ave NW
Washington, DC 20036

International Monetary Fund
Alain Coune
Assistant Director, Office of Internal Audit and Inspection
700 19th Street NW
Washington DC, 20431

Financial Accounting Standards Board
Halsey G. Bullen
Project Manager
Jeannot Blanchet
Project Manager
Teri L. List
Practice Fellow
401 Merritt
Norwalk, CN 06856

Henry Kaufman & Company
Dr Henry Kaufman
660 Madison Avenue
New York, NY 10021

Soros Fund Management
George Soros
Chairman
888 Seventh Avenue, Suite 3300
New York, NY 10106

Carnegie Corporation of New York
Armanda Famiglietti
Associate Corporate Secretary, Director of Grants Management
437 Madison Avenue
New York, NY 10022

Alfred P. Sloan Foundation
Stewart F. Campbell
Financial Vice President and Secretary
630 Fifth Avenue, Suite 2550
New York, NY 10111

Rockefeller Brothers Fund
Benjamin R. Shute, Jr
Secretary

437 Madison Avenue
New York, NY 10022–7001

The Foundation Center
79 Fifth Avenue
New York, NY 10003–4230

Citibank
Daniel Schutzer
Vice President, Director of Advanced Technology
909 Third Avenue
New York, NY 10022

Swiss Re
David S. Laster, PhD
Senior Economist
55 East 52nd Street
New York, NY 10055

Prudential-Bache Securities
Bella Loykhter
Senior Vice President, Information Technology
Kenneth Musco
First Vice President and Director
Management Internal Control
Neil S. Lerner
Vice President, Management Internal Control
1 New York Plaza
New York, NY

Merrill Lynch
John J. Fosina
Director, Planning and Analysis
Paul J. Fitzsimmons
Senior Vice President, District Trust Manager
David E. Radcliffe
Senior Vice President, National Manager Philanthropic Consulting
Corporate and Institutional Client Group
World Financial Center, North Tower
New York, NY 10281–1316

Permal Asset Management
Isaac R. Souede
President and CEO
900 Third Avenue

New York, NY 10022
(telephone interview)

HSBC Republic
Susan G. Pearce
Senior Vice President
Philip A. Salazar
Executive Director
452 Fifth Avenue, Tower 6
New York, NY 10018

International Swaps and Derivatives Association (ISDA)
Susan Hinko
Director of Policy
600 Fifth Avenue, 27th Floor, Rockefeller Center
New York, NY 10020–2302

Standard & Poor's
Clifford Griep
Managing Director
25 Broadway
New York, NY 10004–1064
Mary Peloquin-Dodd
Director, Public Finance Ratings
55 Water Street
New York, NY 10041–0003

Moody's KMV
Askish Das
Analyst
Michele Freed
Analyst
160 Montgomery St, Ste 140
San Francisco, CA 94111

Moody's KMV
Marc Bramer
Vice President, Strategic Clients
130 South Main Street
Suite 300
South Bend, IN 46601

State Street Bank and Trust
James J. Barr
Executive Vice President, U.S. Financial Assets Services

225 Franklin Street
Boston, MA 02105–1992

MBIA Insurance Corporation
John B. Caouette
Vice Chairman
113 King Street
Armonk, NY 10504

Global Association of Risk Professionals (GARP)
Lev Borodovski
Executive Director, GARP, and
Director of Risk Management, Credit Suisse First Boston (CSFB), New York
Yong Li
Director of Education, GARP, and
Vice President, Lehman Brothers, New York
Dr Frank Leiber
Research Director, and
Assistant Director of Computational Finance,
Cornell University, Theory Center, New York
Roy Nawal
Director of Risk Forums, GARP
980 Broadway, Suite 242
Thornwood, NY

Group of Thirty
John Walsh
Director
1990 M Street, NW
Suite 450
Washington, DC, 20036

Broadcom Corporation
Dr Henry Samueli
Co-Chairman of the Board, Chief Technical Officer
16215 Alton Parkway
PO Box 57013
Irvine, CA 92619–7013

Edward Jones
Ann Ficken (Mrs)
Director, Internal Audit
201 Progress Parkway
Maryland Heights, MO 63043–3042

Teachers Insurance and Annuity Association/College Retirement Equities Fund (TIAA/CREF)
John W. Sullivan
Senior Institutional Trust Consultant
Charles S. Dvorkin
Vice President and Chief Technology Officer
Harry D. Perrin
Assistant Vice President, Information Technology
Patty Steinbach
Investment Advisor
Tim Prosser
Lawyer
730 Third Avenue
New York, NY 10017–3206

Sterling Foundation Management
Dr Roger D. Silk
Principal
14622 Ventura Blvd
Suite 745
Sherman Oaks, CA 91403

Grenzebach Glier & Associates, Inc.
John J. Glier
President and Chief Executive Officer
55 West Wacker Drive
Suite 1500
Chicago, IL 60601

Massachusetts Institute of Technology
Ms Peggy Carney
Administrator, Graduate Office
Michael Coen, PhD Candidate
ARPA Intelligent Environment Project
Department of Electrical Engineering
and Computer Science
Building 38, Room 444
50 Vassar Street
Cambridge, MA, 02139

New York University, Stern School of Business
Edward I. Altman
Professor of Finance and Vice Director, NYU Salomon Center
44 West 4th Street
New York, NY 10012–1126

Henry Samueli School of Engineering and Applied Science, University of California, Los Angeles
Dean A.R. Frank Wazzan
School of Engineering and Applied Science
Prof. Stephen E. Jacobson
Dean of Student Affairs
Dr Les Lackman
Mechanical and Aerospace Engineering Department
Prof. Richard Muntz
Chair, Computer Science Department
Prof. Dr Leonard Kleinrock
Telecommunications and Networks
Prof. Chih-Ming Ho, PhD
Ben Rich- Lockheed Martin Professor
Mechancial and Aerospace Engineering Department
Dr Gang Chen
Mechancial and Aerospace Engineering Department
Prof. Harold G. Monbouquette, PhD
Chemical Engineering Department
Prof. Jack W. Judy
Electrical Engineering Department
Abeer Alwan
Bioengineering
Prof. Greg Pottie
Electrical Engineering Department
Prof. Lieven Vandenberghe
Electrical Engineering Department

Anderson Graduate School of Management, University of California, Los Angeles
Prof. John Mamer
Former Dean
Prof. Bruce Miller

Roundtable Discussion on Engineering and Management Curriculum (October 2, 2000)
Dr Henry Borenstein, Honeywell
Dr F. Issacci, Honeywell
Dr Ray Haynes, TRW
Dr Richard Croxall, TRW
Dr Steven Bouley, Boeing
Dr Derek Cheung, Rockwell
Westwood Village
Los Angeles, CA 90024

University of Maryland
Prof. Howard Frank

Dean, The Robert H. Smith School of Business
Prof. Lemma W. Senbert
Chair, Finance Department
Prof. Haluk Unal
Associate Professor of Finance
Van Munching Hall
College Park, Maryland 20742–1815

Gartner Group
David C. Furlonger
Vice President & Research Director, Gartner Financial Services
5000 Falls of the Neuse Road
Suite 304
Raleigh, NC 27609

Accenture
Stanton J. Taylor
Partner
Dr Andrew E. Fano
Associate Partner
Dr Cem Baydar
Analyst
Kishire S. Swaminathan
Analyst
Accenture Technology Labs
161 N. Clark
Chicago, Illinois 60601

Index

ABN-AMRO, 304, 307, 308, 357
Accounting Standards Board, 167
Accruals method, 147
Acid test, 285
Adecco, 271, 272, 338, 339
Adenauer, Konrad, 247
Advance/decline line, 241
Alternative Investment Management
    Association (AIMA), 311, 312, 314
Alternative investments, 9, 206
Amazon.com, 331–3
A.M. Best, 265
American Depository Receipts (ADRs), 343,
    346
American Stock Exchange, 81
Amsterdam's Merchant Exchange, 79
Analogical thinking, 250
Analyst certification, 259
Arbitrageurs, 17
Arpe, Matteo, 355, 356, 369
Ask, 117, 118
Asset management, 15
Asset managers, 40
Asset reallocation, 35
AT&T, 14, 30, 155, 257, 269, 297, 333
Audit committee, 185–7
Average revenue per user (ARPU), 169

BaFin, 351
Baltic Exchange, 105, 106
Banco Ambrosiano, 71, 72
Bank 121, 350
Bank of America, 22, 23, 31, 53, 68, 210, 259,
    346, 352–4, 357
Bank of England, 260, 261
Bank for International Settlements (BIS), 188,
    281
Bank of Italy, 71, 351
Bank One, 36
Barclays Bank, 250
Barings, 69, 70
Basel Committee on Banking Supervision, 163,
    189, 218, 293, 294
Basel II, 135, 150, 163, 177, 293, 304
Basing area hypothesis, 140, 141
Bear Stearns, 68

Beneficial owner, 112
Bid, 117, 118
Bid/ask spread, 72, 117, 118, 266
Black-Scholes, 163
Bloomberg, 314
Bloomberg European 500 Index, 102, 104
Blow-off, 145
Book value, 147, 157, 158, 221, 312
Bondi, Enrico, 351–4, 356
Bonds, 85
Brandeis, Louis, 185
Breakout, 145
Buck, Eugene, 134, 202, 216, 304
Buconero, 347
Buffett, Warren, 3, 168, 203, 209, 221, 233
Bull rate, 36
Business continuity, 324
Business Roundtable, 260
Buybacks, 93
Buy order, 243

CAC 40, 102
Call option, 162
Calpers, 47
Capital asset pricing model, 165
Capital markets, 73
Capital to total assets, 291
Capitalia, 348, 355, 369
Capitalization, 158
Carnegie, Andrew, 47
Cash cost per user (CCPU), 297
Cash flow to share, 157, 166
Cash-out price, 126
Caveat emptor, 19, 21
Charting, 134, 139, 140
Chronos, 221
Churchill, Winston, 245
Cirio, 344, 345, 348, 355, 356, 368, 369
Cisco Systems, 196, 326, 327
Citigroup, 68, 267, 347, 351, 353, 354, 357,
    359, 369
Collateral, 121–3
Collateralized Mortgage Obligations, 358
Commission Houses, 83
Commodities Futures Trading Commission
    (CFTC), 111

Common stock, 83–5
Company risk, 224
Comprehensive income, 249
Comprehensive loss, 249
Comprehensive profit, 249
Confucius, 369
Congestion area, 145
Consob, 351, 353, 365
Consumer price index (CPI), 138
Contingent order, 243, 244
Contrarian opinion, 215–17
Contrarians, 249
Controller of the currency, 76
Convertible bonds, 84–7
Corporate insider activity, 109
Corporate performance management, 296,
    307, 308
Correlation coefficients, 214, 299, 300
Correspondent banking, 70, 71
Corrigan, Gerald, 285
Corruption Perceptions Index, 76
Cost to income ratio, 157
Council of Foreign Relations, 265
Creative accounting, 49, 183, 185, 192,
    263, 343
Credit-linked notes (CLN), 360
Credit rating, 107
Credit risk, 11, 88, 218
Credit Suisse First Boston, 66, 269
Credit Suisse Private Banking, 316
Crossborder M&A, 310, 311
Current assets, 285
Current income risk, 226
Current liabilities, 285, 286
Current profit, 167
CVAR$_{99.97}$, 218, 219, 250

Data insufficiency, 148
DAX, 102, 103, 282
Debentures, 87
Debt equity ratio, 147
Debt instruments, 210
Debt per share (DPS), 133, 147, 293
Debt service coverage, 293
Default probabilities, 135
Deferred tax assets (DTAs), 157
De-leveraging, 292
Deloitte, Touche Tohmatsu, 346, 347, 363, 364
Delta neutral, 268
Demodulation, 162
Demolition Assessment Index, 105
Derivatives, 9, 10, 35, 82, 86, 326
Deutsche Bank, 259, 294, 354, 355, 357, 360,
    361
Deutsche Bundesbank, 135, 208, 315
Deutsche Telekom, 13
Diluted earnings per share, 167
Direct placement, 88

Discretionary portfolio management, 42, 43
Diversification, 38, 39
Dividends, 87
Dodd, David L., 171, 321, 322
Double-bottom, 144
Double-top, 144
Dow Jones Industrial Average (DJIA), 98, 99
Downtrend, 143

Earnings per share (EPS), 133, 157, 316
Earnings revision ratio, 172
EBIT, 161, 168, 170, 308
EBITDA, 161, 167–71, 188, 297
Eccles, Marriner, 283
Economic capital, 301, 302
Eighteenth rule of investment, 274
Eighth rule of investments, 135
Eisenhower, Dwight, 253
Eleventh rule of investment, 215
Entitlement programs, 31
Epicurum, 352, 353
Equity markets, 9, 23
Equity price risk, 15
Equity research, 255, 256
Equity risk premium, 164
Equity-specific risk premium, 158, 159
European Central Bank (ECB), 92, 204, 284,
    285, 310
European Commission (EC), 20, 120, 311
European Union (EU), 19, 73, 119
EURO STOXX 50 index, 280, 281
Eurotunnel, 13, 14
Execution risk, 321, 340
Executive information systems, 196
Executive options, 257

FactSet Research Systems Inc., 299
Failure to deliver, 122
Fed model, 165, 166
Federal Communications Commission
    (FCC), 305
Federal Deposit Insurance Corporation
    (FDIC), 76
Federal Open Markets Committee, 59
Federal Reserve (Fed), 12, 59, 60, 68, 76, 90,
    121, 166
Fermi, Enrico, 193
Fermi principle, 193
Fibonacci ratio, 143
Fifteenth rule on investment, 244
Fifth rule of investment, 41, 204
Financial Accounting Standards (FAS), 128
Financial Accounting Standards Board
    (FASB), 27
Financial Services Authority (FSA), 114,
    285, 351
Financial Times Stock Exchange 100 index
    (FTSE 100), 41, 102, 103
First rule of investment, 3

Fitch Ratings, 48, 265, 359
Fixed income instruments, 26
Floor brokers, 83
Floor traders, 83
Foreign exchange market, 23
Forward Freight Agreements (FFAs), 105, 106
Forward looking statements, 191–3
Fourteenth rule of investment, 240
Fourth rule of investment, 36
Freddy Mac, 344
Freedom of Information Act, 305
Fully diluted earnings per share (FDES), 167
Fund of funds, 9, 42, 47, 48
Fundamental analysis, 131, 135–7, 148–50
Future cost, 232
Future vision, 218
Futures market, 14, 15

GARCH model, 282
Gates, Bill, 154
General loan agreement, 120
General Motors, 48, 49
Generally Accepted Accounting Principles
    (GAAP), 75, 168
Geneva Association, 50
Geometric formation, 143
Geroni, Cesare, 348, 356
Getty, John Paul, 28
Giannini, Amadeo P., 22, 39, 46, 47, 237
Glass-Steagall Act, 65
Golden parachute, 264
Goldman Sachs, 66, 68, 105, 215
Graham, Ben, 90, 171, 321
Grant Thornton, 347, 353, 363, 364
Grasso, Richard, 264
Greenspan, Alan, Dr, 12, 19, 59, 60, 76, 329
Gross domestic product (GDP), 91
Group of Ten, 26, 49, 90
Growth stocks, 219, 220
Growth strategy, 26

Harvard Business School, 264
Head and shoulders, 144
Hedge funds, 22, 23, 30, 42, 47, 276, 346, 356
Hedging, 14, 195, 275, 324, 325
Heisenberg, Werner, Dr, 245
Heisenberg principle, 44–6
High frequency financial data (HFFD), 45,
    46, 148
Holding period, 16
HSBC Shipping Services, 105
Hurst exponent, 223, 224

IAS 32, 311
IAS 39, 311
IBM, 312, 326, 328
Income strategy, 26
Independent rating agencies, 6

Information risk, 231
Initial margin, 121
Inside market, 82
Institutional investors, 3, 16, 18, 32, 82, 88,
    100, 224, 244, 255
Interactive computational finance, 162
Interest rate risk, 15, 26
Internal control, 182, 183, 190
International Accounting Standards (IAS), 75
International Accounting Standards Board
    (IASB), 166, 167, 311
International Maritime Exchange, 105
International Monetary Fund (IMF), 90
International Standards Organization
    (ISO), 100
Internet companies, 205
Internet stocks, 172, 330, 331
Intrinsic value, 158, 221
Investment Management Association (IMA), 6
Investment theory, 140
Investor protection, 107
Italy risk, 350

JP Morgan, 251
JP Morgan Chase, 36, 297, 352, 357, 369
JP Morgan Securities, 68

Kairos, 221, 223
Kaufman, Henry, Dr, 283
Keen, Bob, 6, 26, 32, 44, 131, 135, 202, 205,
    206, 215
Keynes, Maynard, 262
Kuoni, 337
Kyrtosis, 223

Large blocks, 118
Large caps, 41, 51, 204
Legal risk, 231, 232, 260
Leveraging, 10, 120, 275, 276, 291, 292
Levitt, Arthur, 199
Life insurers, 3
Limit order, 244
Limits, 243–7
Liquid assets, 286
Liquidity, 274, 275, 285, 343
Liquidity management, 287
Liquidity risk, 232, 285
Liquidity risk factors, 288
Liquidity risk limits, 287
Liquidity volume, 288
Lloyd's, 105
Loan Pricing Corporation (LPC), 162
London Interbank Offered Rate (LIBOR), 195
London Stock Exchange (LES), 41, 44
Long term investment account, 116
Long term investors, 246
LTCM, 11, 236, 294, 342, 355, 357
Lucent Technologies, 333, 335, 336

Magic Dow 10, 297
Margin account, 121
Margin requirements, 116
Market discipline, 191, 192
Market makers, 95
Market making, 66
Market neutral, 268
Market-on-close order, 244
Market price, 243
Market reversals, 248
Market risk, 11, 88, 218
Market sentiment, 145
Market value, 312
Marking to market, 313
Massachusetts Institute of Technology (MIT),
    312, 314
Mathematical models, 92, 133, 195, 218,
    250–2
Merchant banking, 66, 67, 71
Mergers and acquisitions (M&A), 258
Merrill Lynch, 6, 66, 68, 109, 110, 259, 357
Merton, Robert, Dr, 162, 163
MIB 30, 102, 103
Microsoft, 154, 155, 166, 205, 257
Mid-caps, 204
Midgley, Gordon, 6, 26, 44, 131, 236, 237
Model risk, 231, 252, 313
Momentum analysis, 142
Momentum index, 145
Monte Carlo simulation, 309, 314
Moody's, 265
Morgan Bank, 197, 218
Morgan Stanley, 68, 105, 231, 232, 259, 260,
    271, 354
Morningstar, 50, 51
Moving average, 145
Mutual funds, 5, 30, 52, 210

Net asset value, 311, 312
Net debt over equity, 293
Net present value (NPV), 173
New York Federal Reserve, 342
New York Stock Exchange (NYSE), 41, 73, 82,
    83, 96, 264, 266
Nikkei 225, 103, 104
1996 Market Risk Amendment, 45, 218
Nineteenth rule of investment, 304
Ninth rule of investment, 149
Nomura Securities, 189, 190
Non-purpose loan, 122, 123
Normal market valuation, 160
Norquist, Grover G., 15
Nortel, 333, 334
NASDAQ, 41, 74, 96, 101, 156, 282
Norwegian Options and Futures Clearing
    House, 105

Office of the Controller of the Currency (OCC),
    110, 111
Off-market trades, 120
Off-the-run, 117
Omnibus, 116
On-the-run, 117
Operational leverage, 308
Operating characteristics curve, 214
Operational risk, 11
Opportunity costs, 158
Option pricing, 280
Options market, 207
Ordinary profit, 167
Organization for Economic Cooperation and
    Development (OECD), 182
Oscillator index, 145
Outside market, 82
Over the counter (OTC) market, 81, 82, 181,
    238, 313, 314
Owner of record, 112

Paper Ship Index, 105
Pareto, Vilfredo, 27
Parmalat, 26, 71, 183, 199, 200, 211, 257,
    304, 306, 341, 344, 348, 349, 351,
    358, 361, 362
Pattern analysis, 252, 253
Pension Benefit Guarantee Corporation
    (PBGC), 49
Pension funds, 3, 6, 7, 23, 30, 31, 42,
    47, 50, 51
Ponzi scams, 210
Portfolio repositioning, 247
Position risk, 66
Post-mortems, 242
Preferred stock, 83, 85
Present value, 37, 158
Price/book multiples, 174
Price formation, 96
Price/performance, 151
Price to book value ratio, 158
Price to cash flow (P/CF), 166
Price to earnings (P/E) ratio, 133, 156, 157,
    171–5, 298, 299
Primary dealers, 68, 80
Private banking, 30, 32
Private placements, 41
Professional investors, 3, 6
Pro forma, 161, 192
Proprietary trading, 266
Public Company Accounting Oversight Board
    (PCAOB), 199

Quality of management, 260, 273
Quantitative analysis, 133

Regulation FD, 199
Regulation T, 109
Reputational risk, 180, 305

Resistance level, 143
Retail investors, 3, 9, 32, 36, 131, 247
Return on assets, 177
Return on capital (ROC), 79, 157
Return on equity (ROE), 133, 157, 175–7, 301, 302
Return on funding capital (ROFC), 309
Return on invested capital (ROIC), 309, 310
Return on investment, 158
Return on risk capital, 176
Reversal chart, 143
Reverse forward split, 123, 125, 126
Risk adjusted return on capital, 158
Risk-based pricing, 164
Risk capital, 302
Risk management, 11, 28, 231, 233, 236–40, 248, 249, 255, 273, 276, 299
Risk management officer, 325
Risk tolerance, 233
Rocket scientists, 133, 152–4, 251
Rule 325 from NYSE Constitution and Rules, 116, 117
Russell 200, 101

San Paolo/IMI, 324, 350, 357, 369
Sarbanes-Oxley Act, 89, 180, 197, 198, 200, 202, 259
Savings and loans (S&L), 82
Scientific analysis, 213
Second rule of investment, 22, 23
Secondary distribution, 118
Secondary market, 68, 80
Sector and group analysis, 209
Securities Act of 1933, 61
Securities analysis, 132, 133
Securities and Exchange Commission (SEC), 19, 21, 51, 54, 61, 110, 198, 262, 267
Securities Exchange Act of 1934, 107, 108, 111
Securities Investor Protection Corporation (SIPC), 61
Securities lending, 113
Segregated investment account, 116
Sell order, 243
Senior debt, 85
September 11, 2001, 77
Seventeenth rule of investment, 252
Seventh rule of investment, 131
Short selling, 23, 24, 123–5
Simulation, 132
Sixteenth rule of investment, 247
Sixth rule of investment, 43
Skewness, 223
Sloan, Alfred P. Jr, 217
Small caps, 41, 42, 51, 204
Smith Barney, 267, 269
S&P, 265, 363
S&P/Barro Index, 219
S&P Growth/Value Index, 219

S&P Midcap 400, 99, 100
S&P Smallcap 600, 99
Special offerings, 119
Specialists, 114–16, 266
Specialists book, 83
Speculators, 17, 18, 24, 25, 113, 125
Spinning, 270
Spitzer, Eliot, 51, 53, 54, 262, 268, 270
Standard & Poor's 500 (S&P 500), 99, 281
State Street Bank, 196
Stock market turnover, 97, 98
Stop/loss limits, 246, 247
Stop order, 243, 244
Street name, 112, 125
Stress testing, 132, 161, 190, 309
Structured products, 9, 42
Sun Tzu, 160
Support level, 143
Suspended coverage, 272
Sustainable growth, 272
Swiss Federal Institute of Technology, 251
Swiss Market Index (SMI), 102

Tail events, 252
Tanzi, Calisto, 345, 346, 348, 349, 357, 362, 365, 366
Technical analysis, 131, 133, 136, 137, 141–3, 151
Technology bubble, 205
Tenth rule of investment, 202
Third market, 119
Third rule of investment, 26, 38
Thirteenth rule of investment, 238
Thompson, Tim, 250
Thrice-blessed equity, 142
Tiberius, 283, 284
Ticks, 118
Time horizon, 16, 17, 221–3, 233
Tobin's Q-Ratio, 94, 178
Tokyo Stock Exchange (TSE), 103, 125, 172
Toronto Stock Exchange (TSE), 112
Toxic waste, 35
Trading account, 116
Treasury bills, 225
Tremonti, Giulio, 343, 344
Trend line, 142
Truman, Harry, 215
Tulip bubble, 206
Turnbull Committee, 323
Twelfth rule of investment, 236
Twentieth rule of investment, 309
Twenty rules of investing, 4

Underwriting, 66–8
Unexpected losses (UL), 163
Union Bank of Switzerland (UBS), 75, 354
United Dutch East India Company, 79
University of California, Los Angeles, 36, 156, 203, 259

University of Regensburg, 135
Unregulated lenders, 123
Upper and lower control limits, 245
Upper and lower tolerance limits, 245
Uptick, 118
US Supreme Court, 21
US Treasury securities, 68

Value at risk (VAR), 45, 250, 251
Value stocks, 219, 220
Venture capital firms, 42
Virtual balance sheet, 196
Volatility, 274–82
  implied, 280
Volatility index, 276–8

Warburg, Siegmund, G., 5, 306
Warrants, 85
Wealth management, 33, 34
Weill, Sanford I., 269
Wieleman, Jos, 304, 307, 308
Wilshire 5000, 102
Worst-case valuation, 160

Yamani, Ahmed Zaki, 28
Yardeni, Edward, Dr, 10
Year 200 (Y2K) problem, 322
Yield, 157

Zero tolerance, 245